Charity Law

This work provides an analytical and comparative analysis of the development of charity law, as well as providing a critical commentary on a number of contemporary changes within the charity law field across a range of common law jurisdictions. The book follows earlier studies which cover a similar, and traditional, jurisdictional spread, but which are now dated. It further considers in detail charity law issues within Hong Kong and Singapore, about which there has been historically more limited charity law discussion. The area is growing in terms of practical legal and academic interest.

Juliet Chevalier-Watts is a senior lecturer in law and Associate Dean Research at Te Piringa – Faculty of Law, University of Waikato, New Zealand.

Charity Law
International Perspectives

Juliet Chevalier-Watts

LONDON AND NEW YORK

First published 2018 by Routledge

2 Park Square, Milton Park, Abingdon, Oxfordshire OX14 4RN

52 Vanderbilt Avenue, New York, NY 10017

Routledge is an imprint of the Taylor & Francis Group, an informa business

First issued in paperback 2019

Copyright © 2018 Juliet Chevalier-Watts

The right of Juliet Chevalier-Watts to be identified as author of this work has been asserted by her in accordance with sections 77 and 78 of the Copyright, Designs and Patents Act 1988.

All rights reserved. No part of this book may be reprinted or reproduced or utilised in any form or by any electronic, mechanical, or other means, now known or hereafter invented, including photocopying and recording, or in any information storage or retrieval system, without permission in writing from the publishers.

Notice:
Product or corporate names may be trademarks or registered trademarks, and are used only for identification and explanation without intent to infringe.

British Library Cataloguing in Publication Data
A catalogue record for this book is available from the British Library

Library of Congress Cataloging in Publication Data
Names: Chevalier-Watts, Juliet, author.
Title: Charity law : international perspectives / Juliet Chevalier-Watts.
Description: Abingdon, Oxon [UK] ; New York : Routledge, 2017. | Includes bibliographical references and index.
Identifiers: LCCN 2017014804 | ISBN 9781138656130 (hardback) | ISBN 9781317222040 (adobe reader) | ISBN 9781317222033 (epub) | ISBN 9781317222026 (mobipocket)
Subjects: LCSH: Charity laws and legislation. | Charitable uses, trusts, and foundations. | Nonprofit organizations--Law and legislation. | Charities.
Classification: LCC K797 .C49 2017 | DDC 344.03/17--dc23
LC record available at https://lccn.loc.gov/2017014804

ISBN: 978-1-138-65613-0 (hbk)
ISBN: 978-0-367-87805-4 (pbk)

Typeset in Galliard
by Taylor & Francis Books

This book is for Paul – thank you for your unending love and support.

Contents

1   An introduction to charity law

This chapter introduces some of the concepts of charity law, which will provide the context and parameters for the following chapters. The chapter illustrates many of the interconnections, as well as some key differences, of the jurisdictions that are the focus of this book. The jurisdictions in question are England and Wales, Canada, Australia, New Zealand, Singapore, and Hong Kong.

A Introduction to charity law

Charity is an ancient concept, with its roots buried deeply in history. Charity is said to be a manifestation 'of the better side of human nature',[1] and is 'no doubt as old as mankind itself'.[2] Undoubtedly charity means many things to many people, although in theory, its primary concern is alleviating poverty and the suffering of others. It may also provide and promote opportunities for others to better the human condition, as well as provide for social infrastructures for the well-being of communities. It even extends as far as pursuing aspects of religious worship. Nonetheless, while charity may have taken on many forms, legally speaking, it should be distinguished from benevolence and philanthropy. It has been argued that 'benevolence' should not be determined as being charitable at law because it has a 'somewhat shadowy meaning'.[3] Benevolent gifts have traditionally not been found charitable because they extend beyond that which is exclusively charitable.[4] Indeed:[5]

---

1   Peter Luxton, *The Law of Charities* (Oxford: Oxford University Press, 2001), 3.
2   Ibid.
3   Kerry O'Halloran, Myles McGregor-Lowndes, and Karla W. Simon, *Charity Law & Social Policy: National and International Perspectives on the Functions of Law Relating to Charities* (Netherlands: Springer, 2008), 9.
4   O'Halloran, McGregor-Lowndes, and Simon, *Charity Law & Social Policy*, referring to *Houston* v. *Burns* [1918] AC 337 (HL); *Re Jarman's Estate* (1878) 8 Ch D 584; *Re Rilands Estate* [1881] WN 173; *Chichester Diocesan Fund and Board of Finance In* v. *Simpson* [1944] AC 341 (HL); *A-G for New Zealand* v. *Brown* [1917] AC 393 (PC).
5   O'Halloran, McGregor-Lowndes, and Simon, *Charity Law & Social Policy*, 9, citing Hubert Picarda, *The Law and Practice Relating to Charities*, 3rd edn (London: Butterworths, 1999), 221 (footnotes omitted).

A gift simply to 'benevolent purposes' is objectionable: a benevolent purpose may be (but is not necessarily) charitable. The same is true of gifts to philanthropic purposes, utilitarian purposes, emigration, and public purposes: they all go further than legal charity.

An example of such a void gift was found in *Morice v. Bishop of Durham,*[6] where an estate was left to the Bishop for him to dispose of to 'such objects of benevolence and liberality'.[7] The Court stated, in relation to the concepts of benevolence and liberality:[8]

> Do purposes of liberality and benevolence mean the same as objects of charity? That word in its widest sense denotes all the good affections, men ought to bear towards each other; in its most restricted and common sense, relief of the poor ... Here its signification is derived chiefly from the Statute of Elizabeth (stat. 43 Eliz, c. 4). Those purposes are considered charitable, which that Statute enumerates, or which by analogies are deemed within its spirit and intendment; and to some such purpose every bequest to charity generally shall be applied. But it is clear liberality and benevolence can find numberless objects, not included in that statute in the largest construction of it ... By what rule of construction could it be said, all objects of liberality and benevolence are excluded, which do not fall within the Statute of Elizabeth 1.

This illustrates the issues related to comparing charity with benevolence, and it seems rational to try to distinguish the two concepts entirely to ensure more clarity in charity law. It should be noted that the Statute of Elizabeth, to which the Court makes reference, is one of the key statutes relating to charity law, and it will be discussed in more detail later in the chapter.

Benevolence, therefore, is not the same as charity in legal terms because its terms are too uncertain, and may be too broad for the purposes of charity. What then of the notion of aligning philanthropy with charity?

Just as benevolence fails to align with charity at law, so too, generally speaking, does philanthropy. This is because the 'word 'philanthropic' by itself is undoubtedly too wide',[9] and as a result, it 'implies generality',[10] so will fall outside the construct of charitable purpose.

In the case of *National Provincial and Union Bank of England, Limited* v. *Tetley,*[11] Warrington LJ acknowledged that philanthropy is not charitable at law,

---

6 O'Halloran, McGregor-Lowndes, and Simon, *Charity Law & Social*, citing *Morice* v. *Bishop of Durham* (1804) 32 ER 656, 9 Ves J 399.

7 O'Halloran, McGregor-Lowndes, and Simon, *Charity Law & Social Policy*, 9, citing *Morice* v. *Bishop of Durham*.

8 *Morice* v. *Bishop of Durham*, 658–9.

9 *Eades* v. *Eades* [1920] 2 Ch 353, 356.

10 In *Re Macduff* [1896] 2 Ch 451, 454.

11 *National Provincial and Union Bank of England* v. *Tetley* [1923] 1 Ch 258.

although his Lordship appeared rather bewildered by this. He was 'unable to find any principle which will guide one easily, and safely, through the tangle of the cases as to what is and what is not a charitable gift'.[12] Indeed:[13]

> I confess I find considerable difficulty in understanding the exact reason why a gift for the benefit of animals, and for the prevention of cruelty to animals generally, should be a good charitable gift, while a gift for philanthropic purposes, which, I take it, is for the benefit of mankind generally, should be bad as a charitable gift. The gift for the benefit of animals, apparently, is held to be valid because it is educative of mankind, it being good for mankind that they should be taught not to be cruel but kind to animals, and one would quite agree with that. But if the benefit of mankind on that particular side makes that a good charitable gift it is a little difficult to see why any philanthropic purpose to benefit mankind on all sides is a bad one. But it is so; it has been so decided, and therefore the present case is, made very difficult, as every case is where there is no governing principle which can be applied.

However, it has been acknowledged now that England and Wales have begun to relax their approach to the concept of philanthropy, whereby the Charities Act 1992 stated 'charitable institution' means a charity or an institution (other than a charity) which is established for charitable, benevolent, or philanthropic purposes.[14]

Therefore, charity at law, as a concept, is complex and should be distinguished from the layperson's notions of charity, which has resulted in some judicial criticism. As Lord Wrenbury noted, in *Verge* v. *Somerville*,[15] the legal and popular meanings of charity are 'so far apart that it is necessary almost to dismiss the popular meaning from the mind as misleading before setting out to determine whether a gift is charitable within the legal meaning'. Lord Macnaghten in *Commissioners for Special Purposes of Income Tax* v. *Pemsel*[16] also illustrates this notion of disparate legal and popular meanings of charity:

> No doubt the popular meaning of the words 'charity' and 'charitable' does not coincide with their legal meaning; and no doubt it is easy enough to collect from the books a few decisions which seem to push the doctrine of the Court to the extreme, and to present a contrast between the two meanings in an aspect almost ludicrous. But still it is difficult to fix the point of divergence, and no one as yet has succeeded in defining the popular meaning of the word 'charity'.

12 Ibid., 266.
13 Ibid., 266–7.
14 O'Halloran, McGregor-Lowndes, and Simon, *Charity Law & Social Policy*, 11, referring to the Charities Act 1992, s 58(1) (UK).
15 *Verge v. Somerville* [1924] AC 496 (PC), 502.
16 *Commissioners of Special Purposes for Income Tax v. Pemsel* [1891] AC 531 (HL), 593.

His latter sentence, that 'no one as yet has succeeded in defining the popular meaning of the word "'charity'", generally speaking, still stands true to this day, as Hammond J (as he was) in *D V Bryant Trust Board* v. *Hamilton City Council* noted:[17]

> There is no intrinsic legal definition of charity. As a matter of technique, Courts can only describe the attributes of charities.

There are some exceptions to this, however, one being Australia, which has now set out a statutory definition of 'charity' within the Charities Act 2013, which is discussed later in the chapter. Alongside Australia, England and Wales have also recently introduced a statutory definition of charity:[18]

> Meaning of 'charity'
> (1)For the purposes of the law of England and Wales, 'charity' means an institution which–
> (a) is established for charitable purposes only ...

We will consider in more detail the notion of charitable purposes later on, but sufficient for this stage is that these two jurisdictions are unusual, in comparison with such jurisdictions as Singapore, Hong Kong, Canada and New Zealand, in setting out a statutory definition. What is clear however from these statutory definitions is that 'charity' may still be interpreted broadly, and as we will see in our journey through the concept of charity and charitable purpose, the statutory definition of charity may not offer as much clarity as one may have hoped.

The lack of clarity may also stem from the fact that charity law has 'been built up not logically but empirically'.[19] It has also been said that there is some degree of inconsistency when trying to rationalise the empirical development of charity law.[20] Indeed, in the slightly later case of *Oppenheim v. Tobacco Securities Trust Co Ltd*,[21] it was said '[n]o one who has been versed for many years in this difficult and very artificial branch of the law can be unaware of its illogicalities'.[22]

This 'artificial branch of law', with its 'illogicalities', has led, however, to a diverse range of activities being held as charitable, and being denied charitable status. For instance, in *Re Foveaux*,[23] gifts to the London Anti-Vivisection Society, and the Scottish Society for the Total Suppression of Vivisection were held to be charitable gifts. The objects of the Societies included the total inhibition of the practice of vivisection. This is perhaps not a surprising decision when considered in modern-day times, bearing in mind the keen attention that many jurisdictions give

---

17 *D V Bryant Trust Board* v. *Hamilton City Council* [1997] 3 NZLR 342 (HC), 347.
18 Charities Act 2006, s 1(1).
19 *Gilmour* v. *Coats* [1949] AC 426, 449.
20 Ibid.
21 *Oppenheim* v. *Tobacco Securities Trust Co Ltd* [1951] AC 297.
22 Ibid., 307.
23 *Re Foveaux* [1895] 2 Ch 501 (Ch).

to the protection of animals. However, what is perhaps surprising is the decision relating to anti-vivisection that followed in the next century. In *National Anti-Vivisection Society* v. *Inland Revenue Commissioners*,[24] the House of Lords criticised *Re Foveaux*, holding that a Society for the total suppression of vivisection was not charitable. How could apparently such similar cases be determined to be the total opposite of one another?

The House of Lords in the *National Anti-Vivisection* case considered the issue of cruelty to animals and in relation to vivisection. The Court acknowledged that vivisection does involve pain to animals, notwithstanding the Cruelty to Animals Act 1876. This was thought to be a regrettable necessity, much as a person who eats beef for dinner might reflect on the slaughter of cow that would have suffered pain so that the man may benefit.[25] However, 'all of this must be weighed against the great benefits to humanity as a result of the practice of vivisection'.[26] Thus, a strictly regulated amount of suffering by animals 'may save and avert incalculable suffering to innumerable millions of mankind'.[27] As a result, the Court held that the purposes of the Society would not benefit the community and, in fact, may be detrimental to society generally,[28] therefore the Society was not charitable.

These two cases therefore illustrate some of the challenges being faced by the courts in endeavouring to determine the charitable nature of a gift or entity. While a layperson may innately believe that cruelty to animals should be prevented, the Lordships in the later of the two cases, provided a reasoned rationale as to when cruelty may be warranted, thus negating charitability. This can make for uncomfortable consideration as to the real purpose of charity, which in theory is to relieve suffering, among other purposes. However, as will be addressed in Chapter 4, where public benefit is discussed in detail, and which is a requirement of charitable purposes, if the public benefit is missing, then so is its charitable nature.

The advancement of religion as a charitable purpose has also given rise to some apparently illogical or artificial decisions over the years. In the case of *Gilmour* v. *Coats*,[29] the House of Lords had to determine whether a priory of cloistered nuns, who devoted their lives to prayer, penance and self-sanctification, was charitable. At first sight, one might be forgiven for presuming that such an obvious form of religion should surely fulfil the requirement of advancing religion as a charitable purpose. The issue that arose, however, was that of public benefit. For current purposes, Lord Simonds was bound by the common law and the requirement of public benefit. One of the key issues was that '[t]he faithful must embrace their

---

24 *National Anti-Vivisection Society* v. *Inland Revenue Commissioners* [1948] AC 31 (HL).
25 Ibid., 47.
26 Juliet Chevalier-Watts, *Law of Charity* (Wellington, New Zealand: Thomson Reuters, 2014), 265.
27 Chevalier-Watts, *Law of Charity*, 265, citing *National Anti-Vivisection Society* v. *Inland Revenue Commissioners*, 48.
28 *National Anti-Vivisection Society* v. *Inland Revenue Commissioners*, 48–9.
29 *Gilmour* v. *Coats*.

faith believing where they cannot prove: the court can act only on proof'.[30] The lack of proof meant that:[31]

> A gift to two or ten or a hundred cloistered nuns in the belief that their prayers will benefit the world at large does not from that belief alone derive validity any more than does the belief of any other donor for any other purpose.

As a result, with regard to the notion of edification by example, Lord Simonds thought it 'too vague and intangible to satisfy the prescribed test'[32] of public benefit. In contrast to this case is that of the New Zealand case *Liberty Trust* v. *Charities Commission*,[33] which reflects a more liberal approach to that of public benefit, although the decision has been subject to some criticism.[34] The case concerned the charitable status of the Liberty Trust. This Trust provides a mortgage-lending scheme as a practical outworking of the Christian faith. In other words, the New Testament is concerned with the correct use of money, therefore by the Trust reducing financial burdens of the recipients of the lending scheme, the recipients will be more free to carry out God's work.[35] The Charities Commission (as it was then) determined that while the Trust may be conducive to religion, it did not advance it;[36] rather, it provided private benefits as opposed to a public benefit.

Certainly, a mortgage scheme does not seem like an obvious vehicle for advancing religion,[37] yet Mallon J was persuaded that it did so because:[38]

> While the activities will overlap with secular activities, it is the overt connection with the Christian faith and with the two churches under which Liberty Trust operates that in this case give Liberty Trust's activities their religious purpose. The overwhelming message promoted by Liberty Trust is a religious one.

30 Ibid., 446.
31 Ibid.
32 Ibid.
33 *Liberty Trust* v. *Charities Commission* [2011] 3 NZLR 68 (HC).
34 See Jonathan Barrett and John Veal, 'Social Enterprise: Some Tax Policy Considerations', *Journal of the Australasian Tax Teachers Association* 8(1) (November 2013), 141–68; Juliet Chevalier-Watts, 'Charitable Trusts and Advancement of Religion: On a Whim and a Prayer?', VUWLR 43(3) (2012), 403–42.
35 *Liberty Trust* v. *Charities Commission*, [48].
36 Generally speaking, to advance a religion, there should be a promotion of spiritual teaching in a broad sense, with 'the maintenance of the doctrines on which it rests, and to observances that serve to promote and manifest it' (Picarda, *Law and Practice Relating to Charities*, 99), citing *Keren Kayemeth Le Jisroel Ltd* v. *IRC* [1931] 2 KB 465, 477. Some of the later chapters will address the advancement of religion per jurisdiction.
37 *Liberty Trust* v. *Charities Commission*, [93]
38 Ibid., [96].

What *Liberty Trust* illustrates, therefore, is that the advancement of religion doctrine 'however eccentric it might appear to the general public, is presumptively for the public benefit and therefore worthy of legal and tax privileges'.[39]

What these cases demonstrate, therefore, are some of the eccentricities and challenges relating to charity law, and what is evident is that some elements of charity law appear to be shrouded in obscurity and artificiality. As a result, even with at least two jurisdictions having sought to clarify the meaning of 'charity', it is a concept that is still not easy to explain, even in light of statutory assistance.

Thus, charity does not necessarily correlate with philanthropy or benevolence, and neither does it depend on an organisation's constitutional structure, nor are public-spirited organisations necessarily charitable. Even in modern times, there can still be a 'mismatch between what a layman might think of as charitable and what *is* charitable in law'.[40] For instance, in a survey undertaken in 2005, only 7 per cent of respondents realised that Eton College, often just referred to as 'Eton', the highly prestigious independent school in England, is charitable.[41] This may be because, generally speaking, charity is likely to be more closely associated with the relief of poverty than with prestigious forms of education,[42] which simply reflects some of the key issues for the public in understanding the concepts of charity law, and underpins the issues that have been raised so far in this chapter. In other words, the complexities of the concept of charity at law.

While carrying out acts of humanity will not necessarily be sufficient to be legally charitable, it is true that 'no legal machinery is needed to enable a donor … to put alms in to the hand of the beggar'.[43] So one might still undertake humanitarian acts freely without being concerned as to its legal charitable nature, or not. However, 'once such activity extends beyond gifts to needy individuals … to the provision of groups'[44] to benefit society more generally, then problems can arise as to the effectiveness of the gifts, and to protect against fraud, among other issues. As a result:[45]

> The carrying out and effectiveness of the gift may to a large degree be dependent upon there being in place an appropriate system of law by which such charitable activity can be protected against the fraud and other wrongful acts of those charged with the responsibility of performing it.

---

39 Barrett and Veal, 'Social Enterprise', 8.
40 Mary Synge, *The 'New' Public Benefit Requirement Making Sense of Charity Law?* (Oxford: Hart, 2015), 4.
41 Synge, *New' Public Benefit Requirement*, 4, citing Charity Commission, *Report of Findings of a Survey of Public Trust and Confidence in Charities* (Opinion Leader Research, November 2005), 16–17.
42 Charity Commission, *Report of Findings*, 16–17, cited in Synge, *'New' Public Benefit Requirement*, 4–5.
43 Luxton, *Law of Charities*, 3.
44 Ibid., 4.
45 Ibid.

Therefore, legal systems have evolved to enable facilitation of these good works effectively. In order to give this some context, we will consider the history of charity law that has underpinned the jurisdictions that are the focus of this book. While this book will not provide an exhaustive account of the history, it will illustrate the importance of the history of charity law in some of the key legal journeys from past times to modern day, where the ancient annals of history are still, to be this day, being felt.

B A history of charity law

Charity, from its earliest humanitarian times, and through its subsequent legal governance, has been subject to a multitude of influences and forms throughout the centuries. Prior to the Protestant Reformation that occurred in England in the sixteenth century,[46] pious causes were causes that honoured God and His Church. Gifts might include saying masses; gifts for the church and its upkeep; relieving the poor; and repairing and maintaining hospitals, roads and dykes. Bequests to pious causes were much favoured by the Ecclesiastical courts, and indeed many privileges were granted to charitable legacies that might be denied to private legacies.[47] For instance, 'no charitable legacy was allowed to fail because it was too indefinite, and generous rules of construction were developed to cure the uncertainty'.[48] Charities in England at this time were managed by the Roman Catholic Church, and the Ecclesiastical courts had exclusive jurisdiction over a deceased's personalty. For instance, if a person died intestate, these courts would customarily apply one-third of their personal property to pious purposes.[49] However, the testamentary jurisdiction of the Ecclesiastical courts was becoming unpopular, and such unpopularity stemmed, in part from court fees, and accusations of corrupt court officials. Complainants turned to the Chancellor for aid, and the importance of the role of the Chancellor in the jurisdiction of charity law began to grow.[50]

However, the concept of charity in these times was set to change as a result of the Reformation, with Henry VIII's attack on the power of the Church.[51] One of

---

46 'The Protestant Reformation was the 16th-century religious, political, intellectual and cultural upheaval that splintered Catholic Europe, setting in place the structures and beliefs that would define the continent in the modern era. In northern and central Europe, reformers like Martin Luther, John Calvin and Henry VIII challenged papal authority and questioned the Catholic Church's ability to define Christian practice. They argued for a religious and political redistribution of power into the hands of Bible- and pamphlet-reading pastors and princes. The disruption triggered wars, persecutions and the so-called Counter-Reformation, the Catholic Church's delayed but forceful response to the Protestants' (www.history.com/topics/reformation [accessed 1 Dec. 2015]).

47 Gareth Jones, *History of the Law of Charity 1532–1827* (Cambridge: Cambridge University Press, 1969), 5.

48 Ibid.

49 Gino Dal Pont, *Law of Charity* (Australia: LexisNexis, 2010), 82.

50 Jones, *History of the Law of Charity*, 5–7.

51 Dal Pont, *Law of Charity*, 83.

the key changes was that the objects of charity became more secular in their focus as 'the majority of Englishmen reflected less on the fate of their souls and became more concerned with the worldly needs of their fellow men'.[52] This change in focus was undoubtedly as a result of perhaps one of the most infamous of acts of Henry VIII 1533, with the dissolution of the monasteries, in response to what was described as:[53]

> Manifest sin, vicious carnal and abominable living ... whereby the governors ... consume and utterly waste ... to the high displeasure of Almighty God, slander of good religion and the great infamy of the King's Highness and the realm if redress should not be had thereof.

In 1539, the abbeys were dissolved, and in 1545, colleges were also feeling the effects of such measures, as they too were dissolved for failing to give alms to the poor, and for failing to carry out charitable acts. Such measures, however, came at a high cost, and that was felt most keenly by the poor and needy. In London, the hospital of St Bartholomew's was closed, and the streets became filled with the dead and dying. Maynard Smith noted that:[54]

> It was the poor who suffered the most from the dissolution of the monasteries ... [and] the poor lost the benefactions which the monks were bound to distribute, and also the charity – it may not have been much – which the monks distributed.

While it was evident that the poor were suffering as a result of such undertakings, a number of statutes[55] were introduced in the sixteenth century to reinforce mortmain[56] prohibitions against bequeathing property to Ecclesiastical institutions. While these statutes were partly justified due to the misapplication of endowments to the detriment of the poor,[57] in reality, they were 'designed to bolster the royal treasury'.[58] The Chantries Act 1547 dissolved chantries and directed all property for superstitious purposes to the Crown.[59]

52 Jones, *History of the Law of Charity*, 10.
53 Susan Barker, Michael Gousmett, and Ken Lord, *The Law and Practice of Charities in New Zealand* (Wellington: LexisNexis, 2013), 441, referring to 27 Hen VIII C28 [1535–36].
54 Maynard Smith, *Henry VIII and the Reformation* (London: Macmillan, 1948), 120, cited in Barker, Gousmett, and Lord, *Law and Practice of Charities in New Zealand*, 441.
55 Including the Mortmain Act 1531; Chantries Act 1545; Chantries Act 1547.
56 'Mortmain' translates from the French 'dead hand': an inalienable possession of lands or buildings by an ecclesiastical or other corporation, or the condition of property or other gifts left to a corporation in perpetuity especially for religious, charitable, or public purposes (www.merriam-webster.com/dictionary/mortmain [accessed 3 Dec. 2015]).
57 Dal Pont, *Law of Charity*, 83.
58 Ibid.
59 Ibid.

After Elizabeth I ascended the throne in 1558, the 'diminishing role of the church in charitable work was complemented by an increasing trend towards secularisation and recognition that poverty was a national problem'.[60] Changes began to occur, which included the new merchant class bequeathing money and property to secular concerns such as education and relief of the poor, as opposed to religious bodies. The Poor Law Act 1601 was enacted to provide relief to the poor, although this was a double-edged sword. The Act divided the poor into two categories. First, the employable, who could work, but chose not to, were deemed as undeserving; and, second, the unemployable, in other words, those who could not work due to a variety of circumstances, and were classed as deserving, thus creating a divisive populace. The first category would be punished and compelled to work, while the latter would receive assistance. The Elizabethan State however recognised its lack of money, and thus encouraged private philanthropy to assist the deserving poor. It did this in three ways.[61]

First, the Court of Chancery recognised and enforced charitable use, which established it as the main legal mechanism for ensuring charitable purposes were achieved. Second, legal privileges that were given to charitable institutions were ensured. Third, the Statute of Charitable Uses 1601 was enacted, perhaps one of the most fundamental of all legal instruments in charity law, which encouraged private philanthropy.[62]

The purpose of this Act, entitled 'An Acte to redresse the Misemployment of Landes, Goodes and Stockes of Money heretofore given to Charitable Uses' was twofold. First, it sought to fill the social care role left void by the dissolution of religious entities, and channel gifts to aid the social needs as identified by the government.[63] Second, it 'aimed to reform the abuse of property donated to charities by listing the types of purposes which would thereafter be recognised as charitable'.[64] To assist with this, it also established a body of commissioners with supervisory and inspection powers regarding charitable trusts.[65]

The Preamble of this Act has endured the centuries, even though the Act has long been repealed. This Preamble 'laid the foundations for the legal definition of charitable purposes, which is still recognised today'.[66] The Preamble contained a non-exhaustive list of charitable purposes as follows:[67]

> Whereas land, tenements, rents, annuities, profits, hereditaments, goods, chattels, money, and stock of money, have been heretofore given, limited,

---

60 Ibid.
61 Ibid., 84.
62 Ibid.
63 O'Halloran, McGregor-Lowndes, and Simon, *Charity Law & Social Policy*, 29.
64 Ibid.
65 Ibid.
66 Chevalier-Watts, *Law of Charity*, 7.
67 Donald Poirier, *Charity Law in New Zealand* Wellington: Department of Internal Affairs, 2013), 79–80; Dal Pont, *Law of Charity*, 46–7.

appointed, and assigned as well by the Queen's most excellent majesty, and her most noble progenitors, as by sundry other well-disposed persons: some for relief of aged, impotent, and poor people, some for maintenance of sick and maimed soldiers and mariners, schools of learning, free schools, and scholars in universities; some for repair of bridges, ports, havens, causeways, churches, seabanks and highways; some for education and preferment of orphans; some for or towards the relief, stock, or maintenance for houses of corrections; some for marriages of poor maids; some for supportation, aid, and help of young tradesmen, handicraftsmen, and persons decayed; and others for relief or redemption of prisoners or captives, and for aid or ease of any poor inhabitants concerning payment of fifteens, setting out soldiers, and other taxes; which land, tenement, rents, annuities, profits, hereditaments, goods, chattels, money, and stock of money, nevertheless, have been employed according to the charitable intent of the givers and founders thereof, by reason of frauds, breaches of trust, and negligence in those that should pay, deliver and employ the same

After the Act's enactment, courts would not recognise a purpose as being charitable unless it fell within the purposes of the Preamble, or fell within the spirit and intendment of the Preamble, a phrase that is still utilised in today's courts, and the purpose displayed public benefit.[68] The concept of charitable purposes is still a key consideration in our specified jurisdictions, and it is to the introduction of this concept that we turn.

C Charitable purposes: an introduction

For the purposes of this chapter, probably one of the most influential cases in relation to charitable purposes, following the Preamble's non-exhaustive list of charitable purposes, is that of *Commissioners for Special Purposes of Income Tax* v. *Pemsel*.[69] In this case, Lord Macnaghten produced the now renowned four principal divisions of charity, which, in essence, summarising the Preamble, read as follows:[70]

> Trusts for the relief of poverty; trusts for the advancement of education; trusts for the advancement of religion; and trusts for other purposes beneficial to the community, not falling under any of the preceding heads.

This classification of charitable purposes has traditionally been utilised by many jurisdictions as a basis for discussion and recognition of charitable purposes.[71]

---

68 O'Halloran, McGregor-Lowndes, and Simon, *Charity Law & Social Policy*, 29.
69 *Commissioners for Special Purposes of Income Tax* v. *Pemsel*.
70 Ibid., 583.
71 Elizabeth Cairns, *Charities: Law and Practice*, 3rd edn (London: Sweet & Maxwell, 1997), 2.

Since this classification, charity law has evolved, and, as a result, it is worth-while introducing the concept of charitable purposes in each of the selected jurisdictions, to outline some of the international interconnectedness of the jurisdictions, as well as to illustrate some of the differences. It should be noted that the following section of the chapter will only introduce the notion of charitable purposes in brief because later chapters will consider these purposes in more detail.

D Charitable purposes in England and Wales

England and Wales charity law was subject to numerous statutory changes throughout the nineteenth and twentieth centuries and reform of the legal framework that underpinned charity 'had long been overdue'.[72] The Charities Acts 1960, 1992 and 1993 went some way to modernising charity law, and enhancing the role of the Charity Commission for England and Wales,[73] but one of the most recent, and possibly far-reaching amendments, was the Charities Act 2006. The Act expanded upon the *Pemsel* four heads of charity by creating 13 heads of charity:[74]

> A purpose falls within this subsection if it falls within any of the following descriptions of purposes—
>
> a   the prevention or relief of poverty;
> b   the advancement of education;
> c   the advancement of religion;
> d   the advancement of health or the saving of lives;
> e   the advancement of citizenship or community development;
> f   the advancement of the arts, culture, heritage or science;
> g   the advancement of amateur sport;
> h   the advancement of human rights, conflict resolution or reconciliation or the promotion of religious or racial harmony or equality and diversity;
> i   the advancement of environmental protection or improvement;
> j   the relief of those in need by reason of youth, age, ill-health, disability, financial hardship or other disadvantage;
> k   the advancement of animal welfare;
> l   the promotion of the efficiency of the armed forces of the Crown, or of the efficiency of the police, fire and rescue services or ambulance services;
> m   any other purposes within subsection (4).

---

72 Alison Dunn, 'Lord Hodgson's Charities Act Review', *Voluntary Sector Review* 4(1) (2013), 127.
73 Ibid.
74 Charities Act 2006, s 2(2).

Subsection (4), to which s 2(2)(m) refers, reads as follows:[75]

The purposes within this subsection (see subsection (2)(m)) are—

a   any purposes not within paragraphs (a) to (l) of subsection (2) but recognised as charitable purposes under existing charity law or by virtue of section 1 of the Recreational Charities Act 1958 (c. 17);

b   any purposes that may reasonably be regarded as analogous to, or within the spirit of, any purposes falling within any of those paragraphs or paragraph (a) above; and

c   any purposes that may reasonably be regarded as analogous to, or within the spirit of, any purposes which have been recognised under charity law as falling within paragraph (b) above or this paragraph.

Echoes of the Preamble are still apparent here. It may be recalled from earlier in the chapter, where in the case of *Morice* v. *Bishop of Durham*,[76] the Court stated that: '[t]hose purposes are considered charitable, which that Statute enumerates, or which by analogies are deemed within its spirit and intendment'. Similarly, ss 2(4)(b) and (c) refer to purposes being regarded as analogous to, or falling within the spirit of purposes that have been recognised as charitable, thus reflecting the fundamental relevance still today of the historical context of charity law, even from its earliest days.

However, the retention of the essence of the Preamble has been criticised. One criticism is that s 2 does not remove the Preamble, and while it has been stated that analogy drawing has been legitimated as a result of s 2 of the Act,[77] this raises issues. Not least because as societies evolve, so analogies must become more creative to try to align contemporary purposes with those that were envisaged by the lawmakers of the seventeenth century. For instance, in *Scottish Burial Reform & Cremation Society Ltd* v. *Glasgow Corp*,[78] the House of Lords concluded that maintaining a crematorium was analogous to the repairing of churches in 1601. This may be tenuous, albeit acceptable, but the Canadian case of *Vancouver Regional Freenet Assn* v. *Minister of National Revenue*[79] suggests grave levels of artificiality regarding creating analogies. The Supreme Court held that repairing the internet was analogous to highway maintenance in the time of Elizabeth I! It was asserted that this analogy was 'so unconvincing as to lead to the conclusion that the grant of charitable status … was based on nothing more than general public

75 Charities Act 2006, s 2(4).
76 *Morice* v. *Bishop of Durham*, 658–9.
77 Jordan Frazer, 'Quantity Not Quality: The Failure of the Charities Act 2006', *North East Law Review* 3(1) (2015), 24, referring to Jacob Jaconelli, 'Adjudicating on Charitable Status: A Consideration of the Element', *The Conveyancer*, 77(2) (2013), 96–112.
78 Frazer, 'Quantity Not Quality', 24, referring to *Scottish Burial Reform & Cremation Society Ltd* v. *Glasgow Corp* [1968] AC 138 (HL).
79 Frazer, 'Quantity Not Quality', 24, referring to *Vancouver Regional Freenet Assn* v. *Minister of National Revenue* [1996] 137 DLR (4th) 206 (SC).

utility'.[80] On the other hand, perhaps it is not so unreasonable to align the notions of highways. Both highways move items, and both are deemed essential in their time, therefore while one may criticise the tenuous aspects, logically, there is much to be said for that analogy. What this does illustrate, however, is that charity law still provides many challenges in contemporary times, regardless of the levels of statutory intervention.

The Charities Act 2006 provided, for the first time, a statutory definition of charitable purposes. However, it would be fair to say that this definition made almost no change to the law.[81] In reality, the first three purposes are identical to the *Pemsel* heads, those of the relief of poverty, and the advancement of education and religion. In addition, the thirteenth head, is, in reality, identical to the fourth *Pemsel* head, that of any other purposes beneficial to the community.[82] So the Act 'updates the law, but does not remove any ... current charitable purposes'.[83] While this does maintain the flexibility, 'which was a fundamental feature of the previous categorisation of charitable purposes',[84] regard must be had to case law prior to the Act's enactment.

This highlights the difficulties of drawing a distinction between the *Pemsel* classifications of charitable purposes, and the modern construct given by the Charities Act 2006, illustrating the inherent complexities of charity law. It should also be noted that much of the Charities Act 2006 was consolidated in the Charities Act 2011, which came into force in March 2012.[85]

The Charities Act 2006 also removed the presumption of public benefit. The nature and specifics of public benefit will be discussed in detail in Chapter 4, although for the purposes of this chapter, public benefit has been said to be presumed for the first three heads of charity, where Lord Wright indicated, in *National Anti-Vivisection Society* v. *Inland Revenue Commissioners*.[86]

> The test of benefit to the community goes through the whole of Lord Macnaghten's classification, though as regards the first three heads, it may be prima facie assumed unless the contrary appears.

With regard to the fourth head of charity, prior to the Charities Act 2006 in England and Wales, the public benefit should be expressly indicated.[87]

---

80 Frazer, 'Quantity Not Quality', 24, referring to Jaconelli, 'Adjudicating on Charitable Status', 102.
81 www.inbrief.co.uk/charity-law/defining-charitable-trusts.htm
82 Frazer, 'Quantity Not Quality', 22–3.
83 Frazer, 'Quantity Not Quality', 23, citing A. Talbot, 'The Charities Act 2006: Update on Commencement and Implementation', PCB (2008), 320.
84 www.inbrief.co.uk/charity-law/defining-charitable-trusts.htm
85 Synge, *'New' Public Benefit Requirement*, 10.
86 *National Anti-Vivisection Society* v. *Inland Revenue Commissioners*, 42, and *Re Education New Zealand Trust* CIV-2010-485-924, 22 November 2010, [24].
87 Debra Morris, 'Public Benefit: The Long and Winding Road to Reforming the Public Benefit Test for Charity: A Worthwhile Trip or "Is Your Journey Really Necessary?"', in Myles McGregor-Lowndes and Kerry O'Halloran (eds), *Modernising Charity Law: Recent Developments and Future Directions* (Cheltenham: Edward Elgar, 2010), 104; *New Zealand Computer Society Inc* CIV-2010-485-924, 22 November 2010, [13].

There have always been essential elements of the public benefit requirement,[88] thus a court may ask whether the 'benefits of a trust will accrue to the public is treated as involving a two-fold test'.[89] First, are the purposes of the trust such that they confer a benefit on the public or a section of the public? Second, does the class of persons eligible to benefit constitute the public, or a sufficient section of it?[90] In addition, there should be no undue private benefit that would outweigh the public benefit.[91]

The Charities Act 2006 however now provides that there should be no presumption that any particular purpose is for the public benefit, as follows:[92]

The 'public benefit' test

1   This section applies in connection with the requirement in section 2(1)(b) that a purpose falling within section 2(2) must be for the public benefit if it is to be a charitable purpose.
2   In determining whether that requirement is satisfied in relation to any such purpose, it is not to be presumed that a purpose of a particular description is for the public benefit.

It has been suggested that the rationale for this is to ensure a level playing field for all potential charitable organisations,[93] although as we will see in Chapter 4, when considering public benefit in more detail, issues have been raised with regard to this new statutory requirement.

While the Act itself 'pushes for a more forward-looking approach to regulation'[94] it actually 'holds on to the current case law-based approach to determining charitable purposes and public benefit by backward-looking precedent'.[95] As a result, such reformation may not have clarified the complexities of charity law as might have initially been hoped.

E Charitable purposes in Canada

As with many common law jurisdictions, Canada finds its charitable purposes governed by Lord Macnaghten's four heads of charity, as set out in *Commissioners for Special Purposes of the Income Tax* v. *Pemsel*,[96] which as we know are for the

---

88 Morris, 'Public Benefit', 106.
89 *Re Education New Zealand Trust*, [25].
90 Ibid.
91 Morris, 'Public Benefit', 106.
92 Charities Act 2006, s 3(1)–(2).
93 Synge, *'New' Public Benefit Requirement*, 9.
94 Dunn, 'Lord Hodgson's Charities Act Review', 136.
95 Ibid.
96 *Commissioners of Special Purposes for Income Tax* v.*Pemsel*, 583.

relief of poverty, the advancement of education, the advancement of religion, and any other purposes beneficial to the community.

The Canada Revenue Agency (CRA) 'is the gateway to charitable status',[97] and the Income Tax 1985 'places responsibility for registration in the hands'[98] of the CRA. To be registered as a charity, the CRA must be satisfied that an entity's purposes or objects are exclusively charitable and that its charitable activities support those purposes. There is no statutory definition of 'charitable' in the Income Tax Act, therefore the CRA looks to the common law to determine the charitable nature of an entity.[99]

Therefore, an entity's purposes will be considered charitable if they fall within one of the four *Pemsel* categories of charity. The Supreme Court case of *Vancouver Society of Immigrant and Visible Minority Women* v. *Minister of National Revenue* affirmed this: 'the adoption of the Pemsel categories [w]as a means of determining charitability in Canadian jurisprudence'.[100]

In addition, purposes may fall within the spirit and intendment of the Preamble of the Statute of Elizabeth. This means that purposes must be sufficiently similar to others that have been recognised charitable at law.[101] However, some doubt may have been cast on this, where it was observed about the *Vancouver Society* case:[102]

> Justice Iacobucci commented that 'the court has always had the jurisdiction to decide what is charitable and was never bound by the preamble'. This characterization casts some doubt on the current status of the preamble in Canadian law.

Nonetheless, the CRA does confirm that purposes may be charitable if they fall within the spirit and intendment of the Preamble, suggesting that the CRA approach will be observed.

In line with charity law in England and Wales, all entities wanting to obtain registered charitable status must ensure that their purposes are directed to the public benefit. It will be recalled from earlier that since the enactment of the Charities Act 2006 in England and Wales, any presumption of public benefit has been removed. However, Canadian charity law still follows England and Wales's original stance, that of the presumption of public benefit, at least where the purposes fall within the

---

97 O'Halloran, McGregor-Lowndes, and Simon, *Charity Law & Social Policy*, 455.

98 Ibid.

99 'What Is Charitable?', www.cra-arc.gc.ca/chrts-gvng/chrts/pplyng/cpc/wtc-eng.html [accessed 5 Jan. 2016].

100 Peter Broder, Canadian Centre for Philanthropy Public Affairs, August 2001, 'The Legal Definition of Charity and Canada Customs and Revenue Agency's Charitable Registration Process', 6, citing *Vancouver Society of Immigrant and Visible Minority Women* v. *Minister of National Revenue* [1999] 1 SCR 10, [146].

101 Guidelines for Registering a Charity: Meeting the Public Benefit Test, www.cra-arc.gc.ca/chrts-gvng/chrts/plcy/cps/cps-024-eng.html#N1020F, [3.1.1] [accessed 5 Jan. 2016].

102 Broder, 'Legal Definition of Charity', 6, citing *Vancouver Society of Immigrant and Visible Minority Women* v. *Minister of National Revenue*, [146].

first three categories of charity. This is because the relief of poverty, and the advancement of education and religion have all historically been recognised as benefiting the public.[103] This echoes the early English approach, where:[104]

> The test of benefit to the community goes through the whole of Lord Macnaghten's classification, though as regards the first three heads, it may be prima facie assumed unless the contrary appears.

Nonetheless, this presumption, in Canada, arises only when 'it has been clearly established that the purposes fall within these categories'.[105] This presumption can be rebutted in certain circumstances, for instance, where the contrary is shown, or where there the charitable nature of the organisation is called in to question. In those circumstances, 'the burden of providing public benefit becomes once again the responsibility of the applicant'.[106] The requirement of public benefit, generally speaking, involves the application of a two-stage test, which echoes the England and Wales requirement. The CRA determines that the test is as follows:[107]

- The first part of the test generally requires that a tangible benefit be conferred, directly or indirectly ...
- The second part of the test requires that the benefit have a public character, that is, be directed to the public or a sufficient section of the public.

Further, 'in the Canadian context, this requirement has also been described as an "objectively measurable and socially useful benefit"'.[108] While Canada does follow the more traditional path than some of its fellow jurisdictions, for instance in comparison with England and Wales, and Australia, Canadian charity law is not static. The CRA may consider novel purposes to be charitable 'when the issue of what benefits the public has been altered through a change in legislation or stated government policy',[109] as well as the changes in the needs of the community.[110]

F Charitable purposes in Australia

Up until 2014, Australia 'had been solely a creature of the common law with its antecedents in English common law'.[111] The Australian courts had recognised

---

103 'Guidelines for Registering a Charity', [3.1.1].
104 *National Anti-Vivisection Society* v. *Inland Revenue Commissioners*, 42.
105 'Guidelines for Registering a Charity', [3.1.1].
106 Ibid.
107 Ibid., [3].
108 'Guidelines for Registering a Charity', [3], citing *Vancouver Society of Immigrant and Visible Minority Women* v. *Minister of National Revenue*, [42].
109 'Guidelines for Registering a Charity', [3.1.1].
110 Ibid.
111 Fiona Martin, 'Recent Developments in Australian Charity Law', *Charity Law and Practice Review* 14 (2014), 31.

that the words 'charity' and 'charitable' had technical legal meanings, with their basis in the Preamble of the Statute of Elizabeth, and recognising the relevance of the *Pemsel* heads of charity.[112] Then, in 2013, the Federal Government provided a statutory definition in the Charities Act 2013. However, the Australian Charities and Not-for-Profits Commission (ACNC) notes that there 'are still other definitions of charity that may be applied by state and territory government agencies'.[113] Section 5 of the Act requires that an entity's purposes must be for charitable purposes. Charitable purposes are defined in s 12 of the Act, and loosely follow the pre-existing common law:[114]

a   the purpose of advancing health;
b   the purpose of advancing education;
c   the purpose of advancing social or public welfare;
d   the purpose of advancing religion;
e   the purpose of advancing culture;
f   the purpose of promoting reconciliation, mutual respect and tolerance between groups of individuals that are in Australia;
g   the purpose of promoting or protecting human rights;
h   the purpose of advancing the security or safety of Australia or the Australian public;
i   the purpose of preventing or relieving the suffering of animals;
j   the purpose of advancing the natural environment;
k   any other purpose beneficial to the general public that may reasonably be regarded as analogous to, or within the spirit of, any of the purposes mentioned in paragraphs (a) to (j);

This extended list of charitable purposes, at least in comparison with the four original purposes of *Pemsel*, reflects the England and Wales's contemporary approach. The final head, (k), is actually as a direct result of the High Court case of *Aid/Watch Inc* v. *Commissioner of Taxation*.[115] This case departed from the original position as posited in *Bowman* v. *Secular Society*[116] that charitable purposes cannot include political advocacy. *Aid/Watch* determined that generating public debate with regard to government policy can be charitable. The inclusion of the purpose within (k) reflects charity law's ability to evolve to meet a society's needs.

112   Martin, 'Recent Developments in Australian Charity Law', 31, referring to *Central Bayside General Practice Association Limited* v. *Commissioner of State Revenue* [2006] HCA 43; *Commissioner of Taxation* v. *Word Investments Ltd* [2008] HCA 55; and *Aid/Watch Inc* v. *Commissioner of Taxation* [2010] HCA 42.
113   Australian Charities and Not for Profits Commission, 'Legal Meaning of Charity', www.acnc.gov.au/ACNC/Register_my_charity/Who_can_register/Char_def/ACNC/Edu/Edu_Char_def.aspx [accessed 1 Dec. 2015].
114   Ann O'Connell, Fiona Martin, and Joyce Chia, 'Law, Policy, and Politics in Australia Recent Not-for-Profit Sector Reforms', *Australian Tax Forum* 1(2) (2013), 304.
115   Martin, 'Recent Developments in Australian Charity Law', 33.
116   *Bowman* v. *Secular Society Limited* [1917] AC 406.

Public benefit is still a requirement within Australian charity law, and s 6(1) of the Act defines it as:

> A purpose that an entity has is for the *public benefit* if:
>
> a   the achievement of the purpose would be of public benefit; and
> b   the purpose is directed to a benefit that is available to the members of:
> c   the general public; or
> d   a sufficient section of the general public.

Unlike contemporary England and Wales charity law, Australia permits some purposes to have a presumed public benefit, on the proviso that there is no evidence to the contrary:[117]

a   the purpose of preventing and relieving sickness, disease or human suffering;
b   the purpose of advancing education;
c   the purpose of relieving the poverty, distress or disadvantage of individuals or families;
d   the purpose of caring for and supporting:
e   the aged; or
f   individuals with disabilities;
g   the purpose of advancing religion.

There are additional exemptions from the public benefit requirement, for instance, where the purposes relieve necessitous circumstances,[118] which suggests that, in a number of respects, Australian charity law acknowledges some of the contemporary needs of its society.

G Charitable purposes in New Zealand

Pemsel's four heads of charity remain the basis for assessing that which is charitable in New Zealand. Section 5(1) of the Charities Act 2005 states:

> charitable purpose includes every charitable purpose, whether it relates to the relief of poverty, the advancement of education or religion, or any other matter beneficial to the community.

In 2012, the Act was amended to recognise the promotion of amateur sport as charitable, on the proviso that 'it is the means by which a charitable purpose referred to in subsection (1) is pursued'.[119]

---

117 Charities Act 2013 (Australia), s 7.
118 Ibid., ss 8–9.
119 Charities Act 2005 (NZ), s 5(2A).

It is said that 's 5(1) of the Act codifies the common law',[120] although there is no statutory definition of that which constitutes charitable purpose in New Zealand.

Thus the 'Act builds on the pre-existing common law understanding of "charitable purpose" and it is necessary to make reference to the case-law on the topic'.[121] The Act is the 'appropriate starting point because it provides the framework for consideration of what constitutes 'charitable purpose' in New Zealand law'.[122]

Section 13(1)(b) determines that an entity will qualify as charitable if it:

i   is established and maintained exclusively for charitable purposes; and
ii is not carried on for the private pecuniary profit of any individual[.]

Further, s 14 states that '[t]he purposes of an entity may be expressed in its statement of objects or may be inferred from the activities it undertakes', as s 18 (3) of the Act makes clear.[123] Section 18(3) provides:

> In considering an application, the chief executive must—
>
> a   have regard to—
> b   the activities of the entity at the time at which the application was made; and
> c   the proposed activities of the entity; and
> d   any other information that it considers is relevant;

Public benefit is also a key requirement in New Zealand, and public benefit and charitable purposes do not necessarily coincide. This is because:[124]

> The cases have generally insisted that the purposes of relief of poverty, advancement of education and advancement of religion (all treated as being within the 'spirit and intendment' of the preamble) must also be for the benefit of the public. Conversely, in the case of the fourth head, the common law required objects of benefit to the public still to be charitable within the spirit of the cases based on the 'very sketchy list in the statute of Elizabeth'.

Therefore, public benefit may be assumed until the contrary is shown with regard to the first three heads of charity.[125] There is one aspect of public benefit that is unique to New Zealand that will be considered here briefly. Generally speaking, an entity will not qualify as charitable at law if the beneficiaries are linked by a blood

---

120 *Travis Trust* v. *Charities Commission* (2009) 24 NZTC 23.273, [22].
121 *Re Greenpeace of New Zealand Inc* [2015] 1 NZLR 169 [2014] NZSC 105, [12].
122 Ibid.
123 Ibid., [14].
124 Ibid., [27], referring to *Re Education New Zealand Trust*, [24]; *National Anti-Vivisection Society* v. *Inland Revenue Commissioners*, 42, 65, and 41, respectively.
125 *Re Education New Zealand Trust*, [24]; *Re Greenpeace of New Zealand Inc*, [27].

tie;[126] *Latimer* v. *Commissioner of Inland Revenue*[127] considered that exception. The Court of Appeal held that it would be impossible not to consider Māori beneficiaries as a sufficient section of the community in the context of New Zealand society.[128] This approach has now been underpinned in s 5(2) of the Charities Act 2005, which states:

> the purpose of a trust, society, or institution is a charitable purpose under this Act if the purpose would satisfy the public benefit requirement apart from the fact that the beneficiaries of the trust, or the members of the society or institution, are related by blood;

The effect of this is to ensure, inter alia, that whānau, iwi, or hapū based trusts are capable of being charitable at law.[129]

H Charitable purposes in Singapore

The starting point for defining charitable purposes in the Singapore is the Charities Act 1994,[130] although it is 'not particularly illuminating' as it merely states:[131]

> 'charitable purposes' means purposes which are exclusively charitable according to the law of Singapore ...

Therefore, courts rely on the common law, which has largely been derived from English precedents.[132] It is argued that in fact the definition of charitable purposes is an adapted version of 'charitable purposes' as set out in the England and Wales's Charities Act 2006, and subsequently, the 2011 Act.[133]

Prior to 2005, the Singaporean Government recognised the four *Pemsel* heads of charity.[134] In the Budget Speech 2015, the then Prime Minister and Minister for

---

126 *Oppenheim* v. *Tobacco Securities Trust Co Ltd.*
127 *Latimer* v. *Commissioner of Inland Revenue* [2002] 3 NZLR 195 (PC).
128 Chevalier-Watts, *Law of Charity*, 72.
129 Andrew Butler and Tim Clarke, 'Charitable Trusts', in *Equity and Trusts in New Zealand*, 2nd edn (Wellington: Thomson Reuters, 2009), 304–5. 'Whānau' includes extended family or a community of related families who live closely; 'iwi' includes extended kinship groups or tribes; 'hapū' includes those with a genealogical descent and can include a number of "Whānau" whānau groups.
130 Charities Act 1994, Singapore, revised in 1995, and amended in 1999, 2001, 2004, and 2005.
131 Charities Act 1994, Singapore, s 2(1).
132 Helmut K. Angheier and Stefan Toepler, *International Encyclopaedia of Civil Society* (New York: Springer, 2010), 125.
133 Rachael Leow, 'Four Misconceptions about Charity Law in Singapore', *Singapore Journal of Legal Studies* 1 (2012), 42.
134 Ngoh Tiong Tan, 'Regulating Philanthropy: The Legal and Accountability Framework for Singapore Charities', *Asia Pacific Journal of Social Work and Development* 17(1) (June 2007), 69–70; Ministry of Finance, Singapore 2005, http://unpan1.un.org/intradoc/groups/public/documents/apcity/unpan021594.pdf, [4.26] [accessed 7 Jan. 2016].

Finance, Lee Hsien Loong, made two expansions to the original recognised heads of charity. Echoing the approach taken in New Zealand, he included:[135]

> the advancement of sport as a fifth charitable purpose, where the sport advances the health of individuals. Because this recognises the importance of sports in promoting a healthy lifestyle for all, we will only extend it to sports that require physical skill and exertion.

In addition, the following was announced:[136]

> I will explicitly recognise as charitable purposes several purposes that we now group under 'other purposes beneficial to the community', to encourage the groups undertaking these activities, as well as encourage Singaporeans to donate to these groups. The purposes are:
>
> - the advancement of health;
> - the advancement of citizenship or community development;
> - the advancement of the arts, heritage or science;
> - the advancement of environmental protection or improvement;
> - the relief of those in need by reason of youth, age, ill-health, disability, financial hardship or other disadvantage; and
> - the advancement of animal welfare.

This extended list of charitable purposes 'encompasses eleven out of the thirteen charitable purposes recognized under'[137] English jurisprudence. Although this extended list notably omits two of the English charitable purposes, those of 'the advancement of human rights, conflict resolution or reconciliation or the promotion of religious or racial harmony or equality and diversity'; and 'the promotion of the efficiency of the armed forces of the Crown, or of the efficiency of the police, fire and rescue services or ambulance services'.[138] However, it is beyond the scope of this chapter to consider the underlying reasons for such exclusions.

Interestingly, in the 2014 Court of Appeal case *Koh Lau Keow* v. *Attorney-General*,[139] Chao Hick Tin JA only made specific mention of the original four heads of charity, as opposed to acknowledging that the fourth head had been extended. This may be because this case focused on the relief of poverty and the advancement of religion. Or it may be because the additional purposes are construed as subsidiary legislation;[140] or that they have the legal character of an

---

135 Ministry of Finance, Singapore 2005, [4.27]; Leow, 'Four Misconceptions', 45.
136 Ministry of Finance, Singapore 2005, [4.28]; Leow, 'Four Misconceptions', 45.
137 Leow, 'Four Misconceptions', 45.
138 Leow, 'Four Misconceptions', 45, citing Charities Act 2011, ss 3(1)(h) and (i), respectively.
139 *Koh Lau Keow* v. *Attorney-General* [2014] SGCA 18, [18].
140 Subsidiary legislation is defined under s 2(1) of the Interpretation Act. It is also possible that the proclamation is ultra vires as per s 48 of the Charities Act, as the power

informed rule only. If the latter, then they are non-binding. As a result, the additional purposes actually 'run the risk of being ultra vires, being invalid because of non-compliance with publicity requirements or being of no legal effect as a mere informal rule'.[141] Nonetheless, the Commissioner of Charities (the Singapore regulator) does recognise the additional charitable purposes,[142] even though statute, and apparently case law, is silent on the matter.

With regard to the requirement of public benefit, Singapore retains the presumption of public benefit.[143]

I Charitable purposes in Hong Kong

Hong Kong currently lacks a formal register of charities, although the Inland Revenue Department (IRD), which is the main government body regulating charities in Hong Kong, does maintain the largest list of charities. However, this only includes those entities that have been successfully granted tax exemption under s 88 of the Inland Revenue Ordinance.[144] This means that there is no specific government authority that has overall responsibility for charity law. Therefore, the list of charities exempted from tax under s 88 is not a comprehensive, or even conclusive, list, of all the charities in Hong Kong.[145] Lack of public transparency and accountability led to the Law Reform Commission publishing a report on charities following a six-year review of charity law in Hong Kong, which will be considered in more detail in Chapter 9.

While there is no specific government authority that has overall responsibility for charitable entities, and indeed, no one specific piece of legislation governing such organisations, Hong Kong does recognise specific charitable purposes. A charity must be established exclusively for charitable purposes, and these purposes are exclusively charitable according to law. The law defining the legal attributes of a charity is based on the common law. In line with Hong Kong's fellow jurisdictions mentioned earlier in the chapter, it finds its common law heritage within the *Pemsel* four heads of charity.[146] The IRD states that for practical purposes,

---

to promulgate subsidiary legislation is conferred solely on the Minister of Community Development, Youth and Sports; Leow, 'Four Misconceptions', 47 and fn. 57.

141 Ibid., 47–8.
142 'What Are Charities?', www.charities.gov.sg/setting-up-a-charity/Pages/About-Charities-and-IPCs.aspx [accessed 8 Jan. 2016].
143 Donovan Waters QC, "Singapore and Hong Kong also Retain the Presumption': The Advancement of Religion in a Pluralist Society (Part II): Abolishing the Public Benefit Element', *Trust & Trustees* 17(8) (September 2011), 735.
144 'Charity Law Reform in Hong Kong: What Do the Proposed Changes Mean for You?', Hong Kong Dispute Resolution e-bulletin, file:///Users/juliet/Downloads/20140227%20-%20Charity%20Law%20Reform%20in%20Hong%20Kong%20What%20do%20the%20proposed%20changes%20mean%20for%20you.htm [accessed 8 Jan. 2016].
145 Law Reform Commission of Hong Kong, 'Report on Charities', www.khreform.gov.hk/en/publications/rcharities.htm [accessed 8 Jan. 2016].
146 *Cheung Man Yu* v. *Lau Yuen Ching* [2007] HKCA 171, [24]–[26].

Pemsel can be regarded as an authoritative summary of the purposes that might be accepted as charitable, those being relief of poverty, the advancements of education and religion, and other purposes of a charitable nature beneficial to the community not falling under any of the preceding heads. Interestingly, and in contrast with its fellow jurisdictions, the IRD also notes that while purposes that fall under the first three heads might be in relation to activities being carried out in any part of the world, those that fall under the fourth head will only be regarded as charitable if they are of benefit to the Hong Kong community.[147] The IRD provides a list of purposes that have been found to be charitable:[148]

a   Relief of poor people;
b   Relief of victims of a particular disaster;
c   Relief of sickness;
d   Relief of physically and mentally disabled;
e   Establishment or maintenance of non-profit-making schools;
f   Provision of scholarships;
g   Diffusion of knowledge of particular academic subjects;
h   Establishment or maintenance of a church;
i   Establishment of religious institutions of a public character;
j   Prevention of cruelty to animals;
k   Protection and safeguarding of the environment or countryside.

It also provides examples of purposes that are not charitable:[149]

a   Attainment of a political object;
b   Promotion of the benefits of the founders or subscribers;
c   Provision of a playing field, recreation ground or scholarship fund for employees of a particular company or industry;
d   Encouragement of a particular sport such as angling or cricket.

With regard to the element of public benefit, the IRD provides that a purpose must be directed to the public, or a sufficient section of it, and an institution cannot be charitable, generally speaking, if it was established for the benefit of specific individuals.[150] However, 'it is not possible to lay down any precise definition of what constitutes a sufficient section of the public. Each case must be considered on its merits'.[151] It appears that Hong Kong also embraces the presumption of public benefit, at least with the first three heads of charity, because of its

147 'Tax Guide for Charitable Institutions and Trusts of a Public Character', Inland Revenue Department, www.ird.gov.hk/eng/tax/ach_tgc.htm [accessed 8 Jan. 2016]; see also *Ip (or Yip) Cheung (or Chiang) Kwok* v. *Ip Siu Bun* [1990] HKCA 356.
148 'Tax Guide for Charitable Institutions and Trusts of a Public Character', Appendix A.
149 Ibid.; for information pertaining to political purposes generally, see Chapter 11.
150 'Tax Guide for Charitable Institutions and Trusts of a Public Character'.
151 Ibid.

strong association with historical English common law. Indeed, in *Ip (or Yip) Cheung (or Chiang) Kwok* v. *Ip Siu Bun*, the Court makes specific reference to the assumption of public benefit, and its rebuttal, at least in regard to the advancement of religion.[152]

---

152 *Ip (or Yip) Cheung (or Chiang) Kwok* v. *Ip Sin Bun*, [116]; Mark Hsiao, 'The Beginning and the End of an Era of Charitable Public Benefit in Hong Kong', *Conveyancer and Property Lawyer* 76(3) (2012), 44; see also *Li Kim Sang Victor* v *Chen Chi Hsia* [2015] HKCFI 259; HCA 481/2008 (24 February 2015), [81]; and *Cheung Man Yu* v *Lau Yuen Ching* [2007] KHCA 170, [24]–[26].

2 The nature of charities, charitable entities, not-for-profit organisations, charitable institutions, and governance

Charitable trusts

This chapter will consider the nature of charities within the context of charitable entities and institutions, and distinguish charitable legal entities from other legal entities.

A Trusts and charitable trusts

A trust may be defined as:[1]

> An equitable obligation, binding a ... trustee ... to deal with property over which he has control ... for the benefit of ... beneficiaries ... and any one of whom may enforce the obligation.

A charitable trust is not so much an organisation as it is a relationship:[2]

> [T]he relationship which arises wherever a person call a trustee is compelled in equity to hold property, whether real or personal, and whether by legal or equitable title, for the benefit of ... some [charitable] object permitted by law, in such a way that the real benefit of the property accrues, not to the trustees, but to the [charitable] objects of the trust.

A charitable trust is a species of trust, and there are a number of species within that genus, for instance, resulting trusts, constructive trusts, family trusts, and including charitable trusts. For the most part, the trust genus is governed by characteristics common to all.[3] Therefore, generally speaking, various forms of

---

1 A. Underhill and D. J. Hayton, *Underhill & Hayton: The Law Relating to Trusts and Trustees*, 15th edn (London: Butterworths, 1995), 3.
2 Mark Von Dadelszen, *Law of Societies*, 3rd edn (Wellington: LexisNexis, 2009), 237.
3 Kerry O'Halloran, Myles McGregor-Lowndes, and Karla W. Simon, *Charity Law & Social Policy: National and International Perspectives on the Functions of Law Relating to Charities*, vol. 10 (Netherlands: Springer, 2008), 114.

trust share common elements, and may also be distinguished from one another in a number of regards.

The trustee is the legal owner, while beneficiaries are the equitable owners. Trustees are subject to substantial, and often, onerous obligations. Trusts involve personal and proprietary obligations, and, as a result, beneficiaries can enjoy personal rights against trustees, and may also enjoy rights in respect of the trust property.[4] Trusts may be classified by, inter alia, legislation, intention, or subject matter. Trusts can be divided by their objects, or their beneficiaries.

One point of distinction is that between public and private. Except for charitable trusts, trusts are private by nature, as they are established for the benefit of individuals or a class of persons. On the other hand, charitable trusts are public in nature.[5] Charitable trusts are established to benefit the community, not a specific individual, and thus are public, and are enforced by the Attorney-General. The notion of public benefit is crucial in evaluating the charitability of an entity, which will be explored in greater detail later in the book. Private trusts are enforced by the beneficiaries and are for the benefit of private individuals,[6] and cannot continue indefinitely. One of the most common forms of private trust is an express trust. It has a number of essential elements and its existence is established by the 'three certainties',[7] which are 'sufficient words, to raise it; a definite subject and a certain or ascertained object'.[8] In other words, certainty of intention, certainty of subject matter, and certainty of objects.[9]

Certainty of intention refers to the intention of the settler, or legal person intending to create a trust. In doing so, the transferor is protected by ensuring that their property is applied within their expressed intentions, and protects the transferee by ensuring that they are burdened with the relevant trust obligations, but only when it is apparent that they were to take on the property as a trustee.[10]

If there is no certainty of subject matter, or trust fund, then, generally speaking, there is no trust. This is because a trustee must understand the nature of the trust, and the extent of the trust property being transferred to them, otherwise they will be unable to carry out their obligations and duties correctly.[11] However, if there is merely evidential uncertainty as to the subject matter, for instance, the trust property cannot be located immediately, although its location is capable of being ascertained, then the trust will not automatically fail. On the other hand, if there is

4 Andrew Butler, 'The Trust Concept, Classification and Interpretation', in *Equity and Trusts in New Zealand*, 2nd edn (Wellington: Thomson Reuters, 2009), 44–5.
5 O'Halloran, McGregor-Lowndes, and Simon, *Charity Law & Social Policy*, 114.
6 Butler, 'Trust Concept, Classification and Interpretation', 58.
7 *Knight* v. *Knight* (1840) 3 Beav 148.
8 Hubert Picarda, *The Law and Practice Relating to Charities*, 4th edn (London: Bloomsbury, 2010), 319, referring to, *inter alia*, *Cruwys* v. *Colman* (1804) 9 Ves 319; *Wright* v. *Atkyns* (1823) Turn & R 143, 157
9 Judith Spells, 'Trust Essentials', in *New Zealand Master Trusts Guide*, 3rd edn (Auckland: Wolters Kluwer, 2011), 28; Gary Watt, *Trusts & Equity*, 6th edn (Oxford: Oxford University Press, 2014), 74.
10 Watt, *Trusts & Equity*, 74.
11 Spells, 'Trust Essentials', 30.

evidential difficulty in identifying the subject matter, then conceptual uncertainty may cause the trust to fail.[12] However, in recent times, courts have been more willing to apply a benevolent construction to the words of the gift, so long as the intention to make a gift is sufficiently evident.[13]

It must be possible to ascertain the beneficiaries, or the objects of the trust. While the objects may not be specifically named, it must be possible, generally speaking to identify the beneficiaries. Thus, a class of beneficiaries referred to as 'my old friends' failed for uncertainty as it was not possible to identify the beneficiaries. However, a trust may be declared valid for a class of beneficiaries even if it is not possible to ascertain every member of that class.[14]

B Distinguishing charitable trusts from private trusts

Thus, generally, a private trust will fail for uncertainty if its objects cannot be ascertained. However, if the general intention of an object is to benefit a charity, uncertainty of objects will not necessarily negate its charitability. The key requirement is that of clear charitable intention. Nonetheless, a desire to carry out worthy causes may go beyond the meaning of 'charity'. For instance, in the leading case of *Morice* v. *Bishop of Durham*,[15] the Court held that a trust for 'objects of benevolence and liberality' may be charitable but overall were void for uncertainty.

This decision led to a long line of cases, including declaring void a gift simply to 'benevolent causes', and gifts to philanthropic causes because these purposes go beyond the legal meaning of 'charity'.[16] Indeed, a gift for 'charitable or benevolent' objects also failed because it was not exclusively charitable, thus failed for uncertainty.[17] Nonetheless, a benignant construction should be applied to charitable bequests. This is because this doctrine is an 'overriding principle of construction in relation to gifts to charity'.[18]

The notion of a benignant construction is a well-established maxim whereby a court will try to find in favour of the construction of a charitable gift. Thus, 'there is no better rule than that a benignant construction will be placed upon charitable requests'.[19] This means that where a gift is capable of two constructions, one that might make it void, and one that might make it effectual, the latter should be

---

12 *Palmer* v. *Simmonds* (1854) 2 Drew 221; Watt, *Trusts & Equity*, 82–3.

13 Spells, 'Trust Essentials', 31, referring to *Pennington* v. *Waine* [2002] 4 All ER 215 (CA).

14 Spells, 'Trust Essentials', 31–2, referring to *Brown* v.*Gould* [1972] Ch 53, 57 and *Re Gulbenkian's Settlement Trusts* [1970] AC 508, respectively.

15 *Morice* v. *Bishop of Durham* (1805) 10 Ves 522.

16 Picarda, *Law and Practice Relating to Charities*, 328, referring to *James* v. *Allen* (1817) 3 Mer 17 and *Re Macduff* [1896] 2 Ch 451, respectively.

17 *Chichester Diocesan Fund and Board of Finance (Incorporated)* v. *Simpson* [1944] 2 All ER 60 (HL).

18 Jean Warburton, *Tudor on Charities*, 9th edn (London: Sweet & Maxwell, 2003), 175.

19 Picarda, *Law and Practice Relating to Charities*, 353, citing *Weir* v. *Crum-Brown* [1908] AC 162, 167.

adopted.[20] This is because it is 'better to effectuate than to destroy the intention'.[21] Thus a trust that was dedicated to charitable purposes was held to be valid even though its terms were vague or uncertain.[22] In *Re White*, the testator left a gift to a number of religious societies, but did not name them. The Court saved the gift because it was able to infer the testator's charitable intention, as he had merely failed to name the actual beneficiaries.[23]

Therefore, while it can be said that certainty of objects is not required in a charitable trust, thus differentiating it from private trusts, there must be certainty of exclusive charitable intention. In other words, 'the application of funds to charitable purposes must be obligatory'.[24]

Not only do charitable trusts differ from private trusts in their creation, they also differ in their termination. Where a private trust fails, generally speaking, the trust property reverts to the estate or the settler, by way of a resulting trust. If a charitable trust fails, it will not return to the settler under a resulting trust, and nor will it pass to the Crown under *bona vacantia*. Instead, it can be applied cy-près by the court, or other governing body, in a way that is as near as possible to the intentions of the settler.[25] This chapter only seeks to outline the general principles of this doctrine.[26]

C Cy-près

The ancient equitable doctrine of cy-près permits funds, where applicable, to be applied by the court to objects that were as near as possible to the settler's wishes; it literally translates as 'close as possible'.[27] While its origins might be lost in the mists of time, it was apparently utilised in Roman law where a gift for holding yearly games was held to be impossible because such games were not permitted at the time. Modestinus, a jurist at the time, stated that in those circumstances the gift might be employed in a different manner.[28] While its origins may be ancient, the doctrine is still utilised in modern times in a number of jurisdictions, including England and Wales, and New Zealand.[29]

20 Picarda, *Law and Practice Relating to Charities*, 353, referring to *Bruce* v. *Presbytery of Deer* (1867) LR 1 Sc & Div 96 (HL), 97.
21 Picarda, *Law and Practice Relating to Charities*, 353, referring to *Re Lloyd* (1893) 10 TLR 66.
22 Watt, *Trusts & Equity*, 208, referring to *Chichester Diocesan Fund and Board of Finance (Incorporated)* v. *Simpson* [1944] 2 All ER 60 (HL).
23 *Re White* (1893) 2 Ch 41; *Mills* v. *Farmer* (1815) 1 Mer 55.
24 Picarda, *Law and Practice Relating to Charities*, 326–7, referring to *Morice* v. *Bishop of Durham*.
25 Watt, *Trusts & Equity*, 208.
26 For further information, see Picarda, *Law and Practice Relating to Charities*, ch. 30.
27 Juliet Chevalier-Watts, *Law of Charity* (Wellington: Thomson Reuters, 2014), 320.
28 Chevalier-Watts, *Law of Charity*, 320, referring to Edith L. Fish, 'The cy pres Doctrine and Changing Philosophies', *Michigan Law Review* 51(3) (1953), 375, referring to *Digest of Justinian* 33:2:16.
29 *Re Jenkin's Will Trusts* [1966] Ch 249 and *Alocoque* v. *Roache* [1998] 2 NZLR 250 (CA).

If a gift is to be saved by the cy-près doctrine, then it must comply with some basic principles. First, any modification to be made must be as closely aligned with the settler's intentions as possible.[30] Second, the gift should have failed initially, due to impossibility or impracticability, or failed subsequently due to impossibility or impracticability.[31] Third, the gift must show a paramount charitable intention.

An early example of a gift failing for initial failure due to impossibility is *Attorney-General* v. *The Ironmonger's Company*,[32] which concerned a gift to save British slaves in Barbary or Turkey. From the time of the testator's death, however, there were no British slaves being held in either place, so the gift failed for impossibility. A gift cannot be applied cy-près, however, unless it has been shown that it is impossible to carry out the testator's intention.[33] Further, it cannot be applied because a court believes 'some other scheme will be more beneficial than the testator's'.[34]

An example of a gift initially failing for impracticability is where the gift is to pay for the erection of a building is insufficient, or for which planning permission cannot be obtained, or for which no suitable site can be found.[35]

In *Re Slevin*[36] a gift failed subsequently because an orphanage ceased to exist before a gift could be imparted to it.

In relation to the requirement of a general charitable intention, in the case of initial failure for impossibility or impracticability, cy-près can only operate where there is a paramount charitable intention.[37] However, in situations of subsequent failure, 'it is now firmly established that the property is applicable cy-pres without any need to inquire whether the settler or testator had a general charitable intention'.[38] This is because once the property has been recognised at law as being charitable, the court will presume that the gift was intended to be perpetual, so there is no possibility of a resulting trust. In the case of *Re King*,[39] the will maker left a gift for the erection of a stained-glass window in a church. This was held to be a valid charitable gift, so the surplus funds should be applied cy-près. Romer J observed that with a gift to a 'charitable institution, where such institution ceases to exist before the death of the testator the cy-pres doctrine does not apply unless a general charitable intention can be found',[40] thus affirming our earlier consideration regarding general charitable intention.

---

30 Chevalier-Watts, *Law of Charity*, 320; Watt, *Trusts & Equity*, 232.
31 Andrew S. Butler, 'Charitable Trusts', in Andrew S. Butler (ed.), *Equity and Trusts in New Zealand*, 2nd edn (Wellington: Thomson Reuters, 2009), 295–6; Watt, *Trusts & Equity*, 233.
32 *The Ironmonger's Company* (1840) 2 Beav 313, 48 ER 1201 (Ch).
33 *Re Weir Hospital* [1910] 2 Ch 124, 124.
34 Ibid.
35 Watt, *Trusts & Equity*, 208, referring to *Re Weir Hospital*.
36 *Re Slevin* [1891] 2 Ch 236.
37 For example, *Biscoe* v. *Jackson* (1887) 35 Ch D 460; *Re Richardson's Will* (1887) 58 LT 45.
38 Peter Luxton, *The Law of Charities* (Oxford: Oxford University Press, 2001), 560.
39 *Re King* [1923] 1 Ch 243.
40 Ibid., 246.

However:[41]

> in the case of a legacy to a charitable institution that exists at the death of the testator, but ceases to exist after his death and before the legacy is paid over, the legacy is applied cy-pres, even in the absence of a general charitable intention.

As a result, the surplus was applied cy-près and would be applied in the erection of a further stained-glass window or windows in the same church.

D Privileges of being a charitable entity

Charitable trusts enjoy a number of privileges not available to other trusts, including the above-mentioned matters, as well as other benefits, including social and fiscal privileges.

The rule against perpetuities is also known as the 'rule against remoteness of vesting'.[42] It 'invalidates any future interest under a trust that is not bound to vest, if at all, within a prescribed period of time (the perpetuity period)'.[43] This rule:

> expresses the historical tension that has lain between landowners who wish to ensure that their estates are preserved within their family for generations and the courts trying to constrain the practice of some settlers who seek to tie up their estates indefinitely by 'providing for gifts of property to vest at some distant time in the future'.[44]

The general rule at law is that the perpetuity period extends to the lifetime of the specified person alive at the creation of the trust, and extends 21 years from the date of the death of the last survivor of that person, although the general rule is modified by statutes in many jurisdictions.[45]

However, charitable trusts 'are in most respects exempt from the rule against perpetuities'.[46] This characteristic of charitable trusts is as old as the common law itself.[47] By their very nature, many charitable trusts will be indefinite or will be designed to continue perpetually, and the law accepts this.[48] This means that a

---

41 *Re King* [1923] 1 Ch 243, 246, referring to *Re Slevin* and Amherst D. Tyssen, *The Law of Charitable Bequests*, 2nd edn (London: Sweet & Maxwell, 1921), 202.

42 Gino Dal Pont, *Charity Law in Australia & New Zealand* (OUP: Melbourne, 2000), 85.

43 Ibid.

44 Chevalier-Watts, *Law of Charity*, 25, citing O'Halloran, McGregor-Lowndes, and Simon, *Charity Law & Social Policy*, 113.

45 Dal Pont, *Law of Charity*, 133.

46 *McGovern* v. *Attorney-General* [1982] Ch 321, [1982] 2 WLR 222 (Ch) 331

47 O'Halloran, McGregor-Lowndes, and Simon, *Charity Law & Social Policy*, 115; *Howse* v. *Chapman*, 4 Ves 542, 1799.

48 Dadelszen, *Law of Societies*, 243.

charitable trust can last indefinitely. The reason for this exception to the rule against perpetuities is as follows:[49]

> It is the public interest in encouraging the endowment of charity, which by definition is beneficial to the public, and in securing a donor's bounty to those who were intended to benefit in the future, that can be said to justify this favourable treatment.

This was expressed more fully by an American commentator:[50]

> As a general rule, the state limits dead hand control [over property] through the rule against perpetuities, under which property owners can dictate the use and enjoyment of amassed societal wealth for roughly a century after death. The rule strikes a balance between property owners' desires to exercise control from beyond the grave and a perceived societal interest in having the use of resources determined by the living. In the case of gifts to charity, however, the state strikes a more generous bargain with donors. Donors get to extend their control indefinitely ... [and] the state not only allows [this] ... but monitors and enforces it. The reason ... is an implicit quid prop quo: In exchange for perpetual donor control, society gets wealth devoted to recognizably 'public' purposes.

Private trusts are also subject to another rule against perpetuity – the rule against inalienability, where if there is a possibility that capital will be tied up for longer than the perpetuity period then the disposition will be void for perpetual trusts. Therefore, a non-charitable private trust must spend its capital immediately, or at least within the perpetuity period, if it is not to breach this rule.[51] The reason for this rule is a public policy one. Capital that is owned absolutely can participate unhindered in the economy. Capital that is set aside on trust held solely for the production of income cannot participate in this manner.[52] In contrast, charitable trusts are exempt from this requirement, which means that capital can be tied up indefinitely.[53]

E Fiscal benefits

One of the key benefits for charitable entities is that of fiscal advantages. The history of exemption from some types of tax is ancient, and examples can be found in the eleventh century, at the time of the Crusades,[54] although mention is also

---

49 Dal Pont, *Law of Charity*, 134.
50 Dal Pont, *Law of Charity*, 134, citing R. Atkinson, 'Reforming cy pres Reform', *Hastings Law Journal* 44 (1992), 1114.
51 Luxton, *Law of Charities*, 67; Chevalier-Watts, *Law of Charity*, 26.
52 Watt, *Trusts & Equity*, 187–8.
53 Luxton, *Law of Charities*, 67.
54 Susan Barker, Michael Gousmett, and Ken Lord, *The Law and Practice of Charities in New Zealand* (Wellington: LexisNexis, 2013), 7.

made of exemptions going back to the times of the Old Testament.[55] One early example is in the Duties upon Income Tax 1799, which provided exemption duties to corporations, fraternities, and societies of persons established for charitable purposes only.[56] Today, fiscal exemptions for registered charitable bodies lie within a variety of legislation: in the United Kingdom within the Finance Acts of 1990, 1999, and 2000, and the Income and Corporation Taxes 1988; in New Zealand within the Income Tax Act 2007; and within the Income Tax Act for Singapore.

In the case of Australia, a number of tax concessions are available to charities from the Australian Taxation Office (ATO), as well as from relevant state and territory governments. An entity must be registered with the Australian Charities and Not-for-Profits Commission (ACNC) to apply for tax concessions from the ATO, although an entity does not need to be registered with the ACNC to access state and territory or local government tax concessions.[57] Such tax concessions include exemption from income tax; a number of Goods and Services Tax (GST) concessions; and fringe benefits tax (FBT) rebates.[58]

In the United Kingdom, tax relief for registered charitable entities is available if most of the income and gains is utilised for charitable purposes; this is known as 'charitable expenditure'. This includes tax on donations; profits from trading; rental or investment income, for instance bank interest; profits when an asset is disposed of, for instance property or shares; or when property is purchased.[59] In addition, donations by individuals to charities is tax free, which is called tax relief. The tax goes to the donor or the charity, and how that operates depends on whether the donor donates through Gift Aid; from salary or pension through a payroll-giving scheme; from land, property, or shares; or via a will.[60]

New Zealand also provides numerous fiscal advantages, including: exemption from income tax; eligibility to apply for resident withholding tax; donations through payroll giving; eligibility for exemption for some concessions concerning GST payments; and eligibility for exemption to pay rates on land owned by the charitable entity.[61]

F Non-fiscal advantages

One of the key benefits of being a registered charity is the enhanced public standing. To register with charities institutes, the charity portals make publicly

---

55 Dal Pont, *Law of Charity*, 144.
56 Barker, Gousmett, and Lord, *Law and Practice of Charities in New Zealand*, 17.
57 www.acnc.gov.au/ACNC/Pblctns/Factsheets/ACNC/FTS/Fact_ConcAvail.aspx [accessed 13 Jan. 2016].
58 www.acnc.gov.au/ACNC/Register_my_charity/Why_register/Charity_tax/ACNC/ FTS/Fact_ConcAvail.aspx?hkey=c9347d53-e040-4ab0-81bc-9f3e5193ad40 [accessed 13 Jan. 2016].
59 www.gov.uk/charities-and-tax/tax-reliefs [accessed 13 Jan. 2016].
60 www.gov.uk/donating-to-charity/overview [accessed 13 Jan. 2016].
61 Barker, Gousmett, and Lord, *Law and Practices of Charities in New Zealand*, 28.

available information pertaining to each registered charity. Information may include deeds, trust documents, trustee/officer details, charitable objects, beneficiaries, the sector in which the charity operates, and financial information. As a result, the public can make more well-informed decisions as to where their support may lie. By registering as a charity, entities provide valuable data through the commissions to the charitable sector and relevant governments, which can help inform the sector on relevant policy decisions, which in turn will be of general public benefit. Importantly, funders can ensure, among other matters, that their chosen charity or charities is best matched for their funding criteria; that their chosen entity meets charity law requirements; and funders can target key sections of the charitable sector to ensure best use of their funding money.[62] Of benefit to charities themselves is the ability to avail themselves of the information provided by the various commissions or charity bodies that is made available through the relevant portals or charity teams with regard to matters affecting their charity. This may ensure, inter alia, more effective use of funds; continued legal and policy compliance; and ensuring correct financial reporting. This chapter will introduce, in more detail, the relevant governing bodies in each of the selected jurisdictions.

G Disadvantages of charitable status

While there are evidently numerous advantages to obtaining charitable status, inevitably there are some disadvantages to being a charity. First, registered charities are required to ensure that they meet and comply, at all times, with relevant statutory and common law impositions. While this is not a disadvantage in many ways for the public and beneficiaries, it can be onerous for entities, especially if their objects fall within some contentious areas of law, for instance, advocacy and political purposes, which will be considered later in the book. Charities are also subject, generally speaking, to control by the relevant charities commission, or governing body, and appropriate Attorney-General, which while protecting the public and the charitable sector, means that registered charities must ensure that they comply fully with relevant policies and the law to ensure that they maintain their status.

H Other charitable structures

While this chapter, and Chapter 1, have made reference to charitable trusts, it would be fair to say that charities may assume a number of structures other than charitable trusts, and it is common for entities to utilise other types of legal vehicles to form a charity. However, while every charity must have a legal structure, 'there is no single structure in English law specifically designed for charities'.[63] Thus many charities operate under different legal structures that may be subject

---

62 Chevalier-Watts, *Law of Charity*, 29–30.
63 Luxton, *Law of Charities*, 17.

not just to charity law requirements, but also to their specific structure related requirements.

The following table illustrates some of the different types of charitable entities that can be recognised at law.[64]

Organisation	Objects	Structure	Control	Beneficiaries
Incorporated trust	Charitable	Trust	Trustees	Charitable purposes
Unincorporated trust	Charitable	Trust	Trustees	Charitable purposes
Incorporated society	Charitable	Society	Members and executive	Charitable purposes
Unincorporated society	Charitable	Society	Members and executive	Charitable purposes
Incorporated society	Charitable	Varies	Varies	Charitable purposes
Statutory charity	Charitable	Varies	Varies	Generally, charitable purposes

There are numerous reasons as to why one structure might be chosen over another, and one of those reasons may be the method of operation that is most important for the charity, or perhaps the governance that is most appropriate.[65] Therefore, considerations for a charity may include who will run the charity, and whether it will have a wider membership; whether it can enter into contracts or employ staff of its own; and who has liability.[66]

I Charities and not-for-profits organisations

Charitable organisations may be distinguished from other not-for-profit organisations on the basis of a number of principles and the legal form or structure to give effect to their activities.[67] Although there are also some similarities that will be noted.

Thus, in a similar way to charities, not-for-profit organisations do not distribute their surplus funds to owners or shareholders; rather, they utilise those funds to assist in the pursuit of their purposes. Thus, charities are a type of not-for-profit organisation.[68] The main similarity therefore between charities and not-for-profit

---

64 Dadelszen, *Law of Societies*, 238; recognition of different legal structures may vary from jurisdiction to jurisdiction.
65 Barker, Gousmett, and Lord, *Law and Practices of Charities in New Zealand*, 459–60.
66 www.gov.uk/guidance/charity-types-how-to-choose-a-structure [accessed 14 Jan. 2016].
67 O'Halloran, McGregor-Lowndes, and Simon, *Charity Law & Social Policy*, 23.
68 Donald Poirier, *Charity Law in New Zealand* (2013), www.charities.govt.nz, 68.

organisations is that neither type of organisation is conducted for profit. Both are established to fulfil their purposes for which they were originally established. Another similarity is that not-for-profits may be eligible for some tax exemptions, even if they do not have exclusively charitable purposes. For example, in New Zealand, the Income Tax Act 2007 provides that a number of entities can have tax exemptions, and this includes Māori authority distributions; public authorities, local authorities, friendly societies, and funeral trusts.[69] An example of tax exemption for a not-for-profit organisation in the United Kingdom is community amateur sports clubs (CASCs). This scheme was introduced in April 2002. CASCs are companies or unincorporated associations established to provide facilities and promote amateur sports to the whole community that are recognised by the National Sports Councils. CASCs can claim a limited range of tax exemptions, such as corporation tax if certain principles are met, and gift aid.[70]

While some not-for-profit organisations are charitable, not all will be, and as illustrated in Chapter 1, charity law finds its basis in ancient times and ancient laws and governing principles, thus charity is recognised at law as a creation of equity.[71]

Not-for-profits organisations can take a number of different legal structures, including Industrial and Provident Societies. These exist in New Zealand, Ireland, and the United Kingdom, although recent legislation in the United Kingdom[72] has amended the name to cooperative or community benefit societies. These societies are a member benefit type of non-government organisation that are usually commercial and governed by various statutes respective to their jurisdictions.

Another type is a Friendly Society. This society can include mutual insurance and assurance bodies; benevolent societies; and other societies formed for the promotion of science, literature, and education.[73] As with the previous mentioned society, Friendly Societies will generally be governed by jurisdiction-appropriate legislation. The use of unincorporated associations as a legal structure for charities gained popularity in the eighteenth century, and in the United Kingdom such an association is used mainly by smaller charities with multiple sources of funding for whom membership participation is important. It is not unusual for a charity to commence operation as an unincorporated association, and then change its legal structure to that of a company limited by guarantee, as its activities and possible liabilities to third parties increases.[74]

It has been recognised, generally speaking, that none of the legal structures utilised as charitable entities, including those outlined above, are ideal for charities. All of the legal structures require some kind of adaptation for charities, and some require dual registration. As a result, the Strategy Unit report in the United Kingdom proposed that there should be a new corporate structure specifically for

69 Ibid., 72.
70 www.taxadvisermagazine.com/article/not-profit-not-tax [accessed 14 Jan. 2016].
71 Poirier, *Charity Law in New Zealand*, 72.
72 Co-operative and Community Benefit Societies Act 2014 [UK].
73 O'Halloran, McGregor-Lowndes, and Simon, *Charity Law & Social Policy*, 24.
74 Warburton, *Tudor on Charities*, 163.

charities, the Charitable Incorporated Organisation (CIO).[75] The legislation for CIOs was introduced into the Charities Act 1993 by the Charities Act 2006, but it did not become available as a legal form for charities until further regulations were made that supplemented the statutory provisions, which are now found in Part 11 of the Charities Act 2011. Some of the key features of a CIO are that it is incorporated; the liability of members can be limited; and it has a single constitution that must comply with certain requirements as set out in the Charitable Incorporated Organisations (General) Regulations 2012/2013. The benefit of being a CIO is that it brings the advantages of being incorporated without the burden of dual registration, and with the flexibility to create a constitution aimed specifically at charitable activities and governance.[76]

One key difference between not-for-profit organisations and charities is that charities are established permanently, and are thus exempt from the rule against perpetuity. By contrast, if a not-for-profit organisation is wound up or dissolved, it may distribute its assets among its members. If a charity ceases to exist, it must distribute its assets to charitable purposes.

A charity must meet certain legal requirements that not-for-profit organisations are not obliged to meet. For instance, charities must ensure that their purposes fall under some form of the *Pemsel* heads of charity;[77] that the purposes are exclusively charitable;[78] and that their purposes meet the public benefit test.[79] If these obligations are not met, a charity can be deregistered, which is likely to become public information. Not-for-profit organisations, while certainly being bound by jurisdiction-appropriate statute or governing bodies, are not subject to such stringent duties.

Therefore, while charities and not-for-profit organisations do share some similarities, their legal structures may not necessarily distinguish them, and both can be eligible for tax exemption, although both types of organisations play key roles in the economy of countries, as well as supporting education, communities, social services, and professional activities, among many other very important roles.

Each of the selected jurisdictions has a governing body, or bodies, and legislation associated with governing charities, and it is to these matters that this chapter now turns, to introduce some of the key factors associated with these bodies and the legislation.

International charitable governing bodies and statutory governance

A England and Wales

The Statute of Charitable Uses 1601, or Statute of Elizabeth, with its Preamble, was the original legislative statement of matters pertaining to charitable purposes,

---

75 Ibid., 173.
76 Con Alexander *et al.*, *Charity Governance*, 2nd edn (Bristol: Jordans, 2014), 24–5.
77 This category finds its basis in Lord Macnaghten's dicta in *Commissioners for Special Purposes of Income Tax* v. *Pemsel* [1891] AC 531. (See Chapter 1 for further discussion on the importance of this case in charity law.)
78 See Chapter 3 for further discussion.
79 See Chapter 4 for further discussion.

which formed the common law context of charity law,[80] and was later consolidated by the *Pemsel* classification of the four heads of charity.[81] England's
charity law has been subject to numerous statutory changes throughout the nineteenth and twentieth centuries. The Charities Act 1960 was largely replicated in
the other jurisdictions of the United Kingdom, and 'laid a roughly common
baseline for law and practice in the latter part of the 20th century'.[82] However,
the most far-reaching contemporary change occurred with the Charities Act 2006,
and subsequently the Charities Act 2011, which consolidated the 2006 Act.[83] The
2006 Act provided, for the first time, a statutory definition of charitable purposes,
and removed the presumption of public benefit.[84] In addition to these changes,
the Act also extended the original list of four charitable purposes to thirteen
charitable purposes.[85]

The Charity Commission for England and Wales (in Welsh: Comisiwn Elusennau Cymru a Lloegr) is a non-ministerial government department and body
corporate that regulates charities in England and Wales.[86] The role of the courts in
deciding whether or not a body was charitable was largely transferred to the
Commission by the Charities Act 1993. Courts still remain the forum for ultimate
appeal, and the courts' jurisdiction for administering a charity is concurrent with
that of the Commission.[87] As a result of the Charities Act 2006,[88] the Commission has now been incorporated with an expanded board drawn from a wider
section of the community.[89] The Commission is accountable to Parliament,
through its submission of an annual report and accounts; and to the court or tribunal, as set out below, which may overturn its decisions.[90] However, it is
required to be independent of ministerial influence or control over the exercise of
its functions.[91]

---

80 O'Halloran, McGregor-Lowndes, and Simon, *Charity Law & Social Policy*, 41–2.
81 This category finds its basis in Lord Macnaghten's dicta in *Commissioners for Special
    Purposes of Income Tax* v. *Pemsel* [1891] AC 531. (See Chapter 1 for further discus-
    sion on the importance of this case in charity law.).
82 Kerry O'Halloran *et al.*, 'Charity Law Reforms: An Overview of Progress Since 2001',
    in Myles McGregor-Lowndes and Kerry O'Halloran (eds), *Modernising Charity Law,
    Recent Developments and Future Directions* (Cheltenham: Edward Elgar, 2010), 13.
83 Mary Synge, *The 'New' Public Benefit Requirement: Making Sense of Charity Law?*
    (Oxford: Hart, 2015), 10.
84 Charities Act 2006, s 3 [UK]. For details on charitable purposes and public benefit,
    see Chapters 1, 4, and 5.
85 Charities Act 2006, s 2 [UK]; see Chapter 1 for extended list of charitable purposes.
86 Alexander *et al.*, *Charity Governance*, 43; Synge, *'New' Public Benefit Requirement*,
    10.
87 Watt, *Trusts & Equity*, 231.
88 Now consolidated in the Charities Act 2011 [UK], Part 5 (Charities Act 1993 [UK], s 8).
89 Watt, *Trusts & Equity*, 231.
90 Synge, *'New' Public Benefit Requirement*, 11
91 Charities Act 2011, s 13(4) ('although the members of the Commission are appointed by
    the appropriate government minister, after a public appointments process' (Synge, *'New'
    Public Benefit Requirement*, fn. 68); Synge 'New' Public Benefit Requirement, 11.

The governance framework for the Commission is set out in the 2011 Act.[92] The Commission's objectives include increasing public confidence in charities; promoting awareness and understanding about public benefit; ensuring charitable compliance; and ensuring greater accountability.[93] The Commission has a number of functions, including determining the charitable nature of entities; a watchdog; and encouraging improved administration of charities. The Commission also has a range of statutory duties conferred on it by the 2011 Act, which includes maintaining the register of charities,[94] although it is not permitted to act in the place of any charity trustee, nor to substitute its own views for that of a trustee, nor do anything else that would mean it becomes directly involved with the administration of a charity.[95]

The First-tier Tribunal (Charity) was introduced by the 2006 Act to reduce the costs of appeals against decisions made by the Commission when exercising its statutory duties. The Tribunal's jurisdiction does not extend to the exercise all of the Commission's statutory powers, but many of the Commission's most significant powers are subject to right of appeal to the Tribunal.[96] There is a right of appeal from any decision of the Tribunal to the Upper Tribunal, and a right of appeal from the Upper Tribunal to the Court of Appeal.[97] If it is not possible to challenge a decision of the Commission to the Tribunal, it may be possible to bring an appeal to the High Court.[98]

B Australia

Australia's adoption of a national body for its charity sector, the ACNC, which is the independent national regulator of charities, took place 'after what can best be described as a leisurely and thorough process of reviews and inquiries, dating at least from the *Charities Definition Inquiry* of 2000'.[99]

The Australian Charities and Not-for-Profits Act 2012 (Cth) (ACNC Act) was passed in November 2012, and the ACNC became officially operative in December 2012. As a result of the ACNC Act being an act of the Australian Commonwealth Government, it is only binding on areas within the authority of the Commonwealth Parliament. This means that it does not apply to Australian state laws that relate to charitable fund raising, or licensing of charitable service providers, for instance. Such service providers might include aged care facilities, that is, unless there has been an agreement between the Commonwealth and the state in

---

92 Charities Act 2011, s 13.
93 www.gov.uk/government/organisations/charity-commission/about [accessed 18 Jan. 2016]; Alexander *et al., Charity Governance*, 44.
94 Charities Act 2011, s 29.
95 Alexander *et al., Charity Governance*, 45; Charities Act 2011, s 20.
96 Charities Act 2011, Schedule 6.
97 Charities Act 2011, s 317; Tribunals, Courts and Enforcement Act 2007, ss 11 and 13.
98 Alexander *et al., Charity Governance*, 63–4.
99 Ian Murray, 'The Australian Charities and Not-for-Profits Commission: Reform or Unreform?', *Charity Law and Practice Review* 17(1) (2014–15), 151.

question.[100] The ATO remains responsible for deciding eligibility for charity tax concessions, as well as other commonwealth exemptions and benefits,[101] although it is the ACNC Commissioner who determines whether an entity is a charity, not the Commissioner of Taxation.[102] 'There are a number of other government agencies that regulate charities and other not-for-profits. For example, government agencies may provide grants and other funding. They may also regulate particular services provided by charities, such as aged care or education.'[103]

The ACNC was set up to achieve the following objects:[104]

- maintain, protect and enhance public trust and confidence in the sector through increased accountability and transparency
- support and sustain a robust, vibrant, independent and innovative not-for-profit sector
- promote the reduction of unnecessary regulatory obligations on the sector.

In order to achieve those objects, the ACNC:[105]

- registers organisations as charities
- helps charities understand and meet their obligations through information, guidance, advice and other support
- helps the public understand the work of the not-for profit sector through information, guidance, advice and other support
- maintains a free and searchable public register so that anyone can look up information about registered charities
- is working with state and territory governments (as well as individual federal, state and territory government agencies) to develop a 'report-once, use-often' reporting framework for charities.

The ACNC Act established a Commissioner, and provides that the Commissioner is the national regulator for not-for-profits, including charities. Registration with the ACNC is a requirement if an entity is to take advantage of taxation concessions, including exemption from income tax,[106] as well as a number of other concessions and benefits available under Australian laws.[107]

100 Fiona Martin, 'Recent Developments in Australian Charity Law: One Step Forward and Two Steps Backward', *Charity Law and Practice Review* 17(1) (2014–15), 26.
101 'ACNC's Role'. www.acnc.gov.au/ACNC/About_ACNC/ACNC_role/ACNC/Edu/ACNC_role.aspx?hkey=88635892-3c89-421b-896d-d01add82f4fe accessed 19 Jan 2016.
102 Ian Murray, 'Not-for-Profit Reform: Back to the Future?', *Third Sector Review* 20(1) (2014), 115.
103 'ACNC's Role'.
104 Ibid.
105 Ibid.; Murray, 'Australian Charities and Not-for-Profits Commission?', 153; Australian Charities and Not for profits Commission Act 2012, ss 15–5(2); 15–5(2)(b)(iii); 100–110(1); 15–5(2)(b)(ii); ch 3; ch 4; pt 2–2; s 15–10(f) respectively.
106 Martin, 'Recent Developments in Australian Charity Law', 27; ACNC Act s 15–5(3).
107 Martin, 'Recent Developments in Australian Charity Law', 27; ACNC Act, s 15–5(4).

When exercising powers and functions, the Commissioner must have regard to s 15–10 of the ACNC Act, which establishes a set of comprehensive principles. There are overarching and general guidelines, which include maintaining and protecting public confidence in the sector, and more specific and practical guidelines, including the need for accountability and transparency. The final principle in s 15-10(h) is that the Commissioner must have regard to uniqueness and diversity of not-for-profits, as well as their distinctive role that they play in Australia.[108]

Of significance, and unique to Australia, is that it has six states and two territories. These states and territories have a number of important responsibilities relating to charitable bodies, and the reporting requirements, among other matters, places significant compliance burdens on charitable entities that operate in these jurisdictions. This becomes even more onerous if the charitable entities operate at a multistate level, and the ACNC is not able to override these powers because of the constitutional limitations of the Commonwealth Government.[109] As a result, 'successive governments have recognised that harmonisation of laws and regulations that relate to charities and NFPs, is a long term issue that will need state and territory agreement'.[110]

Until the introduction of the Charities Act 2013 (Cth) in Australia, the definition of charity was traditionally decided by the application of common law principles. As might be imagined, Australia finds its historical reference point for charity in the Preamble of the Statute of Elizabeth 1601.[111] Until the Act, there was no statutory definition of 'charity' for the purposes of Australian law, and with this Act, and also the Charities (Consequential Amendments and Transitional Provisions) Act 2013 (Cth), definitions of 'charity' and 'charitable purpose' were introduced for all Commonwealth legislation.[112] 'Charity' is defined as:[113]

> an entity:
>
> a   that is a not-for-profit entity; and
> b   all of the purposes of which are:
> c   charitable purposes (see Part 3) that are for the public benefit (see Division 2 of this Part); or
> d   purposes that are incidental or ancillary to, and in furtherance or in aid of, purposes of the entity covered by subparagraph (i); and …

108 Martin, 'Recent Developments in Australian Charity Law', 28.
109 Ibid., 31.
110 Martin, 'Recent Developments in Australian Charity Law', 31, referring to Australian Government, *Final Report: Scoping Study for a National Not-for-Profit Regulator*, April 2011, 65 and 68.
111 Martin Kirkness, 'Life Cycle Issues for Charities', *Taxation in Australia* 50(5) (November 2015), 252.
112 See Chapter 1 for the statutory definitions of 'charitable purpose'.
113 Charities Act 2013, s 5 [AU].

e   none of the purposes of which are disqualifying purposes (see Division 3); and
f   that is not an individual, a political party or a government entity.

This codified definition of charity applies for the purposes of federal legislation, unless a contrary intention is specifically provided. The definition actually is largely based upon, and preserves, the common law principles, although it does provide minor modern modifications, and greater clarity.[114] As a result of this definition applying only to federal legislation, and not at state level, the common law meaning will still be relevant 'to state and local government tax concessions in relation to matters such as payroll tax, stamp duty, land tax and council rates'.[115] Thus, in reality, 'the need to understand both the statute and the existing case law indicates'[116] that the notion of reducing the complexities of charity law is likely to be negated, at least in borderline charity cases.[117]

C New Zealand

The late 1950s saw the enactment of the Charitable Trusts Act 1957, which consolidated the various previous statutes. However, it would take nearly half a century before further legislation, and a Charities Commission, was established in New Zealand. In 2005, the Charities Act 2005 was passed, which, inter alia, established the Charities Commission (as it was), a government body, whose purpose was to manage a registration, support, and supervisory system for registered charitable entities.[118] Under ss 21–26 of the Act, the Commission was required to establish and maintain a register of charitable entities, and under ss 31–36 may remove an entity from the register on the grounds as set out in s 32 of the Act.[119] Registration with the Commission was not compulsory, although only those entities that are registered may take advantage of tax exemptions, unless they fall under other provisions administered by Inland Revenue. The fiscal exemptions available to registered charities are found in the Income Tax 2007, and not within the Charities Act 2005.[120]

The Charities Act 2005 retained the *Pemsel* classifications of charitable purpose,[121] and, in contrast with contemporary legislation in Australia and England and Wales, did not broaden the concept of charitable purposes.

114 Murray, 'Australian Charities and Not-for-Profits Commission', 123, referring to Explanatory Memorandum Charities Bill 2013 (Cth) and Charities (Consequential Amendments and Transitional Provisions) Bill 2013 (Cth) (EM Charities Bill 3).
115 Ibid., 128.
116 Ibid., 129.
117 Ibid.
118 O'Halloran, McGregor-Lowndes, and Simon, *Charity Law & Social Policy*, 389.
119 Peter McKenzie, 'Charitable Trusts', in *Master Trusts Guide*, 3rd edn (Auckland: Wolters Kluwer, 2011), 218; Chevalier-Watts, *Law of Charity*, 20.
120 Poirier, *Charity Law in New Zealand*, 95.
121 Charities Act 2005, s 5(1); see Chapter 1 for full discussion on the relevance of the *Pemsel* case and for charitable purposes.

The Charities Act 2005 was amended twice in 2012. The first time to allow registration of amateur sporting clubs as charitable entities,[122] and the second time to replace the Charities Commission with the Department of Internal Affairs – Charities Services.[123]

The purpose of the Act is as follows:[124]

a   to promote public trust and confidence in the charitable sector;

b   to encourage and promote the effective use of charitable resources;

c   to provide for the registration of societies, institutions, and trustees of trusts as charitable entities;

d   to require charitable entities and certain other persons to comply with certain obligations;

e   to provide for the Board to make decisions about the registration and deregistration of charitable entities and to meet requirements imposed in relation to those functions;

f   to provide for the chief executive to carry out functions under this Act and to meet requirements imposed in relation to those functions.

Following the enactment of the 2005 Act, the Income Tax 2004 was amended to ensure that only charities that were registered with the Commission would be exempt from income tax. The responsibility for assessing the donee status of entities operating domestically remains with the Inland Revenue Department, and with Parliament for entities operating overseas.[125]

The Act is unique among jurisdictions selected with respect to its relationship with Māori. The Act gives special recognition to the contribution of Māori, 'the tangtata [*sic*] whenua of Aotearoa New Zealand, to their hapū or iwi' by stating the following:[126]

---

122   Chevalier-Watts, *Law of Charity*, 18; Charities Act 2005, s 5 (2A)
123   Ibid.
124   Charities Act 2005 [NZ], s 3; section 3 replaced, on 1 July 2012, by section 5 of the Charities Amendment Act (No. 2) 2012 (2012 No. 43).
125   O'Halloran *et al.*, 'Charity Law Reforms', 35.
126   Ibid., 33; tangata whenua [correct spelling] is defined as: 'local people, hosts, indigenous people – people born of the whenua, i.e. of the placenta and of the land where the people's ancestors have lived and where their placenta are buried' (*Māori Dictionary*, http://maoridictionary.co.nz/search?keywords=tangata+whenua [accessed 20 Jan. 2016]; hapū: 'kinship group, clan, tribe, subtribe – section of a large kinship group and the primary political unit in traditional Māori society. It consisted of a number of *whānau* sharing descent from a common ancestor, usually being named after the ancestor, but sometimes from an important event in the group's history. A number of related *hapū* usually shared adjacent territories forming a looser tribal federation (*iwi*)' (ibid.); iwi: 'extended kinship group, tribe, nation, people, nationality, race – often refers to a large group of people descended from a common ancestor and associated with a distinct territory' (ibid.); marae: 'courtyard – the open area in front of the *wharenui*, where formal greetings and discussions take place. Often also used to include the complex of buildings around the *marae*' (ibid.). See Chapter 1 for discussion on charitable purpose and the blood-tie exemption; see also Chapter 3.

However, –

a   the purpose of a trust, society, or institution is a charitable purpose under this Act if the purpose would satisfy the public benefit requirement apart from the fact that the beneficiaries of the trust, or the members of the society or institution, are related by blood; and

b   a marae has a charitable purpose if the physical structure of the marae is situated on land that is a Māori reservation referred to in Te Ture Whenua Māori Act 1993 (Māori Land Act 1993) and the funds of the marae are not used for a purpose other than –

c   the administration and maintenance of the land and of the physical structure of the marae;

d   a purpose that is a charitable purpose other than under this paragraph.

The Government indicated that there would be a review of the Charities Act 2005 around its tenth anniversary, however, the review did not take place,[127] due in no small part to a tight fiscal environment and because changes may have tax implications.[128]

Registered charities are not required to take a specific legal form and may be unincorporated, a charitable trust, an incorporated society, a limited liability company, or by a specific Act of Parliament. The register of charities is publicly available, which echoes other jurisdictions, as are the filings of registered charitable organisations, along with their organisational documentation, rules and/or constitution.[129] Such transparency encourages public confidence in the sector, which meets the object of the Act, which states clearly that one of its purposes is 'to promote public trust and confidence in the charitable sector'.[130]

The Charities Amendment Act (No. 2) 2012 disestablished the Charities Commission as of 1 July 2012, moving its core functions to the Department of Internal Affairs. The Commission's registration, education, and monitoring and investigation teams are now part of the Department of Internal Affairs, and operates as the Department of Internal Affairs – Charities Services. The Board makes decisions about the registration and deregistration of charities, and insists that decisions regarding registering or deregistering charities remain independent.[131] The pre-existing processes for registration, obtaining information and guidance

---

127 Barker, Gousmett, and Lord, *Law and Practice of Charities in New Zealand*, 444.

128 'No Review of the Charities Act at this Time', 16 November 2012, www.beehive. govt.nz/release/no-review-charities-act-time [accessed 20 Jan. 2016].

129 Carolyn Cordery, 'Light Handed Charity Regulation: Its Effect on Reporting Practice in New Zealand', working paper no. 83 (Centre for Accounting, Governance, and Taxation Research, December 2011), 8; Chevalier-Watts, *Law of Charity*, 19.

130 Charities Act 2005, s 3.

131 'Charities Commissions Functions Moved to Internal Affairs', www.dia.govt.nz/Cha rities-Commission-functions-moved-to-Internal-Affairs [accessed 20 Jan. 2016].

and complying with the requirements of Charities Act remained unchanged for charitable entities and the public.[132]

D Canada

While the Canadian Constitution[133] established that charities are under the jurisdiction of the provinces, the Constitution empowers the Federal Government to establish the federal tax system, and have administration of the Income Tax Act 1985 (the ITA). The ITA is the federal statute that governs taxation, including individuals, corporations, trusts, partnerships, and estates. It also sets out a regulatory regime under which charities are required to be registered.

As with other jurisdictions, there are fiscal benefits to being a registered charity, and two of the main benefits are firstly, that all income earned is exempt from income tax,[134] and secondly, that registered charities may issue donation tax receipts to their donors.[135] Other advantages to registering as a charity include favourable treatment in relation to Goods and Services Tax; other exemptions from taxes in some provinces, for instance corporation income tax and retail sales tax in Ontario; and the ability to obtain a bingo or a lottery licence.[136]

The ITA creates three types of registered charities: charitable organisations; public foundations; and private foundations. Charitable organisations devote their resources to carrying out charitable activities, while public foundations are primarily funders of charitable activities. Private foundations differ from their public counterparts by way of their governance. In other words, their governance is more tightly controlled (often by family), and their sources of capital are not as diverse.[137]

Canada relies on court decisions that have drawn on legislation and case law, which, unsurprisingly, given its social history, finds its jurisprudential footing in the Statute of Elizabeth, its Preamble, and the *Pemsel* four heads of charity.[138]

In order to register as a charity, an entity must apply to the Canada Revenue Agency (CRA), and the purposes of the entity must fall within one of the four heads of charity. The ITA places responsibility for registration of entities within

---

132 Chevalier-Watts, *Law of Charity*, 21.
133 Constitution Act 1867 [UK], 30 & 31 Vict, c3, reprinted in RSC 1984, App II, No. 5.
134 Income Tax Act, para. 149(1)(f); Terrance S. Carter and Theresa L. M. Man, 'The Evolution of Advocacy and Political Activities by Charities in Canada: An Overview', *The Philanthropist* 23(4) (2011), 535.
135 Individuals who make donations can claim non-refundable tax credits, pursuant to the rules as per section 118.1 of the Income Tax Act. Corporations that make donations can claim tax deductions as per section 110.1 of the same Act (Carter and Man, 'Evolution of Advocacy and Political Activities by Charities in Canada', 535, fn. 6).
136 Richard Bridge, 'The Law Governing Advocacy by Charitable Organizations: The Case for Change', *The Philanthropist* 17(2) (July 2002), 2; for further details on advantages and disadvantages, see Donald J. Bourgeois, *The Law of Charitable and Non-profit Organizations*, 2nd edn (London: Butterworths, 1995), 177–8.
137 Bridge, 'Law Governing Advocacy by Charitable Organizations', 2.
138 See Chapter 1 for further detail on charitable purpose and public benefit.

the remit of the CRA, and the regulation of charities is undertaken by the Charities Directorate of the CRA under the Act. Thus, the CRA has a significant administration role to play with regard to charitable registration and management, although it does not have the power to amend the ITA itself.

The Directorate was established in January 1967 'amid fears of possible abuses committed by charities because no centralized registration or reporting system was in place to regulate them'.[139] The Directorate has undergone significant changes since 2001. Prior to this, it was viewed largely as an organisation that interpreted charity narrowly, thus it would deny charitable status rather than make an error.[140] This would have had a negative impact on the charity sector, in terms of confidence and compliance, and suggests that its assessment procedures fell outside the consideration of the doctrine of benignant construction, as discussed earlier in the chapter. It was further asserted that the Directorate was an understaffed bureaucracy, with limited financial resources, because it was not seen as a priority within the department, that made arbitrary and subjective decisions.[141]

Fortunately, the modern-day Directorate appears to be a different creature, with many seeing it now as being receptive, proactive, and transparent. For example, it has improved its communication processes; developed training programmes to nurture compliance, making publicly available numerous policy documents; and response times have reduced. It is also asserted that its interpretation of 'charity' is more favourable.[142]

However, there is still some work to do yet for the CRA in relation to education, because 'charity education is restricted to meeting regulatory requirements rather than any general form of governance or operational guidance'.[143]

Nonetheless, the Directorate has numerous duties, and its responsibilities include reviewing and registering charities; providing information, guidance, and advice; and ensuring compliance.[144]

The mission of the Directorate is:[145]

> to promote compliance with the income tax legislation and regulations relating to charities through education, quality service, and responsible enforcement,

---

139 Karine Leavasseur, 'In the Name of Charity: Institutional Support for and Resistance to Redefining the Meaning of Charity in Canada', *Canadian Public Administration* 55(2) (June–July 2012), 193.

140 Ibid.

141 Leavasseur, 'In the Name of Charity', 193, referring to Lorne Sossin, 'Regulating Virtue: A Purposive Approach to the Administration of Charities', in Jim Phillips, Bruce Chapman, and David Stevens (eds), *Between State and Economy: Essays on Charities Law and Policy in Canada* (Montreal and Kingston: McGill-Queen's University Press, 2001), 382.

142 Leavasseur, 'In the Name of Charity', 194–5.

143 Peter R. Elson, 'The Origin of Species: Why Charity Regulations in Canada and England Continue to Reflect Their Origins', *International Journal of Not-for-Profit Law* 12(3) (May 2010), 89.

144 Charities Directorate, Canada Revenue Agency, www.cra-arc.gc.ca/chrts-gvng/chrts/bt/mssn_vsn-eng.html [accessed 21 Jan. 2016].

145 Ibid.

thereby contributing to the integrity of the charitable sector and the social well-being of Canadians.

In determining whether an entity meets the charitable requirements, the CRA will assess an entity's purposes and activities because both must be charitable, and all of the organisation's resources must be devoted exclusively to those activities.[146]

In contrast to jurisdictions such as England and Wales and New Zealand, charitable regulation and administration in Canada falls under the auspices of the tax agency, as opposed to operating an independent commission. This means that 'the regulatory goals of the tax agencies are squarely on ensuring charitable funds are spent for charitable purposes'.[147] This inevitably shifts the policy approach of the CRA, although it does mean that Canada is subject to more substantial financial auditing than certainly New Zealand. For instance, Canada requires that entities disclose compensation paid to officers and directors,[148] which New Zealand charities, for example, are not required to do. It could be argued that while New Zealand, for instance, may have a more liberal approach to its charitable administration, Canada's CRA might provide more public confidence due to its more detailed and rigorous assessment requirements.

E Hong Kong

A comprehensive legal framework for regulating charities in Hong Kong does not yet exist, and unlike jurisdictions such as England and Wales, and New Zealand, nor is there a formal or established registration system for charitable entities, with no overall government authority for this area.[149] In addition, there is only a limited statutory definition of what constitutes a 'charity' or a 'charitable purpose'. The Inland Revenue Department (IRD) maintains the largest list of organisations that have successfully applied for tax exemption through being recognised by the IRD as a 'charitable institution or trust of a public character', which is within the scope of s 88 of the Inland Revenue Ordinance (Cap 112).[150]

There is also a limited system of oversight to ensure that donations are properly applied to the purposes for which they have been solicited. Guidelines for best

---

146 See Chapter 3 for further discussion on purposes and activities. This requirement is subject to the 10 per cent rule with regard to political activity (see Chapter 11 for further discussions on political purposes and activities); O'Halloran, McGregor-Lowndes, and Simon, *Charity Law & Social Policy*, 455.

147 Susan D. Phillips, 'Shining Light on Charities or Looking in the Wrong Place? Regulation-by-Transparency in Canada', *Volantas: International Journal of Voluntary and Nonprofit Organisations* 24(3) (September 2013), 885.

148 Ibid.

149 Law Reform Commission of Hong Kong, 'Report on Charities', December 2013, 92 www.hkreform.gov.hk/en/docs/rcharities_e.pdf [accessed 27 Jan. 2016].

150 Law Reform Commission of Hong Kong, Charities Sub Committee Consultation Paper, 'Charities', June 2011, www.gov.hk/en/residents/government/publication/consultation/docs/2011/Charities.pdf, 5–14; Law Reform Commission of Hong Kong, 'Report on Charities', 92.

practice in charity fundraising activities were introduced in recent years, but adoption of these practices is voluntary. In addition, legislation relating to charitable bodies that qualify for tax exemption can be found in various ad hoc provisions.[151]

Thus, an entity will be entitled to tax exemption if it is recognised by the IRD as a charitable institution, or trust of a public character, but the IRD is not responsible for registering charities, nor is it responsible for monitoring their conduct.[152]

In contrast to jurisdictions such as New Zealand and Australia, in Hong Kong, there is no requirement for registered charities to file annual reports or financial accounts. Instead, the IRD will:[153]

> from time to time call for accounts, annual reports or other documents for the purpose of reviewing the exemption status of a particular organisation so as to ensure that the organisation is still charitable and its activities are compatible with its objects.

This inspection of accounts is not mandatory under existing law.[154]

As at December 2013, there were over 7,500 tax-exempt charitable organisations in Hong Kong, and the organisations were most commonly created in one of the following forms:[155]

- a company incorporated under the Companies Ordinance (Cap 32), which may be a company limited by shares or by guarantee, or a company incorporated overseas and registered under Part XI of the Companies Ordinance;
- an unincorporated association which may or may not be required to be registered under the Societies Ordinance (Cap 151);
- a trust; or
- a statutory body established under a specific Hong Kong Ordinance.

As mentioned in Chapter 1, in order for a body to be deemed charitable at law, it must be for exclusively charitable purposes, and these charitable purposes are defined by case law in Hong Kong, thus echoing its fellow jurisdictions in relying on the *Pemsel* categorisation of charitable purpose.[156] A charity will not be defined

---

151 Law Reform Commission of Hong Kong, Charities Sub Committee Consultation Paper, 'Charities', 5; see Inland Revenue Ordinance (Cap 112), ss 2(1) and 88 and Registered Trustee Ordinance (Cap 306), s 2.
152 Law Reform Commission of Hong Kong, Charities Sub Committee Consultation Paper, 'Charities', 1.
153 Law Reform Commission of Hong Kong, 'Report on Charities', 16.
154 A Tax Guide for Charitable Institutions and Trusts of a Public Character, www.ird. gov.hk/eng/tax/ach_tgc.htm [accessed 27 Jan 2016], [17].
155 Law Reform Commission of Hong Kong, 'Report on Charities', 3; Tax Guide for Charitable Institutions, [7].
156 Tax Guide for Charitable Institutions.

by its scale or resources, and a legal charity may be small or run by a limited number of people, and neither does it have to be a public organisation.[157]

It is essential that a charity is established by a written governing document, and the type of instrument adopted will depend on the circumstances of the charity that is proposed, and also the preference of the founders or promoters.

As might be imagined, and similarly to other jurisdictions, there are significant benefits to creating a charitable entity. For example, such an entity will not generally be liable to tax, and donors may claim the amount donated as a deduction from their assessable income. Other benefits may include exemption from stamp duty,[158] and some statutory registration requirements.[159]

Oversight for charitable organisations ranges from stringent statutory overall control to limited scrutiny of specific activities, and oversight will depend upon the type of charity. For instance, for charities established by statute, the imposed controls are established by statute and are generally clear and detailed, as set out in the specific Ordinances. These statutory charities are required to account for all of their proceeds, prepare and keep proper accounts, and be open for reasonable scrutiny. Other non-statutory charities, subject to other types of oversight mechanisms,[160] generally operate autonomously under their own governing bodies, and thus their own rules and regulations. The IRD has no real oversight authority, and is merely responsible for the tax exemption aspects of charities.[161] Thus individuals or organisations must apply to the IRD in order to obtain tax exemption under s 88 of the Inland Revenue Ordinance (Cap 112).

The issues pertaining to lack of accountancy and monitoring, 'has become a matter of major public interest that a system should be put in place to both regulate charities and enhance their transparency'.[162] This lack of accountancy and monitoring creates confusion, and is damaging for the sector.[163] As a result of such criticism, and the wide-ranging issues associated with charity law, the Law Reform Commission of Hong Kong carried out a review of charities law in Hong Kong which was presented in December 2013; Chapter 9 will address this review in more detail.

F Singapore

As noted in Chapter 1, Singapore's charity law is based on that of England and Wales, which is the *Pemsel* categorisation of charitable purposes, albeit with

157 *Li Kim Sang Victor* v. *Chen Chi Hsia* HCA 481/2008 24 February 2015, [81c].
158 Stamp Duty Ordinance (Cap 117), s 44.
159 Societies Ordinance (Cap 151), s 5A(2); Business Registration Ordinance (Cap 310), s 16(a).
160 See generally Law Reform Commission of Hong Kong, 'Report on Charities', 15–18.
161 Ibid., 3.
162 Law Reform Commission of Hong Kong, Charities Sub Committee Consultation Paper, 'Charities', 2.
163 John Kong Shan Ho and Rohan Bruce Edward Price, 'Reform of Charity Law in Hong Kong and Australia: What Lessons Can Be Learned from the United Kingdom', *Asian Journal of Comparative Law* 6(1) (Article 11) (2011), 9.

additional purposes now recognised in England's charity law. Singapore, similarly, also recognises additional heads of charity, alongside the original four charitable purposes.[164]

In 1983, the Charities Act (Cap 37) came into effect in Singapore, and there have been numerous revisions, for instance in 1994, 2002, and 2010. In 1994, Parliament introduced changes, drawing inspiration from English charity law, which included requirements for charities to keep and audit their accounts.[165] This legislation was known as the 1995 Revised Edition. To encourage greater giving to charitable causes, the Government created a new subset of charities, known as Institution of a Public Character (IPC), to be conferred on a not-for-profit organisation that serves only the needs of local communities, and for causes within Singapore. Donations to IPCs are tax deductible.[166]

In an effort to streamline charity governance, the Charities Act was amended in 2006 to establish a Charity Council, whose function is to advise the Commissioner of Charities (CoC); the Charity Council was legally appointed on 1 March 2007.[167]

The CoC has a number of objectives, including maintaining public trust and confidence in the sector, and promoting compliance.[168]

There are five Sector Administrators to assist the CoC in overseeing the charities and IPCs in their respective sectors, which are:[169]

- Ministry of Education – for charitable objects related to the advancement of education;
- Ministry of Health – for charitable objects related to the promotion of health;
- Ministry of Social and Family Development – for charitable objects related to the relief of poverty or those in need by reason of youth, age, ill health, disability, financial hardship, or other disadvantages;
- People's Association – for charitable objects related to the advancement of citizenship or community development;
- Sport Singapore (previously known as Singapore Sports Council) – for charitable objects related to the advancement of sport.

The Charity Council comprises 14 members and its term lasts for two years. It aims to promote and encourage good governance and best practice, and advise the CoC on regulatory issues.[170]

---

164 See Chapter 1 for full details, www.charities.gov.sg/setting-up-a-charity/Pages/About-Charities-And-IPCs.aspx [accessed 28 Jan. 2016].
165 Charities Act, ss 12–17.
166 Anne-Marie Piper, *Charity Law* (London: Sweet & Maxwell, 2012), 198.
167 Ibid.
168 Commissioner of Charities, 'About the Commissioner of Charities', www.charities.gov.sg/about/Pages/About-the-Commissioner-of-Charities.aspx [accessed 28 Jan. 2016]; Charities Act (Singapore), s 4.
169 Ibid.
170 Charity Council, www.charities.gov.sg/about/Pages/About-Charities-Council.aspx [accessed 28 Jan. 2016]; Charities Act 1994, s 4B.

The Charity Council sets out the Charity Transparency Framework, which assists charities with enhancing their disclosure and governance practices. It also acts as a public education tool for charities, and the public, by highlighting key areas of disclosure that will aid in informed giving.[171] Singapore will actively encourage greater transparency, and reward charities' disclosure endeavours, by introducing the Charity Transparency Awards with effect from 2016, which is a novel concept among our selected jurisdictions. Eligible charities will be assessed using the Charity Transparency Scorecard by an independent group of assessors.[172] To assist further with transparency, if an entity is set up exclusively for charitable purposes, and it carries out activities to achieve these purposes, then the entity must, under s 5(6) of the Charities Act, register with the CoC. It is an offence if an entity does not register.[173]

In order to apply for registration as a charity, a body has to be a legal entity set up as:[174]

i A society under the Registry of Society (RoS); or
ii A company limited by guarantee (CLG) under the Accounting and Corporate Regulatory Authority of Company (ACRA); or
iii A trust under the CoC.

It is evident therefore that Singapore's charity institution and its policy framework, like that of fellow jurisdictions such as Australia and New Zealand, are of a progressive and contemporary nature, which is of obvious benefit to the charitable sector and the public.

171 Charity Transparency Framework, www.charitycouncil.org.sg/Charity%20Council/ Our%20Work/Charity%20Transparency%20Framework.aspx [accessed 28 Jan. 2016].
172 Ibid.; see the same link for the eligibility of the award.
173 Charities Act, s 5(6); Piper, *Charity Law*, 200.
174 'Other Requirements for Registration as a Charity or IPC'.

3 Charitable purpose

This chapter will contextualise the notion of charitable purpose within its English heritage, and discusses some key points generally associated with charitable purposes. Thus, the chapter adopts a holistic approach to the challenges associated with charitable purposes in relation to our selected jurisdictions.

A Introduction to charitable purposes

For a body to be charitable at law, its objects must have charitable purpose. While this in itself sounds like a simple requirement, in reality, the definition of 'charity' is fraught with difficulties, not least because charity law has evolved 'not through the application of clearly defined principles but by analogy'.[1] Since the early formulation of charitable purposes by Lord Macnaghten in the now famed *Pemsel* case,[2] there has been a 'steady encrustation of new analogous charitable categories by this means'[3] which suggests that 'these developments have been evolutionary rather than revolutionary'.[4] 'The difficulties of endeavouring to define such a concept'[5] 'evoke[s] the famous description of the capital/revenue distinction in tax law: an intellectual minefield in which the principles are elusive and the analogies treacherous'.[6]

While the definition of 'charitable purpose' 'may cause judicial and academic angst',[7] the origins of this doctrine are to be found in the non-exhaustive list of purposes set out in the Preamble of the Statute of Elizabeth 1601, as set out in Chapter 1, thus while the principles of this body of law are rooted firmly in the past, the nature of charity law lends itself to evolution in line with society, which

---

1 *Scottish Burial Reform & Cremation Society Ltd* v. *Glasgow Corporation* [1968] AC 138 (HL), 144.
2 *Commissioners for Special Purposes of Income Tax* v. *Pemsel*, [1891] AC 531 (HL).
3 *Travis Trust* v. *Charities Commission* [2009] 24 NZTC 23.273 (NZHC) [20].
4 Ibid.; Juliet Chevalier-Watts, *Law of Charity* (Wellington: Thomson Reuters, 2014), 30.
5 Chevalier-Watts, *Law of Charity*, 30.
6 Susan Barker, 'The Presumption of Charitability', *New Zealand Law Journal* October, 9 (2012), 296, citing *Tucker* v. *Granada* [1977] 3 All ER 865 (HL), 869.
7 Chevalier-Watts, *Law of Charity*, 31.

will be evidenced throughout the chapters. While evidently charity law, and charitable purposes, have developed with society, it is worthwhile considering the roots of charitable purposes, to contextualise their evolution within our selected jurisdictions.

As we saw in Chapter 1, while the Statute of Elizabeth 1601 has long since been repealed, the Preamble lives on as 'a source of charitable purposes and as a tool by which courts may endeavour to interpret a "charitable purpose"'.[8] Chapter 1 sets out the Preamble, and while it is generally considered to be the foundations of charitable purposes as we recognise them today, it has been asserted that the Preamble itself took inspiration from a fourteenth-century poem, 'Vision of Piers', by William Langland.[9] Both the poem and the Preamble talk of assisting the poor, providing education, and repairing infrastructure. These are just as relevant today as they were over 700 years ago, when the poem, and, subsequently, the Preamble made reference to them, thus highlighting the timeless quality of charity and its purposes.

The Preamble provided a description of charitable purposes, as opposed to a prescribed definition, thus the uses set out in its text 'were those deemed to be within the equity of the statute and those endowments that could'[10] 'materially contribute to the relief of poverty'.[11] Any other charitable uses, for instance, supporting religious purposes, were outside the scope of the Act and 'had been enforced not by the charity commissioners but by an information brought by the Attorney-General at the relation of a private individual'.[12]

This proved to a useful mechanism, and by the end of the seventeenth century, many purposes were no longer limited to 'cases considered as charities before the statute of charitable uses, but all others are taken to be within the extensiveness of this proceeding in the name of the *Attorney-General*,[13] thus enabling the evolution of charitable purposes within a societal context.

As it was evident that the Preamble could now be interpreted more comprehensively, this paved the way for the common law to develop the concept of charitable purpose. While the *Pemsel* case is considered the forerunner in this matter, actually there was an earlier case, which took that first decisive step in defining 'charity' and enshrined 'the preamble as the fons et origo of all charity'.[14] Sir Samuel Romilly, for the first time in charity law, set out the objects of

---

8 Ibid., 32.
9 Jill Horwitz, 'Nonprofits and Narrative: Piers Plowman, Anthony Trollope, and Charities Law', *Michigan State Law Review* 1(4) (2009), 996–7 citing Rachael Attwater (ed.), *William Langland, the Book Concerning Piers Plowman* (New York: Dent, 1957); see also generally B. H. Smith, *Traditional Imagery of Charity in Piers Plowman* (The Hague: Mouton, 1966).
10 Chevalier-Watts, *Law of Charity*, 34.
11 Gareth Jones, *History of the Law of Charity 1532–1827* (Cambridge: Cambridge University Press, 1969), 120.
12 Ibid.; Chevalier-Watts, *Law of Charity*, 34.
13 *Attorney-General* v. *Brereton* (1752) 2 Ves Sen 425, 426.
14 Jones, *History of the Law of Charity*, 122.

charitable purpose, 'within one of which all charity, to be administered in this Court, must fall',[15] as follows:

1 Relief of the indigent; in various ways: money: provisions: education: medical assistance; &c:
2 The advancement of learning:
3 The advancement of religion; and
4 Which is the most difficult, the advancement of objects of general public utility.

The importance of this classification 'cannot be understated in terms of the evolution of charity law. In particular, charitable purpose',[16] as it became the 'quintessence of legal charity'.[17]

After the *Morice* v. *Bishop of Durham* case:[18]

> the Preamble featured far more prominently and with greater authority in a variety of charity cases and indeed, it became accepted generally that there was no substitute for the Preamble as the source of the definition of legal charity, although in the early nineteenth century even after the case of *Morice*, there are examples of cases where the Court sought to describe charity independently of the Preamble.

It is evident that Lord Macnaghten, in the *Pemsel* case, took inspiration from *Morice* v. *Bishop of Durham*, when compiling the four heads of charity, 'upon which contemporary classifications of charitable purpose still rest',[19] because the later categorisation follows that of Sir Samuel's very closely. Lord Macnaghten's classification is as follows:[20]

> 'Charity' in its legal sense comprises four principle divisions: trusts for the relief of poverty; trusts for the advancement of education; trusts for the advancement of religion; and trusts for other purposes beneficial to the community, not falling under any of the preceding heads.

This classification of charity is now the foundation of charity law in our selected jurisdictions, and similarly to the Preamble, the *Pemsel* classification provides a description rather than a definition of charitable purposes. This classification was

---

15 *Morice* v. *Bishop of Durham* (1804) 9 Ves 399, 532.
16 Chevalier-Watts, *Law of Charity*, 38.
17 Jones, *History of the Law of Charity*, 126.
18 Chevalier-Watts, *Law of Charity*, 38; Jones, *History of the Law of Charity*, 126, referring to *Mellick* v. *President and Guardian of the Asylum* (1821) Jac 180, 184; *Attorney-General* v. *Fowler* (1808) 15 Ves 85, 86–7 and *Doe d Thompson* v. *Pitcher* (1815) 6 Taunt 359, 366–7.
19 Chevalier-Watts, *Law of Charity*, 38.
20 *Commissioners for Special Purposes of Income Tax* v. *Pemsel*, 583.

groundbreaking because in creating it, the 'Law Lords seized the opportunity to develop the law to reflect a modern reality, while still making clear the link to the original Statute of 1601'.[21] This classification has stood the test of time, reflecting its value within charity law, and indeed, in England and Wales, for example, it 'remained unaltered until 2006, a testament to their shrewd judgment'.[22] Indeed, the classification 'is one that has proved to be of value and there are many problems which it solves'.[23]

Nonetheless, this did not mean that the law should remain static within those categories, rather:[24]

> three things may be said about it ... first ... since it is a classification of convenience, there may well be purposes which do not fit neatly into one or other of the headings, secondly ... the words used must not be given the force of a statute to be construed ... thirdly ... the law of charity is a moving subject which may well have evolved even since 1891.

In New Zealand, Hammond J, in *D V Bryant Trust Board* v. *Hamilton City Council*, shared these views, asserting that 'this body of law must keep abreast of changing institutions and societal values'.[25] Canadian law echoes these views. Gonthier J, in *Vancouver Society of Immigrant and Visible Minority Women* v. *MNR*, stated that the *Pemsel* classification is a 'flexible judicial creation, and thus amenable to subsequent change and development'.[26] Thus *Pemsel*'s four heads of charity are still the basis for assessing that which is charitable in our selected jurisdictions, and while a number of the jurisdictions have extended their recognition of purposes, their basis remains the same.

B Benignant construction

What is evident within the law of charity is the notion of benignant construction. This is a well-established maxim, whereby a court will endeavour to find in favour of a charitable bequest. In other words, the 'overriding principle of construction in relation to gifts to charity is that a benignant approach is taken'.[27] Thus 'the

---

21 Robin Hogdson, *Trusted and Independent: Giving back to Charities – Review of the Charities Act 2006* (London: TSO, 2012), 10.

22 Ibid.

23 *Scottish Burial Reform & Cremation Society Ltd* v. *Glasgow Corporation*, 154.

24 *Vancouver Society of Immigrant and Visible Minority Women* v. *Minister of National Revenue* [1999] 1 SCR 10, [146], citing *Scottish Burial Reform and Cremation Society Ltd* v. *Glasgow Corporation* [1968] AC 138, 154; Chevalier-Watts, *Law of Charity*, 40.

25 *D V Bryant Trust Board* v. *Hamilton City Council* [1997] 3 NZLR 342 (HC), 348.

26 *Vancouver Society of Immigrant and Visible Minority Women* v. *Minister of National Revenue*, 26.

27 Jean Warburton, *Tudor on Charities*, 9th edn (London: Sweet & Maxwell, 2003), 175.

question of whether an entity's purposes are charitable should receive a benign construction'.[28] This is because 'society is unlikely to be prejudiced by attempts at public benefaction, however odd they may seem'.[29]

In relation to wills, especially in instances of charitable bequests within wills, the courts are 'even more concerned with preventing intestacy',[30] although the benign approach is applicable in relation to all types of gifts to charities. This is because while the doctrine of benignant construction has been derived from charitable bequests, it 'clearly applies in charities law generally'.[31] There is evidence of such favouritism harking back hundreds of years. In *Attorney-General* v. *Clarke*, the Court noted that it will take into consideration all circumstances, and will incline in favour of a disposition.[32] Thus, courts have 'taken strong liberties on the subject of charities'.[33] These liberties:[34]

> are embodied in definite principles, one of which is that a trust for charitable purposes does not fail for uncertainty and another the assertion of the jurisdiction to give effect to the drift of the ideas embodied in the expression of a gift made on trust for a charitable purpose.

As a result, courts will 'lean in favour of making a charitable bequest effective if it is possible within the limitation of the law'.[35] This is because 'there is no better rule than that a benignant construction will be placed upon charitable bequests'.[36] Therefore if a bequest is capable of being construed to make it void, or to make it effective, then the latter approach should be taken, because it 'is better to effectuate than to destroy the intention'.[37] Thus, in instances where constituting documents 'do not indicate with clarity the main or dominant objects of a body',[38] inferences may be drawn benignly as 'to the over-arching charitable purpose of the entity'.[39] In the New Zealand case *Re Collier (deceased)*, Hammond J

---

28 Susan Barker, 'Are All Charities Equal?', *Chartered Accountants Journal* 90(5) (June 2011), 42.

29 Susan Barker, 'Are All Charities Equal?', 42, citing John Bassett, 'Charity Is a General Public Use', *New Zealand Law Journal* 1(2) (March 2011), 60.

30 *Lecavalier* v. *Sussex (Town)*, 2003 NBQB 430, [18].

31 Susan Barker, 'The Myth of "Charitable Activities"', *New Zealand Law Journal* 1(8) (September 2014), 307.

32 *Attorney-General* v. *Clarke* [1762] 1 Amb 422, 422.

33 *Lecavalier* v. *Sussex (Town)*, [18], citing *Re Robinson* (1976) 15 OR (2d) 286 (Ont HC), 289.

34 Ibid.

35 Ibid.

36 *Weir* v. *Crum-Brown* 1908 SC (HL), 4.

37 Hubert Picarda, *The Law and Practice Relating to Charities*, 4th edn (London: Bloomsbury, 2010), 353, referring to *Re Lloyd* (1893) 10 TLR 66; see also *Re White* (1893) 2 Ch 41.

38 Barker, 'Myth of "Charitable Activities"', 307.

39 Juliet Chevalier-Watts, 'The Public Benefit Requirement in Charity Law: The Mystery of the Balancing Act', *Trust and Trustees* 21(4) (2015), 380.

(as he was then) indicated that there were strong policy reasons for adopting such an approach:[40]

> Charitable bodies have always been distinctly important in socio-economic terms. Charities were a creature of Tudor/Stuart philosophy, and owed their origins to a Christian-ethic system of equity. But, the voluntary sector could go no real distance to meeting the needs of the poor, the sick, and the oppressed, and other needs, in heavily industrialised societies. Welfare systems evolved.
>
> Things then became much more complicated in the twentieth century. Charities have historically been forced to stand on what, in theory, is a bright line between public, and private, concerns. A line of that kind is always hard to define, and to defend. In this, as in other areas of the law, the line has become blurred. In contemporary circumstances, charities often tackle what a conservative bureaucracy or state will not. They are often innovative. And, in some jurisdictions, charities have even become delivery vehicles for state programmes.

In Hammond J's view 'in the public interest there should be an open recognition of a presumption, as opposed to a construction, in favour of charity'.[41] This type of approach is 'more intellectually honest; it is also based on sound policy'.[42] Such views are echoed in the Privy Council case of *Hadaway* v. *Hadaway*:[43]

> where possible, a benignant construction in favour of charity should be adopted ... If there is a real ambiguity, it may be resolved in favour of charity: where there is no ambiguity, no question arises.

Therefore, a benignant construction should be utilised where possible, 'and this is of great assistance where there is ambiguity in the terms of the trust'.[44] As a result, it is clear that where constituting documents 'do not indicate with clarity the main or dominant objects of a body'[45] then inferences may be drawn benignly as to the overarching charitable purpose of the entity.[46]

While it is evident that this doctrine is acknowledged in England and Wales and New Zealand, and to some extent, Canada, Canadian law appears to be a little

---

40 *Re Collier (deceased)* [1998] 1 NZLR 81 (HC) [95].
41 Ibid.
42 Ibid; Chevalier-Watts, 'Public Benefit Requirement in Charity Law', 380.
43 *Hadaway* v. *Hadaway* [1955] 1 WLR 16 (PC), 19; Barker, 'Myth of "Charitable Activities"', 307.
44 Chevalier-Watts, 'Public Benefit Requirement in Charity Law', 380.
45 Barker, 'Myth of "Charitable Activities"', 307.
46 Chevalier-Watts, 'Public Benefit Requirement in Charity Law', 380; Barker, 'Myth of "Charitable Activities"', 307; *Kaikora County* v. *Boyd* [1949] NZLR 233, 261; Donald Poirier 'Charity Law in New Zealand' (Charities Commission, Wellington, 2011), https://charities.govt.nz/assets/Uploads/Resources/Charity-Law-in-New-Zealand.pdf [accessed 10 Feb. 2016], 109.

more reluctant in its application. Canadian courts 'have occasionally applied the principle'.[47] The leading authority is *Jones* v. *T Eaton Co*.[48] In this case, the Supreme Court upheld the validity of the trust on the basis that the will maker was deemed to have expressed charitable intention with the use of the word 'deserving', ensuring that the trust was viewed benignly, according to English authority.[49] Nonetheless, in the Supreme Court case of *Vancouver Society*,[50] the majority viewed the Society's objects in far less benignant terms. In assessing the final object, Iacobucci J stated that while carrying out incidental activities could be treated as a means of fulfilling its purposes, the term 'conducive' implied only that the action contributed to its result, thus negating the Society's overall charitable purpose.[51] It has been asserted that the conclusion 'that begged to be drawn was that the language raised no concerns',[52] and indeed, Gonthier J, for the dissenting, while not explicitly invoking benignant construction, did appear to rely on its spirit. His Honour referred to the obvious intent of the will maker, in that 'conducive' was a mechanism by which the Society's purposes could be achieved, thus it was charitable.[53] Overall, this decision appeared to be at odds with earlier cases in relation to the equitable principle, and as the *Vancouver Society* case is still good law, it may go some way to explain why this doctrine has not been mentioned in the higher courts of Canada since its decision.[54]

Notwithstanding Canada's somewhat more recent reluctant approach, the jurisdictions discussed above are not alone in the recognition of this doctrine. For instance, in the Hong Kong case of *HSBC Trustee (Hong Kong) Ltd* v. *Secretary for Justice*,[55] the Court noted that the first codicil was of no assistance when attempting to construe the intention of the testator, so all that was left was the provisions of the will itself as to meaning of 'British Colony'. The Court relied on *Weir* v. *Crum-Brown*, and Lord Loreburn LC's assertion that '[t]hat there is no better rule than that a benignant construction will be placed upon charitable bequests', confirming that where a bequest is capable of two constructions, the one that would make the bequest effective should be adopted.[56] The more recent

47 Kathryn Chan, 'The Function (or Malfunction) of Equity in the Charity Law of Canada's Federal Courts', *Canadian Journal of Comparative and Contemporary Law* 2(1) (2016), 44.
48 Chan, 'Function (or Malfunction) of Equity', 44, referring to *Jones* v. *T Eaton Co* [1973] SCR 635.
49 Chan, 'Function (or Malfunction) of Equity', 44, referring to *Jones* v. *T Eaton Co*, 642 and 646.
50 Chan, 'Function (or Malfunction) of Equity', 46, referring to *Vancouver Society of Immigrant and Visible Minority Women* v. *MNR*.
51 Chan, 'Function (or Malfunction) of Equity', 46–7, referring to *Vancouver Society of Immigrant and Visible Minority Women* v. *MNR*, [193].
52 Chan, 'Function (or Malfunction) of Equity', 46.
53 Chan, 'Function (or Malfunction) of Equity', 46, referring to *Vancouver Society of Immigrant and Visible Minority Women* v. *MNR*, [118].
54 Chan, 'Function (or Malfunction) of Equity', 47.
55 *HSBC Trustee (Hong Kong) Ltd* v. *Secretary for Justice* [1999] HKCFI 534, [16].
56 *HSBC Trustee (Hong Kong) Ltd* v. *Secretary for Justice*, [16], referring to *Weir* v. *Crum-Brown*, 167 and *Re Lloyd-Greame* (1893) 10 TLR 66; see *Secretary for Justice*

Court of Final Appeal case of *Secretary for Justice (Hong Kong)* v. *Chinachem Charitable Foundation* also confirmed that 'uncertainty can be cured and clarified by the law's benevolent treatment of charitable trusts'.[57]

These approaches reflect the earlier Hong Kong case of *Ng Chi (or Tze) Fong* v. *Hui Ho Pui Fun*, where it was noted that 'a benignant approach ... undoubtedly comes to the assistance of settlers in danger of attack for uncertainty'.[58] In addition, 'there must be a certain bias in the mind of the court in favour of doing what the testator or testatrix obviously wanted to be done'.[59]

Australia also recognises the application of the doctrine. In *Re Municipal Orchestra Endowment Fund*, Williams J observed that 'it is clear that in construing a trust deed with a view to determining whether or not the fund may be applied to some non charitable purpose, the court does not adopt a highly technical approach'.[60] He added that if the words are capable of supporting the gift as being charitable, then that construction should be applied,[61] and his Honour further acknowledged the authority of the Privy Council decision of *Hadaway* v. *Hadaway* in relation to this doctrine.[62]

What is evident therefore is the interconnectedness of the jurisdictions in relation to the doctrine of benignant construction, and thus the doctrine's international value in ensuring that charity is recognised at law, where at all possible, thus benefiting society as a whole.

However, this is not to say that the doctrine is applicable in all circumstances, and courts offer some cautionary words with regard to its application. The doctrine does 'not justify the insertion of words in order to restrict the plain meaning of an expression and thus give validity to an otherwise invalid bequest'.[63] What is recommended is that where there is real ambiguity, then it may be construed as charitable, but where there is no ambiguity, then the plain meaning of the words must be utilised, as must the ensuing legal effects.[64] Thus, while it is true that courts have inferred charitable intent from tenuous indications,[65] a court should not strain the meaning of a gift, as one consequence, in the instance of a

---

v. *Joseph Lo Kin Ching* [2013] HKCFI 233, [36] and [87], referring to *Weir* v. *Crum-Brown*, *IRC* v. *McMullen* [1981] AC 1, and *Guild* v. *IRC* [1992] 2 AC 310.

57 *Secretary for Justice (Hong Kong)* v. *Chinachem Charitable Foundation* (Court of Final Appeal), HKSAR, 18 May 2015, [52].

58 *Ng Chi (or Tze) Fong* v. *Hui Ho Pui Fun* [1987] HKCFI 42, [99], citing *IRC* v. *McMullen* [1981] AC 1, 18.

59 *Ng Chi (or Tze) Fong* v. *Hui Ho Pui Fun* [1987] HKCFI 42, [99], citing *Re Bradbury, Deceased – Needham* v. *Reekie* [1951] 1 TLR 130, 131.

60 *Re Municipal Orchestra Endowment Fund* (1999) QSC 200 (10 August 1999), [19].

61 *Re Municipal Orchestra Endowment Fund*, [19], referring to *Taylor* v. *Taylor* (1910) 10 CLR 218, 225.

62 *Re Municipal Orchestra Endowment Fund*, [19], referring to *Hadaway* v. *Hadaway* [1955] 1 WLR 16 PC.

63 *Re Municipal Orchestra Endowment Fund*, [19].

64 Ibid.

65 Picarda, *Law and Practice Relating to Charities*, 353, referring to *Attorney-General* v. *Skinners' Company* (1827) 2 Russ 407.

will, will be to cheat the residuary legatees or next of kin. In other words, a court should 'not strain the will to gain money for charity'.[66] Indeed, one Judge asserted that 'I will not steal leather to make poor men's shoes',[67] confirming that the doctrine should be applied with caution, and is not a panacea for saving all ambiguous bequests.

While some caution may be required, the overarching principle remains that this doctrine is of great assistance where there is ambiguity as to the terms of a trust in order to find charitability,[68] not only because of its intellectual honesty, but because of sound policy reasons referred to earlier.

C Exclusively charitable, and ancillary purposes

It has long been established that in order for an entity to be charitable, its purposes must be exclusively charitable. Slade J, in *McGovern v. Attorney-General*, noted:[69]

> The third requirement for a valid charitable trust is that each and every object or purpose designated must be of a charitable nature.

If, however, an entity has purposes that are not exclusively charitable, this will not automatically negate its charitability, on the proviso that those non-exclusively charitable purposes are ancillary to its dominant purposes. This was affirmed in England in *Inland Revenue Commissioners v. City of Glasgow Police Athletic Association*:[70]

> if the main purpose of the body of persons is charitable and the only elements in its constitution and operations which are non-charitable are merely incidental to that main purpose, that body of persons is a charity notwithstanding the presence of those elements.

In other words, those purposes 'must be of lesser importance and be in aid of the dominant charitable purpose'.[71] This means that 'a body is a charity even if some of its incidental and ancillary objects, considered independently, are non-charitable'.[72]

---

66 *Koh Lau Keow v. Attorney-General* [2014] SGCA, 18, 21.
67 Picarda, *Law and Practice Relating to Charities*, 353, citing *Attorney-General v. Sutton* (1721) 1 P Wms 754, 765–6, per Lord Harcourt, quoting in part dictum of Twisden J in an unreported case; see fn. 12.
68 Chevalier-Watts, 'Public Benefit Requirement in Charity Law', 380; see *Hadaway v. Hadaway*.
69 *McGovern v. Attorney-General* [1982] 1 Ch 321, 340.
70 *Inland Revenue Commissioners v. City of Glasgow Police Athletic Association* [1953] AC 380, 404; see also *Royal College of Surgeons of England v. National Provincial Bank Ltd* [1952] AC 631.
71 Kerry O'Halloran, Myles McGregor-Lowndes, and Karla W Simon, *Charity Law & Social Policy: National and International Perspectives on the Functions of Law Relating to Charities*, vol. 10 (Netherlands: Springer, 2008), 482–3.
72 O'Halloran, McGregor-Lowndes, and Simon, *Charity Law & Social Policy*, 483, citing *Congregational Union of NSW v. Thistlethwayte* (1952) 87 CLR 375, 442; see

New Zealand relied on the *City of Glasgow Police Athletic Association* case, in *Institution of Professional Engineers New Zealand Inc* v. *Commissioner of Inland Revenue*, where Tipping J approved Lord Normand's dicta:[73]

> This does not mean that the sole effect of the activities of the body must be to promote charitable purposes, but it does mean that that must be its predominant object and that any benefits to its individual members of a non-charitable character which result from its activities must be of a subsidiary or incidental character.

However, it is not sufficient that the purposes are merely ancillary, rather, they must 'lack substance in their own right and amount to no more than something which tends to assist, or which naturally goes with, the achievement of the main purpose'.[74] It has been argued therefore that the distinction is one of means and ends. Thus, a purpose will be ancillary if it assists in achieving the main charitable purpose, but if that purpose is divorced from the main purpose, with its own objectives, then that becomes a main purpose, and negates the overall charitable purpose.[75] As noted, albeit in dissent, by Gonthier J in the Canadian case of *Vancouver Society of Immigrant and Visible Minority Women* v. *MNR*:[76]

> At a certain point, of course, a purpose may grow to assume a collateral rather than incidental nature. If so, it will no longer be a means to the fulfilment of the organization's primary purposes, but will have become an end in itself.

In addition, as stated again by Slade J in *McGovern*:[77]

> in any case where it is asserted that a trust is non-charitable on the ground that it introduces non-charitable as well as charitable purposes, a distinction of critical importance has to be drawn between (a) the designated purposes of the trust; (b) the designated means of carrying out those purposes; and (c) the consequences of carrying them out. Trust purposes of an otherwise charitable nature do not lose it merely because, as an incidental consequence

also *White* v. *White* [1893] 2 Ch 41; *Salvation Army (Vic) Property Trust* v. *Fern Tree Gully Corporation* (1952) 85 CLR 159.

73 *Institution of Professional Engineers New Zealand Inc* v. *Commissioner of Inland Revenue* [1992] 1 NZLR 570 (HC), 573, citing *Inland Revenue Commissioners* v. *City of Glasgow Police Athletic Association*, 402.

74 O'Halloran, McGregor-Lowndes, and Simon, *Charity Law & Social Policy*, 483; see also *Oxford Group* v. *Inland Revenue Commissioners* (1949) 2 All ER 537 and *In re Harpur's Will Trusts* (1962) 1 Ch 78.

75 O'Halloran, McGregor-Lowndes, and Simon, *Charity Law & Social Policy*, 483; see also *Salvation Army (Victoria) Property Trust* v. *Fern Tree Gully Corporation*; *Commissioners of Inland Revenue* v. *Yorkshire Agricultural Society* [1928] 1 KB 611.

76 *Vancouver Society of Immigrant and Visible Minority Women* v. *MNR*, 44–5; see also *Commissioner of Taxation* v. *Word Investments* [2008] HCA 55, [186].

77 *McGovern* v. *Attorney-General*, 340–1.

of the trustees' activities, there may enure to private individuals benefits of a non-charitable nature.

Singapore and Hong Kong also reflect this approach, which is unsurprising, considering their general common law approach to charity law. In the former, the Office of the Commissioner of Charities notes that '[i]t is essential that ... business activities do not undermine the charity's focus and distract the charity from its exclusive purpose'.[78] The recent Court of Appeal case *Koh Lau Keow* v. *Attorney-General*,[79] in making reference to Australian and English authorities, affirmed that ancillary purposes will not necessarily undermine charitable status. In applying those authorities, the Court confirmed that the purposes in question were not merely ancillary to the overriding object of the trust, thus rendering the trust void. Similarly, in the 2013 Hong Kong case of *Secretary for Justice* v. *Joseph Lo Kin Ching*,[80] Hon Poon J confirmed that one of the essential requirements for a charity is to ensure that trustees 'are bound to apply the funds to charitable purposes and not to non-charitable purposes'.

Therefore, while it is evident that our selected jurisdictions all confirm this particular requirement, that a charity must ensure that its purposes are for charitable purposes, albeit with the exception of ancillary non-charitable purposes, a question still remains. That is how one may determine whether or not a purpose is ancillary for non-charitable purposes. New Zealand recently sought to provide some guidance on this matter.[81]

In *Education New Zealand Trust*,[82] Dobson J doubted that 30 per cent of a charity's activities could be said to be 'ancillary, secondary, subordinate or incidental'. This, therefore, provides a specific measurement of what might be more than ancillary. This means that if an object has dominant private purposes, the criteria 'is a situation-specific analysis of the relative relationship between public and private benefits';[83] this was cited with approval in *New Zealand Computer Society Inc*.[84]

Again, New Zealand approved of this approach, where Simon France J in *Grand Lodge of Antient Free and Accepted Masons* recognised Dobson J's measure of dominant purpose. However, although his Honour stated that overall 'there is

---

78 Office of the Commissioner of Charities, Guidance for Charities Engaging in Business Activities, www.charities.gov.sg/about/Pages/About-the-Commissioner-of-Charities. aspx [accessed 26 Feb. 2016].

79 *Koh Lau Keow* v. *Attorney-General*, [40]–[46], referring to *Presbyterian Church (New South Wales) Property Trust* v. *Ryde Municipal Council* [1978] 2 NSWLR 387; *Neville Estates Ltd* v. *Madden* [1962] 1 Ch 832; *Oxford Group* v. *Inland Revenue Commissioners* [1949] 2 All ER 537; and Picarda, *Law and Practice Relating to Charities*, 333–4.

80 *Secretary for Justice* v. *Joseph Lo Kin Ching*, [2013] HKCFI 233, [37].

81 Chevalier-Watts, *Law of Charity*, 83–6; Chevalier-Watts, 'Public Benefit Requirement in Charity Law', 381–5.

82 *Education New Zealand Trust* HC WN CIV-2009-485-2301 [29 June 2010], [43].

83 Ibid., [44].

84 *New Zealand Computer Society Inc* HC WN CIV-2010-485-924 [28 February 2011].

little discussion on what is an ancillary activity',[85] he was of the view that ancillary should have a quantitative component,[86] and quantitively, he did not think that the purposes were ancillary, because conceptually, 'under the Constitution, the expenditure could be 100 per cent of the general funds. Realistically, that cannot amount to an ancillary purpose'.[87]

This appeared to be a positive step forward in the determination of ancillary, and Young J in *Draco Foundation (NZ) Charitable Trust* considered further the ancillary–dominant divide. His Honour cited with approval Simon France J's remarks in the *Grand Lodge* case, that a purpose should be subject to a quantitative and qualitative assessment.[88]

Interestingly, reflecting an implicit reference to Dobson J's actual measure of meeting a 30 per cent ratio in *Education New Zealand Trust*, the appellant in *Draco* stated that the material was incidental to the main charitable purpose. This was because 'it fell well below 30 per cent of the educational material provided on its website'.[89]

What these New Zealand cases show is a response to concerns as to how courts might explicitly quantify whether or not a purpose is ancillary to an overall charitable purpose. As a result:[90]

> it is evident now, at least in New Zealand, that courts are willing to utilise quantitative and qualitative measures to try to measure such purposes'. Where it is not possible to quantify a so-called 'ancillary' purpose quantitively, and thus assess whether it falls below the 30 per cent guideline of the entity's overall activities, a court is able to make enquiries as to the qualitative qualities of the said purpose in terms of its overall value to the entity to try to identify whether a purpose is ancillary for charitable purposes.

Nonetheless, the author is not aware of other jurisdictions necessarily adopting such an explicit methodology, which speaks to recent diverging approaches taken by each jurisdiction in modern times, and also that New Zealand is not necessarily relied upon generally by many of the jurisdictions in question. This is because each of the jurisdictions find their charity law history in England primarily. Their own charitable principles specific to their own charitable functions, and needs, have evolved from there. Adopting New Zealand's approach may not be appropriate at this stage in their evolution of charity law.

Another reason why this approach may not have been explicitly adopted by other jurisdictions may be because the New Zealand methodology has been subject to some criticism. It has been asserted that no authority has been cited 'for the

---

85 *Re Grand Lodge of Antient Free and Accepted Masons* [2011] 1 NZLR 277, [49].
86 Ibid.
87 Ibid.
88 *Draco Foundation (NZ) Charitable Trust* HC WN CIV 2010-485-1275 [3 February 2011], [14].
89 Chevalier-Watts, *Law of Charity*, 85.
90 Ibid., 86.

introduction of these tests in to New Zealand charities law'[91] and 'no mention is made in their introduction of either the presumption of charitability or the doctrine of benign construction',[92] to which this chapter has already made some mention. Therefore, while one might view the New Zealand position as a positive move in assessing ancillary purposes, it probably should not be viewed as a panacea for all ills. First, because it is not always possible to quantify an ancillary purpose, certainly to the extent as to whether or not it might fall below the 30 per cent criterion.[93] Second, because its origins and authority appears to be rather limited to in its own jurisdiction.

D Charitable purposes and charitable activities

The concept of 'charitable purposes' is acknowledged as being a long-recognised one at common law, whereas charitable activities, as a concept, is 'a much more recent innovation'.[94] Gonthier J in *Vancouver Society of Immigrants and Visible Minority Women* v. *MNR* noted[95] that when one is referring to charity law, the primary purpose of a court is to determine whether or not the purposes being pursued are charitable. In other words, it is 'these *purposes* which are essential, not the *activities* engaged in'.[96] However, his Honour added that 'the activities must, of course, bear a coherent relationship to the purposes sought to be achieved'.[97]

This in itself sounds like a straightforward endeavour, because semantically speaking, 'the nature of the distinction between purposes and activities might not appear to create any particular difficulty'.[98] However, the reality is that this often results in confusion among 'judges and commentators alike',[99] as they 'often conflate the concept of "charitable purposes" and "charitable activities"'.[100] Nonetheless, the two can be distinguished, as evidenced by Gonthier J, where his Honour differentiates them as follows:[101]

91 Chevalier-Watts, 'Public Benefit Requirement in Charity Law', 385, citing Barker, 'Myth of "Charitable Activities"', 305.
92 Ibid.
93 Chevalier-Watts, 'Public Benefit Requirement in Charity Law', 385.
94 *Vancouver Society of Immigrants and Visible Minority Women* v. *MNR* [1999] 1 SCR 10, [52]; distinctions made between the two concepts in *Scarborough Community Legal Services* v. *The Queen*, [1985] 2 FC 555, 579; *Toronto Volgograd Committee* v. *MNR* [1988] 3 FC 251; *Guaranty Trust Co of Canada* v. *MNR* 1966 CanLII 40 (SCC) [1967] SCR 133.
95 *Vancouver Society of Immigrant and Visible Minority Women* v. *MNR*, [52].
96 Ibid. (emphasis retained).
97 Ibid.
98 Maurice Cullity, 'Charities and Politics in Canada: A Legal Analysis' (Pemsel Case Foundation, December 2013), 6.
99 *Vancouver Society of Immigrant and Visible Minority Women* v. *MNR*, [52].
100 Ibid.
101 Ibid., [53].

A critical difference between purposes and activities is that purposes may be defined in the abstract as being either charitable or not, but the same cannot be said about activities. That is, one may determine whether an activity is charitable only by reference to a previously identified charitable purpose(s) the activity is supposed to advance. The question then becomes one of determining whether the activity has the effect of furthering the purpose or not ... In determining whether an organization should be registered as a charitable organization, we must ... look not only to the purposes for which it was originally instituted, but also to what the organization actually does, that is, its activities. But we must begin by examining the organization's purposes, and only then consider whether its activities are sufficiently related to those purposes.

Nonetheless, his Honour does later note that 'the precise boundary between an activity and a purpose is rather protean, and so one should not expect a bright line to separate them'.[102] As a result, perhaps then it is unsurprising that the lines between the two concepts have indeed become blurred.

Cullity offers some explanations as to why this blurring of the lines may occur. First, because it has become common for constitution documents to describe the objects or purposes of the entity as carrying on certain activities. When this occurs, perhaps it is unsurprising that judges then use the terms interchangeably. This is evidenced in the Hong Kong Court of Appeal case of *Church Body of the Hong Kong Sheng Kung Hui* v. *Commissioner of Inland Revenue*,[103] where the Court made reference to the charitable activities of the entity, without necessarily defining the meaning of charitable purposes, or distinguishing purposes from activities. The Court noted that it was far from clear when one individual referred to 'charitable purposes' and 'charitable activities', what that individual had in mind as to what the law meant as 'charitable', thus suggesting that the two concepts are interchangeable.[104]

The Hong Kong Final Court of Appeal case of *Chinachem Charitable Foundation Ltd* v. *Secretary for Justice*,[105] also did not distinguish between purposes and activities, and made reference to the main objects of the Foundation being to carry out particular activities. This illustrates Cullity's first explanation as to how the two concepts may become blurred at judicial level.

The second reason Cullity gives for the lack of distinction may be because 'courts have accepted that, properly construed, objects described as such may be characterized as activities'.[106] In the Singapore Supreme Court case of *Life Bible-Presbyterian Church* v. *Khoo Eng Teck Jeffrey*,[107] Judith Prakash J referred to the

102 Ibid., [121].
103 *Church Body of the Hong Kong Sheng Kung Hui* v. *Commissioner of Inland Revenue* [2014] HCCA 445, [12.8], [12.9], and [14.2], for example.
104 Ibid., [16.4].
105 *Chinachem Charitable Foundation Ltd* v. *Secretary of Justice*, [2015] HKFCA 35, [17].
106 Cullity, 'Charities and Politics in Canada', 7.
107 *Life Bible-Presbyterian Church* v. *Khoo Eng Teck Jeffrey* [2010] SGHC 187 (30 June 2010), [76].

college's general charitable purposes being the object of buying land and constructing buildings for the advancement of religion and religious education. Such purposes may also be characterised perhaps as activities.

One further explanation offered by Cullity is the recognition of the courts that the 'nature and extent of an organization's activities may require them to be treated as objects or purposes themselves'.[108] Thus, in the Australian High Court case of *Commissioner of Taxation* v. *Word Investments Ltd*,[109] the Court noted that the inquiry 'so far as it is directed to activities, must centre on whether it can be said that the activities are carried on in furtherance of a charitable purpose'. The Court determined that:

> So far as the actual activities of Word in furtherance of its purposes are relevant, it is plain that, subject to the Commissioner's contentions in relation to the second and third issues, the funds paid out by Word were paid to bodies fulfilling charitable purposes.

As a result, it was held that Word's activities of commercial fundraising, while not intrinsically charitable, were actually 'charitable in character because they were carried out in furtherance of a charitable purpose'.[110] Therefore Word's activities were treated as charitable purposes, illustrating Cullity's third point. The *Word* case is not the only Australian case to consider the issue of activities in relation to charitable purposes. In *Salvation Army* v. *Shire of Fern Tree Gully*,[111] the Court was concerned with whether land was being used exclusively for charitable purposes. The focus of the Court was actually in the sense of the activities. The land in question was being used as a training farm for delinquent boys, and for homes for difficult, wayward, or underprivileged boys. The Court found that the sole object of the organisation in carrying out the various activities was to achieve the charitable purpose of the education of the boys. The *Salvation Army* case also made reference to the case of *Nunawading Shire* v. *Adult Deaf and Dumb Society of Victoria*.[112] The Court in *Nunawading Shire* focused on the activities undertaken by the Society, asserting that:[113]

> The inquiry, however, is not what was the motive for bringing ... the sequence of ideas that brought, the land into use, but whether that use was exclusively for charitable purposes. It is not enough that the primary or main

---

108 Cullity, 'Charities and Politics in Canada', 7.
109 *Commissioner of Taxation* v. *Word Investments*, [26].
110 Ibid.
111 *Commissioner of Taxation* v. *Word Investments Ltd* [2007] FCAFC 171 (14 November 2007), [21], referring to *Salvation Army* v. *Shire of Fern Tree Gully* [1952] HCA 4.
112 *Commissioner of Taxation* v. *Word Investments Ltd* [2007], [22], referring to *Nunawading Shire* v. *Adult Deaf and Dumb Society of Victoria* [1921] HCA 6.
113 *Nunawading Shire* v. *Adult Deaf and Dumb Society of Victoria*, 6.

object of the use of the land was for charitable purposes, unless it can be affirmed that the land was used for these purposes only.

While this case was distinguished in *Salvation Army*, and indeed, it was held not to be charitable, the point remains that the Court in *Nunawading Shire* focused their attention firmly on the activities of the Society.

Canada has adopted a similar approach, holding that what makes an activity charitable is not something to be considered in isolation. It can only turn on whether the activity has the effect of furthering the entity's charitable purpose.[114] Indeed, Canada's Income Tax Act defines a charitable organisation as one where 'all the resources of which are devoted to charitable activities carried on by the organisation itself'.[115] The registration status of an entity can be revoked if an entity fails to expend above a certain level on its charitable activities, although 'charitable activities' is not defined.[116]

England and Wales adds to this confusion. Its Charity Commission, since the 1990s, has routinely asked for information pertaining to an entity's proposed, as well as actual, activities, as well as its purposes.[117] Nonetheless, the United Kingdom Upper Tribunal decision of *R (on the application of Independent Schools Council)* v. *Charity Commission*[118] stated that charitable status ultimately turns on 'what it is that the institution was set up to do, not … how it would achieve its objects or whether its subsequent activities are in accordance with what it was set up to do'. While this approach reflects the orthodox position, an entity's purposes should be the focus of its charitability, not its activities undertaken in pursuit thereof. The Tribunal then asserted that it is legitimate to insist that its 'activities overall are for the public benefit',[119] thus simply adding more confusion to the notion of distinguishing between the two concepts.

New Zealand has not been exempt from issues arising between these two concepts. While Canadian legislation may make reference to charitable activities, New Zealand's Charities Act 2005 makes no reference to such a notion. Rather, s 13(1) states that an entity will qualify for registration if its purposes are charitable, not its activities. Nonetheless, 'a myth of charitable activities appears to be plaguing New Zealand charities law'.[120] This is because the Charities Commission,[121] appears to

---

114 *Vancouver Society of Immigrant and Visible Minority Women* v. *MNR*, [53]–[54] and [152]; Jonathan Garton, 'Charitable Purposes and Activities', *Current Legal Problems* 67(1) (2014), 387.
115 Income Tax Act 1985, s 149(1) (Canada).
116 Barker, 'Myth of "Charitable Activities"', 304.
117 Garton, 'Charitable Purposes and Activities', 373.
118 Garton, 'Charitable Purposes and Activities', 374, citing *R (on the application of Independent Schools Council)* v. *Charity Commission* [2011] UKUT 421 (TCC, [2012] Ch 214, [188].
119 Garton, 'Charitable Purposes and Activities', 374, citing *R (on the application of Independent Schools Council)* v. *Charity Commission*, [195].
120 Barker, 'Myth of "Charitable Activities"', 304.
121 Now the Department of Internal Affairs – Charities Services.

have denied registration to organisations on the basis of their activities not being charitable.

The source of this difficulty appears to stem from s 18(3) of the Act, which states:

In considering an application, the chief executive must –

a   have regard to –
b   the activities of the entity at the time at which the application was made; and
c   the proposed activities of the entity; and
d   any other information that it considers is relevant;

Barker asserts, however, that the intention of this section was to ensure that charities, once registered, continue to act in the furtherance of their charitable activities. In other words, it was not intended to require charities to engage in charitable activities, and nor was its intention to change the meaning of 'charitable purpose', as the Act 'includes every charitable purpose, whether it relates to the relief of poverty, the advancement of education or religion, or any other matter beneficial to the community'.[122] Indeed, it has been confirmed that the definition of 'charitable purpose' has not been changed.[123]

However, it could be argued that New Zealand does intend activities to be taken into consideration when considering charitable purposes, because s 18 of the Act is contained in Part 2 of the Act, which refers to Registration of Charitable Entities, and, in particular, Applications for Registration. Regardless of the intentions, it is evident that New Zealand courts, and the Department of Internal Affairs – Charities Services,[124] do take into consideration the activities of an entity. For instance in *Re the Grand Lodge of Antient Free and Accepted Masons in New Zealand*, the Court found that the Grand Lodge was not charitable because of its activities, as they did not appear to be charitable in their own right.[125] It has also been argued that the use of activities and purposes were used interchangeably in this case.[126] Similarly, in the case of *Draco Foundation (NZ) Charitable Trust*,[127] the Court considered its purposes and activities in relation to its overall charitable purposes. However, even prior to the Charities Act 2005, and the issue of s 18, it was evident that New Zealand courts paid attention to purposes and activities in charity law cases. In

---

122 Charities Act 2005, s 5(1) (NZ).
123 Barker, 'Myth of "Charitable Activities"', 305, referring to New Zealand Parliament, *Report of the Social Services Select Committee Considering the Charities Bill 108–2*, government report (17 December 2004), 3 and *Re Education New Zealand Trust*, [13].
124 See, for example, Registration Decision: Society for the Protection of Auckland Harbours (SOC51367) 1 September 2016, [31]–[33].
125 *Re the Grand Lodge of Antient Free and Accepted Masons in New Zealand* [2011] 1 NZLR 277 (HC), [48].
126 Barker, 'Myth of "Charitable Activities"', 305.
127 *Draco Foundation (NZ) Charitable Trust*, [23].

Molloy v. *Commissioner of Inland Revenue*, the Court of Appeal referred to the activities of the Society in question as being within the ambit of its stated objects.[128]

What is evident therefore is that in jurisdictions based on the English model, of which our considered jurisdictions are just that, then the extent to which it is appropriate for a court to consider an entity's activities, as well as its purposes, is still a matter of controversy. What we can feasibly say is that while the 'distinction between ends and means is fundamental in the law of charity',[129] it is perhaps the case that while it is not necessarily the nature of the activity that is relevant, it is the activity's role in supporting the charitable purpose that is in question. For instance, this might be the case where there is doubt over the original purpose stated in the constitution or deed, because its purposes may have changed over the years, and referring to its activities may indicate whether an entity is acting ultra vires the powers vested in it.[130]

Therefore, while purposes lie at the heart of the legal concept of charity, for they are the 'foundation of a valid [charitable] trust',[131] activities are not necessarily going to be irrelevant, especially if it is not always clear as to the entity's overall purposes. Therefore, while 'there is a kernel of truth in the orthodoxy that it is a charity's purposes, and not the proposed or actual activities carried on it purpose of those purposes, that count',[132] the reality is that activities may play a role in determining the charitability of an organisation, thus leading to the lack of overall distinction between the two concepts.

E Charitable purposes and motives

Charity may be said to be a manifestation 'of the better side of human nature',[133] and, as a result, it is unsurprising that altruistic motives are closely associated with charitable purposes. However, as Chapter 1 confirmed, benevolent gifts have traditionally been found not charitable because they extend beyond that which is exclusively charitable.[134] Indeed:[135]

---

128 *Molloy* v. *Commissioner of Inland Revenue* [1981] 1 NZLR 688 (CA), 693, citing *Molloy* v. *Commissioner of Inland Revenue* (1977) TRNZ 211 (SC), 214; Chevalier-Watts, *Law of Charity*, 75.

129 Barker, 'Myth of "Charitable Activities"', 306, referring to *Latimer* v. *Commissioner of Inland Revenue* [2004] 3 NZLR 157 (PC), [34]; Garton, 'Charitable Purposes and Activities', 375, referring to Maurice Cullity, 'The Myth of Charitable Activities', *Estates Trust Journal* 10(1) (1990–1), 10.

130 Chevalier-Watts, *Law of Charity*, 75; O'Halloran, McGregor-Lowndes, and Simon, *Charity Law & Social Policy*, 483–4.

131 Garton, 'Charitable Purposes and Activities', 375, citing *A-G of New South Wales* v. *Perpetual Trustee Co (Ltd)* (1940) 63 CLR 209, 223.

132 Garton, 'Charitable Purposes and Activities', 406.

133 Peter Luxton, *The Law of Charities* (Oxford: Oxford University Press, 2001), 3.

134 O'Halloran, McGregor-Lowndes, and Simon, *Charity Law & Social Policy*, 9, referring to *Houston* v. *Burns* [1918] AC 337 (HL); *Re Jarman's Estate* (1878) 8 Ch D 584; *Re Rilands Estate* [1881] WN 173; *Chichester Diocesan Fund and Board of Finance In* v. *Simpson* [1944] AC 341 (HL); *A-G for New Zealand* v. *Brown* [1917] AC 393 (PC).

135 O'Halloran, McGregor-Lowndes, and Simon, *Charity Law & Social Policy*, 9, citing Picarda, *Law and Practice Relating to Charities*, 221 (footnotes omitted).

A gift simply to 'benevolent purposes' is objectionable: a benevolent purpose may be (but is not necessarily charitable). The same is true of gifts to philanthropic purposes, utilitarian purposes, emigration, and public purposes: they all go further than legal charity. Likewise gifts for encouraging of general utility, for hospitality, for such societies as should be in the opinion of trustees 'most in need of help' and for such purposes, civil or religious, as a class of persons should appoint, are too wide ... the permutations are endless.

Equally so, laudable motives as to the intent of the donor are, on the face of it, not relevant to an entity's charitable status, because such inquiries may be subjective, although the motives of the donor may be incorporated into the purpose of the gift.[136] Gonthier J in *Vancouver Society of Immigrant and Visible Minority Women* v. *MNR*, illustrated this:[137]

I pause to emphasize that motive and purpose are not synonymous. The courts are not, in general, concerned with the motive of a donor or volunteer, only with the purpose being pursued.

This was echoed in *Nunawading Shire* v. *Adult Deaf & Dumb Society of Victoria*, where the Court noted:[138]

The inquiry, however, is not what was the motive for bringing ... the sequence of ideas that brought the land into use, but whether that use was exclusively for charitable purposes.

Therefore, it can be argued that motives may align with purposes, although they should not necessarily be the focus for a court in assessing charitability. This was emphasised by Lord Normand in *Inland Revenue Commissioners* v. *City of Glasgow Police Athletic Association*, where he stated:[139]

This is not a matter of the motive of the members of the association or of the high police officials who took part in furthering the association, though there is a natural probability that their motives agree with the purposes of the association.

Nonetheless, as observed by Roxburgh J in *Re Delius*, while 'one must be careful to distinguish motive from purpose, because motive is not relevant in these cases except so far as it is incorporated into the purpose ... [it] is, of course rather subtle'.[140] This point on subtlety is well made by his Honour, because it highlights a difficulty in distinguishing between motive and purpose.

136 Gino Dal Pont, *Law of Charity* (Chatswood: LexisNexis, 2000), 21.
137 *Vancouver Society of Immigrant and Visible Minority Women* v. *MNR*, [52].
138 *Nunawading Shire* v. *Adult Deaf and Dumb Society of Victoria*, 6.
139 *Inland Revenue Commissioners* v. *City of Glasgow Police Athletic Association*, 396.
140 *Re Delius* [1957] 1 Ch 299, 307.

Indeed, as Roxburgh J states, it 'is a question which is the cart and which is the horse'.[141] This was a valid point, because the trust in question in this case was a trust for the advancement of the widow's husband, that of the famous composer Frederick Delius, and it was possible to approach the purposes of the trust 'upon the hypothesis that their intention was … to enhance her husband's reputation'.[142] The cart-and-horse analogy refers then to the notion that the greater the aesthetic appreciation of Delius's music, the greater his reputation will become. Both objectives are going to be achieved, and are both clearly entwined, but one is a motive, and one is a purpose. Thus, Roxburgh J imagined himself in the position of the widow to try to distinguish the two principles:[143]

> I think that there is every reason to suppose that the testatrix took the view, and was well advised to take it, that if the work of Delius was brought before the public in an efficient manner, the aesthetic appreciation of the public would grow and, inherent in that growth, would be the enhancement of Delius's reputation, which was in itself a desirable thing, and I for my part refuse to disentangle it.

Therefore, his Honour isolated the motive from the purpose, and approached the question of charitability not from the motive of the widow, but from viewing the overall purpose of the trust. However, he was clear that the two concepts, at least in this instance, are inherently bound, and the motive will be achieved inevitably as a result of the purpose of the trust. This inherent binding of the two concepts is also evident in the earlier case of *Re Corelli*,[144] where Cohen J referred at length to the testatrix's motives behind a gift, and what her dominant motive may have been in the bequest. His Honour found his inquiry 'not without difficulty',[145] no doubt because of the possible subjectivity that is associated with assessing motives, although he did conclude that the testatrix's dominant motive rendered the gift void.

Such inherent binding of motive and purpose is evident in other jurisdictions. MacKenzie J, in the New Zealand High Court case of *Re Queenstown Community Housing Trust*,[146] had to consider whether a trust to promote and/or provide housing in Queenstown in New Zealand was charitable:

> I accept that the Council, in supporting the formation of the Trust, and in facilitating its funding, was motivated by a desire to address the impact of housing affordability on the community in its district, through its effect on the ability of the community to attract and retain key workers vital to the functioning and operation of the community.

141 Ibid.
142 Ibid.
143 Ibid.
144 *Re Corelli* [1943] 1 Ch 332, 336–7.
145 Ibid., 337.
146 *Re Queenstown Community Housing Trust* BC201162649 CIV-2010-485-1818 17 March, 24 June 2011, [75].

However, 'motive is not, in this context, the same as purpose', thus acknowledging their link, while at the same time recognising the difference between the two concepts. Nonetheless, the use of the words 'in this context' suggests that in some circumstances, motive and purpose may be construed as the same, which does add another level of uncertainty to this issue. However, in the earlier New Zealand Court of Appeal case of *Commissioner of Inland Revenue* v. *Medical Council of New Zealand*, McKay J was clear that:[147]

> just as with charitable trusts the purposes are not identified by reference to the motives of those responsible for settling the trusts and the charitable or non-charitable purposes of bodies privately established are not identified by reference to the motives of the founders.

In the Hong Kong Court of Final Appeal case of *Chinachem Charitable Foundation Ltd* v. *Secretary for Justice*,[148] Lord Walker of Gestingthorpe NPJ referred extensively to the will maker's intentions, or motives, but his Lordship did not necessarily align motive with purposes, as other courts have done. He determined that Wang's intentions were matters to be considered carefully, 'but what is essential is that the Chinese prize should be a proper charitable purpose'. In other words, the two concepts appear to be entirely separate from each other, which is in stark contrast to other courts' approaches.

While there is evidence, therefore, of the differing judicial considerations of the concepts of purpose and motive, what can be said is that the test is objective, and motive, while inevitably aligned with purpose, will incidentally be realised through the charitable purpose being achieved. Thus, the motive of the donor is 'frequently reflected in the application of the gift for purposes that are charitable at law',[149] but the actual motive is irrelevant in determining whether or not a gift is charitable,[150] 'except so far as it is incorporated into the purpose of the gift'.[151]

147 *Commissioner of Inland Revenue* v. *Medical Council of New Zealand* [1997] 2 NZLR 297, 306, referring to *Keren Kayemeth Le Jisroel Ltd* v. *Inland Revenue Commissioners* [1932] AC 650, 661.
148 *Chinachem Charitable Foundation Ltd* v. *Secretary of Justice*, [58] and [61].
149 Dal Pont, *Law of Charity*, 21.
150 Picarda, *Law and Practice Relating to Charities*, 24.
151 Dal Pont, *Law of Charity*, 21.

4 Public benefit

Public benefit is a concept that has elicited much judicial, academic, and public commentary with regard to its meaning, and then its application. The following discussion will consider some general public benefit themes, as well as addressing some of the key jurisdiction-specific public benefit considerations.

History of public benefit

Generally speaking, a purpose will not be charitable unless it is directed to public benefit, but difficulties can arise when determining what may be sufficient to satisfy this test.[1] This is because, while it 'is easy to state',[2] it has 'been stated in a variety of ways'.[3] To be 'a charity there must be some public purpose, something tending to the benefit of the community'.[4] Therefore, public benefit is 'an interminably broad concept, which spills over from the pure altruism of a community welfare at one end of the spectrum into the realm of collective self-interest at the other'.[5] It is a court's role to decide how this should be determined.

To understand public benefit generally, we have to look to the English common law model, which can be traced back to the Statute of Charitable Uses 1601, where the Preamble set out a non-exhaustive list of charitable purposes.[6] As charity law developed, it was apparent that courts tended to the view that a common thread 'running through the wide range of purposes accepted as charitable was public benefit', as opposed to any direct link to the Preamble. Although it is worth noting that early cases, from, for instance, the eighteenth century, 'are not on the whole, characterized by comprehensiveness or lucidity'.[7] The Statute

1 Hubert Picarda, *The Law and Practice Relating to Charities*, 4th edn (London: Bloomsbury, 2010), 29.
2 *Oppenheim* v. *Tobacco Securities Trust Co Ltd* [1951] AC 297 (HL), 305.
3 Ibid.
4 *Re Foveaux* [1895] 2 Ch 501, 504.
5 *Vancouver Regional FreeNet Association* v. *MNR* 1996 CarswellNat 1463, [44].
6 Jonathan Garton, *Public Benefit in Charity Law* (Oxford: Oxford University Press, 2013), 1–2.
7 Garton, *Public Benefit in Charity Law*, 3, citing Gareth Jones, *History of the Law of Charity 1532–1827* (Cambridge: Cambridge University Press, 1969), 122.

and its Preamble made no direct reference to public benefit but the characteristics of the latter tended to the benefit of the public.[8]

Early evidence public benefit is found in *Jones* v. *Williams*, where Lord Chancellor Hardwicke stated: 'Definition of charity: a gift to a general public use, which extends to the poor as well as to the rich'.[9] In *Vezey* v. *Jameson*, the Court 'confirmed the fundamental distinction between the trust which is charitable and for the public benefit, and the trust which merely benefits the public'.[10] *Goodman* v. *Mayor of Saltash* similarly confirmed the concept of public benefit:[11]

> Such a condition would create that which in the very wide language of our courts is called a charitable, that is to say a public, trust or interest for the benefit of the free inhabitants of ancient tenements ... if it creates a charitable, that is to say a public, interest, it will be free from any obnoxiousness to the rule regard to perpetuities.

Re Foveaux confirmed this approach, noting:[12] '[t]o be a charity there must be some public purpose – something tending to the benefit of the community'. So 'it was clear, even in the nineteenth century, that the concept of public benefit was fully established'.[13] The mid-twentieth-century case of *Oppenheim* v. *Tobacco Securities Trust Company Limited* affirmed this, where Lord Simonds observed:[14]

> It is a clearly established principle of the law of charity that a trust is not charitable unless it is directed to the public benefit.

While there 'has never been an attempt comprehensively to define what is, or is not, of public benefit', it is possible to discern two related aspects of public benefit'.[15] Therefore, the public benefit test requires two questions to be answered, which are closely related:[16]

> The first aspect is that the nature of the purpose itself must be such as to be a benefit to the community: this is public benefit in the first sense ... The

---

8 Garton, *Public Benefit in Charity Law*, 18.
9 *Jones* v. *Williams* (1767) 1 Ambler 651, [652], referring to *Attorney-General* v. *Heelis*, 2 S. & S. 76. *British Museum* v. *White*, 596.
10 Jones, *History of the Law of Charity*, 127, citing *Vezey* v. *Jamson* (1822) 1 Sim and Stu 69.
11 *Goodman* v. *Mayor of Saltash* (1882) App Cas 633, 650; see also *Verge* v. *Somerville* [1924] AC 496; Juliet Chevalier-Watts Law of Charity (Wellington: Thomson Reuters, 2014), 45.
12 *Re Foveaux*, 504.
13 Chevalier-Watts, *Law of Charity*, 46.
14 *Oppenheim* v. *Tobacco Securities Trust Co Ltd*, 305.
15 *R (on the application of Independent Schools Council)* v. *Charity Commission* [2011] UKUT 421 (TCC); [2012] Ch 214, [44].
16 Hilary Biehler, 'Trusts for the Relief of Poverty and Public Benefit: Time for a Reappraisal?', *Trust Law International* 28(3) (2014), 145, citing *R (on the application of Independent Schools Council)* v. *Charity Commission* [44].

second aspect is that those who may benefit from the carrying out of the purpose must be sufficiently numerous, and identified in such manner as, to constitute what is described in the authorities as 'a section of the public': this is public benefit in the second sense.

The test of public benefit therefore has two related limbs, or senses. We will consider each test in turn generally, although more discussion on public benefit can be found in the jurisdiction-specific chapters.

A Public benefit in the first sense

Lord Green MR in *Re Compton* addressed the issue of public benefit, where he referred to Chitty J's dictum in *Re Foveaux*,[17] confirming that to 'be a charity there must be some public purpose – something tending to the benefit of the community', and then to Lord Wrenbury in *Verge* v. *Somerville*, where his Lordship asserted:[18]

> To ascertain whether a gift constitutes a valid charitable trust so as to escape being void on the ground of perpetuity, a first inquiry must be whether it is public – whether it is for the benefit of the community or of an appreciably important class of the community.

By way of example, Lord Wrenbury confirmed that:[19]

> The inhabitants of a parish or town, or any particular class of such inhabitants, may, for instance, be the objects of such a gift, but private individuals, or a fluctuating body of private individuals, cannot.

In reality, this does not mean that every gift that tends to the public will be charitable; rather, it means that a gift can be charitable at law if it has the necessary public character.[20] It has been asserted that this 'general principle is now beyond question'.[21]

Slade J, in *McGovern* v. *Attorney-General*[22] affirmed the rather vague concept of public benefit, by stating that the 'question whether a purpose will or may operate for the public benefit is to be answered by the court forming an opinion on the evidence before it'. His Honour confirmed that there are likely to be some cases where 'a purpose may be so manifestly beneficial to the public that it would be

---

17 *Re Compton* [1945] 1 Ch 123, 129, citing *Re Foveaux*, 504.
18 *Re Compton* [1945] Ch 123, 129, citing *Verge* v. *Somerville* [1924] AC 496, 499.
19 Ibid.
20 *Re Compton*, 129
21 *Re Pinion* [1963] 3 WLR 778, 783.
22 *McGovern* v. *Attorney-General* [1982] 1 Ch 321, 333; see also *National Anti-Vivisection Society* v. *Inland Revenue Commissioners* [1948] AC 31, 44.

absurd to call evidence on this point'.[23] However, in many other situations, the public benefit element 'may be much more debatable'.[24]

In situations where courts cannot prove this requirement of public benefit, the entity will fail as charitable;[25] this may occur if there is a public disadvantage. In *National Anti-Vivisection Society* v. *Inland Revenue Commissioners*,[26] the House of Lords held that political campaigning would fail the public benefit test.[27] In *Re Pinion*,[28] Wilberforce J provided another example. In this case, a testator gave his studio and the contents, which included personal paintings, furniture, china, glass, and bric-a-brac, to be used to endow the studio as a museum for the display of his collection. The question for the Court was whether a valid charitable trust had been created. His Honour noted that, in some circumstances, a court should call upon expert evidence to assist in the determination of the public benefit. Although 'it must be cautious in the receipt of such evidence … "the court will not be astute … to defeat on doubtful evidence the avowed benevolent intention of a donor"'.[29] This is of particular relevance where a court is dealing with matters of art or aesthetics, because of issues pertaining to subjectivity and changes in fashion and taste.[30] Nonetheless, in:[31]

> making all these necessary allowances, there must come a point when the court, on the evidence, is impelled to say that no sufficient element of benefit to the public is shown to justify the maintenance in perpetuity of the subject-matter given. A strong and a clear case has to be made before such a conclusion can be reached: Is this case sufficiently strong and clear?

Unfortunately, at least for the testator, the Court held that the evidence did not establish with sufficient certainty that a recognisable benefit to the public was secured, thus the charitable gift failed.[32]

Therefore, it can be said that public benefit is generally interpreted broadly, and objectively, so as to advantage a community.[33]

---

23 *McGovern* v. *Attorney-General*, 333–4.
24 Ibid., 334.
25 Ibid.
26 *National Anti-Vivisection Society* v. *Inland Revenue Commissioners*.
27 This is a controversial and evolving area of law, which will be addressed in detail in Chapter 11.
28 *Re Pinion*.
29 *Re Pinion*, 785, citing *National Anti-Vivisection Society* v. *Inland Revenue Commissioners*, 65.
30 *Re Pinion*, 785.
31 Ibid.
32 Ibid., 788.
33 Chevalier-Watts, *Law of Charity*, 49, referring to Kerry O'Halloran, Myles McGregor Lowndes, and Karla Simon, *Charity Law and Social Policy* (Netherlands: Springer, 2008), 159; and Fiona Martin, 'Charities for the Benefit of Employees: Why Trusts for the Benefit of Employees Fail the Public Benefit Test', *Social Science Research Network* 1(1) (2009), 9.

B *Public benefit in the second sense*

Public benefit, in the second sense, refers to the requirement that the purpose must benefit the public in general, or a sufficient section of it, and not to give rise to more than incidental private benefit.[34] However, as the Charity Commission for England and Wales notes, the 'benefit' and 'public' can overlap,[35] which evidently may lead to complexities in the application of the concepts.

It is said[36] that the public benefit element can be traced back to the English Court of Appeal case of *Re Compton*,[37] where it was held that a trust for the education of the lawful descendants of named persons was not charitable. Lord Greene MR stated:[38]

> In the case of many charitable gifts it is possible to identify the individuals who are to benefit, or who at any given moment constitute the class from which the beneficiaries are to be selected.

His Lordship did note, however, that this would not necessarily 'deprive the gift of its public character'.[39] This is explained by the example of a gift 'to relieve the poor inhabitants of a parish'. Certainly, 'the class to benefit is readily ascertainable'.[40] However, the argument is that they do not enjoy the benefit because of them as individuals; rather, they enjoy it because of their membership of a specified class.

Consequently, 'the common quality which unites the potential beneficiaries into a class is essentially an impersonal one'.[41] In other words, it is defined by reference to that which they have in common, not their individual status.[42]

This approach was approved in *Oppenheim* v. *Tobacco Securities Trust Company Limited*:[43]

> the question is whether that class of persons can be regarded as such a 'section of the community' as to satisfy the test of public benefit. These words 'section of the community' have no special sanctity, but they conveniently indicate first, that the possible ... beneficiaries must not be numerically negligible, and secondly, that the quality which distinguishes them from other members of the community, so that they form by themselves a section of it, must be a quality which does not depend on their relationship to a particular individual.

34 Gary Watt, *Trusts & Equity*, 6th edn (Oxford: Oxford University Press, 2014), 210.
35 Watt, *Trusts & Equity*, 210, referring to 'Public Benefit: The Public Benefit Requirement (PB1)' (Charity Commission for England and Wales, September 2013).
36 Andrew Butler and Tim Clarke, 'Charitable Trusts', in *Equity and Trusts in New Zealand*, 2nd edn (Wellington: Thomson Reuters, 2009), 289.
37 *Re Compton*, 123.
38 Ibid., 129.
39 Ibid.
40 Ibid.
41 Ibid.
42 Ibid.
43 *Oppenheim* v. *Tobacco Securities Trust Co Ltd*, 306.

Thus, a group of beneficiaries may be numerically numerous but, if the connection between them is their personal relationship 'to a single propositus or to several propositi',[44] this will void them being a community, or a section of a community for charity law.[45]

Therefore, *Compton* and *Oppenheim* do offer some clarity as to what may constitute a sufficient section of the community, although they are not without criticism,[46] and indeed, may not be applicable in some circumstances. One such a circumstance arises in relation to a class of beneficiaries and their blood-tie connection, which is demonstrated in the context of New Zealand jurisprudence.

C Public benefit and blood tie: the anomalies

It is a truism that, generally speaking, a purpose will fail the public benefit test if the class of beneficiaries are linked by a blood tie. However, New Zealand created an exception in *Latimer* v. *Commissioner of Inland Revenue*[47] with regard to Māori-based tribal claims.[48] The question for the Court in *Latimer* was whether certain income of the Crown Forestry Rental Trust was for charitable purposes. As part of an agreement, the Crown sold tree crops on Crown forestry land to third party commercial buyers. These buyers were to make a capital payment, and then pay annual rent. Any interest on these payments was to be made available to assist Māori in the preparation, presentation, and negotiation of claims before the Waitangi Tribunal.[49]

It was evident that the Māori claimants were connected by blood tie, which would place their group outside the *Oppenheim* test of public benefit, because it would not be a sufficient section of the community for charitable purposes. However, the Court of Appeal held that such claims might be an exception to this test because:[50]

> To understand the nature of the purpose of the assistance to be given to Māori claimants it is necessary to understand the Waitangi Tribunal process. When that process is understood, it is apparent that the assistance purpose is not a mere matter of funding litigants in the preparation, presentation and negotiation of their cases. If that were all, it could have been achieved through normal legal aid arrangements.

44 Ibid.
45 Ibid.
46 Chevalier-Watts, *Law of Charity*, 60–4; Picarda, *Law and Practice Relating to Charities*, 32–3; Donald Poirier, *Charity Law in New Zealand* (www.charities.govt.nz, 2013), 132–3.
47 *Latimer* v. *Commissioner of Inland Revenue* [2002] 3 NZLR 195.
48 The indigenous people of New Zealand.
49 *Latimer* v. *Commissioner of Inland Revenue*, 195.
50 Ibid., 207.

It could be argued therefore 'the purpose had far reaching consequences and was not just limited in the funding of litigation'.[51] The research would enable claimants to 'finally determin[e] the truth about grievances long held by a significant section of New Zealand society ... for the benefit of all members of New Zealand society'.[52]

> If this research were not conducted in such a manner, the Tribunal's findings may not be seen as having such solid foundations, which may not therefore be accepted by the Crown, nor Māori, and perhaps most importantly, by the public. As a result, settlements may not occur, or if they do, then the results might not be regarded as full and final.[53] Such research endeavours to end such grievances and without such research grievances are likely to 'lead to social ferment at a future time'.

Consequently, the public benefit was evident because it reflected the 'large public benefit in the assistance purpose'.[54] The public benefit could also be found in 'proper presentation of the research to the tribunal and its utilisation during the negotiation process'[55] 'from which lasting and detailed settlements can be achieved'.[56]

However, the Court still had to determine whether the beneficiaries constituted a sufficient section of the community. In response, the Court stated that:[57]

> the common descent of claimant groups is a relationship poles away from the kind of connection which the House of Lords must have been thinking of in the *Oppenheim* case.

The Court stated that the House of Lords could not have had in their 'contemplation tribal or clan groups of ancient origin'.[58] It was far more likely that their Lordships actually had in mind 'the paradigmatic English approach to family relations'. Therefore, the Court in *Latimer* recognised a context-specific recognition of a public benefit that was exempt from the tests set out in *Compton* and *Oppenheim*, which reflected the cultural and social expectations of the time.[59]

New Zealand, however, has not been alone in the matter of blood tie and public benefit. The Australian Charities Act 2013 provides another exception to the public benefit requirement with respect to purposes directed to indigenous

---

51 Chevalier-Watts, *Law of Charity*, 69.
52 Chevalier-Watts, *Law of Charity*, 70, citing *Latimer* v. *Commissioner of Inland Revenue*, 207.
53 *Latimer* v. *Commissioner of Inland Revenue*, 207.
54 Ibid., 208.
55 Ibid.
56 Chevalier-Watts, *Law of Charity*, 70.
57 *Latimer* v. *Commissioner of Inland Revenue*, 208.
58 Ibid.
59 This is now codified in s 5(2) of the Charities Act 2005 (NZ).

Australians where the 'entity receives, holds or manages an amount, or non-cash benefit ... that relates to native title ... or traditional Indigenous rights of ownership, occupation, use or enjoyment of land'.[60]

In the past, Australia has followed the conventional English approach with regard to blood tie and family relationships, as established in *Compton* and *Oppenheim*. Thus, in the Privy Council case of *Davies* v. *Perpetual Trustee Co Ltd*,[61] the Court held that although the trust in question was for the advancement of education, there was no public benefit because the class of persons who would benefit was defined through their descent through their ancestors, in other words, the blood-tie relationship negated the public benefit. However, while the Australian common law still does follow the English common law in relation to the public benefit being negated if the class of beneficiaries depends on their relationship to a person, Australian legislation now creates an exemption for indigenous Australians. Although it is worth noting that the charity in question must be in receipt of money or non-cash benefits with respect to the indigenous traditional lands, so the exemption does have caveats.[62]

This chapter has focused on much common law emanating from England in order to contextualise the general principles of public benefit. Now we turn to each of the jurisprudential-specific approaches, where an overview of key matters will be considered. Further discussion on public benefit, including issues relating more extensively to the presumption, and lack of, public benefit, can be found in the jurisdiction-specific chapters.

Overview of international approaches to public benefit

A England and Wales and public benefit

It is evident that each of the selected jurisdictions have been influenced in many respects by their historical relationship with England, and in many respects, their jurisprudence is still closely linked with their historical roots. So, it is perhaps ironic that it is England that such an apparent dramatic development in its statutory provisions in relation to charitable purposes has occurred, and indeed, public benefit, in recent times, in comparison with some of its fellow jurisdictions.

Prior to the statutory changes in 2006, it was said that the public benefit was presumed for purposes that fell within the first three heads of charity, those of the relief of poverty, and the advancements of education and religion.[63] With the

---

60 Charities Act 2013, s 9 (AU).
61 Fiona Martin, 'Recent Developments in Australian Charity Law: One Step Forward and Two Steps Backward', *Charity Law and Practice Review* 17(1) (2014–15), 35–6, referring to *Davies* v. *Perpetual Trustee Co Ltd* (1959) 59 SR (NSW) 112; see also *Aboriginal Hostels Ltd* v. *Darwin City Council* (1985) 75 FLR 197. See also Chapter 6 for further discussion.
62 Charities Act 2013, s 9(2); Martin, 'Recent Developments in Australian Charity Law', 36.
63 Con Alexander *et al.*, *Charity Governance* (Bristol: Jordans, 2014), 4–5; Mary Synge, *The 'New' Public Benefit Requirement: Making Sense of Charity Law?* (Oxford: Hart, 2015), 9.

enactment of the Charities Act 2006, consolidated in the Charities Act 2011, this so-called presumption was said to be removed from all the heads of charity. Thus, s 3(2) of the 2006 Act states 'In determining whether that requirement is satisfied in relation to any such purpose, it is not to be presumed that a purpose of a particular description is for the public benefit'.[64] The rationale for this apparent change appears to have been 'to ensure a level playing field for all potentially charitable organisations'.[65] Public benefit is not defined in this Act, nor in the later 2011 Act, and merely states:[66]

> In this Part any reference to the public benefit is a reference to the public benefit as that term is understood for the purposes of the law relating to charities in England and Wales.

It has been argued therefore that this lack of clear definition 'undermines arguments that the Act reformed and modernised charity law by its focus on public benefit'.[67] It is not difficult to understand this apparent frustration when the new statutory provisions were much anticipated, and came in the face of many challenging principles of charity law that have developed throughout the centuries. Thus, the absence of straightforward definitions within the 2006, and 2011, Acts may, inevitably, pave the way for continued varying interpretations of public benefit.

While it has been a long and commonly held view that public benefit is presumed for the first three heads of charity, the decision of the Upper Tribunal (Tax and Charity) in *Independent Schools Council* v. *Charity Commission for England & Wales*[68] suggests that the presumption did not exist before the 2006 statutory changes. One of the questions raised in that case was whether the schools had always been subject to the legal duty to demonstrate how they deliver public benefit, or whether this was a new obligation introduced by the 2006 Act.[69] What this meant was that 'the historic position for those charities did not in fact fundamentally change with the coming into force of the 2006 Act'.[70] Nevertheless, what is of note now in England is that an entity must be able to demonstrate that its purposes are for the public benefit if it is to be registered as a charity. Although with the lack of statutory definition of public benefit, the Acts confirm that public benefit is understood by reference to pre-existing case law.[71]

64 Charities Act 2011, s 4.
65 Synge, *'New' Public Benefit Requirement*, 9.
66 Charities Act 2006, s 3(3); Charities Act 2011, s 4(3).
67 Mary Synge, 'A State of Flux in the Public Benefit Across United Kingdom, Ireland and Europe', *Charity Law and Practice Review* 16(1) (2013), 164.
68 *Independent Schools Council* v. *Charity Commission for England & Wales* [2011] UKUT 421 (TCC).
69 Synge, *'New' Public Benefit Requirement*, 9.
70 Alexander *et al.*, *Charity Governance*, 5.
71 Charities Act 2006, s 3(3); Charities Act 2011, s 4(3).

What can be said in relation to public benefit in England and Wales is that there are two aspects of public benefit:[72]

> The first aspect is that the nature of the purpose itself must be such as to be a benefit to the community: this was referred to as public benefit in the first sense ... The second aspect is that those who may benefit from the carrying out of the purpose must be sufficiently numerous, and identified in such manner, as to constitute what is described in the authorities as 'a section of the public': this is public benefit in the second sense.

In other words, there is a benefit aspect, and a public aspect that must be satisfied without it being presumed, regardless of whether that presumption existed prior to 2006. The 'benefit aspect' may be satisfied if the purpose is beneficial and any detriment or harm does not outweigh the benefit. The 'public aspect' may be satisfied if the purpose benefits the public generally, or a sufficient section of the community; and the benefit does not give rise to more than incidental private benefit.[73]

B Canada and public benefit

The Canada Revenue Agency (CRA) notes that in order for an organisation to become a registered charity, it must, inter alia, meet a public benefit test. This test mirrors that of the England and Wales, prior to its 2006 changes:[74]

- Purposes and activities provide a measurable benefit to the public; and
- The people who are eligible for benefits are either the public as a whole, or a significant section of it. Beneficiaries cannot be a restricted group, or one where members share a private connection.

The CRA Policy Statement on Public Benefit refers extensively to English law,[75] although it also provides Canadian common law as authority for the two-stage public

---

72 *Attorney-General* v. *Charity Commission for England and Wales* 2011 UKUT 421 TCC, [30] and [33], referring to *Williams' Trustees* v. *Inland Revenue Commissioners* [1947] AC 447; *Verge* v. *Somerville* [1924] AC 496; and *Gilmour* v. *Coats* [1949] AC 426.

73 Alexander *et al.*, *Charity Governance*, 7–8; 'Public Benefit: The Public Benefit Requirement (PB1)', pt. 2, September 2013, www.gov.uk/government/uploads/system/uploads/attachment_data/file/383871/PB1_The_public_benefit_requirem ent.pdf [accessed 15 Apr. 2016]

74 Canada Revenue Agency, 'What Is Charitable?', www.cra-arc.gc.ca/chrts-gvng/chrts/pplyng/cpc/wtc-eng.html [accessed 8 Mar. 2016].

75 Canada Revenue Agency, 'Guidelines for Registering a Charity: Meeting the Public Benefit Test', policy statement CPS-024, [3.0]–[3.3], referring to *Verge* v. *Somerville* [1924] AC 496; *National Anti-Vivisection Society* v. *Inland Revenue Commissioners* [1948] AC 31; *IRC* v. *Baddely* [1955] AC 572; and *McGovern* v. *AG* [1982] 3 All ER 439, by way of example, www.cra-arc.gc.ca/chrts-gvng/chrts/plcy/cps/cp s-024-eng.html [accessed 8 Mar. 2016].

benefit test. In *Vancouver Society of Immigrant and Visible Minority Women* v. *MNR*,[76] the Supreme Court confirmed the application of English authority in relation to public benefit in Canada, noting that one of the central principles of charity law is that of 'public welfare or benefit in an objectively measurable sense,' which underlies the existing categories of charitable purposes.

This approach was affirmed in *Alliance for Life* v. *MNR*,[77] where the Court observed that a charitable purpose must be 'for the benefit of the community or an appreciably important class of the community'. These cases echo *Vancouver Regional Free Net Association* v. *MNR*,[78] where the Court, in referring to English law, observed that '[p]ublic benefit ... spills over from the pure altruism of community welfare'.

It is evident, therefore, that Canada continues to reflect its historical alignment with England in a contemporary setting with regard to the concept of public benefit. This is perhaps not surprising because:[79]

> The regulatory regimes for charities in England and Canada both emerged under a general climate of economic and social upheaval, one in the context of the industrial revolution, the other one hundred years later during the Great Depression.

Unlike jurisdictions such as Australia and New Zealand, Canada has resisted regime change, albeit with some peripheral changes, which will be discussed in Chapter 7, and its core regulatory regime remains true to its origins. This is perhaps because the regimes share a similar emergence pattern, and, more importantly, the history and the institutionalisation of two regimes demonstrates that the origins have led to positive reinforcement, regardless of the extent of external factors or efficiencies that may change. This may explain why Canada's jurisprudence reflects so closely its origin of species, and it appears that this is unlikely to change any time soon.[80]

C Australia and public benefit

Section 6 of the Charities Act 2013 defines public benefit as:

1   A purpose that an entity has is for the *public benefit* if:
2   the achievement of the purpose would be of public benefit; and

76 *Vancouver Society of Immigrant and Visible Minority Women* v. *MNR* [1999] 1 SCR 10, [37], referring to *Commissioners for Special Purposes of the Income Tax* v. *Pemsel* [1891] AC 531. See also *Vancouver Society*, [147] and *Guaranty Trust Company of Canada* v. *MNR* [1967] SCR 133.
77 *Alliance for Life* v. *MNR* [1999] 3 FC 504, 32, referring to *Vancouver Society of Immigrant and Visible Minority Women* v. *MNR*.
78 *Vancouver Regional Free Net Association* v. *MNR*, [44], referring also to *Re Scowcroft* [1898] 2 Ch 638.
79 Peter R. Elson, 'The Origin of Species: Why Charity Regulations in Canada and England Continue to Reflect Their Origins', *International Journal of Not-for-Profit Law* 12(3) (May 2010), 89.
80 Ibid.

3   the purpose is directed to a benefit that is available to the members of:
4   the general public; or
5   a sufficient section of the general public.

For certain charitable purposes, the Act sets out where the presumption of public benefit is presumed:[81]

a   the purpose of preventing and relieving sickness, disease or human suffering;
b   the purpose of advancing education;
c   the purpose of relieving the poverty, distress or disadvantage of individuals or families;
d   the purpose of caring for and supporting:
e   the aged; or
f   individuals with disabilities;
g   the purpose of advancing religion.

There are also two exceptions to the public benefit requirement. First, where the purpose is the relief of necessitous circumstances or one or more individuals in Australia. Second, where purposes are directed to indigenous Australians and the entity holds, receives, or manages benefits related to native title, or the traditional rights of the ownership, occupation, use, or the enjoyment of the land,[82] as considered earlier.

Aside from the indigenous persons' exemptions, it is evident that the Australian common law follows the English common law in relation to public benefit, thus it 'is sufficient if the public benefit is in fact for an appreciable section of the public'.[83] While Australia may follow its English heritage on this matter, the principle of public benefit is not without its issues. Bleby J observed, in relation to the concept of a 'section of the public', that it is a 'vague phrase which may mean different things to different people'.[84] This means that 'public benefit is an elusive quality. It is not always open to sound reason, but is a quality often plainly recognised when it exists'.[85] While this may not assist a court in determining whether purposes meet the requirement of public benefit, what it does speak to is the complexity of the principle, and even the frustration of the court in endeavouring to ascertain it.

This view is given weight in *Tasmanian Electronic Commerce Centre Pty Ltd* v. *Commissioner of Taxation*,[86] where it was confirmed that what is for the public

---

81   Charities Act 2013, s 7 (AU).
82   Ibid., ss 8 and 9 respectively; Martin, 'Recent Developments in Australian Charity Law', 34–5.
83   *Strathalbyn Show Jumping Club Inc* v. *Mayes* [2001] SASC 73 (16 March 2001), [93], referring to *Oppenheim* v. *Tobacco Securities Trust Co Ltd*.
84   *Strathalbyn Show Jumping Club Inc* v. *Mayes*, [95].
85   Ibid., [97].
86   *Tasmanian Electronic Commerce Centre Pty Ltd* v. *Commissioner of Taxation* [2005] FCA 439 (18 April 2005), [37], referring to *Scottish Burial Reform and Cremation Society* v. *Glasgow Corporation* [1968] AC 138, 154 and *Vancouver Regional FreeNet Association* v. *MNR* [1996] 3 FC 880.

benefit now may change in accordance with changing social needs. The social needs at the time were of key relevance in this case, where the Court had to consider whether the Tasmanian Electronic Commerce Centre (TECC) was a charitable institution. Of importance was the notion that the genesis of the TECC was the provision of funding to economically disadvantaged areas of Australia. In other words, those areas that were poor in comparison with the rest of the nation, Tasmania being the case in point. Tasmania combines a small population, and long distances from markets and raw materials. Consequently, conventional manufacturing would be disadvantaged, resulting in Tasmania becoming a 'poor relation of the rest of the nation'.[87] Therefore, the TECC's objects were of benefit to the public because they would enable Tasmania to develop economically in line with the rest of the nation. This is evidence, therefore, of a public benefit of its time. It is possible that with time and changing socio-economic circumstances, this public benefit may become obsolete.

D New Zealand and public benefit

Under the Charities Act 2005, the public benefit requirement is as follows:[88]

> the purpose of a trust, society, or institution is a charitable purpose under this Act if the purpose would satisfy the public benefit requirement.

There is, however, no statutory definition of public benefit. Consequently, courts utilise case law to determine the public benefit requirement. New Zealand affirms that there must be a benefit that accrues to the public, which requires the application of the twofold test. That test being, as addressed earlier, that purposes confer a benefit on the public, or a section of the public; and the class of persons eligible to benefit constitutes the public, or a sufficient section of it.[89] This, of course, echoes the English approach, unsurprising considering New Zealand's historic connections with its colonial cousin. New Zealand courts, similarly to the English courts, reflect the difficulties in establishing public benefit. The Supreme Court, in *Re Greenpeace of New Zealand Inc*, noted that:[90]

> The *Pemsel* classification ... does not ... treat 'public benefit' and 'charitable purpose' as coinciding entirely. The cases have generally insisted that the purposes of relief of poverty, advancement of education ... and ... religion ... must also be for the benefit of the public. Conversely, in the case of the fourth head ... objects of benefit to the public [are] still to be charitable within the spirit of the cases based on the 'very sketchy list in the statute of Elizabeth'.

---

87 *Tasmanian Electronic Commerce Centre Pty Ltd* v. *Commissioner of Taxation*, [61].
88 Charities Act 2005, s 5(2)(a) (NZ).
89 *Travis Trust* v. *Charities Commission* HC WN CIV-2008-485-1689 [3 December 2008], [54].
90 *Re Greenpeace of New Zealand Inc* [2015] 1 NZLR 169, [27].

Further, the Court observed that this '[i]dentifying whether a purpose is charitable or not has always been difficult'.[91] This difficulty may arise from the origin of the classification, as suggested in *Greenpeace*, but it may also be that the difficulty is 'inherent in the subject-matter under consideration'.[92]

While New Zealand recognises the difficulties in assessing public benefit, what has been confirmed is that under the first three heads of charity, unless there is evidence to the contrary, public benefit is assumed,[93] because purposes are 'all treated as being within the "spirit and intendment" of the preamble'.[94] With regard to the fourth head of charity, the public benefit should be expressly established. Further to this, any private benefits 'derived from an entity's activities must be a means of achieving an ultimate public benefit'.[95]

E Hong Kong and public benefit

Echoing its historical ancestry, in Hong Kong a purpose cannot be charitable unless it is directed to the public, or a sufficient section of the public. However, there is no one precise definition of what may constitute a sufficient section of the public, and instead, each case will be decided on its own merit.[96] Thus a public benefit may be found even if the charity is small and run by one or a few people; this is because a charity is not defined by its size or its resources.[97]

In reality, this means that the courts will invariably turn to case law to assess the public nature of a purpose because 'charities law in Hong Kong … largely remains governed by common law jurisprudence'.[98]

This is evidenced in *Ip Cheung-Kwok* v. *Sin Hua Bank Trustee Ltd*,[99] which followed *Oppenheim* v. *Tobacco Securities Trust Co Ltd* in relation to establishing what may constitute a public benefit as either benefiting an appreciably important or substantial section of the public. The purpose in the *Ip Cheung-Kwok* case 'fell squarely within the single propositus test'[100] set out earlier, meaning the requirement of common relationship to Sze-Shing as an attribute for selection of class rendered the trust non-charitable.

91 Ibid., [28].
92 *Re Greenpeace of New Zealand Inc*, [28], referring to *National Anti-Vivisection Society* v. *Inland Revenue Commissioners*, 52.
93 *Re Family First New Zealand* [2015] NZHC 1493 [30 June 2015], [21].
94 *Re Greenpeace of New Zealand Inc*, [27].
95 *Re Family First New Zealand*, [21].
96 'A Tax Guide for Charitable Institutions and Trusts of a Public Character', [5], www. ird.gov.hk/eng/tax/ach_tgc.htm [accessed 8 Apr. 2016]; *Li Kim Sang Victor* v. *Chen Chi Hsia* HCA 481/2008 24 February 2015, [71]; *Cheung Man Yu* v. *Lau Yuen Ching* [2007] 4 KHC 314, [24].
97 *Cheung Man Yu* v. *Lau Yuen Ching*, [90].
98 Stefano Mariani, 'Traditional Chinese Religion Trusts in Hong Kong', *Trust and Trustees* 21(5) (June 2015), 539.
99 *Ip Cheung-Kwok* v. *Sin Hua Bank Trustee Ltd* [1990] HKCU 0403.
100 Mark Hsiao, 'The Beginning and the End of an Era of Charitable Public Benefit in Hong Kong', *Conveyancer and Property Lawyer* 76(3) (2012), 48.

The more contemporary case of *Li Kim Sang Victor* v. *Chen Chi Hsia* also reflects a continued application of the *Oppenheim* approach to public benefit. Here, the Court referred to that English approach in relation to establishing that a public benefit either benefits an appreciably important, or substantial section, of the public.[101]*Li Kim Sang Victor* confirmed that, in the Hong Kong context, a trust for the welfare of relatives, rather than for a village, is not charitable, because of the blood-tie nexus between the beneficiaries, thus failing the public element.[102]

Therefore, Hong Kong charity law still reflects its early English charity heritage, and this reflection is evident even after the transfer of sovereignty to the Chinese from the United Kingdom in July 1997, which marked the end of British rule in Hong Kong.[103]

F Singapore and public benefit

Charity law in Singapore is derived primarily from English law, and it is evident that English law is still an important reference point for the Singaporean courts, although as will be seen in the chapter dedicated to Singapore charity law, while English law still plays a prominent part, its application can be challenging in relation to cases that must take into account particular religions, customs, and cultures prevalent in Singapore.

Nonetheless, in relation to public benefit, and the first three heads of charity, Singapore presumes the public benefit,[104] thus retaining English law interpretation, at least prior to 2006, when England and Wales still retained the presumption of public benefit. While Singapore retains the presumption of public benefit,[105] where gifts for beneficiaries may be related by blood, or contract to an individual person, these will not be charitable because of the lack of public benefit.[106] Where purposes are of a religious nature, while the public benefit is presumed, it will be negated if the purpose is said to be subversive of morality, illegal, or otherwise contrary to public policy.[107] Evidently such an approach echoes Singapore's historical association with England.

---

101 *Li Kim Sang Victor* v. *Chen Chi Hsia*, [75], referring to *Oppenheim* v. *Tobacco Securities Trust Co Ltd*.
102 *Li Kim Sang Victor* v. *Chen Chi Hsia*, [76], referring to *Ip Cheung-kwok* v. *Ip Siu-bun* [1988] 2 HKLR 247, 253C.
103 https://en.wikipedia.org/wiki/Transfer_of_sovereignty_over_Hong_Kong [accessed 8 Apr. 2016].
104 Ter Kah Lang, *The Law of Charities: Cases & Materials Singapore and Malaysia* (Singapore: Butterworths, 1985), 10, 30, 38, and 59.
105 Donovan Waters QC, '"Singapore and Hong Kong also Retain the Presumption": The Advancement of Religion in a Pluralist Society (Part II): Abolishing the Public Benefit Element', *Trust & Trustees* 17(8) (September 2011), 735.
106 Lang, *Law of Charities*, 30–1.
107 Lang, *Law of Charities*, 30, referring to *Thornton* v. *Howe* (1862) 31 Beav 14; *O'Hanlon* v. *Logue* [1906] 1 IR 247; *Re Caus* [1934] Ch 162; and *Re Watson* [1973] 1 WLR 1472.

The Court of Appeal case of *Koh Lau Keow* v. *Attorney-General* provides a useful illustration of contemporary courts still relying on English law to determine issues relating to charitable purposes.[108] Here, the Court had to determine the charitable nature of trusts under the heads of the relief of poverty, and the advancement of religion.

In relation to the relief of poverty, the Court stated that no assumption could be made that Chinese vegetarian women of the Buddhist faith were destitute or poor. This meant that the English case of *In re Isabel Joanna James* should be distinguished, because, in that case, Farwell J was influenced by the fact that the religious sisters, or clergy, were either without means themselves, or were carrying on charitable work. It therefore would be charitable to provide them with a home.[109] Interestingly, while Singapore does claim to recognise a presumption of public benefit in relation to three of the four heads of charity, the Court in this case appears to utilise the word 'assumption' interchangeably with 'presumption', and denies that the charitable purpose of relief of poverty can be assumed to be of public benefit. This appears to be contrary to the notion of presumption of public benefit, and illustrates the complexities of charity law, and its interpretation in the various jurisdictions.

This apparent removal of the presumption is also echoed later in the case when the Court considered the advancement of religion. The Court refers at length to the English cases of *Cocks* v. *Manners* and *Gilmour* v. *Coats*,[110] in which the Courts found the public benefit requirement was missing in relation to the advancement of religion. In the present case, the Court stated that one of the purposes was to create a long-term residence for individuals, and not a temporary religious retreat to which Buddhist Chinese vegetarian women could resort. This failed to meet the public benefit requirement, even though there was some mingling between residents and the public when the retreat opened its doors to the public four times a year to take part in religious activities. While it is likely that this was the correct decision for the Court to make, because the trust was not required to open the property to the public, it seems that the Court did not presume public benefit in the purpose in the first instance, as the common law requires. Rather, the Court stated that it could not find the public benefit, which is entirely different from presuming public benefit, and its being negated.[111]

So, while it appears, prima facie, that Singapore follows the English method of assessing charitable purpose, the reality may be that Singapore Courts have in fact adapted that approach and there may be a separation of jurisdiction-specific methods.

---

108 *Koh Lau Keow* v. *Attorney-General* [2014] SGCA 18.
109 *Koh Lau Keow* v. *Attorney-General*, [27], referring to *In re Isabel Joanna James* [1932] Ch 25.
110 *Koh Lau Keow* v. *Attorney-General*, [33]–[35], referring to *Cocks* v. *Manners* (1871) LR 12 Eq 574 and *Gilmour* v. *Coats*; see also reference to *Re Warre's Will Trusts* [1953] 1 WLR 725.
111 See also *Re Chionh Ke Hu, Deceased* [1964] MLJ 270.

5 England and Wales

A Introduction

As previous chapters indicate, within the common law jurisdictions of the world, England and Wales 'has historically carried the lead role, forging ahead with developments in the field'.[1] One of the focuses of charity law has been regulatory power to enforce the law, and to prevent abuses or misuses of powers or funds. The majority of regulatory functions are found in legislation, and the agencies associated in the exercise of those supervisory powers.

This chapter, and the following jurisdiction-specific chapters, begin by introducing key policing and legislative developments. This chapter, inter alia, then develops discussion relating to the Charity Commission for England and Wales; public benefit; and then considers jurisprudential milestones.

This chapter focuses on England and Wales, as have earlier chapters, as opposed to the United Kingdom as a whole because the latter does not have one single legal system. England and Wales applies English law, and has its own Charity Commission, while Scotland, for instance, applies Scots law. Each jurisdiction in the United Kingdom has its own charity law, although they share similarities.[2]

Charities have a long history within England and Wales. The oldest charity is the King's School Canterbury, which was established in AD 597, and exists today as a thriving educational establishment.[3] This charity is not alone in its longevity – other examples include the Hospital of St Cross, in Winchester, Hampshire, established in 1136 by the grandson of William the Conqueror. It still operates today providing care and support to the elderly and travellers.[4] The Laugharne

1 Kerry O'Halloran, *The Profits of Charity: International Perspectives on the Law Governing the Involvement of Charities in Commerce* (New York: Oxford University Press, 2012), 141.
2 Clive Cutbill, Alison Paines, and Murray Hallam, *International Charitable Giving* (Oxford: Oxford University Press, 2012), 222.
3 Robin Hogdson, *Trusted and Independent: Giving back to Charities – Review of the Charities Act 2006* (London: TSO, 2012), [1.1], http://www.kings-school.co.uk/about/history [accessed 20 Apr. 2016].
4 Hogdson, *Trusted and Independent*, [1.2].

Corporation Lands in Wales can trace its origins back to 1290, and still operates for the benefit of those within the Laugharne and Llansadurnen areas.[5]

Charities today in England and Wales are wide-ranging and diverse in nature and benefits, and, at the time of writing, there were 181,823 charities registered with the Charity Commission.[6] From early times, the charitable regulatory system has endeavoured to ensure that charities do not undermine the agenda of the government, and that they benefit the public as appropriately as possible. These factors have been 'the driving concern of government since well before the Statute of Charitable Uses 1601'.[7]

It is true that the charity law of England is rich in judicial precedent, but alongside that runs a raft of statutory interventions and reforms that have helped to shape charity law in England, and this chapter now considers some of those milestones.

B A potted history of charitable regulation in England and Wales

Up until the Middle Ages, charities were mainly the domain of the Roman Catholic Church, which provided substantial assistance through hospitals, almshouses, doles, and general relief to the poor and needy. However, with Henry VIII's dissolution of the monasteries, and the stripping of power of the Church, much change was to come with regard to the poor, and with it came state regulation. Early statutes included the Mortmain Act 1531 and the Chantries Act 1545, which reinforced mortmain prohibitions against bequeathing land to chantries and other ecclesiastical bodies.[8] Come the reign of Elizabeth I, alongside the lasting effects of the Reformation, the effects of urbanisation, rapid population growth, and dispossession of peasant land, all led to substantial increases in levels of poverty and suffering.

The Statute of Charitable Uses 1601, or the Statute of Elizabeth, was born out of this difficult period, and was a necessitous regulatory framework. It sought to rationalise and clarify the role of state and private charitable donations;[9] its overall intent was to ensure accountability for funds for charitable purposes.[10] The Act has long since been repealed but its Preamble,[11] which set out a non-exhaustive list of charitable purposes, is the heritage of the current common charitable purposes found in the Charities Acts 2006 and 2011.

---

5 Cutbill, Paines, and Hallam, *International Charitable Giving*, 222; http://opencharities.org/charities/218121 [accessed 20 Apr. 2016].
6 http://apps.charitycommission.gov.uk/showcharity/registerofcharities/SectorData/SectorOverview.aspx [accessed 20 Apr. 2016].
7 Kerry O'Halloran, Myles McGregor-Lowndes, and Karla W. Simon, *Charity Law & Social Policy: National and International Perspectives on the Functions of Law Relating to Charities*, vol. 10 (Netherlands: Springer, 2008), 134.
8 Gino Dal Pont, *Law of Charity* (Chatswood: LexisNexis, 2000), 82–3.
9 Hodgson, *Trusted and Independent*, [1.3].
10 O'Halloran, McGregor-Lowndes, and Simon, *Charity Law & Social Policy*, 135.
11 See Chapter 1 for further information.

The continued presence of this ancient Act is also still to be found in the present Charity Commission for England and Wales. Its terms of reference, while clearly much evolved, evidently originated from the Act's 'initial bare outline of regulatory powers'.[12] This is because the 'regulatory role and powers of the Charity Commissioners for England & Wales were first statutorily assigned to such a non-judicial body in 1601'.[13] However, while that body was established at that time to ensure that charitable gifts were utilised for their intended purposes, practically speaking, the costs of seeking legal remedies actually made this process impractical. Thus, a Charity Commission was formally created in 1853 by the Mortmain and Charitable Uses Act, which was based on progressive reform.[14]

One key non-legislative change was brought into being by the Industrial Revolution in the nineteenth century, alongside great social dislocation and poverty – the Brougham Inquiry. This was headed by Lord Brougham in 1819, lasting nearly 20 years, and resulting in the prosecution of nearly 400 charities. Its initial aim was to address access to education, especially by the poor, although other aspects of the inquiry focused on more general charity abuses, such as fraud and misallocation of funds.[15]

The twentieth century saw further reforms – in 1952 the Nathan Commission[16] was established. Its remit was to consider and report on proposed changes in the law and practice relating to charitable trusts. Its report led to a number of changes, including reforms to investment rules; reform of the Board of Charity Commissioners; and improving information available on charitable trusts.[17] In 1960, the Charities Act 1960 was implemented, and this laid a 'largely common baseline for law and practice in the latter part of the 20th century'.[18] It contained many of the major recommendations of the Nathan Committee, and it extended the powers of the Charity Commissioners over all organisations devoted to exclusively charitable purposes, not just charitable trusts. Additionally, all old and new charities were required to register with the Commission, unless excluded by the Act.[19]

The early 1990s saw the passing of the Charities Acts 1992 and 1993, and much of the authority previously vested in the office of the Attorney-General was directed to the Commissioners.[20]

---

12 O'Halloran, McGregor-Lowndes, and Simon, *Charity Law & Social Policy*, 136.

13 Ibid., 137.

14 Peter R. Elson, 'The Origin of Species: Why Charity Regulations in Canada and England Continue to Reflect Their Origins', *International Journal of Not-for-Profit Law* 12(3) (May 2010), 83.

15 Elson, 'Origin of Species', 83–4, referring to M. Gilbert, 'The Work of Lord Brougham for Education in England' (doctoral thesis, University of Pennsylvania, 1922).

16 Committee on the Law and Practice relating to charitable trusts (the Nathan Committee), established 1949, reported 1952.

17 Hogdson, *Trusted and Independent*, [1.9].

18 Kerry O'Halloran *et al.*, 'Charity Law Reforms: An Overview of Progress Since 2001', in *Modernising Charity Law, Recent Developments and Future Directions* (Cheltenham: Edward Elgar, 2010), 13.

19 O'Halloran *et al.*, 'Charity Law Reforms', 13–14; Dal Pont, *Law of Charity*, 94–5.

20 O'Halloran, McGregor-Lowndes, and Simon, *Charity Law & Social Policy*, 151; Hogdson, *Trusted and Independent*, [1.13].

Then began another era of legislative reform. In 2001, the then-Prime Minister, Tony Blair, announced a review of charities and the not-for-profit sector, which was undertaken by the Cabinet Office's Strategy Unit, along with the Home Office. The final report of the project, *Private Action, Public Benefit*, was published in September 2002. The report, and the results of its consultation, formed the basis of the Charities Bill 2004, which was largely intended to reform charity law. The Charities Act 2006 was passed in November 2006,[21] creating numerous reforms, including increasing the policing functions of the Commission; extending the list of charitable purposes; and considering the lists of exempt and excepted charities.[22]

This was also the first Act to have built into it an automatic review procedure, with the review's terms of reference being found in s 73(2)). The review was undertaken by Lord Hodgson of Astley Abbotts, who presented his findings to Parliament in 2012. The review 'clearly set its sights beyond a mere legislative review and took its wide terms of reference to heart'.[23] It traversed:[24]

> the regulatory framework in England and Wales and sets over 100 recommendations on matters from the determinants of charitable status, charity registration, accounting, the roles of and support for trustees, the regulator and principal regulators, through to investment and fundraising.

Some of the recommendations are controversial, and some 'display a restraint that borders on timidity'.[25] The recommendations can be condensed into four key themes:[26]

- The need for regulatory balance;
- Prioritisation of regulatory choices;
- Education of the public and trustees through information and transparency; and
- The need to take responsibility.

This much-anticipated review can be seen as yet one 'more milestone along the continuing road to reform',[27] following on from the 2006 Act, and illustrates the fact that 'the reforming spirit is alive and well in the sector'.[28] Indeed, the spirit of

---

21 Hogdson, *Trusted and Independent*, [2.1]–[2.3].
22 The extension of the list of charitable purposes is considered later in the chapter.
23 www.withersworldwide.com/news-publications/review-of-the-charities-act-2006-%E2%80%93-giving-charity-back-to-charities–2 [accessed 22 Apr. 2016].
24 Alison Dunn, 'Lord Hogdson's Charities Act Review', *Voluntary Sector Review* 4(1) (2013), 127.
25 Ibid., 128.
26 Ibid.
27 Ibid., 137.
28 www.withersworldwide.com/news-publications/review-of-the-charities-act-2006-%E2%80%93-giving-charity-back-to-charities–2 [accessed 22 Apr. 2016].

additional reform continued, as it was 'always the intention to consolidate the statute law of England and Wales',[29] for instance the Recreational Charities Act 1958, and the Charities Acts 1993 and 2006. As a result, the Charities Act 2011 came into force in March 2012, which, while not making any changes to the law, consolidated existing legislation.[30]

Its coming into force suggests that charity law in England and Wales is 'in a state of flux'.[31] Indeed, with the 2006 Act under review, and to be considered by the Law Commission, it is likely that further legislative or regulatory reform is to come.

C Charity Commission for England and Wales

These are difficult economic times for charity regulators.[32] In Australia, regulators are being instituted, while in New Zealand the short-lived Charities Commission was disestablished under the Charities Amendment Act (No. 2) 2012, with its functions being transferred to the Department of Internal Affairs – Charities Services. A similar 'bonfire of the quangos'[33] occurred in the United Kingdom as a result of economic deficits, but the Charity Commission for England and Wales (the Comisiwyn Elusennau Cymru a Lloegr)[34] was 'spared the flame'.[35]

Nonetheless, the Commission was subject to significant budgetary cuts in the spending review period of 2014–15, because it is not considered a frontline public service. The cuts resulted in strategic prioritisation of work programmes and departments, alongside a raft of redundancies.[36] As part of its review in 2011, the Commission acknowledged that it would need to focus on its core regulatory roles, as opposed to a more hands-on approach to support charities. Lord Hodgson made similar recommendations in his review of the Charities Act 2006.[37]

---

29 Frank Cranmer, 'Government and Parliament 2010–2011', *Christian Law Review* 80 (1) (2011), 80.
30 Juliet Chevalier-Watts, *Law of Charity* (Wellington: Thomson Reuters, 2014), 15–16; 'About the Charities Act', www.charitycommmission.gov.uk [accessed 22 Apr. 2016].
31 Hubert Picarda, 'Charities Act 2011: A Dog's Breakfast or Dream Come True? A Case for Further Reform', in Matthew Harding, Ann O'Connell, and Miranda Stewart (eds), *Not-for-Profit Law: Theoretical and Comparative Perspectives* (Cambridge: Cambridge University Press, 2014), 135; for criticisms of the 2011 Act, see ibid., 134–58.
32 Alison Dunn, 'Regulatory Shifts: Developing Sector Participation in Regulation for Charities in England and Wales', *Legal Studies* 34(4) (2014), 660.
33 Ibid.
34 Welsh translation.
35 Dunn, 'Regulatory Shifts: Developing Sector Participation in Regulation for Charities in England and Wales', 660, referring to Strategy Unit Public Bodies Reform – Proposals for Change (December 2010), at 4, www.direct.gov.uk/prod_consum_dg/groups/dg_digitalassets/@en/documents/digitalasset/dg_191543.pdf [accessed 1 June 2013].
36 Dunn, 'Regulatory Shifts', 661.
37 Con Alexander *et al.*, *Charity Governance*, 2nd edn (Bristol: Jordans, 2014), 43; Hogdson, *Trusted and Independent*, 45–6.

One far-reaching regulatory shift for the Commission will be its rebalance of relationships with charities by encouraging greater self-regulation. This change will enable the Commission to streamline its operations and target resources more efficiently. There is nothing new in this type of regulatory approach, and it is the favoured approach of the European Commission to protect the European Union's non-profit sector from misuse. This strategy has been utilised extensively as a sector regulatory tool within a number of the European Union's member states, thus, the Commission's approach 'corresponds with a wider regulatory agenda'.[38]

Regardless of reforms, the Commission remains, regulating all charities in England and Wales. It is a statutory corporation established under the Charities Act 2011,[39] performing functions on behalf of the Crown. Its governance framework is set out in s 13 of the Act, and is established in line with a number of statutory objectives, functions, and duties. Its objectives include increasing public confidence; ensuring charity compliance; and enhancing charities' accountability. Its general functions include determining the charitability of institutions; facilitating improved administration of charities; and identifying and investigation alleged misconduct or mismanagement of charities.[40] The Commission maintains the register of charities,[41] and this is part of its general function of obtaining, evaluating, and disseminating information in relation to achieving its objectives.[42]

While the Commission carries out vital regulatory functions and duties within the charity industry, it has been subject to criticism. One criticism focuses on the Commission's approach to public benefit. The Charities Act 2006 required the Commission to publish guidance on public benefit, and it undertook this by issuing extensive general guidance and supplemental guidance relating to individual sectors. These were only intended to be guidance and summary of the law, with no force of law. However, during the consultation process leading to the publication of its guidance, the Commission rejected challenges to the legal basis of its draft documents, and rejected calls for the guidance to be written by charity law experts. Instead, its Policy Division wrote the 2008 guidance, whose members were responsible for proposing and developing the Commission's own policies and strategies, raising questions of conflict of interest.[43]

The Commission asserted that its key principles in its 2008 guidance were 'distilled … from the relevant case-law',[44] but it has been asserted that its interpretation was legally flawed, or just plain wrong.[45]

---

38 Dunn, 'Regulatory Shifts', 664.
39 Also, the Charities Act 2006.
40 Alexander *et al.*, *Charity Governance*, 44; Charities Act 2011, s 15.
41 Charities Act 2011, s 29.
42 Alexander *et al.*, *Charity Governance*, 46; Charities Act 2011, s 15(4).
43 Mary Synge, *The 'New' Public Benefit Requirement: Making Sense of Charity Law?* (Oxford: Hart, 2015), 11–12; it should be noted that the Commission has made a number of changes in its 2013 guidance.
44 Synge, *'New' Public Benefit Requirement*, 12, citing *Charities and Public Benefit* (Commission, January 2008), Foreword.
45 Picarda, 'Charities Act 2011', 145.

Further criticisms of the Commission include its guidance being admonitory, with overemphasis on risk management. Further, endeavouring to explain to charities the consequences of overstepping regulatory boundaries, it has tended to draw those boundaries tightly, especially in legal grey areas. Thus, the guidelines have appeared to move from good practice to legal principle, which is beyond the Commission's remit. However, while the Commission has been subject to criticism, it revised its guidance in 2013. The law that is being interpreted by the Commission is said to be imprecise and confusing, therefore it is not surprising that issues have arisen with such guidelines law is imprecise and confusing. It is perhaps not surprising, therefore, that issues arise with such guidelines.[46]

Overall therefore the Charity Commission operates in tricky waters – it is subject to political agendas; budgetary reforms; and lack of legal clarity. At the same time, it operates transparently and supportively as a regulator of a sector that is fundamental within society. It has an unenviable, and 'almost impossible'[47] task, but one that is necessary to ensure accountability, compliance, and regulation.

D Public benefit

As noted in Chapter 2, charities enjoy many privileges not afforded to other types of organisations, including fiscal benefits, and high levels of public trust and confidence. Having such privileged status means that charities must, and should, operate for the benefit of the public. Nonetheless, there has been much debate over the decades as to the notion of public benefit, and it would be fair to say that it is a controversial doctrine.[48] Chapter 4 focuses on public benefit and its requirements. This section does not aim to repeat such matters; rather, the focus is to consider England and Wales's contemporary approach to this doctrine.

While legislative reform has brought public benefit to the fore in England and Wales, in reality, the meaning of public benefit is still far from clear. The doctrine was a central part of the 'long anticipated statutory definition of charity',[49] introduced by the Charities Act 2006, and largely consolidated in the subsequent 2011 Act, but no definition was given, beyond stipulating that the doctrine should be understood according to that which has been attributed by decades of case law.[50]

One of the key reforms of the 2006 Act was the reversal of the public benefit presumption traditionally granted to the first three heads of charity within the *Pemsel* construct, meaning all charitable purposes in England and Wales are now subject to mandatory application of the public benefit test.

46 Alison Dunn, 'Charities and Restrictions on Political Activities: Developments by the Charity Commission for England and Wales in Determining Regulatory Barriers', *International Journal of Not-for-Profit Law* 11(1) (November 2008), 59–62.
47 Debra Morris, 'The Charity Commission for England and Wales: A Fine Example or Another Fine Mess?', *Chicago-Kent Law Review* 91(3) (2016), 965.
48 Hogdson, *Trusted and Independent*, 27.
49 Mary Synge, 'A State of Flux in Public Benefit across UK, Ireland and Europe', *Charity Law and Practice Review* 16(1) (2013–14), 164.
50 Ibid.; Charities Act 2011, s 4(3).

It has been argued that such a reversal has possible implications for the Commission. This is because it is considered an independent body, although it is government funded, staffed by government-approved staff, and, while not directly accountable to government ministers, it is subject to their oversight. Thus, it could be vulnerable to political pressures in respect of finding, or not, the public benefit in a variety of health, educational, and social facilities, depending on the politics in play at the time. The alternative argument is that s 6(4) of the 2006 Act prevents such pressure from coming to bear.[51]

There has been considerable debate about whether or not a statutory definition of public benefit would be desirable in this jurisdiction, but governments have continually resisted this approach, no doubt in part due to the considerable difficulties of 'condensing several hundred years of case-law into a straightforward definition that would reflect the diversity of the sector and would enable the law to continue to evolve'.[52] Regardless of the lack of definition, when an entity's purposes are scrutinised for public benefit, this public benefit requirement is to be tested against the entity's purposes as set out in its governing documents, not what the entity does, or will do, to further those purposes.[53] This means that the Commission and the courts have limited scope to review that which the entity will do, or does, when determining charitable status. Nonetheless, if the governing documents are not clear on the matter, then the activities may be taken into consideration to determine charitability.

The 2011 Act gave the Commission a public benefit objective 'to promote awareness and understanding of the operation of the public benefit requirement'.[54] As part of this objective, the Commission was charged with producing guidelines on the operation of this doctrine, and it has subsequently produced substantial guidance, starting from 2008. In doing so, it was asserted that the Commission made 'de facto, if not de jure, changes to charity law',[55] thus taking advantage of its remit in this area. Even though the Commission stated that its guidance did not constitute the law on public benefit, the *Independent Schools Council* case[56] actually successfully challenged the status of the guidance in the Upper Tribunal in 2011. This case is discussed later in the chapter, but suffice to say, as a result of that decision, the Commission published revised public benefit

51 O'Halloran, *Profits of Charity*, 151–2; Charities Act 2006, s 6(4) states: 'In the exercise of its functions the Commission shall not be subject to the direction or control of any Minister of the Crown or other government department'.
52 Alexander *et al.*, *Charity Governance*, 5.
53 Alexander *et al.*, *Charity Governance*, 5, referring to *Independent Schools Council* v. *Charity Commission for England and Wales* [2011] UKUT 421 (TCC).
54 Charities Act 2011, s 14.
55 Jonathan Garton, *Public Benefit in Charity Law* (Oxford: Oxford University Press, 2013), 26, referring to (1993) 1 Decision of the Charity Commissioners 4, where it refused to register two rifle clubs as charities, and the later negotiation of the voluntary removal of similar clubs from the register of charities. This, despite High Court authority that teaching of shooting is charitable, see *Re Stephens* [1892] 8 TLR 792 (Ch); *Re Good* [1905] 2 Ch 60 (Ch); *Re Driffill* [1950] 1 Ch 93 (Ch).
56 *Independent Schools Council* v. *Charity Commission for England and Wales*.

guidance in September 2013. Thus, it has been confirmed that the role of the Commission and public benefit is to clarify the law, not to advance it.[57]

It has been stated that the 2006 and 2011 Acts removed the presumption of public benefit,[58] however, it is uncertain what effect these words may have on the law of public benefit. The Commission is clear that every entity entered on the register of charities must show explicitly that its purposes are for the public benefit. This will mean, for example, that schools and churches will have to establish this. This will, in effect, change the law, because previous case law shows that public benefit has been presumed. On the other hand, it is argued that the removal of the presumption will have no effect because s 3 of the 2011 Act makes it clear that these purposes are charitable, thus of public benefit. This therefore follows the original *Pemsel* classifications, where the first three heads of charity were said to be presumed for the public benefit. Therefore, the only issue to determine is whether such purposes affect a sufficient section of the public to give it its required public character.[59]

It has been further argued that the presumption of public benefit has little legal basis, and therefore, does not exist. The presumption was said to be based primarily on Lord Wright's dictum in *National Anti-Vivisection Society* v. *IRC:*[60]

> The test of public benefit to the community goes through the whole of Lord Macnaghten's classification, though as regards the first three heads, it may be *prima facie assumed* unless the contrary appears.

His Lordship utilised 'assumed' not 'presumed', thus immediately challenging the notion that a presumption exists, and 'it goes too far to conclude from this that those purposes were presumed to be for the public benefit as a matter of law'.[61] If, therefore, the presumption did not exist,[62] then the legislative reforms change nothing, and are merely procedural, resulting in the courts being likely to articulate clearly their conclusions as to the charitability of an entity.[63]

Thus, the issue of public benefit appears to be just as complex, even after regulatory reform. However, it cannot be ignored that the 2011 Act states 'any reference to the public benefit is a reference to the public benefit as that term is

---

57 Garton, *Public Benefit in Charity Law*, 26–7; Alexander *et al.*, *Charity Governance*, 6; Guidance includes: 'Public Benefit: The Public Benefit Requirement (PB1)', www. gov.uk/government/uploads/system/uploads/attachment_data/file/383871/PB1_ The_public_benefit_requirement.pdf [accessed 6 May 2016].

58 Charities Act 2006, s 3(2); Charities Act 2011, s 4(2).

59 Debra Morris, 'Public Benefit: The Long and Winding Road to Reforming the Public Benefit Test for Charity: A Worthwhile Trip or "Is Journey Really Necessary?"', in *Modernising Charity Law: Recent Developments and Future Directions* (Cheltenham: Edward Elgar, 2010), 112–13.

60 Synge, 'New' *Public Benefit Requirement*, 22, citing *National Anti-Vivisection Society* v. *IRC* [1948] AC 31 (HL), 42 (emphasis in original).

61 Synge, 'New' *Public Benefit Requirement*, 22.

62 Garton, *Public Benefit in Charity Law*, 26, referring to Hubert Picarda, *The Law and Practice Relating to Charities*, 4th edn (London: Bloomsbury, 2010), 39B.

63 Synge, 'New' *Public Benefit Requirement*, 24.

understood for the purposes of the law relating to charities in England and Wales'.[64] In other words, the law relating to charities could be said to be those purposes as set out in s 3(1) without the need to presume a public benefit, if such a presumption exists, so any reference to a presumption, or lack of, is irrelevant. The fact that these are established charitable purposes suggests that public benefit is present. Nonetheless, this is not the approach being taken by the Commission,[65] so questions remain as to the development and interpretation of public benefit in this jurisdiction.

E Charitable purposes

Charitable purpose is defined by s 2(1) of the Charities Act 2011:

> a charitable purpose is a purpose which –
>
> a   falls within section 3(1), and
> b   is for the public benefit

Section 3 states:

> A purpose falls within this subsection if it falls within any of the following descriptions of purposes –
>
> a   the prevention or relief of poverty;
> b   the advancement of education;
> c   the advancement of religion;
> d   the advancement of health or the saving of lives;
> e   the advancement of citizenship or community development;
> f   the advancement of the arts, culture, heritage or science;
> g   the advancement of amateur sport;
> h   the advancement of human rights, conflict resolution or reconciliation or the promotion of religious or racial harmony or equality and diversity;
> i   the advancement of environmental protection or improvement;
> j   the relief of those in need because of youth, age, ill-health, disability, financial hardship or other disadvantage;
> k   the advancement of animal welfare;
> l   the promotion of the efficiency of the armed forces of the Crown or of the efficiency of the police, fire and rescue services or ambulance services;
> m   any other purposes –

---

64 Charities Act 2011, s 4(3).
65 Charity Commission for England & Wales, 'Public Benefit: The Public Benefit Requirement'; Morris, 'Public Benefit', 113.

n   that are not within paragraphs (a) to (l) but are recognised as charitable purposes by virtue of section 5 (recreational and similar trusts, etc.) or under the old law,

o   that may reasonably be regarded as analogous to, or within the spirit of, any purposes falling within any of paragraphs (a) to (l) or sub-paragraph (i), or

p   that may reasonably be regarded as analogous to, or within the spirit of, any purposes which have been recognised, under the law relating to charities in England and Wales, as falling within sub-paragraph (ii) or this sub-paragraph.

This list of charitable purposes represents significant additions to the traditional four heads of charity, in contrast to jurisdictions such as New Zealand and Canada, which were originally reflected in England and Wales. While this list is extensive, s 3(1)(m) enables the door to remain open on the development of further charitable purposes.

This list of purposes largely gives statutory recognition to purposes that have already been legally acknowledged as charitable, and represents the Government's 'new partnership agenda with charity'.[66] For instance, ss 3(1)(d), (e), and (f) send a clear message that the Government 'will encourage organizations to become established in these areas and will reward them with charitable status'.[67]

While it is not possible, within the confines of this book, to address every head of charity in England and Wales, this chapter will consider a selection of key cases and Charity Commission decisions that incorporate some of the charitable purposes. Such "leading cases" are a vital part of the chaotic-looking case law tradition',[68] providing a valuable insight into the jurisprudential trends in England and Wales.[69] Other chapters discuss the importance of many cases emanating from England and Wales, such as *Commissioners for Special Purposes of Income Tax* v. *Pemsel*, *National Anti-Vivisection Society* v. *Inland Revenue Commissioners*, and *Oppenheim* v. *Tobacco Securities Trust Co Ltd*,[70] and as a result, this chapter will consider other cases that have played an important role in English jurisprudence.

F Dingle v. Turner

Dingle v. *Turner*[71] has been regarded as 'the most important pronouncement of the House of Lords in the field of charities since 1891',[72] in other words, since the

66 O'Halloran, *Profits of Charity*, 152.

67 Ibid.

68 John Mummery, '*The Commissioners for Special Purposes of the Income Tax* v. *Pemsel*', *Charity Law and Practice Review* 16(1) (2013–14), 1.

69 Additional cases related to political purposes are considered in Chapter 11.

70 *Commissioners for Special Purposes of Income Tax* v. *Pemsel* [1891] AC 531 (HL); *National Anti-Vivisection Society* v. *Inland Revenue Commissioners; Oppenheim* v. *Tobacco Securities Trust Co Ltd* [1951] 1 AC 297 (HL).

71 *Dingle* v. *Turner* [1972] 1 AC 601 (HL).

72 Peter Luxton, '*Dingle* v. *Turner* Forty Years on', *Charity Law and Practice Review* 16 (1) (2013–14), 43, citing S. E. A. Johnson, 'A New Look for Public Benefit in the Law of Charities', *Modern Law Review* 36(5) (1973).

Pemsel case. It will be recalled from earlier chapters the importance of *Re Compton*[73] and *Oppenheim* v. *Tobacco Securities Trust Co Ltd*,[74] in which the 'nexus' test emerged from the former, and was affirmed in the latter. Both these cases involved the advancement of education, but *Dingle* v. *Turner* held that a trust for the relief of poverty among employees was valid, even though, contrary to the other two cases, the beneficiaries were employees of a particular company, and so defined by a particular nexus.

The testator, Dingle, was the part owner of E Dingle & Co Ltd company. After his wife's death, her husband's shares in the company fell to the residuary estate on trust to provide pensions for poor employees of the company.

It will be recalled from *Oppenheim*, that the Court affirmed that a group of beneficiaries may be numerically numerous but if the connection between them is their personal relationship 'to a single propositus or to several propositi',[75] this will void their being a community, or a section of a community for charitable purposes.[76]

However, the Court in *Dingle* sanctioned the earlier decision of *Gibson* v. *South American Stores (Gath and Chaves) Ltd*,[77] where the beneficiaries were limited to those employed by a particular employer. Lord Cross submitted that there was a practical reason, although not necessarily a historical explanation, as to why 'poor members and the "poor employees" decisions were a natural development of the "poor relations" decisions'.[78] First, to draw distinctions between different forms of poverty would be illogical,[79] and, second, cases like *Compton* and *Oppenheim* were influenced by suggestions that if the trusts were held as valid, then the beneficiaries would receive underserved fiscal immunity. In other words, education could be seen as a benefit that would not have public purpose. The companies involved were offering a private benefit under the guise of company purpose, thus providing fringe benefits to employees, making the conditions of their employment more attractive.[80] 'In the field of poverty the danger is not so great as in the field of education';[81] trying to alleviate poverty does not offer similarly attractive fringe benefits, thus its public benefit is recognised. As a result, this case is important because it upholds the charitable status of poor-employee cases, in spite of the confirmation of the approved nexus test in education cases.[82]

G Independent Schools Council v. Charity Commission for England and Wales

One of the most recent, and perhaps controversial cases, on the concept of public benefit, is *Independent Schools Council* v. *Charity Commission for England and*

---

73 *Re Compton* [1945] 1 Ch 123 (CA).
74 *Oppenheim* v. *Tobacco Securities Trust Co Ltd*.
75 Ibid., 306.
76 Ibid.
77 *Gibson* v. *South American Stores (Gath and Chaves) Ltd* [1950] Ch 177 (CA).
78 *Dingle* v. *Turner*, 623.
79 Ibid.
80 Ibid., 624–5.
81 Ibid., 625.
82 Luxton, '*Dingle* v. *Turner*', 56.

Wales.[83] The Charity Commission published guidance on public benefit first in 2008. According to the Commission, it did not constitute the law on public benefit, but was a guide as to how it is interpreted and applied at law. This guidance was successfully challenged in the Upper Tribunal (Tax and Chancery Chamber) in this case.[84] Two sets of proceedings came before the Tribunal and were fast-tracked to the Upper Tribunal. The first argued that the Commission's guidance exhibited errors of law, and sought judicial review to quash the guidance. The second was a reference to the Tribunal by the Attorney-General, concerning a hypothetical independent school. The main question posed by the Attorney-General was whether an institution established for the sole purpose of advancing education for those who can pay full fees can be charitable.[85]

This case was 'hugely significant and expectations were high that it would bring much needed clarity to the law',[86] however, criticism was levelled at this decision. The main reaction has been that of 'dissatisfaction at what appeared to be a compromise decision exhibiting a failure to deliver the desiderated, longed-for clarity'.[87] Although it was praised for clarifying that it should be trustees, not the Commission, nor the judiciary, to decide how to administer a trust.[88] Nonetheless, the case ran to over 100 pages, and 'lacked any clear summary and demanded careful study in order to establish quite what was decided'.[89]

What the Tribunal did state was that the Commission's guidance on public benefit applied to independent schools was not correct. '[I]t is not possible to be prescriptive about the nature of the benefits which a school must provide to the poor nor the extent of them'.[90] In particular, the Tribunal referred to principle 2b of the guidance, which referred to benefits being unreasonably restricted by an ability to pay. It concluded that the focus of reasonableness was wrong.[91] It 'is not a question of reasonableness. It is a question of the proper exercise of the trustees' powers'.[92] It followed therefore that the guidance should be corrected. While the Tribunal had some sympathy for the Commission in producing the guidance, it did not believe it was right to leave matters to the Commission to correct the guidance without giving relief to the Independent Schools Council (ISC). The Tribunal ordered the parties to agree on what relief should be afforded to the ISC.[93] The parties did not agree, and a further decision was published in December 2011, declaring the relevant parts of the guidance would be quashed, unless

83 *Independent Schools Council* v. *Charity Commission for England and Wales*.
84 Alexander *et al.*, *Charity Governance*, 6, referring to Charity Commission for England and Wales, 'Charities and Public Benefit', first published in January 2008, amended in December 2011, and withdrawn in September 2013.
85 Picarda, 'Charities Act 2011', 139–40.
86 Synge, *'New' Public Benefit Requirement*, 185.
87 Picarda, 'Charities Act 2011', 141.
88 Ibid.
89 Synge, *'New' Public Benefit Requirement*, 185.
90 *Independent Schools Council* v.*Charity Commission for England and Wales*, [217].
91 Ibid., [234].
92 Ibid.
93 Ibid., [236].

withdrawn by the Commission. The Commission withdrew the affected parts later that month.[94]

The Tribunal was undoubtedly aware that this decision would be subject to criticism as it acknowledged that the 'decision will not ... give the parties the clarity for which they were hoping'.[95] However, it has been called a 'landmark ruling',[96] perhaps because of its assistance to the many school governors on what may amount to public benefit, and to 'remove the notion that the Commission can strip an independent school's charitable status'[97] if it feels that the school is not meeting its public benefit requirement. While this decision only applies to educational charities, it may have broader implications for other fee-charging charities, and result in further guidance amendments.[98]

H Advancement of religion

The last two cases, or rather decisions of the Charity Commission, that of the *Gnostic Centre*, and the *Druid Network*, are important jurisprudentially because they were the Commission's first reported decisions with regard to the advancement of religion, following the coming into force of the relevant provisions of the Charities Act 2006, and thus the 2011 Act, which included most of the provisions on the meaning of charity and charitable purposes within ss 1–3 of the Act.[99] While the legal meaning of public benefit was unchanged, s 4(2) of the 2011 Act states 'it is not to be presumed that a purpose of a particular description is for the public benefit'.

Both of the organisations had applied to the Commission to register as charities and both refer to the advancement of religion, which falls under the purposes set out in s 3(1) of the 2011 Act. Charity law has always accepted the advancement of religion as charitable, and '[a]s between different religions the law stands neutral, but it assumes that any religion is at least likely to be better than none'.[100] Indeed,

94 Synge, *'New' Public Benefit Requirement*, 187, referring to *ISC* v. *Charity Commission* TCC-JR/03/2010.
95 *Independent Schools Council* v. *Charity Commission for England and Wales*, [260].
96 Margaret Craton, 'Independent Schools v. Charity Commission – and the Winner Is?', Asblaw, 13 March 2012, http://www.asb-law.com/what-we-say/articles/articles/2012/independent-schools-v-charity-commission-and-the-winner-is#.V19E_ih96Uk [accessed 14 June 2016].
97 Ibid.
98 '*Independent Schools Council* v. *Charity Commission for England & Wales*', DWF Law, 17 November 2011, www.dwf.law/news-events/legal-updates/2011/11/independent-schools-council-v-charity-commission-for-england-wales [accessed 14 June 2016].
99 Peter Luxton and Nicola Evans, 'Cogent and Cohesive? Two Recent Charity Commission Decisions on the Advancement of Religion', *Conveyancer and Property Lawyer* 75(2) (2011), 144.
100 *Hester* v. *Commissioner of Inland Revenue* [2005] 2 NZLR 172 (CA), [6], citing *Neville Estates Ltd* v. *Madden* [1962] Ch 832, 853.

the relevance of religion in still today can be found in many of jurisdictions where freedom of religion is a fundamental human right.[101] Thus:[102]

> The liberal acceptance of trusts for the advancement of religion as being for the public benefit is consistent with the attitude and views of the court that would extend toleration to the need to support religion as a 'valuable constituent in the character of our citizens'.

Centuries of case law reflect judicial tolerance of a wide variety of ancient and contemporary religions that comprise multi-cultural, and multi-belief societies, and the Commission's decision with regard to the Gnostic Centre, in light of the reversal of the presumption of public benefit, is perhaps a preview of what is to come with regard to similar future decisions.

I Gnostic Centre

This decision has been subject to some criticism. The Gnostic Centre was established to 'promote and advance and research on Gnosticism, both ancient and modern'.[103] This object fell under the head of advancement of religion. The Commission considered that the characteristics of a religion for charitable purposes are:[104]

- the belief system involves belief in a god (or gods) or goddess (or goddesses), or supreme being, or divine or transcendental being or entity or spiritual principle, which is the object or focus of the religion (referred to in this guidance as 'supreme being or entity');
- the belief system involves a relationship between the believer and the supreme being or entity by showing worship of, reverence for or veneration of the supreme being or entity;
- the belief system has a degree of cogency, cohesion, seriousness and importance;
- the belief system promotes an identifiable positive, beneficial, moral or ethical framework

---

101 For instance: Human Rights Act 1998, s 13 (UK); New Zealand Bill of Rights Act 1990, s 13 (NZ); Commonwealth of Australia Constitution Act, s 116 (AU).

102 Hubert Picarda, 'Charities Act 2011: A Dog's Breakfast or Dream Come True? A Case for Further Reform', in Matthew Harding, Ann O'Connell, and Miranda Stewart (eds), *Not-for-Profit Law: Theoretical and Comparative Perspectives* (Cambridge University Press, Cambridge, 2014), 143, citing *Gass* v. *White* 32 Ky 170 (CA, 1834).

103 *Application for Registration of the Gnostic Centre* (Charity Commission for England and Wales, 16 December 2009), [19].

104 *Application for Registration of the Gnostic Centre*, [22], referring to 'Advancement of Religion for the Public Benefit', s C2 and Annex A, www.gov.uk/government/uploads/system/uploads/attachment_data/file/358531/advancement-of-religion-for-the-public-benefit.pdf [accessed 15 June 2016].

The first two are said to be a defensible summary of that which the law requires,[105] and thus are justified criteria; the Gnostic Centre met those criteria. The third criterion is more problematic, because there is no clear authority in English law that requires it to be met. What is evident in these criteria is the form of words in relation to those used by the European Court of Human Rights when interpreting the meaning of 'convictions' under Article 2 of the First Protocol.[106] Interestingly, the case on which this qualification was claimed was not concerned with the meaning of religion or belief, and, indeed, questions have been asked as to why the European Convention on Human Rights is being utilised in this capacity.[107] It has been suggested, however, that such a move may be beneficial because it reflects an early emergence of a common definition of religion under English law, based on principles within the European Convention on Human Rights.[108]

Regardless, the Commission found that the core beliefs of Gnostics may be sufficient to demonstrate the requisite degree of cogency, cohesion, seriousness, and importance of the beliefs, but only if adequately expressed.[109]

The more concerning matter lies with the fourth criteria, that the belief system promotes an identifiable positive, beneficial, moral, or ethical framework, as there is no evidence to support this in case law. The Commission does not set out on what authority it relies upon to support these criteria, merely making reference to its own guidance, except for the case of *Gilmour* v. *Coats*[110] in relation to the notion of public benefit (where the benefits have to be described and evidenced in a way that can be evaluated legally, although this case does not make specific reference to the fourth criteria). The Commission noted that while the applicants may have sincere beliefs, there was only anecdotal evidence that the belief system would be promoted in the required way. This would not satisfy the requirements as laid down by the courts, although it is not clear to which authorities the Commission is making reference, though there is a tenuous link to *Gilmour* v. *Coats*. It is asserted that the Commission was wrong in this approach given that the 'meaning of religion goes to the nature of a charitable purpose'.[111] Therefore, the primary focus should be on the conceptual nature of public benefit. The fourth criteria are consequently at odds with the realities and complexities of religion.

105 Luxton and Evans, 'Cogent and Cohesive?', 146.
106 Luxton and Evans, 'Cogent and Cohesive?', 146, referring to *Campbell* v. *United Kingdom* (1982) 4 EHRR 293 ECtHR, [36], where 'convictions' had a meaning akin to 'beliefs' in art 9 of the European Convention on Human Rights, where the article refers to 'religion or beliefs' that are 'views that attain a certain level of cogency, seriousness, cohesion and importance'.
107 Picarda, 'Charities Act 2011', 145; Luxton and Evans, 'Cogent and Cohesive?', 146.
108 Russell Sandberg, 'Defining the Divine', *Ecclesiastical Law Journal* 16(2) (2014), 200.
109 *Application for Registration of the Gnostic Centre*, [42].
110 *Application for Registration of the Gnostic Centre*, [46], referring to *Gilmour* v. *Coats* [1948] Ch 340 (CA).
111 Garton, *Public Benefit in Charity Law*, 176.

It can therefore be said that the Commission's approach to public benefit is controversial, and has been asserted as being plain wrong.[112] It has been stated that evidently the advancement of religion is for the public benefit, because it is listed in the 2006/2011 Acts,[113] but perhaps the real difficulty is that a court is not the appropriate place to determine matters of religious doctrine, let alone make a determination on moral or ethical frameworks, whatever those frameworks may be.[114] Indeed, as noted earlier '[a]s between different religions the law stands neutral, but it assumes that any religion is at least likely to be better than none'.[115] The Commission stated that the Centre showed no evidence of the beneficial impact flowing from its core beliefs to the public because to advance the moral or spiritual welfare, or improvement to the community in ways to have public benefit, there must be an ethical or moral code that is promoted, which can be evidentially of public benefit. It is entirely unclear how such things can indeed be evidentially proven, yet the Commission asserted the Centre failed on this matter.

It is possible that the Commission may have confused the fourth category of advancing religion with its interpretation of public benefit, although it is not clear overall as to its reasoning, nor of the basis of its authorities. It has been suggested that the reason the Commission may have done this is because it is a practical way of evaluating the benefit to the public,[116] although there is no apparent evidence that this was the in the mind of the Commission. Overall, therefore, this decision raises a number of questions, and unfortunately for the Centre, citing financial concerns, it did not appeal to the Tribunal, so the decision stands.[117]

J Druid Network

By contrast, the Commission took a different stance in the *Application for the Registration of the Druid Network*.[118] This too has elicited criticism, even though the organisation was held to be charitable.

---

112 Luxton and Evans, 'Cogent and Cohesive?', 147, referring to, inter alia, Hubert Picarda, *Written Evidence on the Joint Committee on the Draft Charities Bill 2004*, Government Report No. 167–2; 662, DCH 297 (2004); Jeffrey Hackney, 'Charities and Public Benefit', *Law Quarterly Review* 124(1) (2008); Anne Sanders, 'The Mystery of Public Benefit', *Charity Law and Practice Review* 10(2) (2007).

113 Luxton and Evans, 'Cogent and Cohesive?', 147, referring to Peter Luxton, 'Making Law: Parliament v. the Charity Commission', *Politeia* 64 (June) (2009), 3.

114 Luxton and Evans, 'Cogent and Cohesive?', 147.

115 *Hester* v. *Commissioner of Inland Revenue*, [6], citing *Neville Estates Ltd* v. *Madden*, 853.

116 Suzanne Owen and Teemu Taira, 'The Category of Religion in Public Classification: Charity Registration of the Druid Network in England and Wales', in Trevor Stack, Naomi R. Goldenberg, and Timothy Fitzgerald (eds), *Religion as a Category of Governance and Sovereignty* (Chester: Brill, 2015), 100.

117 Luxton and Evans, 'Cogent and Cohesive?', 149.

118 *Application for the Registration of the Druid Network* (Charity Commission for England and Wales, 21 September 2010).

The objects of the Druid Network are to, inter alia, provide information on the principles and practice of Druidry, and to facilitate the practice of Druidry.[119] Again, the Commission relied on the four criteria, as set out above, although unlike the former decision, the Commission confirmed that the Network met all four criteria.

In relation to the fourth criteria, on which we will focus, the Commission found evidence that the Druid Network promoted its ethical codes in such a way as to be an integral and central part of their belief system. It did this, inter alia, through provision of information about ethical living and caring for the environment, and promoting access to ancient monuments and artefacts.[120] The Commission asserted that this was sufficient evidence of 'an identifiable positive beneficial ethical framework ... that is capable of having a beneficial impact on the community at large'.[121]

The only case cited by the Commission as authority for the fourth criteria is a surprising one – *Cocks* v. *Manners*.[122] It is not evident to which particular principle in this case the Commission is referring, but it is presumed to be the following:[123]

> It is said, in some of the cases, that religious purposes are charitable, but that can only be true as to religious services tending directly or indirectly towards the instruction or the edification of the public; an annuity to an individual, so long as he spent his time in retirement and constant devotion, would not be charitable, nor would a gift to ten persons, so long as they lived together in retirement and performed acts of devotion, be charitable.

However, this 'statement hardly provides support for the Commission's fourth characteristic, as not only do the words 'identifiable', 'beneficial', 'moral', 'ethical', or 'framework' not appear anywhere in the judgment, the Court held that the gift was not charitable. This was because the benefits were restricted to a group of nuns working for their own salvation, rather than being available to the public.[124] If, however, the religious activities are undertaken in public, inter alia, then the public benefit test is satisfied. At no stage has it been seen necessary to go beyond assessing the beneficial nature of religion beyond those exclusions set out in *Thornton* v. *Howe*. In other words, the public benefit would not be satisfied if the doctrines of the religion were adverse to the foundations of all religion, or were subversive to morality.[125] While it seems unlikely that the Commission is suggesting that the Druid Network may have strayed into such territory, the

---

119 Ibid., [5].
120 Ibid., [51]–[52].
121 Ibid., [53].
122 *Cocks* v. *Manners* (1871) LR 12 Eq 574.
123 Luxton and Evans, 'Cogent and Cohesive? Two Recent Charity Commission Decisions on the Advancement of Religion', 149, citing *Cocks* v. *Manners*, 585.
124 Luxton and Evans, 'Cogent and Cohesive?', 150; referring to *Gilmour* v. *Coats* [1949] 1 AC 426 (HL).
125 Luxton and Evans, 'Cogent and Cohesive?', 150 and 147, referring to *Thornton* v. *Howe* 54 ER 1042; (1862) 31 Beav 14, 20.

Commission made no reference to the exclusions in *Thornton*, and instead confirmed its novel approach, as set out in the *Gnostic Centre* decision.

Overall, what can be observed about the Commission's current treatment of advancement of religion applications is that it is now adopting a different approach in its decision-making, and the approach appears to have limited legal authority. Indeed, is said to be 'relatively brief and formulaic', with much apparent weight given to its own guidance. This is in contrast to earlier decisions, such as that of *Church of Scientology (England and Wales)*,[126] in which there was much evidence of reliance on case authority and detailed analysis of the relevant principles and laws. Until such times as there is an appeal of such a decision to the Tribunal, which would provide much needed clarity, it is likely that the Commission's approach has simply added uncertainty to this already complex area of law.

---

126 Luxton and Evans, 'Cogent and Cohesive?', 150–1, referring to *Application for the Registration of the Church of Scientology (England and Wales)* (Charity Commission for England and Wales, 17 November 1999).

6   Australia

A Introduction

Similarly to England and Wales, Australia has undergone significant charity law reforms in the last few years, and charities are becoming more significant to the Australian way of life. According to the Australian Bureau of Statistics, there are almost 57,000 not-for-profits (NFPs) that are economically significant, and as a proportion of the economy, they accounted for around 3.8 per cent of the gross domestic product, which was up from previous years. Further, they generated about $107bn in revenue, had total assets worth about $176bn, and a net worth of about $123bn at the end of June 2013. In addition, around 1.1 million people are employed in economically significant NFPs.[1] Therefore, the significance of charity in the Australian context is evident, and thus is its governance and regulation.

This chapter will look at, inter alia, some of the key regulatory reforms and legislative milestones, as well as a selection of some jurisprudentially important cases.

B A potted history of charitable regulation in Australia

Law reform initiatives can take decades to come to fruition. A number of issues, policies, and political streams must align to initiate changes to existing laws, thus policymaking can be characterised as reflecting long periods of stability, followed by brief periods of major policy changes, resulting in key legislatory reforms.[2] Australia's charities and NFP sector reflects these assertions.

1 Martin Kirkness, 'Life Cycle Issues for Charities', *Taxation in Australia* 50(5) (November 2015), 251; Kim Weinert, 'Is It a Not-for-Profit Organisation or a For-Profit Organisation? The Case for a CIC Structure in Australia', *Journal of Australasian Law Teachers Association* 7(1) (2014), 2, referring to the Australian Bureau of Statistics, Australian National Accounts: non-profit institutions satellite account, 2012–13, cat no. 5256.0 ASB Canberra 2014, referring to 2012–13 statistics.
2 Elen Seymour and Marina Nehme, 'The ACNA, the Senate, the Commission of Audit and the Not-for-Profit Sector', *UNSW Law Journal* 38(3) (2015), 1186, referring to John W. Kingdon, *Agendas, Alternatives and Public Policies*, 2nd edn (New York: Harper Collins, 1995), 116 and 165–8; and Frank B. Baumgarnter and Bryan D.

Inquiries and reviews into the NFP sector date back to at least 1995, with the Industry Commission on the NFP sector: Industry Commission 'Charitable Organisations in Australia',[3] followed by a raft of state and government inquiries.[4] While there have been many reports and inquiries, they have not always been welcomed. For instance, the Industry Commission's Inquiry was met with some hostility and scepticism. This was partly because of the Commission's economic and industry-orientated perspective, and partly because the motives of the inquiry were not clear.[5] Nonetheless, this inquiry made some 31 recommendations for reform of the charitable sector, including its regulation, legal structures, and taxation, but these were largely left unimplemented because of a change in federal government.[6]

The later inquiry into the Definition of Charities and Related Organisations Report in 2001, also known as the Sheppard Inquiry, was given a warmer reception. This was perhaps because it was an independent ad hoc inquiry, chaired by a federal court judge, and included members with significant sector involvement.[7] This inquiry specified a draft statutory definition, which was generally well received by the sector, although the subsequent Exposure Draft, produced by the Liberal Government on the basis of the recommendations of that inquiry, received significant opposition. In particular, the provision purporting to state the common law restriction on political advocacy, as well as concerns about removing the presumption of public benefit. A further inquiry was held on the Exposure Draft by the Board of Taxation, and the Government opted for minimum changes, such as extending the definition of charitable purpose to certain disputed organisations,

---

Jones, 'Agenda Dynamics and Policy Subsystems', *Journal of Politics* 53(4) (1991), 1044.

3 Seymour and Nehme, 'ACNA, the Senate', 1186, referring to Federal Senate of Australia, *Industry Commission on the Not-for-Profit Sector: Industry Commission: 'Charitable Organisations in Australia'*, Government Report No. 45 (1995).

4 Seymour and Nehme, 'ACNA, the Senate', 1186, referring to Commonwealth, Inquiry into the Definition of Charities and Related Organisations, Report (2001) ('Definition of Charities Report'); Senate Standing Committee on Economics, Parliament of Australia, Disclosure Regimes for Charities and Not-for-Profit Organisations (2008) ('Disclosure Regimes for Charities Report'); Victoria State Services Authority, Review of the Not-for-Profit Regulation (Final Report, September 2007); Productivity Commission, Contribution of the Not-for-Profit Sector (Research Report, January 2010) ('Contribution of the Not-for-Profit Sector Report'); Australia's Future Tax System Review Panel, Report to the Treasurer (Report, December 2009) ('Australia's Future Tax System Report'), also known as the Henry Review; Senate Economics Legislation Committee, Parliament of Australia, Tax Laws Amendment (Public Benefit Test) Bill 2010 (2010).

5 Ann O'Connell, Fiona Martin, and Joyce Chia, 'Law, Policy and Politics in Australia's Recent Not-for-Profit Sector Reforms', *Australian Tax Reform* 28(2) (2013), 292.

6 Kerry O'Halloran *et al.*, 'Charity Law Reforms: An Overview of Progress Since 2001', in Myles McGregor-Lowndes and Kerry O'Halloran (eds), *Modernising Charity Law, Recent Developments and Future Directions* (Cheltenham: Edward Elgar, 2010), 37.

7 O'Connell, Martin, and Chia, 'Law, Policy and Politics', 292.

such as NFP childcare and low-cost housing under the national rental affordability scheme.[8]

A number of the reports endorsed concerns by the sector with regard to complexities and incoherence associated with tax concessions and the Industry Commission, the Productivity Commission, and the Henry Review all concluded that the business income of NFPs should not be taxed.

On the matter of regulation, a key issue was whether a regulatory model similar to that of the Charity Commission for England and Wales should be adopted. The Industry Commission Report initially rejected such a proposal, on the basis of being too bureaucratic, duplicative, and ineffective to be able to address state issues or damaging behaviours, but the Sheppard Inquiry, Disclosure Inquiry, and Productivity Commission all endorsed the proposal.[9] For instance, the Productivity Commission observed that:[10]

> The current regulatory framework … is characterised by uncoordinated regimes at the Commonwealth and state/territory levels. Disparate reporting and other requirements add complexity and cost.

As a result, it recommended establishing a national registrar that would bring together national regulatory functions.[11]

Alongside these reports and inquiries, there were two major High Court decisions that also formed part of the historical context of reforms – the *Commissioner of Taxation* v. *Word Investments Limited* and *Aid/Watch Incorporated* v. *Commissioner of Taxation*, which will be considered later in the chapter.[12] In the former case, the High Court ruled that an entity that had been established to distribute funds to a bible translation services was charitable, even though it did not carry out any charitable activities itself. In the latter case, the High Court ruled that the political purpose doctrine, an internationally recognised doctrine, no longer applied in Australia in relation to advocacy, thus an entity may engage in political advocacy without negating its charitable status.

In 2011, the Australian Treasury (a federal government agency) opened up the debate once more as to the benefits, or otherwise, of instituting a national

---

8 O'Connell, Martin, and Chia, 'Law, Policy and Politics', 293, referring to the Board of Taxation, Consultation on the Definition of a Charity (December 2003) www.ta xboard.gov.au/content/content.aspx?doc=reviews_and_consultations/definition_ of_a_ charity/default.htm&pageid=007 and Extension of Charitable Purpose Act (2004) (Cth), ss 4 and 4A.

9 O'Connell, Martin, and Chia, 'Law, Policy and Politics', 294.

10 'Not-for-Profit Reform and the Australian Government', 2013 Australian Charities and Not-for-profits Commission, September 2013, Australian Government, 17, www. acnc.gov.au/ACNC/Pblctns/Rpts/NFP/ACNC/Publications/Reports/NFPreport. aspx [accessed 20 June 2016], citing 'Contribution of the Not-for-Profit Sector' (January 2010), Productivity Commission report, 113.

11 Ibid., 17.

12 O'Connell, Martin, and Chia, 'Law, Policy and Politics', 294, referring to *Commissioner of Taxation* v. *Word Investments Limited* (2008) 236 CLR 204 and *Aid/Watch Incorporated* v. *Commissioner of Taxation* [2010] HCA 42.

regulator of charities and NFPs, in its *Consultation Paper: Scoping Study for a National Not-For-Profit Regulator.* This paper indicated that an Australian regulatory body would be similar to the Charity Commission for England and Wales.[13]

The numerous inquiries, reports and recommendations eventually led to the implementation of a new Act of great legal and regulatory significance – the Australian Charities and Not-for-Profits Act 2012 (Cth) (ACNC Act). It became officially operative on 3 December 2012,[14] and, among other purposes, established a Commission, which is the first consideration in this chapter, followed by a consideration of the Act itself.

C Australian Charities and Not-for-profits Commission

The ACNC Act introduced this national regulatory system in order to promote transparency, accountability, and good governance. The Australian Charities and Not-for-profits Commission (ACNC) commenced operation on 3 December 2012,[15] as the first federal regulator for the NFP sector. Prior to the commencement of the ACNC, the Australian Tax Office (ATO) determined an entity's charitable status, for instance determining if an entity was a charity, or a Public Benevolent Institution, and then assessed whether that entity had entitlement to be endorsed to access commonwealth tax concessions. Since the commencement of the ACNC, it is now the ACNC that determines the charitability of an entity. Those entities must register with the ACNC before the ATO can endorse them to access charity tax concessions.[16]

The objects of the ACNC are:[17]

- To maintain, protect and enhance public trust and confidence in the sector;
- To support and sustain a robust, vibrant, independent and innovative sector; and
- To promote the reduction of unnecessary regulatory obligations within the sector.

In administering the new regulatory framework, the ACNC's tasks include determining charitable status; providing an educational role for registered charities; maintaining a public register; and monitoring and enforcing compliance by

---

13 Fiona Martin, 'Recent Developments in Australian Charity Law: One Step Forward and Two Steps Backward', *Charity Law and Practice Review* 17(1) (2014–15), 26, referring to Commonwealth of Australia, consultation paper, 'Scoping Study for a National Not-For-Profit Regulator' (2011).
14 Martin, 'Recent Developments in Australian Charity Law', 26.
15 Marina Nehme, 'Regulation of the Not-for-Profit Sector Is Another Change Really Needed?', *Alternative Law Journal* 39(1) (2014), 24, referring to Australian Charities and Not-for-profits Commission Act 2012, ss 5–10 (AU).
16 Australian Charities and Not-for-profits Commission, 13.
17 Ibid., 14.

registered charities.[18] Thus, the ACNC determines the charitability of an entity, although the Commissioner of Taxation still plays a role in determining and monitoring additional tax endorsements obligations for charities and NFPs.[19]

The Act established a single reporting framework, but this is proportional to the size of the registered charity, which is designed to minimise compliance costs, and provide appropriate levels of accountability and transparency. Once a charity is registered, it is required to provide an annual information statement for a financial year, and the set format for this statement has different levels of reporting, depending on whether a charity is deemed small, medium, or large.[20]

Thus a small charity will be one that has an annual revenue of $250,000 or less, and while it does have to provide an information sheet, it does not have to provide financial reports. A medium-sized charity is one that has revenue between $250,000 and $1m, and will have to provide an information sheet, and financial reports. A large charity is deemed as such if its revenue is $1m or greater, and must provide audited financial reports.[21]

As part of the overarching compliance requirements related to registration with the ACNC, the 'ACNC governance standards have been considered part of the regulatory and compliance reforms'.[22] Thus, before an entity can register with the ACNC, it must comply with these five governance standards, which are:[23]

- Governance Standard 1: this relates to the purposes and NFP nature of the entity, meaning the entity must be NFP and work towards their charitable goals;
- Governance Standard 2: refers to accountability of members of the charity, thus members of the charity must take reasonable steps to ensure their accountability and to enable members adequate opportunity to raise concerns about governance;
- Governance Standard 3: requires compliance with national laws and charities must not commit serious offences under any national law;
- Governance Standard 4: requires charities to ensure that their responsible persons, such as directors and trustees, are not disqualified from acting in their capacity, and if they are disqualified, the charity must take reasonable steps to remove said persons;

18 Ian Murray, 'Not-for-Profit Reform: Back to the Future?', *Third Sector Review* 20(1) (2014), 114–15, referring to Australian Charities and Not-for-profits Commission Act 2012, s 15, chs 3–4, and pt 2.
19 Murray, 'Not-for-Profit Reform', 115.
20 Martin, 'Recent Developments in Australian Charity Law', 28, referring to Australian Charities and Not-for-profits Commission Act 2012, s 60–5(1).
21 Fiona Martin, 'Recent Developments in Australian Charity Law', *Charity Law & Practice Review* 17 (2014), 28, referring to the Australian Charities and Not-for-profits Act 2012 (Cth), ss 205–25(4), 205 25(2), and 202–25(3), respectively.
22 Murray, 'Not-for-Profit Reform', 119.
23 Martin, 'Recent Developments in Australian Charity Law', 29, referring to the Australian Charities and Not-for-profits Commission Regulation 2013 (Cth) (the ACNC Regulations), division 45, subdivision 45B, 45.5–45.25.

- Governance Standard 5: requires charities to take reasonable steps to ensure that responsible persons undertake their duties honestly, responsibly, and in the best interests of the charity.

These Governance Standards ensure minimum outcomes with regard to practices in relation to charities carrying out their purposes, although it is worth bearing in mind that these standards have some limitations. For instance, some transitional rules provide exemptions in some circumstances thus permitting some entities to register even though their governing rules to not comply with a standard, which may exist until July 2017.[24] In addition the standards have been worded generally, meaning that they can be applied flexibly where required, which appears to be beneficial, although, in reality, it may generate uncertainty as to compliance for entities.[25]

D The ACNC and the Charity Commission for England and Wales

As might be imagined, such similar bodies share similar functions. Both bodies were designed with multiple purposes in mind. For instance, both register charities and maintain registers of charities, as well as requiring charities to provide annual reports, and both undertake enforcement of charitable governance. However, the types of regulation and enforcement that is undertaken by both bodies may differ to some extent.[26] The Charity Commission asserts that it registers and regulates charities in England and Wales,[27] whereas the ACNC is said to have a more 'softly, softly touch and a more educative role'.[28] However, it may not always be easy to strike a balance between regulation and advising charities because it is reported that, at least in England, some charities may be reluctant to approach the Commission for advice for fear that this may lead to investigations into their charitable activities.[29] Such fears may also be prevalent in Australian charities.

Other differences between the two bodies include the fact that the Charity Commission has a number of quasi-judicial functions, where it may utilise powers similar to the High Court in England and Wales. For instance, the Commission has the power to create cy-près schemes to amend a charity's objects, which the ACNC is not able to undertake.[30]

---

24 Murray, 'Not-for-Profit Reform', 120, referring to ACNC Regulations, division 45, subdivision 45D, 45.130.
25 Murray, 'Not-for-Profit Reform', 120.
26 Helen Andrews, 'Charities Regulator Reprieve a Call to Get Back to Work', The Mandarin, 9 April 2014 www.themandarin.com.au/28930-acnc-charities-regula tor-reprieve/?pgnc=1 [accessed 20 June 2016].
27 Charity Commission for England and Wales, www.gov.uk/government/organisa tions/charity-commission [accessed 20 June 2016].
28 Martin, 'Recent Developments in Australian Charity Law', 31.
29 Andrews, 'Charities Regulator'.
30 Martin, 'Recent Developments in Australian Charity Law', 31; for discussion on the cy-près doctrine, see Juliet Chevalier-Watts and Sue Tappenden, *Equity, Trusts and Succession* (Wellington: Thomson Reuters, 2013), 295–8, and *Re Wilson* [1913] 1 Ch 314 and *Biscoe* v. *Jackson* (1887) 35 Ch D 460 (CA).

E Abolishment of the ACNC

Prior to the establishment of the ACNC, it had been difficult to capture the size and the scale of the charity and NFP sector,[31] but now it is possible to monitor and recognise the value of this sector within the Australian context. This was because Australia did not have a regulatory system that dealt with the sector in a uniform manner. The Commonwealth, states, territories, and local governments all regulated varying parts of the sector differently, and it was the role of the ATO to determine relevant tax concessions. However, the regulatory model of the ACNC provides transparency, accountability, and promotes good governance.[32]

Regardless, the Federal Government, under Tony Abbott, in 2014, announced its intention to abolish the ACNC, and repeal the ACNC Act, and transfer some of the functions to the ATO, and to a National Centre for Excellence, which had not, at the time, been established. The Abbott Government asserted that the ACNC, and its legislation, have implemented a heavy-handed regulatory approach,[33] and that this had led to increased red tape and duplication of compliance measures, as well as its powers and penalties being too draconian.[34]

As a result, the Government introduced to Parliament in March 2014, the Australian Charities and Not-for-profits Commission (Repeal) (No. 1) Bill 2014 (Cth). It was argued that such an abolition would likely result in removal of Governance Standards, and lead to lack of effective governance regulation.[35] On the other hand, the Charities Commission of New Zealand, which was created in 2005, was also disestablished in 2012, with its core functions being transferred to the Department of Internal Affairs – Charities Services, under the guise of cost savings and streamlining services.[36] To all intents and purposes, this disestablishment has not undermined the regulatory or governance imposed upon the charitable sector in New Zealand, although it is not possible to explore the realities of that matter within the confines of this chapter.

Interestingly, this Bill, while providing for the abolition of the ACNC and its Act, failed to set out any replacement arrangements, which evidently is 'productive of uncertainty'.[37] While the Bill did refer to a transfer of provisions, it merely notes that this would be to an unidentified recipient agency to be decided upon by

---

31 Kirkness, 'Life Cycle Issues for Charities', 252.
32 Nehme, 'Regulation of the Not-for-Profit Sector?', 24.
33 Ibid.
34 Joanne Dunn, 'What Is the Future of the ACNC under the New Government?', *The Lawyer* (31 October 2013), www.thelawyer.com/what-is-the-future-of-the-acnc-under-the-new-government [accessed 20 June 2016]; Bill d'Apice and Anna Lewis, 'Government to Repeal the ACNC', 19 March 2014, *Charities & Not-for-Profits Law in Australia*, www.charitiesnfplaw.com.au/2014/03/19/government-to-repeal-the-ACNC [accessed 20 June 2016].
35 Murray, 'Not-for-Profit Reform', 120.
36 Juliet Chevalier-Watts, *Law of Charity* (Wellington: Thomson Reuters, 2014), 21.
37 Ian Murray, 'The Australian Charities and Not-for-profits Commission: Reform or Unreform?', *Charity Law and Practice Review* 17(1) (2014–15), 154.

the relevant minister.[38] The accompanying materials do refer to the Centre of Excellence, but this appears to be focused on self-help, as opposed to self-regulation,[39] which again appears to undermine the notion of stringent governance and transparency.

Nonetheless, the Turnbull Government, led by Malcolm Turnbull, who took office in September 2015, appears to have different plans for the ACNC. It was reported that the ACNC will have an ongoing role in the Turnbull Government, and while this does not mean that the ACNC has a guaranteed future, it does provide some evidence that it still plays an important role within the NFP sector. As a result, bodies are still be required to register with the ACNC and comply with the ACNC's governance and regulatory requirements.[40]

F The Australian Charities and Not-for-profits Commission Act 2012

Of great significance was the implementation of the Australian Charities and Not-for-Profits Act 2012 (Cth) (ACNC Act). Until this Act, the definition of charity was traditionally decided by common law, unsurprisingly, 'with its antecedents in English common law'.[41] Prior to this Act, there had been no statutory definition of 'charity', so the concept of charity developed from the common law.[42]

Section 5 of the Act defines 'charity' as:[43]

an entity:

a   that is a not-for-profit entity; and
b   all of the purposes of which are:
c   charitable purposes (see Part 3) that are for the public benefit (see Division 2 of this Part); or
d   purposes that are incidental or ancillary to, and in furtherance or in aid of, purposes of the entity covered by subparagraph (i); and
e   none of the purposes of which are disqualifying purposes (see Division 3); and
f   that is not an individual, a political party or a government entity.

---

38 Murray, 'Australian Charities', 154, referring to Australian Charities and Not-for-profits Commission (Repeal) (No. 1) Bill 2014 (Cth), sch 1, pt 2.
39 Murray, 'Australian Charities', 154, referring to 'Explanatory Memorandum to the ACNC Repeal Bill: Regulation Impact Statement', 3.
40 Xavier Smerdon, 'Turnbull Government Makes Plans for ACNC's Future', Probono Australia, 23 December 2015, http://probonoaustralia.com.au/news/2015/12/turnbull-government-makes-plans-for-acncs-future [accessed 20 June 2016]; Bill d'Apice and Anna Lewis, 'The ACNC's Future Becoming More Certain', *Charities & Not-For-Profits Law in Australia* (9 February 2015), www.makdap.com.au/publications/acnc%E2%80%99s-future-becoming-more-certain [accessed 20 June 2016].
41 Martin, 'Recent Developments in Australian Charity Law', 31.
42 Kirkness, 'Life Cycle Issues for Charities', 252.
43 Charities Act 2013, s 5.

Evidently obtaining successful registration of a charity brings with it access to a number of tax concessions at state and commonwealth levels; such concessions are of great value to organisations. With the statutory definition of charity, there was a presumption that an application for registration would be granted by the ACNC without further consideration because it was thought that the objects would reflect the objects of the charity in line with definition of charity at s 5, the charitable purposes at s 12, and the public benefit requirement at s 6. However, the reality is that the ACNC may still require further evidence as to how the objects are to be achieved, meaning that simple compliance with the Act will not automatically result in registration,[44] reflecting the realities of the complexity of charity law, even with statutory definitions.

The definition of 'charity' within the Act applies for the purposes of all federal legislation, unless a contrary intention is provided specifically, and the ACNC notes that there 'are still other definitions of charity that may be applied by state and territory government agencies'.[45] The definition was largely based upon, and intended to preserve the common law principles, although it was also designed to provide more clarity and certainty to the meaning of charity, and also charitable purpose.[46]

Section 12(1) of the Act sets out purposes that are considered to fall within the existing common law:[47]

a   the purpose of advancing health;
b   the purpose of advancing education;
c   the purpose of advancing social or public welfare;
d   the purpose of advancing religion;
e   the purpose of advancing culture;
f   the purpose of promoting reconciliation, mutual respect and tolerance between groups of individuals that are in Australia;
g   the purpose of promoting or protecting human rights;
h   the purpose of advancing the security or safety of Australia or the Australian public;
i   the purpose of preventing or relieving the suffering of animals;
j   the purpose of advancing the natural environment;
k   any other purpose beneficial to the general public that may reasonably be regarded as analogous to, or within the spirit of, any of the purposes mentioned in paragraphs (a) to (j);
l   the purpose of promoting or opposing a change to any matter established by law, policy or practice in the Commonwealth, a State, a Territory or another country, if … the change is in furtherance or in aid of one or more of the purposes

44 Kirkness, 'Life Cycle Issues for Charities', 254.
45 Australian Charities and Not-for-profits Commission, 'Legal Meaning of Charity', www.acnc.gov.au/ACNC/Register_my_charity/Who_can_register/Char_def/ ACNC/Edu/Edu_Char_def.aspx [accessed 1 December 2015].
46 Murray, 'Not-for-Profit Reform', 114–15, referring to Explanatory Memorandum Charities Bill 2013 (Cth) and Charities (Consequential Amendments and Transitional Provisions) Bill 2013 (Cth) (EM Charities Bill 3).
47 Murray, 'Not-for-Profit Reform', 124, referring to Charities Act 2013, s 12(1).

mentioned in … (a) to (k); or … in the case of opposing a change – the change is in opposition to, or in hindrance of, one or more of the purposes mentioned in those paragraphs.

Of brief note here is that (l) was a direct result of the High Court case of *Aid/ Watch Inc* v. *Commissioner of Taxation*,[48] which will be discussed later in the chapter.

In addition, the Act also purports to set out purposes that expand beyond the common law definitions:[49]

Purpose of advancing health
Purpose of advancing social or public welfare
Purpose of advancing culture
Purpose of advancing the security or safety of Australia or the Australian public

The Act provides, in some instances, extensive information pertaining to the meaning of these purposes. While this may appear to reflect a progressive approach to defining charity, it has been argued that the purposes listed are more numerous and 'largely differently worded to those accepted at common law', thus making it difficult to judge whether those purposes listed in s 12 do fall within the common law meanings.[50]

In spite of the statutory provisions, the common law principles are still applicable. Two reasons are immediately apparent. First, for interpreting some purposes, such as 'advancing education', whereby common law consideration will be necessary because statute does not provide sufficient explanation. Second, the statutory definition applies only to federal legislation, thus common law meanings will be relevant to state and local government tax concessions. Therefore, the need to understand both the statute and the common law suggests that charity law in Australia is unlikely to be any less complex than it was prior to the enactment of the Act, especially if the ACNC is to consider novel or borderline cases.[51]

G Public benefit

The public benefit requirement is still fundamental within Australian charity law, and s 6(1) of the Act defines it as:[52]

A purpose that an entity has is for the *public benefit* if:

a the achievement of the purpose would be of public benefit; and
b the purpose is directed to a benefit that is available to the members of:

48 Martin, 'Recent Developments in Australian Charity Law', 33.
49 Charities Act 2013, ss 14–17.
50 Murray, 'Not-for-Profit Reform', 124.
51 Ibid., 128–9.
52 Charities Act 2013, s 6(1).

    c   the general public; or

    d   a sufficient section of the general public.

This confirms the common law approach to public benefit, and in particular, the concept of including a 'sufficient section of the public'. This acknowledges the general common law exclusion from charitability of benefits through blood tie or some contractual relationships, as determined in *Oppenheim* v. *Tobacco Securities Trust Company Limited*[53] (as discussed in earlier chapters).

Interestingly, and unlike the other selected jurisdictions, Australia also now provides a specific provision about the size of a section of the general public, as follows:[54]

a   the numerical size of that section of the general public; and

b   the numerical size of the section of the general public to whom the purpose is relevant.

It has been asserted that this provision may mean that where there is a sufficient section of the public to which the purpose is directed, and a different-sized section to which the purpose is relevant, then their respective sizes should be compared. For instance, where a grammar school offers scholarships for a certain number of pupils to attend the school free of charge, and this scholarship is determined through academic ability, then s 6(4) requires the number of available scholarships to be compared with the number of pupils in the community able to apply.[55]

As discussed in earlier chapters, England and Wales has removed the presumption of public benefit, notwithstanding assertions that the presumption of public benefit is a fallacy,[56] but Australia retains the presumption of public benefit for some purposes. For instance:[57]

a   the purpose of preventing and relieving sickness, disease or human suffering;

b   the purpose of advancing education;

c   the purpose of relieving the poverty, distress or disadvantage of individuals or families;

d   the purpose of caring for and supporting:

53 *Oppenheim* v. *Tobacco Securities Trust Co Ltd* [1951] AC 297 (HL), 306; see also *Re Compton* [1945] Ch 123 (CA).

54 Charities Act 2013, s 6(4).

55 Fiona Martin, 'Has the Charities Act 2013 Changed the Common Law Concept of Charitable "Public Benefit" And, If So, How?', *Australian Tax Forum* 30(1) (2015), 79; see also House of Representatives, Explanatory Memorandum to the Charities Bill 2013 and Charities (Consequential Amendments and Transitional Provisions) Bill 2013, [1.63].

56 See generally Mary Synge, *The 'New' Public Benefit Requirement: Making Sense of Charity Law?* (Oxford: Hart, 2015) and *Independent Schools Council* v. *The Charity Commission for England and Wales* [2011] UKUT 421 (TCC).

57 Charities Act 2013, s 7 (AU).

e   the aged; or
f   individuals with disabilities;
g   the purpose of advancing religion.

In addition, the Act continues the provisions of the Extension of Charitable Purpose Act 2004 (Cth), whereby open and non-discriminatory self-help groups, and closed or contemplative religious orders are not subject to the public benefit requirement.[58] The latter point is in contrast to cases such as *Gilmour* v. *Coats*[59] and *Cocks* v. *Manners*[60] in England, where closed orders were found to lack the requisite public benefit.

An additional point of interest to be found within the Act is that of s 8, where the public benefit requirement has also been removed for the relief of necessitous circumstances:[61]

> Disregard the requirement in paragraph 6(1)(b) that a purpose be directed to a benefit that is available to the members of the general public, or of a sufficient section of the general public, if the purpose is the purpose of relieving the necessitous circumstances of one or more individuals who are in Australia.

This appears to continue the concept that the relief of poverty is exempt from the requirement of being open to a sufficient section of the public, but 'the relief of poverty' is specifically mentioned in s 7(c) as being a charitable purpose, and being presumed to be of public benefit. Therefore, it is not clear whether the 'relief of necessitous circumstances' has a different meaning to that of 'relief of poverty'[62] and how it may be interpreted, thus leading to a possible lack of clarity.

H Indigenous Australians and the Charities Act 2013

Aboriginal peoples of Australia 'have suffered a long and arduous journey of recognition in Australia',[63] but the Charities Act 2013 has gone some way 'in dealing with this traditional problem and now recognizes that a charitable trust can be for the benefit of the public in the native title context where it has a defined class of beneficiaries by reference to descendants of named ancestors'.[64]

The background to this, as discussed in Chapter 4, is the restriction on a gift or trust being charitable if it benefits beneficiaries defined by a personal nature. In other words, 'the number of potential beneficiaries of a charity must not be numerically negligible, and there must be no personal relationship between

58 Martin, 'Charities Act 2013', 78.
59 *Gilmour* v. *Coats* [1949] AC 426.
60 *Cocks* v. *Manners* [1871] LR 12 Eq 574.
61 Charities Act 2013, s 8.
62 Martin, 'Charities Act 2013', 79–80.
63 Adam Levin, 'Observations on the Development of Native Title Trusts in Australia', *Trusts and Trustees* 22(2) (March 2016), 241.
64 Ibid., 256.

beneficiaries and any named person or persons'.[65] This finds its history in the English decisions of *Re Compton*,[66] and later *Oppenheim* v. *Tobacco Securities Trust Co Ltd*.[67] In the former case, the Court of Appeal refused to find the public benefit in a trust for the education of the descendants of three named persons because such a gift 'defined by reference to a purely personal relationship to a named propositus ... cannot be a charitable gift'[68] due to 'the inherent vice of the personal element'.[69]

Six years later, the House of Lords in *Oppenheim* confirmed this principle, finding a trust for the education of the children of employees, or former employees, not charitable because members of a family and employees of a particular employer were, by way of illustration, on the same footing as *Re Compton*. Thus 'neither in common kinship nor in common employment the sort of nexus which is sufficient'.[70]

This approach was followed in Australia. In *Davies* v. *Perpetual Trustee Co Ltd*,[71] the Privy Council had to determine the charitability of a trust for the education of descendants of Presbyterians from Northern Ireland. It was held that even though the trust advanced education, there was no public benefit because the class of persons was defined through their ancestry. This principle was applied in respect to indigenous Australians in *Aboriginal Hostels Ltd* v. *Darwin City Council*.[72] The Supreme Court of the Northern Territory confirmed that the Aboriginal Hostels Ltd had to benefit a section of the community that was not defined through family relationships, noting that 'the character that marks the potential beneficiary must not be a relationship to a particular person or persons such as one of blood or employment'.[73]

That meant that under the common law, NFPs in Australia were not 'for the benefit of a section of the public if the quality that distinguishes the class of beneficiaries from other members of the public depends on their relationship to a person and it is impossible for anyone outside this relationship to enter'.[74]

While it was confirmed that indigenous Australians were a sufficient section of the community for charity law purposes,[75] the blood-tie relationship precluded native title groups from being charitable, as envisaged under the Native Title Act

65 Paul Harpur, 'Charity Law's Public Benefit Test: Is Legislative Reform in the Public Interest?', *Queensland University of Technology Law Journal* 3(2) (November 2003), 424.

66 *Re Compton* [1945] 1 Ch 123 (CA).

67 *Oppenheim* v. *Tobacco Securities Trust Co Ltd*.

68 *Re Compton*, 131.

69 Chevalier-Watts, *Law of Charity*, 58, referring to *Re Compton*.

70 *Oppenheim* v. *Tobacco Securities Trust Co Ltd*, 306–7, referring to *Re Compton*, 131 and *Re Hobourn Aero Components Air Raid Distress Fund* [1946] Ch 194 (CA).

71 *Davies* v. *Perpetual Trustee Co Ltd* (1959) 59 SR (NSW) 112.

72 *Aboriginal Hostels Ltd* v. *Darwin City Council* (1985) 75 FLR 197.

73 Ibid., 209.

74 Martin, 'Charities Act', 82.

75 Martin, 'Charities Act', 82, referring to *Aboriginal Hostels Ltd* v. *Darwin City Council*.

1993 (Cth) (NTA), and owners of traditional lands under other Australian land rights, for instance the Aboriginal Land Rights (Northern Territory) Act 1976 (Cth). The claims to traditional land invariably are determined through kinship or descendancy, thus would fail for charitable purposes under the common law, unless solely for the relief of poverty.[76]

However, s 9 of the Charities Act 2013 has gone some way to addressing this matter, stating:

1   This section applies to a purpose that an entity has if:
2   the purpose is directed to the benefit of Indigenous individuals only; and
3   the purpose is not for the public benefit under this Division (disregarding this section) only because of the relationships between the Indigenous individuals to whose benefit the purpose is directed.
4   The purpose is treated as being for the public benefit if the entity receives, holds or manages an amount, or non-cash benefit (within the meaning of the *Income Tax Assessment Act 1997*), that relates to:
5   native title (within the meaning of the *Native Title Act 1993*); or
6   traditional Indigenous rights of ownership, occupation, use or enjoyment of land.

The limits of s 9(1) are that there must be an entity, and its purpose is directed to benefit only indigenous individuals, and cannot have purposes that benefit indigenous individuals, among others. This means that some entities will fail under this provision. For instance, NFPs established for the protection of traditional lands, or school-based trust programmes who do not differentiate between indigenous peoples are who members of specific groups, as these would not be directed to the benefit of indigenous individuals. The latter may be a key concern for remote communities where various claim groups reside together.[77]

Section 9(2) also provides an additional narrowing of the exception to public benefit, whereby it has linked the modification of the public benefit test to receipt of money or non-pecuniary benefit by the entity. Further, 'receives, holds or manages an amount, or non-cash benefit'; 'native title'; or 'traditional Indigenous rights of ownership' are not defined in any legislation, thus there is a scope of uncertainty and ambiguity in their interpretation.[78]

Therefore, the Act has removed the barrier for a number of charities in relation to indigenous Australians, reflecting New Zealand's approach with regard to Māori claims, who would otherwise be precluded because of historic blood-tie restrictions. This is clearly a progressive step for Australian charity law, notwithstanding some possible limitations associated with provisions within s 9. Thus,

76 Ibid.
77 Ibid., 83, and Levin, 'Observations on the Development of Native Title Trusts in Australia', 16 and 17. See also Levin re economic development issues for indigenous peoples and charitable purposes, ibid, 17.
78 Martin, 'Charities Act 2013', 83–4; see also 84–5 for further issues pertaining to limitations to the s 9 provision.

legislation recognises 'that Indigenous customs have always placed family relationships at the centre of their legal and social structures and that this should be accepted as a valid way of organising the ultimate benefit from payments in respect of native title and traditional lands'[79] by relaxing the public benefit requirement.

I Charitable purposes

As stated above, s 12(1) of the Charities Act 2013 sets out charitable purposes, and similarly to that of English Charities Act 2006, it provides a contemporary extended list of such purposes.

While it is not possible, within the confines of this book, to address every head of charity in Australia, this chapter will consider a small selection of key cases because such '"leading cases" are a vital part of the chaotic-looking case law tradition'[80] and provide a useful insight into the jurisprudential trends of charitable purposes in Australia.

The first case is the High Court decision in *Central Bayside General Practice Association Limited* v. *Commissioner of State Revenue*.[81]

J Central Bayside General Practice Association Limited v. Commissioner of State Revenue

This case represents a recent example of courts' acknowledging the evolving role of charities within society.[82]

Central Bayside is part of a General Practice Program that enables general practitioners to, inter alia, work towards improving community healthcare; it receives government funding and commonwealth grants to fund its activities. The Victorian State Revenue Office refused Central Bayside a payroll exemption scheme under the Payroll Tax Act 1971 (Vic) because it found that it was not a charitable body under that Act. This was upheld by, inter alia, the Court of Appeal, on the basis that the entity was so much under the control and influence of the Government that it was furthering Government objectives rather than carrying out its own.[83]

Historically, there is evidence that courts have distinguished between charitable purposes and government purposes, with the assumption being that government purposes were outside the scope of charity.[84] This is perhaps because of the lack of

79 Ibid., 87.
80 John Mummery, 'The Commissioners for Special Purposes of the Income Tax v. Pemsel', *Charity Law and Practice Review* 16(1) (2013–14), 1.
81 *Central Bayside General Practice Association Limited* v. *Commissioner of State Revenue* [2006] HCA 43.
82 Ian Murray, 'Charity Means Business: *Commissioner of Taxation* v. *Word Investments Ltd*: Case Note', *Sydney Law Review* 31(2) (June 2009), 312.
83 *Central Bayside General Practice Association Limited* v. *Commissioner of State Revenue*, [25].
84 Gino Dal Pont, 'Charity Law: "No Magic in Words"?', in Matthew Harding, Ann O'Connell, and Miranda Stewart (eds), *Not-for-Profit Law: Theoretical and Comparative Perspectives* (Cambridge University Press, Cambridge, 2014), 100, referring

altruism in the provision of goods and services provided by the government, and also it could be because it may allow charities to pursue government objectives that have traditionally been precluded because historically political purposes have negated charitability.[85]

Regardless of the apparent distinctions between the first sector (government) and the third (charity), this situation is less clear in contemporary times. For instance, it is not uncommon for governments to outsource some of their functions to charities, and those charities may then tender for government funding to supply the services to fulfil those purposes.[86] Indeed, the High Court in *Central Bayside* confirmed that this distinction is less precise today, noting that in *Brisbane City Council* v. *Attorney-General for Queensland*,[87] it was held that a trust, which was entirely a creature of state legislation, was charitable.

As a result, the High Court in *Central Bayside* acknowledged that 'objects of government and its creatures are by no means necessarily antithetical to charitable objects and activities',[88] thus:[89]

> The mere fact that the appellant and the government both have a purpose of improving patient care and health does not establish that the appellant has the purpose of giving effect to government purposes, abdicating any independent fulfilment of its own. The appellant's purpose is charitable. It remains charitable even though the government is the source of the funds it uses to carry out that purpose. Its consent to the attachment by the government of conditions to the employment of those funds does not establish that the appellant is not independently carrying out its purpose.

As a result, the High Court found that the entity was charitable under the fourth *Pemsel* head, which, while not entirely removing the distinction between the first and third sectors, may actually suggest 'a porosity in the relevant concepts',[90] and an expansion of our understanding of the legal concept of charity.

There are further factors associated with this case. The Court left open the question of whether a body can be charitable even if it is subject to substantial or government control, which is yet to be answered, and it also has some

---

to *Trustees for the Roll of Voluntary Workers* v. *Commissioners of Inland Revenue* [1942] 1 SC 47; see also *National Trustees Executors and Agency Company of Australasia Ltd* v. *Jeffrey*, [1950] 1 VLR 382 (VSC).

85 Dal Pont, 'Charity Law: "No Magic in Words"?', 100–1. See Chapter 11 for discussion relating to political purposes.

86 Dal Pont, 'Charity Law', 101.

87 *Central Bayside General Practice Association Limited* v. *Commissioner of State Revenue*, [173], referring to *Brisbane City Council* v. *Attorney-General for Queensland* [1979] AC 411; see also *Monds* v. *Stackhouse* [1948] HCA 47 and *Bathurst City Council* v. *PWC Properties Pty Ltd* [1998] HCA 59.

88 *Central Bayside General Practice Association Limited* v. *Commissioner of State Revenue*, [176].

89 Ibid., [42].

90 Dal Pont, 'Charity Law', 102.

implications. First, that entities set up independently from government can receive government funding and retain charitable status, even if the funding constitutes all or most of the body's income. Second, governments might impose conditions for funded bodies to be accountable for funding, which may impact on the governance of such bodies.[91]

While this was a welcome decision, because it challenged one of the historical constraints on the legal concept of charity law, it still left some unanswered questions, which may not be such a welcome addition to charity law.

Just as *Central Bayside* challenged legal concepts, a few short years later, so too did the groundbreaking case of *Aid/Watch Incorporated* v. *Commissioner of Taxation*.[92]

K Aid/Watch Incorporated v. Commissioner of Taxation

This is a fundamental case in the jurisprudence of Australia, as it not only changed the common law in relation to political purposes, as will be discussed below, and further in Chapter 11, it also formed part of the historical context of legislative charity law reform in Australia,[93] and s 12(1)(l) of the Charities Act 2013 recognises this High Court decision. This is one of the significant expansions on the types of charitable purpose, and in particular, the fourth type, that of any other purposes beneficial to the community.[94]

Aid/Watch endorses the competent use of national and international aid that is directed to the relief of poverty. Its campaigns encourage public debate and instigate changes of government policy and activity in relation to granting of foreign aid.

The High Court's starting point was that the, now much familiar, remarks of Lord Parker in *Bowman* v. *Secular Society* 'were not directed to the Australian system of government established and maintained by the Constitution itself'.[95] In other words, 'a trust for the attainment of political objects has always held to be invalid'.[96] This doctrine has been widely acknowledged in many common law jurisdictions, and, indeed, by Australia, up until this case.[97]

The majority of the Court determined that 'the generation by lawful means of public debate ... is a purpose beneficial to the community within the fourth head in *Pemsel*'.[98] This is because, in relation to Australia:[99]

---

91 'Does Government Funding with Strings Attached Affect a Body's Charitable Status?', Clayton Utz, 12 December 2006, www.claytonutz.com/publications/news/ 200612/12/does_government_funding_with_strings_attached_affect_a_bodys_cha ritable_status.page [accessed 28 June 2016].

92 *Aid/Watch Incorporated* v. *Commissioner of Taxation*.

93 O'Connell, Martin, and Chia, 'Law, Policy and Politics', 294.

94 Martin, 'Charities Act 2013', 77.

95 *Aid/Watch Incorporated* v. *Commissioner of Taxation*, [40]; Chevalier-Watts and Tappenden, *Equity, Trusts and Succession*, 286.

96 *Bowman* v. *Secular Society Limited* [1917] AC 406 (HL), 442.

97 See Chevalier-Watts, *Law of Charity*, ch. 7.

98 *Aid/Watch Incorporated* v. *Commissioner of Taxation*, [47].

99 *Aid/Watch Incorporated* v. *Commissioner of Taxation*, [44], referring to respectively, *Royal North Shore Hospital of Sydney* v. *Attorney-General* (1938) 60 CLR 396; *Lange* v. *Australian Broadcasting Corporation* [1997] HCA 25 (1997) 189 CLR 520,

the foundation of the 'coherent system of law' ... is supplied by the Constitution. The provisions ... mandate a system of representative and responsible government with a universal adult franchise ... Communication between electors and legislators and the officers of the executive, and between electors themselves, on matters of government and politics is 'an indispensable incident' of that constitutional system.

Therefore 'it is assumed to be indispensable regarding communication between the executive, legislature and electors on government and policy matters'.[100] The system of law that operates in Australia 'thus postulates for its operation in the very "agitation" for legislative and political changes'.[101] This, therefore, acknowledges that public benefit is to be found in holding governments to account and the public benefit arises because the public has a legitimate interest in the exercise of public functions and powers.[102] In other words, this implied freedom of politically communicating 'is premised on the idea that democracy works most effectively and legitimately if citizens are engaged in the democratic process'.[103]

This had the effect of determining that 'in Australia there is no general doctrine which excludes from charitable purposes "political objects" and has the scope indicated in England by *McGovern* v. *Attorney-General*'.[104] In addition, the majority concluded that any lawful generation of debates concerning changes to the law, and that fall under the four heads of charity, are of public benefit and should be charitable.[105]

One of the most profound effects of the *Aid/Watch* decision was that 'advocacy has been accepted as a legitimate charitable activity. This will no doubt shape the charity sector's self-conception and its future engagement with government'.[106]

557–9; *Roach* v. *Electoral Commissioner* (2007) 233 CLR 162, 174–5 [7]–[8], 186–8 [44]–[49]; *Kruger* v. *The Commonwealth* [1997] HCA 27 (1997) 190 CLR 1, 46–7, 93, 125–6, 146–8; *Bivens* v. *Six Unknown Named Agents of Federal Bureau of Narcotics* [1971] USSC 133 403 US 388 (1971); *Australian Broadcasting Corporation* v. *Lenah Game Meats Pty Ltd* (2001) 208 CLR 199 220 [20]; [2001] HCA 63; *Mulholland* v. *Australian Electoral Commission* [2004] HCA 41 (2004) 220 CLR 181, 245 [180]–[181]; *Coleman* v. *Power* [2004] HCA 39 (2004) 220 CLR 1, 50 [92] 77–8 [196], 82 [211] (footnotes deleted).

100 Chevalier-Watts and Tappenden, *Equity, Trusts and Succession*, 287; Juliet Chevalier-Watts, 'Charitable Trusts and Political Purposes: Sowing the Seeds of Change? Lessons from Australia', *Canterbury Law Review* 19(1) (2013), 62.

101 *Aid/Watch Incorporated* v. *Commissioner of Taxation*, [45].

102 Matthew Turnour and Elizabeth Turnour, 'Archimedes, *Aid/Watch*, Constitutional Leavers and Where We Now Stand', in Harding *et al.*, *Not-for-Profit Law*, 52.

103 Jenny Beard, 'Charity Law from a Public Law Perspective: The *Aid/Watch* Case Revisited', *Charity Law and Practice Review* 18(1) (2015–16), 85.

104 *Aid/Watch Incorporated* v. *Commissioner of Taxation*, [48], referring to *McGovern* v. *Attorney-General* [1982] Ch 321, 340.

105 Beard, 'Charity Law from a Public Law Perspective', 89–90.

106 Joyce Chia, Matthew Harding, and Ann O'Connell, 'Navigating the Politics of Charity: Reflections on *Aid/Watch Inc* v. *Federal Commissioner of Taxation*', *Melbourne University Law Review* 35(2) (August 2011), 378.

This will enable charities to carry out increased levels of campaigning and advocacy, and indeed, the Charities Act 2013 subsequently endorsed this decision by including s 12(1)(l) in the Act. The courts now have the jurisdiction to determine whether a proposed change in the law has the requisite public benefit, 'but not beyond a consideration of the concepts of public benefit enumerated in one of more of the purposes defined as charitable in the Act'.[107]

While this was undoubtedly a groundbreaking case, there are still some questions left unanswered. The extent of the implied freedom of political communication under the Constitution is not clear, nor yet whether other forms of the political purpose doctrine may not be included. For instance, whether political campaigning for the spread of doctrines such as socialism would place too much strain on the constitutional system of government of the Commonwealth.[108] Nonetheless, what this case demonstrates is Australia's commitment to ensuring that charity law principles are applied in the context of contemporary society,[109] and that charity law has an important role to play in a contemporary and functioning democracy.[110]

What is also important about this decision is that it is consistent with the 2008 decision of *Commissioner of Taxation of the Commonwealth of Australia* v. *Word Investments Limited*,[111] which demonstrated that the Australian High Court 'is open to applying the principles of charity law in the context of the values and expectations of modern society'.[112]

L Commissioner of Taxation of the Commonwealth of Australia v. Word Investments Limited

In today's difficult economic climate, it is important for charities to understand what they are permitted to do in order to raise funds without the risk of losing their charitable status, and ultimately the benefits that come with that status. In December 2008, the High Court of Australia provided some much-needed certainty as to whether charities can engage in commercial activities as part of its charitable purposes.[113] That decision was *Commissioner of Taxation of the Commonwealth of Australia* v. *Word Investments Limited.*

Wycliffe Bible Translators (International) is a missionary organisation who seeks to spread the Christian religion through missionaries. The missionaries, inter alia,

---

107 Beard, 'Charity Law from a Public Law Perspective', 106.
108 Ibid., 107.
109 Fiona Martin, '"Advocacy in Charity: A Breakaway from the Common Law" (Impactful Advocacy)', *Lien Centre for Social Innovation (Singapore Management University)* 1(1) (2012), 79.
110 Beard, 'Charity Law from a Public Law Perspective', 107.
111 *Commissioner of Taxation* v. *Word Investments Ltd.*
112 Fiona Martin, 'The Legal Concept of Charity and Its Expansion after the *Aid/Watch* Decision', *Cosmopolitan Civil Societies Journal* 3(2) (2011), 32.
113 Claire Russell, 'A Word to the Wise', *Keeping Good Companies* 61(3) (April 2009), 17.

translate the Bible into local languages, and then teach people how to read the Bible. Word was founded to raise money within Australia and give it to Wycliffe to enable it to carry out its purposes.

The issues in the appeal centred on the fact that Word does not carry out training of missionaries, publishing of the Bible, or preaching the Gospel, but rather gives its profits to Wycliffe, and other similar entities, to enable them to carry out these activities. This decision required the Court to reconsider its long-standing position on a variety of permissible trading activities that charities may undertake.[114]

One of the key submissions by the Commissioner was that Word's activities were commercially focused, thus not merely ancillary to Word's religious purposes. However, the majority of the Court rejected this submission, and asserted that while Word did endeavour to make a profit, this was only in aid of its charitable purposes, and to 'point to the goal of profit and isolate it as the relevant purpose is to create a false dichotomy between characterisation of an institution as commercial and characterisation of it as charitable'.[115]

The Court also considered whether an institution can be charitable when it does not engage in charitable activities beyond making a profit, which is directed to entities that do carry out charitable activities. The majority determined that the charitable purposes of a company can be found in purposes that bring about natural and probable consequences 'of its immediate and expressed purposes, and is charitable activities can be found in the natural and probable consequence of its immediate activities'.[116]

Therefore, the majority confirmed that Word had solely charitable purposes, and only conducted commercial activities in order to effectuate those purposes.[117]

The Court recognised that this area of law required modernising, and the decision did exactly that. This is beneficial because as 'government funding dries up and a push to privatisation and self-funding is advanced, many charities will rely on entrepreneurial activities to remain viable'.[118]

As a result of this decision, and no doubt to limit the impact of the judgment, the ATO issued a Decision Impact Statement that confined the decision to its facts,[119] and in the Federal Budget, the then Labour Government stated that there would be reforms to charity law to ensure that income tax exemptions would not apply to unrelated business income.[120] The Government further announced that it would delay the start for these changes until 2012, and draft legislation was

---

114 Murray, 'Charity Means Business', 309–10.
115 *Commissioner of Taxation* v. *Word Investments Ltd*, [24].
116 *Commissioner of Taxation* v. *Word Investments Ltd*, [38], referring to *Baptist Union of Ireland (Northern) Corporation Ltd* v. *Commissioners of Inland Revenue* (1945) 26 TC 335, 348. This also echoes the New Zealand decision *Hester* v. *Commissioner of Inland Revenue* [2005] 2 NZLR 172 [83].
117 *Commissioner of Taxation* v. *Word Investments Ltd*, [27].
118 Russell, 'A Word to the Wise', 18.
119 Martin, 'Recent Developments in Australian Charity Law', 37.
120 Martin, 'Recent Developments in Australian Charity Law', 37, referring to Australian Government, Budget 2011–12, Not-for-profit sector reforms.

prepared for release in late 2012, although this did not materialise before the Federal election. In 2013, the then Federal Government stated that it would not make these proposed amendments, and would instead look to other measures to address risks to revenue. As far as the author can determine, there have been no further suggested changes by the Federal Government.[121]

Evidently the impact of the *Word* case has been felt within the charitable and NFP sector, as well as causing ripples of concern within governments, but what it represents is a significant boost to charities in being able to undertake broader activities that can encompass commercial activities,[122] in order to remain buoyant in a challenging environment.

121 Martin, 'Recent Developments in Australian Charity Law', 38, referring to Arthur Sinodinos, Assistant Treasurer, media release, 'Integrity Restored to Australia's tax system' (14 December 2013).
122 Murray, 'Charity Means Business', 328.

7 Canada

A Introduction

Charity and charities plays an important role in the social structure of Canada, generally speaking, and often, in surprising ways. For instance, in the third leg of the rock band U2's 2011 tour, during the Winnipeg concert in 2011, the lead singer, Bono, chronicled the history of Amnesty International, a renowned human rights charity, leading the fans to sing 'Happy Birthday' to celebrate the charity's 50-year history, and urging the crowd to support its human rights causes. While such charities may be close to the hearts of Canadians, charity law generally, in Canada, receives little attention in relation to its policies. It is said that Canadian charity law is viewed conservatively, and may even restrict certain groups from receiving charitable status. This is certainly true of those organisations that engage actively in political activities and advocacy, which will be discussed in Chapter 11. In brief, for the purposes of this chapter, Canadian courts have not favoured finding purposes as being charitable if charities engage in political activities, because, it is alleged that this enters in to a debate over whether policies may, or may not, lack public benefit.[1]

In addition to the notion that Canadian charity law is conservative, it is asserted that multicultural and ethnic cultural groups, umbrella organisations, and community broadcasting organisations, while being recognised as charitable in other jurisdictions, have not always been so in Canada.[2]

The basis, and much of the development of charity law in Canada, and the notion of charity, derives its origins from the Charitable Uses Act 1601, and the centuries of charity jurisprudence arising from England. The definition of the four heads of charity, as summarised by Lord Macnaghten in *Commissioners for Special*

---

1 Andrew Kitching, 'Charitable Purpose, Advocacy, and the Income Tax Act' (Parliamentary Information and Research Service (Canada), 28 February 2006), 2–3, http://sectorsource.ca/sites/default/files/resources/files/2458_Book.pdf [accessed 1 Aug. 2016]. See generally *Alliance for Life* v. *Minister of National Revenue* 1999 CarswellNat2489 [1999] 3 FC 504; *Positive Action Against Pornography* v. *Minister of National Revenue* 1988 CarswellNat 274 [1988] 1 CTC 232 [1988] 2 FC 340.
2 Karine Levasseur, 'In the Name of Charity: Institutional Support for and Resistance to Redefining the Meaning of Charity in Canada', *Canadian Public Administration* 55 (2) (2012), 181–2.

Purposes of Income Tax v. *Pemsel*,[3] as set out in earlier chapters, 'has received general acceptance in'[4] Canada. While the common law ability has the ability to evolve over time, it is said that this evolution is rather limited in Canada.[5]

Unlike New Zealand and England and Wales, Canada has an integrated relationship between tax policy and charity regulation.[6] Thus, Canada is a 'classic example of a state-dominated regulatory regime focused on the goal of ensuring charitable funding is dedicated to charitable purposes while protecting the integrity of the tax system'.[7]

Charities receive preferential treatment under the Income Tax Act (the Act), whereby, inter alia, a charity's income is exempt from taxes. Registered status is thought to convey legitimacy on the charitable entity because such entities are subject to the regulatory oversight provided by the Canada Revenue Agency (CRA).[8] In order to obtain the benefits of being a registered charity, an organisation must register with the CRA, and registration means that the entity has met the CRA's requirements, and is compliant with the Act. The Charities Directorate of the CRA makes determinations on which entities qualify as charities, requiring annual reporting, making reports publicly available on its website, and ensuring auditing compliance under the Act.[9]

The Act creates three types of registered charities: charitable organisations, public foundations, and private foundations. Charitable organisations devote their resources to carrying out charitable activities. Foundations are primarily funders of charitable activities.[10] This chapter will focus on charitable organisations.

The Act provides rules for the tax treatment of registered charities, but does not provide a definition of charity. In the absence of such a statutory definition, courts rely on the various common law tests to determine charitability;[11] the Supreme Court adopted the *Pemsel* classification in *R* v. *Assessors of the Town of Sunny Brae*.[12]

---

3 *Commissioners for Special Purposes of Income Tax* v. *Pemsel* [1891] AC 531 (HL), 583.
4 Trevor C. W. Farrow, 'The Limits of Charity: Redefining the Boundaries of Charitable Trust Law', *Estates and Trust Journal* 13(1) (1999), 310, citing *Guaranty Trust Company of Canada* v. *MNR* (1967) 60 DLR (2d) 481, 486.
5 Levasseur, 'Name of Charity', 182.
6 Richard Bridge, 'The Law Governing Advocacy by Charitable Organizations: The Case for Change', *The Philanthropist* 17(2) (2002), 2.
7 Susan D. Phillips, 'Shining Light on Charities or Looking in the Wrong Place? Regulation-by-Transparency in Canada', *International Journal of Voluntary and Nonprofit Organisations* 24(3) (2013), 881.
8 Kitching, 'Charitable Purpose', 1.
9 Phillips, 'Shining Light', 886.
10 Bridge, 'Law Governing Advocacy by Charitable Organizations', 1–2.
11 Kitching, 'Charitable Purpose', 1–2.
12 Adam Parachin, 'Legal Privilege as a Defining Characteristic of Charity', *Canadian Business Law Journal* 48(1) (2009), 39, referring to *R* v. *Assessors of the Town of Sunny Brae*, 2 SCR 76; see also *Guaranty Trust Company of Canada* v. *Minister of National Revenue* [1967] SCR 133; *Vancouver Society of Immigrant and Visible Minority Women* v. *MNR* [1999], 1 SCR 10.

While many jurisdictions, such as Australia and New Zealand, have undergone major policy and legislative changes, Canada continues to resist such changes. This is despite attempts to push for such changes, including the separation of tax policy and charitable regulation, and establishing a specific charity commission, which would echo some fellow jurisdictions.

This chapter critically explores, inter alia, Canadian charity law and its regulatory regimes, beginning with a brief foray into the historical and contemporary regulatory regimes and changes to have occurred within Canada.[13]

B A potted history of charitable regulation in Canada

(i) Calls for reform

The legal definition of charity in Canada, which has evolved from the English common law, and has been modified by statute, 'is widely seen as both unfair and out-of-step with contemporary Canadian values'.[14] It is said that much of the dissatisfaction comes from the current legal definition of charity, which has been asserted as being 'antiquated, inconsistent and inflexible'.[15] As a result, it is further asserted that charities 'live within a tethered ... regime which acts a de facto muzzle on legal dissent and social justice issues'.[16]

Indeed, the current issues facing charity law in Canada have been subject to criticism by the judiciary. For instance, Iacobucci J, in the Supreme Court case *Vancouver Society of Immigrant and Visible Minority Women*, recognised the inherent problems of continuing to rely on the common law definition of a charity:[17]

> Considering that the law of charity in Canada continues to make reference to an English statute enacted almost 400 years ago, I find it not surprising that there have been numerous calls for its reform, both legislative and judicial.

In the same Supreme Court case, the Court was encouraged to accept a new definition of charity, and while the Court acknowledged that such a definition would respect the precedents developed in the jurisprudence,[18] it declined to adopt the approach because 'suddenly to adopt a new and more expansive definition of charity, without warning,

---

13 Peter R. Elson, 'The Origin of Species: Why Charity Regulations in Canada and England Continue to Reflect Their Origins', *International Journal of Not-for-Profit Law* 12(3) (May 2010), 75.

14 Peter Broder, *The Legal Definition of Charity and Canada Customs and Revenue Agency's Charitable Registration Process* (Canadian Centre for Philanthropy Public Affairs, August 2011), 1.

15 Ibid.

16 Peter R. Elson, 'A Short History of Voluntary Sector–Government Relations in Canada', *The Philanthropist* 21(1) (2007), 60.

17 *Vancouver Society of Immigrant and Visible Minority Women* v. *Minister of National Revenue*, [126].

18 Kitching, 'Charitable Purpose', 7, citing *Vancouver Society of Immigrant and Visible Minority Women* v. *Minister of National Revenue*, [197].

could have a substantial and serious effect on the taxation system'.[19] Instead, the Court suggested that such a change would be better effected by Parliament.[20]

It is perhaps not surprising, therefore, that there have been numerous calls for reform to realign charity regulation in Canada, and not least, within the area of political purposes, although, this controversial topic will be addressed fully in Chapter 11. It suffices to say here, by way of example, on the matter of political purposes, that a report released by the University of Victoria's Environmental Law Centre in 2015 found that the CRA's definition of political activity is unclear, leading to an 'intolerable state of uncertainty' and having a 'chilling effect' among charities.[21]

A series of reports and policy initiatives have proposed changes to the legal definition of charity, as well as liberalising the rules governing political purposes. For instance, in 1998, the distinguished charity lawyer, Arthur Drache, called for statutory reform to bring the definition of charity law in line with contemporary Canadian society.[22] In 1999, the Panel on Accountability and Governance in the Voluntary Sector, chaired by the Hon. Ed Broadbent, the Broadbent Report, released their report. This report recommended that the Federal Government could establish a legislated definition of which organisations would be charitable.[23] The Report not only laid out recommendations for improved self-regulation and governance, it also set out proposed steps for the Government to create a stronger relationship with the voluntary sector.[24]

In 2002, the Volunteer Sector Initiative Secretariat, a working group funded by the Canadian Government, released a report asserting that contemporary charities do not sit within the Elizabethan concepts of charity, and concluded that it would be necessary to broaden the scope of advocacy by charities.[25]

On the other hand, there has also been call for the status quo in charity law. The Carter Commission commented that, at least for tax purposes, the *Pemsel* definition of charity appeared to be satisfactory.[26] Although this is perhaps not a

19 Kitching, 'Charitable Purpose', 8, citing *Vancouver Society of Immigrant and Visible Minority Women* v. *Minister of National Revenue*, [197].
20 Kitching, 'Charitable Purpose', 8, citing *Vancouver Society of Immigrant and Visible Minority Women* v. *Minister of National Revenue*, [197].
21 Emma Gilchrist, 'Canada's Charity Law Needs Reform: Report', Desmog, Canada, *The Tyee: News, Culture, Solutions,* 25 March 2015. http://thetyee.ca/News/2015/03/25/Charity-Law-Report-2015/ accessed 1 August 2016.
22 Kitching, 'Charitable Purpose', 8, referring to Arthur Drache and Frances K. Boyle, *Charities, Public Benefit and the Canadian Income Tax System* (Brisbane/Ottawa: Commercial Services Office (Queensland University of Technology), 1998).
23 Kitching, 'Charitable Purpose', 8–9, referring to Panel on Accountability and Governance in the Voluntary Sector, *Building on Strength: Improving Governance and Accountability in Canada's Voluntary Sector* (1999). http://sectorsource.ca/sites/default/files/resources/files/2458_Book.pdf accessed 1 August 2016.
24 Elson, 'Short History', 54–5.
25 Kitching, 'Charitable Purpose', 9, referring to Volunteer Sector Initiative Secretariat, 'Advocacy – The Sound of Citizen's Voices', September 2002, www.vsi-isbc.org/eng/policy/pdf/position_paper.pdf [accessed 1 Aug. 2016].
26 Broder, *Legal Definition of Charity*, 9, referring to Government of Canada, *Royal Commission on Taxation*, Ottawa, Government Report (Ottawa: Queen's Printer, 1966), vol. 4, 132.

surprising conservative stance, considering that, generally speaking, the Carter Commission favoured equitable tax treatment for revenue sources, so to permit charities to receive favourable treatment, would not meet this requirement.[27]

A 1983 research paper for the Policy Coordination Directorate of the Federal Secretary of State Department canvassed arguments in favour, and against, of the legislative codification of the definition of charity, although it did not explicitly favour or reject either contention.[28]

The Ontario Law Reform Commission, in 1996, concluded that it would be simpler to permit charity law to evolve through the common law, rather than impose legislative reform, and concluded generally that attempting to define exactly what a charity is would likely hinder judicial making, rather than assist it.[29] However, there are issues with this approach, because Canadian courts have asserted that they can only make incremental changes, and will leave comprehensive legal changes to Parliament.[30] Further, historically, the Supreme Court rarely considers charity law cases, having only dealt with three cases where status as a charity has been an issue. Thus, this appears to be a self-limiting approach.[31] Indeed, when courts have been able to consider such issues, they have tended to express their views in line with the conservative position of the CRA, as opposed to taking a liberal view of the legislation.[32]

Thus, charity law in Canada remains rather more conservative than some of its fellow jurisdictions, with the scope of accepted purposes of charities often being narrowly construed, and as the law stands, 'may encourage charitable resources to be committed to a narrow range of non-controversial endeavours'.[33] Indeed, the litigation costs of challenging for a more expansive charitable mandate may in fact serve to discourage development of charity law.[34]

(ii) Canadian charity law legislation

One of the key legislative milestones in Canadian charity law was the introduction of the Income War Tax Act in 1917. This Act was introduced because it was

27 Broder, *Legal Definition of Charity*, 9.
28 Broder, *Legal Definition of Charity*, 9, referring to Neil Brooks, *Charities: The Legal Framework* (Ottawa: Policy Coordination Directorate (Secretary of State – Canada), 1983).
29 Broder, *Legal Definition of Charity*, 10, referring to Ontario Law Reform Commission, *Report on the Law of Charities*, 165; and Kitching, 'Charitable Purpose', 9, referring to the same report.
30 Kitching, 'Charitable Purpose', 9.
31 Peter Broder, 'Pemsel Case Foundation Launched to Foster Canadian Charity Law', *The Philanthropist* 25(4) (2014), 209, referring to *Guaranty Trust Company of Canada* v. *Minister of National Revenue; Vancouver Society of Immigrant and Visible Minority Women* v. *Minister of National Revenue; Amateur Youth Soccer Association* v. *Canada (Revenue Agency)* [2007] 3 SCR 217.
32 David Stevens and Margaret Mason, 'Tides Canada Initiatives Society: Charitable Venture Organizations: A New Infrastructure Model for Canadian Registered Charities', *The Philanthropist* 23(2) (2010), 102.
33 Kitching, 'Charitable Purpose', 4.
34 Ibid.

evident to the Federal Government that funds were needed for the First World War veterans and their families, and the Act provided unlimited income tax deductions for donations to designated war charities. While the portion pertaining to war charities was repealed in 1920, the precedent had been set, and a limited tax deduction to hospitals, asylums, and related charities continued. An amendment to the Income War Tax Act made in 1930 made provision for tax deductions for donations to churches, universities, colleges, schools, or hospitals. Fewer than 30 days after this amendment was introduced, the Government moved to replace the named institutions with the expression 'any charitable organization', which was defined by English law. That meant that, for the first time, a universal tax deduction was introduced for any type of charitable donation in Canada.[35]

In response to a proliferation of foundations, some of which were set up to benefit benefactors, charitable foundations were defined explicitly in An Act to Amend the Income Tax Act 1950,[36] and the Income Tax Act reforms 1972 made some minor amendments to the 1950 Act, in response to the report of the Carter Commission. Further reforms were made resulting in the Income Tax Act reforms 1976, and An Act to Amend the Income Tax Act and related statutes 1984.[37]

To this day, charity law in Canada does not have its own legislation. Instead, the federal Income Tax Act 1985 (ITA),[38] which is a large and complex document, makes provision for tax exemptions and tax deductibility for registered charities, and dictates the process by which an organisation can seek charitable status in Canada.[39] It is the current sole related statute with federal application within Canada relating to charity law.[40] It places responsibility for registration in the hands of the CRA, meaning the CRA has key policing functions.[41]

The rules governing the regulation of charities within the Act are sparsely stated, and have also built up over several major and minor legislative reforms. It is said that these reforms have paid insufficient attention to policy coherence, or logical flow, leading to a conceptually complex and vague regulatory regime, which is subject to overt administrative discretion.[42] The Act itself may also limit the evolution of charity law because 'the scheme of the ITA does not support a

35 Elson, 'Short History', 43–4.
36 Kerry O'Halloran, *Charity Law and Social Inclusion: An International Study* (Oxon. and New York: Routledge, 2007), 348–49.
37 Kerry O'Halloran, Myles McGregor-Lowndes, and Karla W Simon, *Charity Law & Social Policy: National and International Perspectives on the Functions of Law Relating to Charities*, vol. 10 (Netherlands: Springer, 2008), 438, also referring to Government of Canada, 'Royal Commission on Taxation', 1966.
38 Income Tax Act RSC 1985.
39 Kathryn Bromley, 'The Definition of Religion in Charity Law in the Age of Fundamental Human Rights', *The International Journal of Not-for-Profit Law* 3(1) (September 2000), 3–4.
40 Kerry O'Halloran, *The Profits of Charity: International Perspectives on the Law Governing the Involvement of Charities in Commerce* (New York: Oxford University Press, 2012), 325.
41 O'Halloran, McGregor-Lowndes, and Simon, *Charity Law & Social Policy*, 455.
42 Stevens and Mason, 'Tides Canada Initiatives Society', 102.

wide expansion of the definition of charity',[43] which echoes earlier concerns regarding Canada's alleged antiquated charity laws. When coupled with the CRA's alleged 'predilection for over-cautious interpretation of the law',[44] this leads inevitably to a limited way of achieving real policy change within charity law, even though there does appear to be evidence to support a more proactive approach for institutional and legislative evolution.

Section 149.1 of the ITA provides rules for the tax treatment of registered charities, although it does not provide a definition of charity. In the absence of statutory definition they rely on common law tests for charitable purposes that have their basis in the historical English legislation, the Statute of Charitable Uses 1601, and its Preamble,[45] and the House of Lords' case *Commissioners for Special Purposes of Income Tax* v. *Pemsel*; charitable purposes will be addressed later in the chapter.[46]

There are two basic requirements for registration under the ITA that may be deduced under s 248(1), those being the purposes and activities of an entity must be charitable, and all of the entity's resources must be devoted to those activities.[47]

(iii) Canadian Revenue Agency

The Canadian Revenue Agency (CRA) 'is the gatekeeper to charitable status'.[48] It is asserted that Canada reflects the 'classic state-dominated regulatory regime focused on the goal of ensuring charitable status funding is dedicated to charitable purposes while protecting the integrity of the tax system'.[49] Indeed, it is only since 2000 that the Charities Directorate of the CRA has initiated any type of 'soft' regulations, general charity education, or intermediary sanctions. Even with such introductions, it is said that the CRA still restricts charity education to ensuring that entities meet regulatory requirements, as opposed to general governance or operational guidance.[50] Thus, for instance, in comparison with the Charity Commission for England and Wales, the CRA is seen as more focused on regulatory control than providing support to entities.[51]

---

43 Parachin, 'Legal Privilege', 67, citing *Amateur Youth Soccer Association* v. *Canada (Revenue Agency)*, [13].

44 Levasseur, 'Name of Charity', 185.

45 See Chapters 1 and 3 for further discussion.

46 *Commissioners for Special Purposes of Income Tax* v. *Pemsel*, 583; Kitching, 'Charitable Purpose', 1–2; Broder, *Legal Definition of Charity*, 4.

47 Bromley, 'Definition of Religion', 4; see also *Vancouver Society of Immigrant and Visible Minority Women* v. *Minister of National Revenue*, 109; General Requirements for Charitable Registration, Canada Revenue Agency, Guidance CG-017, www.cra -arc.gc.ca/chrts-gvng/chrts/plcy/cgd/gnrlrqrmnts-eng.html [accessed 4 Aug. 2016].

48 O'Halloran, McGregor-Lowndes, and Simon, *Charity Law & Social Policy*, 455.

49 Phillips, 'Shining Light', 888.

50 Elson, 'Origin of Species', 88–9.

51 Susan D. Phillips, '"Canadian Leapfrog": From Regulating Charitable Fundraising to Co-Regulating Good Governance', *Voluntas* 23(3) (2012), 819.

In determining the charitability of an organisation, the CRA will consider the purposes and activities of the organisation, as all, generally speaking, must be charitable, and the requisite number of its resources must be devoted exclusively to those charities.[52] The CRA also requires registered charities to provide annual reporting, which are made publicly available on is website, and it audits for compliance, and sanctions for non-compliance.[53] Therefore, the CRA acts as the key charity regulator, although, its primary function is in relation to the administration of the ITA, as opposed to 'a broader role of nurturing, governance and accountability of the sector'.[54] For instance, the publicly available financial reports, called T3010s, while at first sight, reflect greater transparency, have a primary focus on financial data, with only limited information on programming, and no requirement to report on governance or public benefit results. Thus, with a tax agency as a regulator, while there is a growing emphasis on transparency, the focus still remains on financial reporting and ensuring regulatory compliance.[55]

However, such a focus is not necessarily to be criticised. The CRA is responsible for preserving the integrity of the federal income tax base, and if such matters are not managed appropriately, or balanced incorrectly, then tax burdens may shift unfairly to others, and a healthy tax system is key to ensuring the financial health of a state.[56]

Nonetheless, having a tax authority as the relevant decision-maker and regulator with regard to charity regulation is not always thought to be the best approach. It has been argued that tax officials will inherently focus on tax, as opposed to charitability, thus potentially causing a conflict of interest. For instance, the Supreme Court of British Columbia case of *Blair Longley* v. *MNR*[57] demonstrates the possible conflicts of interest between the two bodies. In this case, Blair Longley developed a scheme whereby individuals could make payments to a registered political party and have the funds flow back for their personal benefit. This would reduce personal tax liabilities. On inquiring with the tax authorities as to their view on such a scheme, he was informed that it was illegal, although the case reports that this was not in fact correct. Longley later discovered this error, and alleging that he had been misled, sued successfully. This illustrates a possible institutional bias against tax expenditures, although it could also be argued that this is merely a lack of correct training and/or expertise in tax officials, as opposed to deliberate bias.

52 O'Halloran, McGregor-Lowndes, and Simon, *Charity Law & Social Policy*, 455.
53 Phillips, 'Shining Light', 888.
54 Helen Irvine, Christine Ryan, and Myles McGregor-Lowndes, 'An International Comparison of Not-for-Profit Accounting Regulation', Queensland University of Technology, conference proceedings, 2010, http://apira2010.econ.usyd.edu.au/conference_proceedings/APIRA-2010-092-Irvine-Not-for-profit-accounting-regulation.pdf [accessed 4 Aug. 2016].
55 Phillips, 'Shining Light', 888–900.
56 Bridge, 'Law Governing Advocacy by Charitable Organizations', 8.
57 Arthur BC Drache, 'Canadian Charity Tribunal: A Proposal for Implementation' (Brisbane: Queensland University of Technology, 1996), 16, referring to *Blair Longley* v. *MNR* 1999 Carswell BC 1657.

Another issue with the CRA being the lead regulator is the inherent confidentiality associated with tax information. While it is acknowledged that this is generally required when it comes to an entity's financial matters, this lack of transparency can spill over into matters such as guidelines for registration, administrative issues, and a general lack of transparency within the sector.[58] While it is acknowledged that the CRA has made concerted efforts to be more transparent in its administrative and decision-making duties, there are still inherent limitations with regard to tax, and as such, 'it is still required to maintain privacy on certain tax-related items'.[59]

Nonetheless, there are signs that the CRA appears more willing to adopt a more positive administrative function, and to undertake policy discussion on charitable criteria, as well as endeavouring to act more transparently and proactively. One such change is awareness of the need to work across federal government departments, not just financial departments. For instance, the CRA now consults with the Department of Health, not just the Department of Finance in relation to alternative medicine as a purpose that may fall under the fourth head of charity in relation to the promotion of health. This consultation occurred to diversify the knowledge base of the CRA in order to make informed decisions about the benefits, or otherwise, of alternative medicine in a contemporary society.[60]

In addition, the CRA has not only improved its handling times and responses for charitable applications through improved channels of communication and training programmes, it has also posted many hundreds of policy documents on its website to assist its organisational and administrative processes. While the CRA is still required to apply the ITA, and cannot change the legislation, its attempts at issuing policy statements and guides do assist in developing more transparent registration guidelines and thus better understanding within the sector.[61]

Thus, while the CRA may still be subject to criticism, there is evidence that the institutional machinery that supports charity in Canada is endeavouring to improve its administrative and policy processes, which must go some way to restoring credibility and public support within the sector.

C Charitable purposes

The CRA assesses eligibility for charity registration under the ITA using a two-stage test to determine if an organisation:[62]

- is constituted for purposes (sometimes referred to as 'objects') that are exclusively charitable and define the scope of activities that can be engaged in by the organization; and

---

58 Drache, 'Canadian Charity Tribunal', 19.
59 Levasseur, 'Name of Charity', 194.
60 Ibid.
61 Ibid.
62 CRA, 'How to Draft Purposes for Charitable Registration', CG-019, 25 July 2013, www.cra-arc.gc.ca/chrts-gvng/chrts/plcy/cgd/drftprpss-eng.html#N103DF [accessed 15 Aug. 2016].

- subject to limited exceptions, devotes its resources to charitable activities that further those purposes.

'It remains the law of Canada today that no purpose is charitable at law unless it fall under one of the *Pemsel* categories',[63] which are the relief of poverty, the advancement of education, the advancement of religion, or 'certain other purposes beneficial to the community in a way the law regards as charitable'.[64] As determined in earlier chapters, these categories derive from the Preamble to the Statute of Charitable Uses 1601, and subsequently from Lord Macnaghten's determination of the heads of charity in *Commissioners for Special Purposes of the Income Tax* v. *Pemsel*.[65]

The Canadian approach to interpreting the four heads of charity, unsurprisingly, echoes many of the common law approaches in our respective jurisdictions. For instance, relieving poverty 'means providing relief to the poor. The poor are not only the destitute, but anyone lacking essential amenities available to the general public'.[66] To advance education, the CRA requires that a purpose should be 'formally training the mind, advancing the knowledge or abilities of the recipient, or improving a useful branch of human knowledge'.[67]

Purposes that advance religion will manifest, promote, sustain, or increase 'belief in a religion's three key attributes, which are: faith in a higher unseen power such as a God, Supreme Being, or Entity; worship or reverence; and a particular and comprehensive system of doctrines and observances'.[68]

With regard to the fourth head the CRA acknowledges that '[c]ommon law courts have identified various purposes that are beneficial to the community in a way the law regards as charitable under the broad fourth category,'[69] and as a result, Canadian courts observe the same approach. In addition, and in line with common law approaches, a purpose must be exclusively charitable.[70]

Utilising the same methodology of earlier chapters relating to specific jurisdictions, this chapter will consider a selection of key cases to consider charitable purposes in Canada. This is because such '"leading cases"' are a vital part of the chaotic-looking case law tradition'[71] and provide a useful insight into the jurisprudential trends of charitable purposes in Canada.

It has been said that the first three heads of charity represent a prima facie early obstacle to organisations' obtaining charitable status, even though they may

63 Parachin, 'Legal Privilege', 39.
64 CRA, 'How to Draft Purposes for Charitable Registration'.
65 *Commissioners for Special Purposes of Income Tax* v. *Pemsel*.
66 CRA, 'How to Draft Purposes for Charitable Registration'.
67 Ibid.
68 Ibid.
69 Ibid.
70 Parachin, 'Legal Privilege', 39, referring to *Vancouver Society of Immigrant and Visible Minority Women* v. *Minister of National Revenue*, [154]–[158].
71 John Mummery, '*The Commissioners for Special Purposes of the Income Tax* v. *Pemsel*', *Charity Law and Practice Review* 16(1) (2013–14), 1.

appear deserving of it. This is because these purpose 'encompass historical social priorities that do not necessarily reflect current needs'.[72] Further, the 'scope of the accepted purposes of charities is often narrowly defined, and encompasses engagement only in non-contentious societal problems carried out in conventional ways'.[73] This means that as the law stands in Canada, the 'law does not promote innovation in the delivery of services within ... charity'.[74]

It should also be noted, as mentioned earlier, that charity cases are rarely litigated in Canada. This may be in part due to the large expense required to do so, but also it may be because when litigation has occurred, it is common for the Government to be victorious,[75] which may dissuade claimants. This too may lessen the opportunity for Canadian charity law to reflect the realities of contemporary society.

We will begin with perhaps one of the most cited charity cases in Canada, that of *Vancouver Society of Immigrant and Visible Minority Women* v. *MNR*,[76] perhaps in part because it was the first decision of the Supreme Court with regard to the interpretation of the meaning of 'charity' in over 25 years. Importantly, it also addressed the question as to whether the current definition of 'advancement of education' needed to be updated in light of advancements within contemporary society.[77] As a result, this is a fundamental case within Canadian charity jurisprudence.

D Vancouver Society of Immigrant and Visible Minority Women v. MNR

Iacobucci J, delivering the judgment for the majority, stated that this case presented an opportunity to reconsider Canadian charity law for the first time in 25 years, and also that the Court faced 'the interesting questions of whether the time for modernization has come, and if so, what form that modernization should take'.[78] Thus the stage was set as to the appropriateness of Canadian charity law in a contemporary context, and we will focus specifically on advancement of education to consider this matter.

Of relevance to this chapter, the Society's purposes included, inter alia, the provision of educational forums, classes, and workshops, to immigrant women in order to assist them with finding or obtaining employment.

His Honour noted that Canada has traditionally given 'advancement of education' a fairly restricted meaning. For instance, in *Positive Action Against*

---

72 Kitching, 'Charitable Purpose', 4.
73 Ibid.
74 Ibid.
75 O'Halloran, McGregor-Lowndes, and Simon, *Charity Law & Social Policy*, 435.
76 *Vancouver Society of Immigrant and Visible Minority Women* v. *Minister of National Revenue*.
77 O'Halloran, McGregor-Lowndes, and Simon, *Charity Law & Social Policy*, 436.
78 *Vancouver Society of Immigrant and Visible Minority Women* v. *Minister of National Revenue*, [127].

Pornography v. *MNR*,[79] Stone JA observed that it has generally been limited to the 'formal training of the mind', or the 'improvement of a useful branch of human knowledge'. However, his Honour was of the view that the law in this area should be modified, and that it was worth considering a more expansive approach, as considered in *IRC* v. *McMullen*:[80]

> Both the legal concept of charity, and within it the educated man's ideas about education, are not static, but moving and changing. Both change with changes in ideas about social values. Both have evolved with the years. In particular in applying the law to contemporary circumstances it is extremely dangerous to forget that thoughts concerning the scope and width of education differed in the past greatly from those which are now generally accepted.

Such an approach has meant that, at least in England, trusts for the promotion of physical education alongside formal education, as well as trusts for the promotion of conferences, have been found to be educational.[81] However, as Iacobucci J pointed out, Canada too has, on occasion, recognised non-traditional educational activities as charitable, for instance, a summer camp to teach children about their heritage and ancestral culture.[82] Therefore, he believed there was much to be gained by adopting a more inclusive approach to education, because the traditional Canadian approach appeared unduly restrictive. Indeed, there seemed no logical or reasoned principle why the purpose could not include informal training initiatives that might include teaching necessary life skills. This ruling is important, therefore, because of the finding that the advancement of education is not restricted to teaching, but also includes research, so long as this is of educational value to the person carrying out the research, or advancing knowledge, which could then be taught. It may also include advancing education through, for instance, workshops and seminars, as well as the provision of information and information for narrowly defined purposes, such as obtaining employment.[83]

This, therefore, suggests a progressive approach in Canadian jurisprudence, and while this might be correct, prima facie, Iacobucci J, in *Vancouver Society*, was

79 *Vancouver Society of Immigrant and Visible Minority Women* v. *Minister of National Revenue*, [161], referring to *Positive Action Against Pornography* v. *Minister of National Revenue* 1988 CarswellNat 274, 1988 CarswellNat 689, [1988] 1 CTC 232, [1988] 2 FC 340, 29 ETR 92, 49 DLR (4th) 74, 83 NR 214, 99 TTC 6186, 9 ACWS (3d) 52.

80 *Vancouver Society of Immigrant and Visible Minority Women* v. *Minister of National Revenue*, [166], citing *Inland Revenue Commissioners* v. *McMullen* [1981] 1 AC 1, 15; see also *Re Hopkins' Will Trusts* [1964] 3 All ER 46.

81 *Vancouver Society of Immigrant and Visible Minority Women* v. *Minister of National Revenue*, [167], referring to *Inland Revenue Commissioners* v. *McMullen and Re Koeppler Will Trusts* [1986] 1 Ch 423 (CA), respectively.

82 *Vancouver Society of Immigrant and Visible Minority Women* v. *Minister of National Revenue*, [167], referring to *Re Societa Unita and Town of Gravenhurst* (1977) 16 OR (2d) 785 (HC), aff'd (1978) 6 MPLR 172 (Ont Div Ct).

83 O'Halloran, *Profits of Charity*, 336, referring also to *Wood* v. *R* [1977] 6 WWR 273 (Alta TD) and *Seafarers Training Institute* v. *Williamsburg* (1982) 39 OR (2d) 370 (TD).

quick to note that such an approach would actually amount to no more than an incremental change to the common law, and Canada had already approved such changes.[84] Therefore, Canadian charity jurisprudence still appears to be more restrictive in its characterisation of advancement of education in comparison with other jurisdictions, thus doing little to assuage the concerns about Canadian charity law.

Then, in 2007, the Supreme Court, in *Amateur Youth Soccer Association* v. *Canada Revenue Agency*,[85] once again demonstrated its conservative stance regarding charity.

E Amateur Youth Soccer Association v. Canada Revenue Agency

Despite the apparent brevity of the judgment, this is still an important case jurisprudentially within Canadian charity law.[86]

The case concerned an amateur soccer association, the AYSA. The CRA denied it registration, asserting that courts had not held the promotion of sports to be a charitable purpose.

The AYSA claimed its purposes fell under the fourth head of charity, that of other purposes beneficial to the community. It did concede that older English cases supported the contention that 'mere sport' cannot be charitable, as recognised in *Re Nottage*,[87] but it argued that the time was ripe for Canada to recognise the promotion of amateur sports that involved the pursuit of physical fitness.[88] While the consensus is that 'mere sports' cannot be charitable, the Court in *AYSA* did acknowledge that *Re Laidlaw Foundation*[89] held that the promotion of amateur sport involving the pursuit of physical fitness could be charitable. However, the Court in *AYSA* stated '*Laidlaw* appears to be an anomalous case, based on statutory provision which adopts only part of the common law test, and inconsistent with this Court's holding in *Vancouver Society* that public benefit alone is not enough'.[90]

Further, the Court added that while *Re Nottage* was rather perfunctory, and should not perhaps be regarded as 'an unsurmountable barrier',[91] the common link between all the sporting cases, *Laidlaw* notwithstanding, is that while participating in a sport is generally beneficial, those benefits alone are not sufficient to demonstrate charitability.

---

84 *Vancouver Society of Immigrant and Visible Minority Women* v. *Minister of National Revenue*, [168], referring to *Watkins* v. *Olafson* [1989] 2 SCR 750 and *R* v. *Salituro* [1991] 3 SCR 654.
85 *Amateur Youth Soccer Association* v. *Canada (Revenue Agency)* 2007 SCC 42, [2007] SCR 217; O'Halloran, McGregor-Lowndes, and Simon, *Charity Law & Social Policy*, 437.
86 Parachin, 'Legal Privilege', 44.
87 *Amateur Youth Soccer Association* v. *Canada (Revenue Agency)*, [33] and [34], referring to *re Nottage* [1895] 2 Ch 649 (CA).
88 *Amateur Youth Soccer Association* v. *Canada (Revenue Agency)*, [33] and [34].
89 Ibid., [34] and [37]; *Re LaidLaw Foundation*, 13 DLR (4th) 491, 523 (Ontario Divisional Court (ODC)).
90 *Amateur Youth Soccer Association* v. *Canada (Revenue Agency)*, [38], referring to *Re LaidLaw Foundation; Vancouver Society of Immigrant and Visible Minority Women* v. *Minister of National Revenue*.
91 *Amateur Youth Soccer Association* v. *Canada (Revenue Agency)*, [40].

Indeed, the Court was not unsympathetic to the proposition that promoting fitness should be charitable, but in addition to there being limited authority to support this, the AYSA's objects did not reflect that fitness was a main object; it was a by-product. Finding a by-product to be charitable would risk the definition of charity growing beyond that which is recognised at common law.[92]

Indeed, the Court acknowledged that the ITA 'does not support a wide expansion of the definition of charity',[93] thus the Court appeared to be limited in its ability to broaden the definition beyond that which was currently recognised and thus the AYSA failed in its appeal.

This appears to be a rational interpretation of charity law, but it has been criticised. Absent from the *AYSA* judgment is any consideration by the Court of how amateur sport 'falls short of a conceptual or philosophical ideal of "charity"'.[94] Further, the Court failed to 'apply the analogical method of reasoning that is normally applied when courts are called upon to resolve whether the fourth *Pemsel* head should be expanded to include a novel purpose'.[95] In other words, the usual approach for a court is to consider whether the purpose at issue is within the spirit and intendment of the Preamble of the Statute of Elizabeth, or analogous to other purposes within the Preamble, or one found charitable at common law.[96]

It is true that the Court in *AYSA* did make reference to the trend of sports cases, but it is asserted that this was done solely to establish that courts had previously never found the promotion of sports to be a charitable purpose under the fourth head. There was no evidence that the Court considered any contemporary social, moral, or economical contexts so that an incremental analogy may be drawn to establish a charitable purpose.[97] As just one example, for instance, soaring obesity levels in Canada may have been a sufficient contemporary social pressure for the Court to consider. According to the Canadian Obesity Network, six million Canadians are said to be obese, and one of the key Government concerns is the levels of stress this places on healthcare in funding obesity-related disorders, among other issues.[98]

It is asserted that the basis on which the Court ultimately made its conclusions rested on issues with potential tax revenue losses:[99]

> The government submits that 21 percent of all non-profit organizations in the country are sports and recreation organizations, and that the potential recognition of these organizations as charities could have a significant impact on the income

92 Ibid., [40]–[41].
93 Ibid., [43].
94 Parachin, 'Legal Privilege', 47.
95 Ibid.
96 Parachin, 'Legal Privilege', 47–8, referring to *Vancouver Society of Immigrant and Visible Minority Women* v. *Minister of National Revenue*, fn. 12.
97 Parachin, 'Legal Privilege', 48.
98 Canadian Obesity Network, 'Obesity in Canada', Canadian Obesity Network (2017), www.obesitynetwork.ca/obesity-in-canada [accessed 22 Aug. 2016].
99 Parachin, 'Legal Privilege', 48, citing *Amateur Youth Soccer Association* v. *Canada (Revenue Agency)*, [44].

tax system. I agree with the government that this would seem to be closer to wholesale reform than incremental change, and is best left to Parliament.

Indeed, while it may be desirable to recognise sports associations as being charitable, for policy reasons, the Court concluded that this is a decision best left to Parliament, not courts.[100] Although it is a pity that the Court did not expand on what type of policy reasons, as this may have provided some answer to the criticism that it did not consider 'any contemporary social, moral or economical contexts'.

What this suggests is that the Court could not expand the definition of charitable purpose within this context because of the possible tax revenue repercussions, indicating that financial 'expenditure considerations played an overt and decisive role in this reasoning'.[101]

This is perhaps not surprising – Canada reflects the 'classic state-dominated regulatory regime focused on the goal of ensuring charitable status funding is dedicated to charitable purposes while protecting the integrity of the tax system'.[102] In other words, tax revenue is of paramount importance in charity law governance. Thus, it is not inconceivable that a Canadian court, when faced with such an apparent decision to make an incremental change to the law will defer to the legislature. Further, it could be argued that unfortunately the AYSA itself did not enable such a change in charitable purpose. This was because its objects did not reflect that health and fitness were its main object; perhaps if they had, then the Court may have approached the question differently. The reality may be that the Court in *AYSA* had limited room to expand charitable purpose in sporting activities with this specific case.

Regardless of the specific factors involved in this case, what it does do is reflect the continued trend in Canadian charity law of adopting a conservative approach to charitable purpose.

F Aboriginal populations

Judicial discussion on matters relating to aboriginal populations also provide opportunities to examine charitable purposes within a unique context-specific environment, to which we turn now. Two cases are of interest – *Gull Bay Development Corporation* v. *R*,[103] and *Native Communications* v. *Minister of National Revenue*.[104]

G Gull Bay Development Corporation v. R

In this case, 'the special role of Aboriginal peoples'[105] was discussed within a charitable context. The objects of the organisation were to, inter alia, promote the

100 *Amateur Youth Soccer Association* v. *Canada (Revenue Agency)*, [44].
101 Parachin, 'Legal Privilege', 48.
102 Phillips, 'Shining Light', 888.
103 *Gull Bay Development Corporation* v. *R* [1984] 2 FC 3.
104 *Native Communications* v. *Minister of National Revenue* [1986] 3 FC 471.
105 O'Halloran, McGregor-Lowndes, and Simon, *Charity Law & Social Policy*, 436.

economic and social welfare of members of the Gull Bay Indian Reserve; and provide support for charitable organisations engaged in assisting their economic and social development. The plaintiffs established a commercial logging operation that provided employment; trained Indian students; maintained public buildings; provided funds for programmes to assist those in need on the reserve; and funding for educational and other assistance activities. The defendant contended that the Corporation carried out a logging business with a view to profit, meaning that, if that were correct, the plaintiff organisation was not a not-for-profit organisation under s 149(1)(f) of the Income Tax Act.

There was no doubt, for Walsh J, that the logging operations of the Corporation were extensive, and that they provided considerable revenue, of which much was held in surplus. However, for Walsh J, the real issue in this case appeared to be that the Corporation was not set up for commercial activities, although the motive for forming a corporation may have been that it was desirable to provide employment and training to those Indians on the Reserve who were previously unemployed. This would be done through commercial activities, which would provide not just employment, but also valuable social and charitable activities on the Reserve. It was actually more effective to carry on these activities through a corporation, for instance through enabling effective negotiations on how the lumber was cut.

Indeed, it was the policy of the Department of Indian Affairs to encourage Indian bands to become self-reliant, and to improve their social and living conditions on reserves. This case provided evidence that many social and living improvements had been made within the Reserve as a result of the funds derived from the lumbering operations, as well as providing employment opportunities for those who would have been receiving state welfare.[106]

In his Honour's view, the 'social and welfare activities of [the] plaintiff are not a cloak to avoid payment of taxation on a commercial enterprise but are the real objectives of the corporation'.[107] As a result the special position of the Aboriginal peoples in this case was fundamental in the Court's determination of the charitability of the Corporation, and it was held that because of the particular facts of the case, the Corporation was operated exclusively for charitable purposes, even though it raised funds for this purpose through its commercial lumbering operations.

H Native Communications v. Minister of National Revenue

In this case, the Federal Court of Appeal 'placed the common law definition of charity within a twentieth century Canadian context'.[108] In this case, the appellant was a non-profit organisation, whose purposes included developing radio and television productions relevant to the native people of British Columbia; training native people as communication workers; and delivering information pertinent to

106 *Gull Bay Development Corporation* v. *R*, [34]–[38].
107 Ibid., [38].
108 Ellen Zwiebel, 'A Truly Canadian Definition of Charity and a Lesson in Drafting Charitable Purpose', *The Philanthropist* 7(1) (1987), 4.

native people. The registration was refused because it was said that their objects went beyond being exclusively charitable.

Stone J, echoing the earlier considerations of Walsh J *Gull Bay Development Corporation*, noted the special position of Aboriginal peoples within a Canadian context. He observed that this case cannot be decided 'without taking account of the special legal position in Canadian society occupied by the Indian people'.[109]

The objects of this organisation were directed towards members of Indian bands scattered throughout British Columbia, and while the respondent argued that the newspaper merely provided news, Stone J rejected this contention, specifically in relation to the cultural context of the Indian peoples. He noted that the newspaper made its Indian readers aware of cultural activities in the wider Indian community, and of attempts to foster native languages, ancient crafts, music, and storytelling. This is likely to instil ancestral pride and promote cohesion among the native communities that may otherwise be missing. The radio and television programmes were also designed along similar lines.[110]

Of note is that his Honour chose to reject English authorities, because they did not concern 'activities directed to aboriginal people'.[111] Rather, he chose to acknowledge Lord Wilberforce's comments in *Scottish Burial Reform and Cremation Society Ltd* v. *Glasgow Corporation* where his Lordship stated 'the law of charity is a moving subject'.[112] As a result, Stone J concluded that 'our duty must be to see whether in the circumstances ... the purposes fall within ... the fourth head of charities'.[113] He noted that there was no Canadian case law to assist because of the specific circumstances of this case, although the Australian case of *Re Mathew* provided assistance, where O'Bryan J observed that 'Australian aborigines are notoriously ... a class which ... is in need of protection and assistance'.[114]

Stone J concluded that the Canadian state is authorised, and does play a role in protecting and assisting Indian people because, unlike the majority of Canadian citizens, Indians are a people 'set apart for particular assistance and protection in many aspects of their lives'.[115] That was a chief factor in determining whether the purposes of the organisation fell within the fourth head of charity. As a result, his Honour concluded that the purposes in question were beneficial to the Indian community within the spirit and intendment of the Statute of Elizabeth, and thus charitable.[116]

---

109 *Native Communications* v. *Minister of National Revenue* [1986] 3 FC 471 (CA), 481, referring to Constitution Act, 1982 [Schedule B, Canada Act 1982, 1982 c. 11 (UK)].
110 *Native Communications* v. *Minister of National Revenue*, 481–2.
111 Ibid., 482.
112 *Native Communications* v. *Minister of National Revenue*, 480, citing *Scottish Burial Reform & Cremation Society Ltd* v. *Glasgow Corporation* [1968] AC 138 (HL), 154.
113 *Native Communications* v. *Minister of National Revenue*, 482.
114 *Native Communications* v. *Minister of National Revenue*, 482, citing *Re Mathew* [1951] VLR 226 (Aust SC) 232.
115 Ibid., 483.
116 Ibid., 484.

This case echoes the approach taken by the New Zealand Court of Appeal in *Latimer* v. *Commissioner of Inland Revenue*, in which Blanchard J stated, in relation to the indigenous peoples of New Zealand and established English law:[117]

> The common descent of claimant groups is a relationship poles away from the kind of connection which the House of Lords must have been thinking of in the *Oppenheim* case ... There is no indication that the House of Lords had in its contemplation tribal or clan groups of ancient origin. Indeed, it is more likely that the Law Lords had in mind the paradigmatic English approach to family relations.

Thus, Blanchard J, in *Latimer*, indicated that charity law should be considered within its own social context, exactly as Stone J in *Native Communications* endeavoured to do, reflecting the relevance of charity law in a contemporary society.

It is also said that this case emphasised the notion that a charitable purpose may be more easily found where the beneficiaries of the activities that result from the purposes are individuals from groups or communities that are in actual need of charitable assistance.[118] The *Native Communications* case therefore was undoubtedly 'a major step towards modernizing the judicial process of determining what are charitable purposes',[119] which must be welcomed when criticism has been levelled at the Canadian courts for their apparent conservative approach in developing charity law within a modern context.

The final case to be considered is the recent Federal Court of Appeal case of *Credit Counselling Services of Atlantic Canada Inc* v. *Canada (National Revenue)*,[120] in relation, inter alia, to the relief of poverty, the first head of charity.

I Credit Counselling Services of Atlantic Canada Inc v. Canada (National Revenue)

The objects of the appellant included the prevention of poverty and the provision of financial and debt counselling to the community. The Minister of National Revenue had earlier concluded that prevention of poverty was not a recognised charitable purpose.

The Court asserted that the requirement that a purpose for the relief of poverty will be satisfied when the person receiving assistance is in poverty, which is a relative term.

---

117 *Latimer* v. *Commissioner of Inland Revenue* [2002] 3 NZLR 195, [38], referring to *Oppenheim* v. *Tobacco Securities Trust Co Ltd* [1951] AC 297, and *Dingle* v. *Turner* [1972] AC 601.
118 *News to You Canada* v. *Minister of National Revenue* 2011 FCA 192, [22] and [24] (FCA).
119 Zwiebel, 'Canadian Definition of Charity', 4.
120 *Credit Counselling Services of Atlantic Canada Inc* v. *Minister of National Revenue*, 2016 FCA 193.

Thus, counselling, or providing some type of assistance to those in serious financial trouble, may relieve poverty, even if the individuals are not destitute.[121]

The Court dealt with this matter, disappointingly, in a summary manner. It observed that the appellant assisted people who were employed, and had assets, who would not necessarily be thought to be in poverty. The Court gave no further consideration as to what may be construed as being in poverty, whereas in reality there is evidence that a person who 'suffers hardship from a reduction in his circumstances may be a proper object of charity'.[122]

Therefore, it is possible that those individuals may fall within that definition of poverty. However, the Court precluded their inclusion on limited evidence. Further, the Court stated that the activities of the appellant could best be described as relating to the prevention of poverty. Interestingly, the Charities Act 2011 of England and Wales now includes the prevention of poverty as a charitable purpose, to which the Court made reference.[123] However, the Court stated that while England may have taken steps to include such a purpose as being charitable, 'it will require an act of Parliament to add the prevention of poverty as a charitable purpose',[124] thus it was not charitable.

This is an unsurprising decision, because of the generally conservative approach that has traditionally been taken by the Canadian courts, and this case simply reflects that stance. Additionally, what it also does is 'underscore the fact that if there is going to be substantive progress made in expanding the parameters of what is considered to be charitable, it will have to be at the initiative of Parliament;[125] change is unlikely to occur at judicial level.

It could be argued that, from a 'legal perspective, the court's findings in the above decision were correct'.[126] However, 'the result may be considered less than satisfactory from the broader societal perspective'[127] because there is a lack of clarity as to what constitutes relief of poverty in a contemporary context. This means that, in Canada at least, the 'legal distinction between the relief and prevention of poverty is here to stay'.[128]

---

121 *Credit Counselling Services of Atlantic Canada Inc* v. *Minister of National Revenue*, [16], referring to *Vancouver Society of Immigrant and Visible Minority Women* v. *Minister of National Revenue*.

122 Jean Warburton, *Tudor on Charities*, 9th edn (London: Sweet & Maxwell, 2003), 38, referring to *Re Coulhurst* [1951] 1 Ch 661.

123 *Credit Counselling Services of Atlantic Canada Inc* v. *Minister of National Revenue*, [18], referring to Charities Act 2011, s 3(1)(a).

124 Ibid.

125 Jacqueline M. Demczur and Terrance S. Carter, 'FCA Holds That the Prevention of Poverty Is Not a Charitable Purpose', Charity and NFP Law Bulletin No. 390, 25 August 2016, www.carters.ca/pub/bulletin/charity/2016/chylb390.pdf [accessed 31 Aug. 2016].

126 'Prevention vs. Relief of Poverty: Not a Difference without a Distinction in the Eyes of the Law', Bull Housser, July 2016, www.bht.com/resources/prevention-vs-relief-poverty-not-difference-without-distinction-eyes-law [accessed 31 Aug. 2016].

127 Ibid.

128 Ibid.

J Public benefit

The CRA confirms that if an organisation wishes to be registered as a charity under the ITA, it must ensure that its purposes are directed to the public benefit for all the heads of charity, and this involves a two-stage test:[129]

- The first part of the test generally requires that a tangible benefit be conferred directly or indirectly. ...
- The second part of the test requires that the benefit have a public character, that is, to be directed to the public or a sufficient section of the public.

As might be expected, considering the heritage of Canadian charity law, this echoes its fellow jurisdictions, such as New Zealand and England and Wales. In line with this, the CRA confirms that where purposes fall within the first three heads of charity, there is a presumption of public benefit. The presumption, however, will only arise when it has been established that the purposes do fall within these categories.[130] A similar presumption may arise for purposes falling within the fourth head, such as for those purposes that are clear and the benefit is apparent. For example, for provision of healthcare services, or services for the relief of the aged. In other circumstances, it is accepted that the benefit must be proven in relation to purposes under the fourth head.[131]

In assessing purposes under the fourth head, courts, and the CRA, will generally assess purposes following reasoning by analogy. Thus, if an analogy can be found in a factually similar previous case, then benefit will be established.

This is illustrated in the Supreme Court case of *Vancouver Society of Immigrant and Visible Minority Women* v. *MNR*:[132]

> the purpose must be beneficial to the community 'in a way which the law regards as charitable' by coming within the 'spirit and intendment' of the preamble ... if not within its letter, and whether a purpose would ... for the public benefit is to be answered ... the basis of the record before it.

In other words, 'more is required than simple "public benefit"'.[133] This is a narrow task, because a court is 'not called upon "to decide what is beneficial to

---

129 CRA, 'Guidelines for Registering a Charity: Meeting the Public Benefit Test', CPS-024, [3.0], www.cra-arc.gc.ca/chrts-gvng/chrts/plcy/cps/cps-024-eng.html [accessed 31 Aug. 2016]; see also *Vancouver Society of Immigrant and Visible Minority Women* v. *MNR*, [174].

130 CRA, 'Guidelines for Registering a Charity', [3.1.1]; see also Chapter 5 for discussion on the presumption of public benefit.

131 CRA, 'Guidelines for Registering a Charity', [3.1.1], referring to *Everywoman's Health Centre Society* (1988) MNR [1992] 2 FC 52, 60.

132 *Vancouver Society of Immigrant and Visible Minority Women* v. *Minister of National Revenue*, [175], referring to *Native Communications* v. *Minister of National Revenue*, 471, 479–80; see also *Amateur Youth Soccer Association* v. *Canada (Revenue Agency)*, [27].

133 *Vancouver Society of Immigrant and Visible Minority Women* v. *Minister of National Revenue*, [176].

the community in a loose sense, but only what is beneficial *in a way the law regards as charitable*"[134] Thus, Canada confirms that while there are many purposes and activities that may appear, prima facie, to be beneficial to the community in a popular, or general sense, they will not necessarily be beneficial in the legal sense[135] – in other words, 'objects of general public utility'.[136]

134 *Vancouver Society of Immigrant and Visible Minority Women* v. *Minister of National Revenue*, [176], citing *Positive Action Against Pornography* v. *Minister of National Revenue*, 352 (emphasis as source).
135 *Positive Action Against Pornography* v. *Minister of National Revenue*, [11], referring to *Commissioners for Special Purposes of Income Tax* v. *Pemsel*.
136 *Positive Action Against Pornography* v. *Minister of National Revenue*, [11], citing *Morice* v. *Bishop of Durham* (1805) 10 Ves 522.

8 New Zealand

A Introduction

New Zealand was a colony of Great Britain, consequently, 'there are social, legal and political inheritances that followed from the formalisation of this link after the various signings of the Treaty of Waitangi and the British declaration of sovereignty in 1840'.[1]

While New Zealand retains many links with its colonial origins, it has undergone significant charity law reforms in the last few years, and charity is a growing and valuable sector within New Zealand. For example, there are, at the time of writing, 27,919 registered charities in New Zealand, with New Zealand having more registered charities per capita worldwide,[2] reflecting the importance of charitable institutions within New Zealand society.

However, the early days of the New Zealand charitable sector reflected a more laissez-faire philosophy, which may have been in part due to its colonial heritage. For instance, it has been suggested that at the time of colonisation in the 1800s, there was a dichotomy of communalism and pride in self-sufficiency, which was then reflected in New Zealand's charitable regulatory processes. Echoing England's early periods, charitable matters were dealt with on an ad hoc basis, and no regulatory body existed to monitor activities or compliance.[3]

The first charitable organisations to appear were religious in nature, for instance, the Anglican Church Missionary Society, and the Roman Catholic Church, but more secular associations began to emerge in the mid 1800s, including friendly societies, craft unions, and benevolent societies. However, the notion of 'strong individualism and a belief in New Zealand as a "new society", free of entrenched

---

1 Margaret Tennant, Mike O'Brien, and Jackie Sanders, *The History of the Non-Profit Sector in New Zealand* (Wellington: Office for the Community and Voluntary Sector, 2008), 3; Juliet Chevalier-Watts, *Law of Charity* (Wellington: Thomson Reuters, 2014), 16.

2 Andrew Phillips, 'Charities Services "Registration, Deregistration and Applying the Eligibility Test"', Lecture given at Te Piringa – Faculty of Law, University of Waikato, 4 October 2016.

3 Donald Poirier, *Charity Law in New Zealand* (www.charities.govt.nz, 2013), 88–9.

poverty and the ills of the "old world""[4] appeared to work against any emergence of formal and organised charities.

In the early colonial days, the focus, therefore, appeared to be on self-sufficiency with limited state intervention. Nonetheless, altruism was widespread within communities, and in the absence of state assistance, private philanthropy stepped into the breaches,[5] and self-help and family support were thought to be more important than government assistance or formal charity when it came to meeting social needs.[6]

Even in modern times, it is said that the charitable sector 'remains characterised by a "partnership ethos between government and community"'.[7] It is asserted that government has sufficient resources to deliver many of the services that are performed by charities, but government appears to prefer to pay, and subsidise charities. Indeed, much of charities' income is derived directly from government.[8] This approach is apparently consistent with 'neoliberal doctrines whereby government purchases services from various and competing agencies, including traditional charities, rather than providing them directly'.[9]

That is not to say, however, that there are no statutory provisions relating to charitable regulation in New Zealand, even in the early colonial days, and it is to this that the chapter now turns.

B A potted history of charitable regulation in New Zealand

The early colonial experiences of promoting self-sufficiency and self-reliance, and with the encouragement of government to look after their families, led to an early proliferation of societies and associations. This led to the Unclassified Societies Registration Act 1895, and the Incorporated Societies Act 1908. The notion of self-reliance was also reflected in the Destitute Persons Ordinance 1846, which imposed obligations on relatives of the needy, and enforced deductions from wages to assist their relatives.[10]

---

4 Margaret Tennant *et al.*, 'Defining the Non-Profit Sector: New Zealand', www.parliament.nz/resource/0000115088 [accessed 7 Sept. 2016], 4–5.
5 Poirier, *Charity Law*, 89.
6 Gino Dal Pont, *Charity Law in Australia and New Zealand* (Melbourne: Oxford University Press, 2000), 78.
7 Jonathan Barrett and John Veal, 'Charities' Tax Privileges in New Zealand: A Critical Analysis', *Journal of Australasian Tax Teachers Association* 7(1) (2012), 5, citing Kerry O'Halloran, *Charity Law and Social Inclusion: An International Study* (Oxon. and New York: Routledge, 2007), 280.
8 Barrett and Veal, 'Charities' Tax Privileges', 5, referring to charities' income of approximately NZ$15 bn in 2011 consisted of: government grants (NZ$4.997 bn); donations (NZ$1.040 bn); income from service provision (NZ$5.667 bn); and other income, including investments (NZ$3.214 bn); and Charities Commission, Annual Report 10/11.
9 Barrett and Veal, 'Charities' Tax Privileges', 5, referring to Tennant *et al.*, 'Defining the Non-Profit Sector'.
10 Kerry O'Halloran, Myles McGregor-Lowndes, and Karla W Simon, *Charity Law & Social Policy: National and International Perspectives on the Functions of Law Relating to Charities*, vol. 10 (Netherlands: Springer, 2008), 376.

Nonetheless, while there was strong focus on community support, there were still a number of charity legislative milestones. The English common law, based on the Statute of Charitable Uses 1601, provided the foundations of this early charity law. The Religious, Charitable and Educational Trusts Acts 1856 and 1865 recognised, and encouraged, charitable trusts that were for the public benefit. In particular, the later Act was designed to make 'more simple and effectual the titles by which property was held for charitable purposes'.[11]

The Charitable Funds Appropriation Act 1871 specified 11 categories of charitable purpose in s 2, including educational services for the needy; reformation of criminal prostitutes; and provision of public services. It also provided the first statutory provision for the doctrine of cy-près, where gifts for one purpose that have become inexpedient, impossible, or impracticable may be applied to another charitable purposes.[12]

The Charitable Trust Extension Act 1886 reaffirmed the application of the cy-près doctrine, providing a 'statutory procedure to enable charities to redirect charitable assets to other [charitable] ends when original purposes had become impossible, impractical, uncertain or illegal'.[13]

With the Religious, Charitable and Educational Trusts Act 1905, many of the earlier statutes were consolidated, which was then amended in the Religious, Charitable and Educational Trusts Act 1928. The first amendment of note in that later Act was in s 3, where 'charitable purpose' was defined as every other purpose in accordance with English law as a charitable purpose. The second amendment of note was captured within s 5. Here the Attorney-General, or a judge of the Supreme Court (as was at the time), could alter the purposes of an approved scheme and even restore the original purposes.[14]

One of the most familiar statutory provisions, and still in force today, is the Charitable Trusts Act 1957. This Act consolidated previous statutes relating to charitable trusts, and in 1963, the Charitable Trusts Amendment Act 1963 added two more sections to the 1957 Act. Section 61A concerned facilities that improved the conditions of lives of people, which have always been held to be charitable, and s 61B was re-enacted from s 82 of the Trustee Act 1956. This permitted a court to 'blue pencil' non-charitable purposes if the main purpose was to create a charitable trust.[15]

The 1957 Act, however, was not the last statutory provision within New Zealand relating to charity law. There was a lack of a general system for the supervision and

11 Carolyn Cordery, Carolyn J. Fowler, and Gareth G Morgan, 'The Development of Incorporated Structures for Charities: A 100-Year Comparison of England and New Zealand', *Accounting History* 21(2–3) (2016), 7, citing Tennant, O'Brien, and Sanders, *History of the Non-Profit Sector*, 17.

12 Cordery, Fowler, and Morgan, 'Development of Incorporated Structures', 7; for the cy-près doctrine, see generally Chevalier-Watts, *Law of Charity*, 319–27.

13 Cordery, Fowler, and Morgan, 'Development of Incorporated Structures', 7, citing O'Halloran, McGregor-Lowndes, and Simon, *Charity Law & Social Policy*, vol. 10 [note: spelling error corrected in the quote].

14 Dal Pont, *Charity Law*, 81.

15 Poirier, *Charity Law*, 94.

control of charities in the country, and although the 1957 Act did provide much needed administration powers, for instance under ss 32 and 33,[16] it was unsurprising perhaps that the 1980s saw calls being made for a charity regulator in New Zealand.

Parliament responded by setting up a working party to discuss the regulation of charities, with the resulting report, the *Report to the Minister of Finance and the Minister of Social Welfare*, asserting that a commission for charities should be established, and that the current definition of charity should be actioned.[17]

The decision to establish a commission, however, was many years coming. It took until the passing of the Charities Act 2005 to create the Charities Commission of New Zealand.[18] This Act, alongside the Income Tax 2007, and in conjunction with the Incorporated Societies Act 1908, and the Charitable Trusts Act 1957, provided the new legislative framework for New Zealand charity law. Its focus was primarily on registration and regulation to improve accountability and transparency within the sector. It also provided for donor incentive schemes, and simplifying fiscal matters.[19] This Act was seen as 'a symbol of this government's commitment to growing the relationship between government and the charitable sector'[20] and the Act retained the traditional four *Pemsel* classifications of charitable purpose.[21]

The Act was amended twice in 2012. First, to permit registration of amateur sporting clubs as charitable organisations,[22] and, second, to replace the Charities Commission with the Department of Internal Affairs – Charities Services (DIACS).[23] The pre-existing processes for registration, guidance, and other compliance matters pertaining to the 2005 Act remained unchanged for entities and the public.[24]

The Act's purpose 'is implemented by provisions imposing both procedural and substantive requirements for the registration and monitoring of charities'.[25] These are reflected in the functions of the Chief Executive, which include educating and assisting

---

16 Dal Pont, *Charity Law*, 82.
17 Kate Tokeley, 'A New Definition of Charity?', *Victoria University of Wellington Law Journal* 21(1) (February 1991), 41, citing Working Party on Charities and Sporting Bodies, *Report to the Minister of Finance and the Minister of Social Welfare* (1989), 59 and 79, respectively; Chevalier-Watts, *Law of Charity*, 17.
18 Chevalier-Watts, *Law of Charity*, 17; the Charities Commission has since been disestablished and its services and functions transferred to the Department of Internal Affairs – Charities Services in 2012.
19 Kerry O'Halloran, *The Profits of Charity: International Perspectives on the Law Governing the Involvement of Charities in Commerce* (New York: Oxford University Press, 2012), 407.
20 O'Halloran, *Profits of Charity*, 406, citing media statement by the Hon Judith Tizard, Associate Minister of Commerce, announcing the legislation, 14 April 2005.
21 Charities Act 2005, s 5(1); *Commissioners for Special Purposes of the Income Tax* v. *Pemsel* [1981] AC 531 (HL), 583.
22 *Greenpeace of New Zealand Incorporated* [2012] NZCA 533, [2013] 1 NZLR 339, [35] referring to the Charities Amendment Act 2012, s 5; see also Michael Gousmett, 'Fiscal Issues for Charities' 3 *NZLJ* (2014).
23 *Greenpeace of New Zealand Incorporated*, [35], referring to Charities Amendment Act 2012, ss 7–16.
24 Chevalier-Watts, *Law of Charity*, 21.
25 *Greenpeace of New Zealand Incorporated*, [37], citing the Charities Act 2005, s 10; Chevalier-Watts, *Law of Charity*, 18.

charities in relation to good governance and management;[26] receiving and processing applications for registration as charitable entities;[27] and ensuring that the register of charitable entities is compiled and maintained.[28]

While the DIACS, and previously the Commission, took over from the Inland Revenue Department (IRD) as decision maker with regard to the charitable status of entities for income tax purposes, 'an existing ruling of the IRD is protected in relation to previous binding rulings only in the limited respect provided for by s 13(2) of the Charities Act'.[29] However, with regard to all other matters, the DIACS is not affected by the previous decisions of the IRD regarding charitable status of an entity, and is not required to have regard to those rulings.[30]

The Government indicated that there would be a review of the Charities Act 2005 around its tenth anniversary, although it later announced that this review would not be taking place.[31] A number of reasons were given, including possible fiscal consequences following the widening of any definitions, and that the current definition of charitable purposes appeared to be working well.[32]

Registration as a charitable entity is voluntary, although only those bodies that are registered with the DIACS can take advantage of benefits including income tax exemption status; providing tax rebate to private donors; and deductions for Māori authorities and companies. The charities register is publicly available, as are the filings of registered charitable organisations, along with their organisational documentation, rules, and/or constitution.[33] This transparency encourages public confidence in the sector.

It has been said that this Act is restrained in terms of legislator reform, indicating that the Government and the sector are cautious in their endeavours to progress,[34] although as the consideration of charitable purposes, and public benefit, later suggests, New Zealand does reflect a certain level of progression in a number of areas within charity law.

26 *Greenpeace of New Zealand Incorporated*, [37], citing the Charities Act 2005, s 10(c); Chevalier-Watts, *Law of Charity*, 18.
27 *Greenpeace of New Zealand Incorporated*, [37], citing the Charities Act 2005, s 10(c).
28 *Greenpeace of New Zealand Incorporated*, [37]; citing the Charities Act 2005, s 10(e).
29 Peter McKenzie, 'Charitable Trusts', in *Master Trusts Guide*, 3rd edn (Auckland: Wolters Kluwer, 2011), 217, referring to *Re Grand Lodge of Antient Free and Accepted Masons* [2011] 1 NZLR 277 (HC).
30 McKenzie, 'Charitable Trusts', 217, referring to *Re Grand Lodge of Antient Free and Accepted Masons*; Chevalier-Watts, *Law of Charity*, 18.
31 Susan Barker, Michael Gousmett, and Ken Lord, *The Law and Practice of Charities in New Zealand* (Wellington: LexisNexis, 2013), 444.
32 Chevalier-Watts, *Law of Charity*, 18–19, referring to 'No Review of the Charities Act at This Time', www.national.org.nz/Article.aspx?ArticleId=39839 [accessed 16 Nov. 2012]; see also Michael Gousmett, 'The History of Charitable Purpose Tax Concessions in New Zealand Part I', *New Zealand Journal of Taxation Law and Policy (NZJTLP)* 19(2) (2013), 19.
33 Carolyn Cordery, *Light Handed Charity Regulation: Its Effect on Reporting Practice in New Zealand*, working paper no. 83 (Centre for Accounting, Governance, and Taxation Research, December 2011), 8.
34 O'Halloran, *Profits of Charity*, 407.

C The Charities Act 2005 and Māori

The 2005 Act is unique in giving special recognition to the contribution of Māori, the indigenous peoples of New Zealand, to their iwi, or hapū, and recognition of the importance of maraes.[35]

Section 5(2)(a) illustrates the importance of blood-tie relationships within Māori and New Zealand culture:

> the purpose of a trust, society, or institution is a charitable purpose under this Act if the purpose would satisfy the public benefit requirement apart from the fact that the beneficiaries of the trust, or the members of the society or institution, are related by blood.

This reflects the Court of Appeal case of *Latimer* v. *Commissioner of Inland Revenue*,[36] which confirmed that the Māori claimant group were a section of the public, in public benefit terms. This was even though 'there is a relationship of common descent for each claimant group'. This approach was in contrast to the House of Lords decision in *Oppenheim* v. *Tobacco Securities Trust Company Limited*,[37] where it was noted that 'there is no public element in the relationship of parent and child'. However, in *Latimer*, the Court asserted this 'approach might be thought insufficiently responsive to values emanating from outside the mainstream of the English common law, in particular as a response to the Māori view of the importance of whakapapa and whānau to identity, social organisation and spirituality'.[38] The Act therefore entrenches New Zealand's progressive approach with regard to acknowledging context-specific cultural needs.

In relation to s 5(2)(b), a marae will be charitable, therefore, if the marae is on Māori reservation land; its funds are used for administering or maintaining the land or the marae; and it has public benefit.[39]

---

35 Charities Act 2005, s 5(2)(a) and (b); Kerry O'Halloran *et al.*, 'Charity Law Reforms: An Overview of Progress Since 2001', in *Modernising Charity Law, Recent Developments and Future Directions* (Cheltenham: Edward Elgar, 2010), 33. Māori terms defined as: 'iwi': Māori tribe; 'hapū': Māori subtribe at Statistics New Zealand, www.stats.govt.nz/methods/classifications-and-standards/classification-related- stats-standards/iwi/definition.aspx [accessed 16 Sept. 2016]; 'marae': a fenced-in complex of carved buildings and grounds that belongs to a particular iwi, hapū, or whānau (family); a focal point of Māori communities, http://www.newzealand.com/int/feature/marae-maori-meeting-grounds [accessed 16 Sept. 2016].

36 *Latimer* v. *Commissioner of Inland Revenue*, [2002] 3 NZLR 195; see Chapter 4.

37 *Oppenheim* v. *Tobacco Securities Trust Co Ltd* [1951] 1 AC 297, 310.

38 *Latimer* v. *Commissioner of Inland Revenue*, [38]; 'whakapapa': the recitation in proper order of genealogies, and also to name the genealogies, http://maaori.com/whakapapa/whakpap2.htm [accessed 16 Sept. 2016].

39 DIAC, 'Charitable Purpose', https://charities.govt.nz/apply-for-registration/charitable-purpose [accessed 16 Sept. 2016].

D The Department of Internal Affairs – Charities Services

On the 31 May 2012, Parliament passed the Charities Amendment Act (No. 2) 2012. This disestablished the Charities Commission on 1 July 2012, which had been created as an Autonomous Crown Entity in July 2005, pursuant to the Charities Act 2005. The Board of the Commission comprised seven members. The Commission's core functions were transferred to the Department of Internal Affairs. Its registration, education, and monitoring and investigation teams now operate as the Department of Internal Affairs – Charities Services (DIACS).[40]

The now three-person board makes decisions about the registration and deregistration of entities, and the DIACS insists its decision-making process remains independent.[41] The Government elected to disestablish the Commission because it wanted to 'reduce spending on administration, while improving services. Merging agencies is one way of achieving this'.[42]

It has been argued that disestablishing the Commission, and moving its functions to the DIACS, was a 'retrograde step'[43] for the sector, especially when comparing with its neighbour Australia, which appears to be taking the opposite approach.[44] However, there may be benefit for the sector in consolidating the functions of the Commission, and the Office for the Community and Voluntary Sector all under the roof of the Ministry of Internal Affairs.[45] Any potential legislative reviews may 'provide a fresh context within which to reconsider a future role for an independent Charities Commission'.[46]

E Charitable purposes

Charitable purposes are embedded in s 5(1) of the Charities Act 2005:[47]

> In this Act, unless the context otherwise requires, charitable purpose includes every charitable purpose, whether it relates to the relief of poverty, the advancement of education or religion, or any other matter beneficial to the community.

Evidently these purposes find their history in New Zealand's colonial connection with England, and Lord Macnaghten's determination of the heads of charity in

---

40 Chevalier-Watts, *Law of Charity*, 19–21.
41 Chevalier-Watts, *Law of Charity*, 21, referring to DIA, 'Charities Commission Functions Moved to Internal Affairs', www.charities.govt.nz [accessed 16 Sept. 2016].
42 Chevalier-Watts, *Law of Charity*, 21, referring to DIA, 'Charities Commission Functions Moved to Internal Affairs'.
43 O'Halloran, *Profits of Charity*, 407.
44 See Chapter 6 on Australia for further discussion and a comparative approach.
45 www.dia.govt.nz/Decommissioned-websites—Office-of-the-Community-and-Voluntary-Sector-website [accessed 16 Sept. 2016].
46 O'Halloran, *Profits of Charity*, 407–8.
47 Charities Act 2005 (New Zealand NZ), s 5(1); Charities Services New Zealand, Charitable Purposes https://charities.govt.nz/apply-for-registration/charitable-purpose [accessed 16 Sept. 2016].

Commissioners for Special Purposes of the Income Tax v. *Pemsel.*[48] Thus, the well-established common law tests for charitable purposes continues under the 2005 Act.[49] Indeed, the Act 'builds on the pre-existing common law understanding of charitable purpose'.[50]

These means that even though New Zealand has a regulatory framework, and a government body responsible for registering, monitoring, and administering charitable entities, 'the institutional infrastructure relating to charities',[51] and charitable purposes, 'is of a traditional common law character'.[52]

As a result, and echoing other chapters, we will consider a selection of key cases to evaluate charitable purposes in New Zealand. This is because such '"leading cases" are a vital part of the chaotic-looking case law tradition'[53] and provide a useful insight into the jurisprudential trends of charitable purposes in a New Zealand context. It should be stated at the outset that the author acknowledges the importance of two cases in particular within New Zealand jurisprudence, although this part of the book will not discuss them in detail. This is because they are addressed in detail in other chapters. The first is the Court of Appeal case of *Latimer* v. *Commissioner of Inland Revenue.*[54] The second is the Supreme Court decision of *Re Greenpeace of New Zealand Inc.*[55] The latter heralded a new era in New Zealand in relation to political purposes and public benefit, and although a relatively new case, its effects are already being jurisprudentially.[56]

We begin with two cases that illustrate the jurisprudential journey that appears to have been taken with regard to the relief of poverty. The cases are *D V Bryant Trust Board* v. *Hamilton City Council,*[57] and *Re Queenstown Lakes Community Housing Trust,*[58] beginning with the former.

F D V Bryant Trust Board v. Hamilton City Council

While the Preamble of the Statute of Elizabeth has as its opening lines the relief of the aged, the impotent, and poor persons, illustrating that this purpose is at the

48 *Commissioners for Special Purposes of Income Tax* v. *Pemsel* [1891] AC 531.
49 O'Halloran, McGregor-Lowndes, and Simon, *Charity Law & Social Policy*, 379.
50 *Re the Foundation for Anti-Aging Research and the Foundation for Reversal of Solid State Hypothermia*, [2016] 27 NZTC 22, [15], citing *Re Greenpeace of New Zealand Inc* [2015] 1 NZLR 169, [12].
51 O'Halloran, McGregor-Lowndes, and Simon, *Charity Law & Social Policy*, 10:379.
52 Ibid.
53 John Mummery, '*The Commissioners for Special Purposes of the Income Tax* v. *Pemsel*', *Charity Law and Practice Review* 16(1) (2013–14), 1.
54 *Latimer* v. *Commissioner of Inland Revenue*.
55 *Re Greenpeace of New Zealand Inc*.
56 See generally Juliet Chevalier-Watts, 'Post *Re Greenpeace* Supreme Court Reflections: Charity Law in the 21st Century in Aotearoa (New Zealand)', *Bond Law Review* 28 (1) (2016), 63–82; also *Re Family First New Zealand* [2015] NZHC 1493; and Rex Tauati Ahdar, 'Charity Begins at the Politically Correct Home? The Family First Case', *Otago Law Review* 14(1) (2015), 171–90.
57 *D V Bryant Trust Board* v. *Hamilton City Council* [1997] 3 NZLR 342 (HC).
58 *Re Queenstown Community Housing Trust* [2011] 3 NZLR 502 (HC).

very heart of charity law,[59] it provides little in the way of determining the meaning of 'poverty', nor the extent to which a person should be 'poor' in order to be relieved. The case of *D V Bryant Trust Board* however is useful in providing some much-needed context.[60]

In this case, the plaintiffs were the trustees of a retirement village in Hamilton, which was owned by a trust. The Council determined that the land was now be subject to rates. If the village was held to be charitable, then the land would be exempt from rates.

Hammond J, as he was, asserted that poverty should not be equated with destitution, rather '[p]overty is a relative term which extends to comprise persons of moderate means'.[61] His Honour also confirmed that courts have long interpreted '[r]elief of aged, impotent and poor people' disjunctively, so while the relief of the elderly is in itself charitable, the mere provision of amenities will not in relieve poverty.[62] However, his Honour held that the circumstances of the instant case went beyond the mere provision of amenities[63] and 'when the concept of the village is properly understood ... it is seen to address the deepest kind of human needs, particularly of the aged'.[64] He further criticised the defendant for suggesting that the village did not relieve the needs of the aged, asserting that the Council was not just wrong in law, but also 'downright churlish'[65] because the 'spectre of a retreat of the state, coupled with a harsh view of the law of charity, is unthinkable in both human and legal terms'.[66]

Hammond J also considered whether there was a need to be relieved, and was the relief to be afforded real, or was it 'fanciful, or trifling, or insubstantial?'.[67] He concluded that while the needs of the residents in question was intangible, that should not preclude the need from being enough to be relieved. This was because other elements of humanity, such as spirituality and art, give rise to charitable activities, and these too are intangible elements of humanity.[68]

---

59 *D V Bryant Trust Board* v. *Hamilton City Council*, 348.

60 Juliet Chevalier-Watts and Sue Tappenden, *Equity, Trusts and Succession* (Wellington: Thomson Reuters, 2013), 231.

61 *D V Bryant Trust Board* v. *Hamilton City Council*, 349, citing *Re Bethel* (1971) 17 DLR (3d) 652, 666; *Protestant Hold Ladies' Home* v.*Provincial Treasurer of Prince Edward Island* [1941] 2 DLR 534; *Re Cottam's Will Trusts* [1955] 3 All ER 704; *Joseph Rowntree Memorial Trust Housing Association Ltd* v. *Attorney-General* [1983] Ch 159.

62 *D V Bryant Trust Board* v. *Hamilton City Council*, 349, referring to *Re Cole* [1958] Ch 877 (CA); *Inland Revenue Commissioners* v. *Baddeley* [1955] AC 572, 585; and *Re Mitchell* [1963] NZLR 934.

63 *D V Bryant Trust Board* v. *Hamilton City Council*, 349.

64 Ibid.

65 Ibid., 350.

66 Ibid.; Chevalier-Watts and Tappenden, *Equity, Trusts and Succession*, 232.

67 *D V Bryant Trust Board* v. *Hamilton City Council*, 350, referring to *Joseph Rowntree Memorial Trust Housing Association Ltd* v. *Attorney-General* [1983] Ch 159 and *Re St Anne's Tower Corp of Toronto and City of Toronto* (1973) 41 DLR (3d) 481.

68 *D V Bryant Trust Board* v. *Hamilton City Council*, 350; Chevalier-Watts and Tappenden, *Equity, Trusts and Succession*, 232.

Further, there is often a relationship between poverty and distress, thus the relief of the needs of the aged, and relief from distress caused by solitariness, overlap in this case.[69] Consequently, while the needs were intangible, they were no less real, reflecting the realities of humanity, and relieving such needs surely must go the heart of charity law per se. Therefore, Hammond J provided a liberal interpretation of relief of poverty by recognising the realities of the needs of the aged, and this contemporary approach was approved in *Re Centrepoint Community Growth Trust*.[70]

While *D V Bryant* provides a liberal consideration of the relief of poverty, the more recent case of *Re Queenstown Lakes Community Housing Trust* appears, prima facie, to do just the opposite.

G Re Queenstown Lakes Community Housing Trust

This case considered the relief of poverty in relation to modern-day housing issues. The Trust's objects, inter alia, promote or provide housing at manageable costs through shared ownership programmes. The Trust asserted that housing is a basic human necessity, not a luxury, and 'central to the right to an adequate standard of living ... recognised in art 25 of the Universal Declaration of Human Rights'.[71] Indeed, the Court confirmed that housing may be a basic requirement; however, home ownership in itself is not. Therefore, the key issue was whether a person could afford particular housing in a particular location. Further, the Court asserted that many people who would fall into the Trust's eligibility criteria may take offence at being deemed to be in poverty. Additionally, there were other reasonable alternatives to home ownership, such as, renting in other areas within the district.[72]

However, the Trust argued that the poverty element related to expense of living in the Queenstown district. Consequently, if housing assistance was not available, then those who fell within the Trust's eligibility criteria would simply be unable, or unwilling, to settle in the district; the Court rejected this. It stated that eligible individuals have realistic alternative housing available to them, thus they did not fulfil the criterion of need under the head of relief of poverty. The Trust asserted that alternative housing disadvantaged the community because it would be difficult to attract and retain key workers. However, the Court considered that, under the head of relief of poverty, the consequences for the community were not a relevant factor in assessing whether the assistance provided by the Trust is addressing the needs of individuals. This is because they fell under the fourth head of charity. As a result, the Court believed that the Trust's purposes were not charitable under the relief of poverty.[73]

---

69 *D V Bryant Trust Board* v. *Hamilton City Council*, 350.
70 *Re Centrepoint Community Growth Trust* [2000] 2 NZLR 325.
71 *Re Queenstown Lakes Community Housing Trust* [2011], 3 NZLR 502, [34]; Chevalier-Watts and Tappenden, *Equity, Trusts and Succession*, 233.
72 *Re Queenstown Lakes Community Housing Trust*, [42]; Chevalier-Watts and Tappenden, *Equity, Trusts and Succession*, 234.
73 *Re Queenstown Lakes Community Housing Trust*, [41]–[46].

While, prima facie, this may appear to be a reasoned decision, it is not always easy to reconcile, particularly considered against *Liberty Trust* v. *Charities Commission*.[74] Here the Court held that providing interest-free mortgages constituted a charitable purpose, albeit under the head of advancement of religion, which will be discussed later in the chapter. Such opposing findings, especially when considering that public benefit is presumed under these heads, makes the *Queenstown* case difficult to reconcile with charity law principles. This is because the Court in *Queenstown* stated that while assisting the poor is an inherent public good, this will only be so if 'poverty' is not interpreted too liberally.[75] This is a surprising approach, because it is well established that poverty does not mean destitution,[76] and, further, poverty could be equated to a lack of affordable accommodation.[77] One underlying rationale for the decision of *Queenstown* is that the general public may not recognise a general social responsibility for assisting those that appear already to be able to assist themselves in some regard.[78] This argument appears to fail however if contrasted with the beneficiaries of Liberty Trust, who might appear to be well off, or better off than some members of the general public. Further, the Court in *Queenstown* asserted that the law must be flexible to address new categories of need within poverty as they arise.[79] It is said that New Zealand is currently in a housing crisis, and lack of affordable housing is causing homelessness and inequality throughout the country.[80] If that is correct, then rejecting an affordable housing scheme that may assist the prevention of such community issues appears contrary to the needs of a contemporary society.

Two more cases, *Travis Trust* v. *Charities Commission*[81] and *Canterbury Development Corporation* v. *Charities Commission*,[82] this time under the fourth head of charity, also reflect a more conservative approach of the courts. We begin with *Travis Trust*.

H Travis Trust v. Charities Commission

This is an important case in New Zealand jurisprudence because it was the first appeal against a decision of the Charities Commission (as it was). Williams J had

---

74 *Liberty Trust* v. *Charities Commission* [2011] 3 NZLR 68.

75 *Re Queenstown Lakes Community Housing Trust*, [39].

76 *Re Queenstown Lakes Community Housing Trust* [2011] 3 NZLR 502 (HC), [35], referring to *Re Coulthurst Deed Coutts and Company* v. *Coulthurst* [1951] 1 Ch 661.

77 *Re Queenstown Community Housing Trust*, [35], referring to *Re Centrepoint Community Growth Trust*.

78 *Re Queenstown Community Housing Trust*, [39].

79 Ibid., [40].

80 www.labour.org.nz/housing_crisis_affecting_more_than_98_per_cent_of_nz [accessed 20 Sept. 2016]; Philippa Howden-Chapman, *Home Truths Confronting New Zealand* (Wellington: Bridget Williams, 2015); www.theguardian.com/world/2016/may/17/new-zealand-housing-crisis-forces-hundreds-to-live-in-garages-tents-and-cars [accessed 20 Sept. 2016].

81 *Travis Trust* v. *Charities Commission* (2009) 24 NZTC 23, 273, (2008) 2 NZTR 18-030.

82 *Canterbury Development Corporation* v. *Charities Commission* [2010] 2 NZLR 707.

to determine whether the provision of prize money for a horse race was charitable within the fourth head of charity.[83] His Honour confirmed that 'English, Canadian, Australian and New Zealand courts have dealt with the question of whether trusts for the promotion of sport and leisure are charitable under the "general benefits" heading on a number of occasions',[84] with *Re Nottage* being the leading decision regarding sports and charitable purposes.[85] None of those cases, however, refer specifically to horse racing.

The Australian case of *Re Hoey*[86] did address horse racing in relation to a racecourse, but Williams J stated that it was 'not on all fours with the present facts where the gift is not for land or physical plant'.[87] Nonetheless, the Court in *Re Hoey* did confirm that the purposes in question did not meet the required public benefit.[88] As a result, therefore Williams J, in *Travis Trust*, confirmed that the principles in *Re Hoey* were analogous to the instant case as its purposes 'lacked the requisite character and the benefit was not public because horse racing is conducted for the benefit of the racing industry and not the protection of public interest'.[89]

One New Zealand case that was on all fours with *Travis Trust*, was in *Re Beckbessinger*,[90] where it was held that providing a stake to a trotting club was 'beyond doubt non-charitable'. As a result, 'the weight of authorities runs powerfully against a finding that a gift toward the prize in the Travis Stakes'[91] as being charitable.[92]

It is perhaps surprising that the Court in *Travis Trust* was not able to take a more liberal approach in relation to sports and charities, considering how important sporting activities are within New Zealand as a nation, especially in such a contemporary context. However, Williams J did acknowledge that 'that categories of charitable purpose can evolve, and although case law suggests that mere sport is not charitable, contemporary New Zealand cases support the notion of charitable purpose evolving to meet changing social circumstances and New Zealand's unique legal culture'.[93] So while this case shows perhaps limited advancement in charitable principles, it acknowledges that 'New Zealand supports the evolution of legal principles where it most appropriate', and, unfortunately, previous authorities did not enable evolution with regard to sporting activities at the time of *Travis Trust*. However, Parliament has now acknowledged the importance of sports

83 *Travis Trust* v. *Charities Commission*, [29].
84 Ibid., [36].
85 Ibid., [37], referring to *In re Nottage* [1895] 2 Ch 649; Chevalier-Watts, *Law of Charity*, 233.
86 *Re Hoey* [1994] 2 Qd r 510.
87 *Travis Trust* v. *Charities Commission*, [42].
88 Ibid., referring to re Hoey.
89 *Travis Trust* v. *Charities Commission*, [42], referring to *Re Hoey*, 513–14.
90 *Travis Trust* v. *Charities Commission*, [43], citing *Re Beckbessinger* [1993] 2 NZLR 362, 376.
91 *Travis Trust* v. *Charities Commission*, [44].
92 Chevalier-Watts, *Law of Charity*, 235.
93 *Travis Trust* v. *Charities Commission*, [45].

within the New Zealand context, with the following amendment to the Charities Act 2005 made in 2012, whereby:[94]

> The promotion of amateur sport may be a charitable purpose if it is the means by which a charitable purpose referred to in subsection (1) is pursued.

In other words, the promotion of amateur sport may be charitable if it falls within one of the four heads of charity. Thus, while Williams J was unable to expand charity law at the time, Parliament has now addressed the issue, reflecting a more contemporary charity law landscape.

While it is evident that New Zealand charity law is becoming more expansive in relation to sporting activities, *Canterbury Development Corporation* v. *Charities Commission* reflects a conservative approach in relation purposes under the fourth head of charity, that of economic development.

I Canterbury Development Corporation v. Charities Commission (CDC)

This case provided an opportunity for the High Court to consider the charitable nature of the promotion of industry and economic development in a contemporary context. The Canterbury Development Corporation, the Canterbury Development Corporation Trust, and the Canterbury Economic Development Fund are interrelated organisations. Their main purposes promote economic development in the Canterbury area through, inter alia, supporting and promoting the establishment and development of businesses in Canterbury.

Ronald Young J considered each of the three appeals separately but a number of findings had common application across the appeals. His Honour noted that what 'must be kept in mind is ... that purpose of benefit to the community is a community benefit to assuage need'.[95] The requirement, therefore, is to provide a 'community benefit where an identified need is established'.[96] However, his Honour observed:[97]

> No such claim of deprivation is made with respect to Canterbury or Christchurch. The objects and work of the CDC are commendable. Its

---

94 Charities Act 2005, s 5(2A); the provision of recreational facilities is also recognised under s 61A of the Charitable Trusts Act 1957, so long as the facility is for recreation or leisure-time occupation, is in the interests of social welfare, and is for the public benefit; see *Registration Decision: Northern Region Equestrian Trust* (NOR44300) 15 April 2013, New Zealand, [25].

95 *Canterbury Development Corporation* v. *Charities Commission*, [42], relying on *Re Tennant* [1996] 2 NZLR 633 and *Tasmanian Electronic Commerce Centre* v. *Commissioner of Taxation* [2005] FCA 439.

96 *Canterbury Development Corporation* v. *Charities Commission*, [42].

97 Chevalier-Watts and Tappenden, *Equity, Trusts and Succession*, 275–280; *Canterbury Development Corporation* v. *Charities Commission*, [43]–[44].

intention is to help fledgling businesses. By itself this does not establish the CDC as having the necessary focus on charitable intent ... These are essentially the provision of help to individual businesses in the hope they will grow ... This help may promote these individual businesses. It may make them more profitable. This promotion and profitability is not incidental to the work of the CDC. It is at its core.

In other words, 'the spirit and intendment of charitable purpose is not central to CDC's function',[98] meaning that CDC's purposes were not charitable.

While this appears to be a logical approach, it has been subject to criticism. This appears to be on the basis of how CDC's purposes can be given effect. For example, CDC's purposes include assisting individuals and businesses in order to promote economic development, but it is difficult to see how these purposes can be given effect in any other way. Indeed, *Commissioner of Taxation* v. *Triton Foundation* and *Tasmanian Electronic Commerce Pty Ltd* v. *Commissioner of Taxation* confirm that such assistance is not inconsistent with charitable status.[99]

It should be noted, however, that with regard to the latter case, Ronald Young J in *CDC*, stated that there was a need to be assuaged in Tasmania, due to its economically deprived status, thus it was distinguished because there was no claim for economic deprivation in the Canterbury region.[100] Ronald Young J further distinguished the *Triton* case because in that case the Court was satisfied that the overarching object of the Foundation, promoting a culture of innovation and entrepreneurship through supporting innovations to commercialise products, was charitable, although it was acknowledged that this was a 'question of perspective'.[101]

He further noted that the provision of business support provided by CDC would be done with the 'hope and belief that their economic success would be reflected in the economic wellbeing of the Canterbury region'.[102] The Triton Foundation's provision of support, however, was contrasted with CDC's because the Foundation's had a 'broad public benefit'.[103] With respect, it is difficult to see how these economic purposes differ from each other, as both are broad, and both assist individuals and businesses specifically. Therefore, it is not difficult to see why the *CDC* decision has been subject to criticism.[104] Indeed, it has been considered,

---

98 *Canterbury Development Corporation* v. *Charities Commission*, [44].
99 Susan Barker, 'The Myth of "Charitable Activities"', *New Zealand Law Journal* 1(8) (September 2014), 306, referring to *Commissioner of Taxation* v. *Triton Foundation* [2005] FCA 1319 and *Tasmanian Electronic Commerce Pty Ltd* v. *Commissioner of Taxation*.
100 *Canterbury Development Corporation* v. *Charities Commission*, [61].
101 Ibid., [65].
102 Ibid., [66].
103 Ibid.
104 Barker, 'Myth of "Charitable Activities"', 306, referring to, among others, John Bassett, 'Charity Is a General Public Use', *New Zealand Law Journal* 1(2) (March 2011); Mark Von Dadelszen, 'Moving the Charitable Goal Posts', *NZLawyer* (March 2011); Susan Barker and Kate Yesberg, 'Charities Act Review', *NZLawyer* (April 2011); Michael Gousmett, 'Charity and Economic Development', *New Zealand Law Journal* 1(2) (2011).

but specifically not followed in Australia.[105] This emphasises the challenging nature of the decision in *CDC* when there does appear to be authority that when an 'organisation plays a significant role in support for the business community generally and its constitutional objects are directed to that end',[106] this can fulfil the requirement of charitable purpose.

Interestingly, it is worth noting that *CDC* was decided before the devastating earthquake that struck Christchurch in 2011, which killed 185 people, causing millions of dollars of damage, and 'untold damage to the economic prosperity of the area'.[107] If *CDC* had been heard subsequent to this earthquake, it is possible that 'the Court would have identified a community need that could have been assuaged by the objects of CDC' because Ronald Young J did state that the 'position may be different in an identifiably economically deprived area in New Zealand'.[108] If that were the case, his Honour may have come to a different conclusion.[109]

While the cases of *Travis Trust* and *CDC* reflect a conservative judicial approach towards charitable purposes under the fourth head of charity, the same cannot necessarily be said with regard to such purposes under the head of advancement of religion. Two cases illustrate this trend, beginning with *Liberty Trust* v. *Charities Commission*.[110]

J Liberty Trust v. Charities Commission

While secular activities will not necessarily negate religious purposes at charity law,[111] this High Court case offered a contemporary, and controversial, perspective in relation to advancement of religion and secular activities.

This Trust was registered[112] but its money-lending scheme led the Charities Commission (as was) to deregister the Trust, which was appealed. The Trust is described as a Christian charitable community that enables people 'to own their own homes, churches and ministries without long term debt, so that they can be free to fulfil God's call upon their lives'.[113] People may contribute to the Trust for five to ten years and are then eligible for an interest-free loan. Repayments of the loans are made to the pool of funds and these are available to other donors who may seek financial assistance from the Trust. The scheme is available to persons of

105 Barker, 'Myth of "Charitable Activities"', 306, referring to *Chamber of Commerce and Industry of Western Australia (Inc) and Commissioner of State Revenue* [2012] WAS 146 [33] and [99].
106 Barker, 'Myth of "Charitable Activities"', 306, citing *Chamber of Commerce and Industry of Western Australia (Inc)* v. *Commissioner of State Revenue*, 90 and 99.
107 Chevalier-Watts and Tappenden, *Equity, Trusts and Succession*, 280.
108 *Canterbury Development Corporation* v. *Charities Commission*, [61].
109 Chevalier-Watts and Tappenden, *Equity, Trusts and Succession*, 280.
110 *Liberty Trust* v. *Charities Commission*.
111 Chevalier-Watts, *Law of Charity*, 196.
112 Under the Charities Act 2005.
113 www.libertytrust.org.nz/questions; Chevalier-Watts and Tappenden, *Equity, Trusts and Succession*, 254.

any creed or faith, and it seeks to support them by demonstrating Christian care. The Trust states that its scheme teaches Biblical financial principles through, inter alia, its loan scheme.[114]

In relation to teaching Biblical financial principles, Mallon J referred to *Roman Catholic Archbishop of Melbourne* v. *Lawlor*,[115] which concerned the establishment of a Catholic newspaper. Her Honour observed that the Trust's teachings of financial matters were presented as being the word of God, as opposed to secular activities that may be likened to the Catholic newspaper in *Lawlor*. Consequently, her Honour confirmed that teaching biblical financial principles did advance religion.[116] The question remained, however, as to whether the loan scheme advanced religion. Mallon J stated that a 'difficulty with accepting practical out-workings as advancing religion is that they may embrace activities that are carried out by non-religious organisations which do not enjoy the legal and fiscal benefits that apply to charities'.[117] She referred to *Presbyterian Church (New South Wales) Property Trust* v. *Ryde Municipal Council*[118] to consider this issue in that context. This case concerned a church trust that bought land adjoining the church, and set up a retirement village on that land. The Court in that case asserted that activities of a church can extend beyond its usual activities,[119] thus:[120]

> where a church or analogous body has as one of the purposes to which its property may be applied a purpose which is not a mere ulterior secular, but one directs at and able to be seen as assisting in the advancement of its religious purpose, then the purpose of that religion will be held to be religious for present purposes.

This meant that the church trust 'was intimately connected with the Presbyterian Church and so within this principle'.[121]

Mallon J, in *Liberty Trust*, confirmed that in the *Ryde* case, the activities were carried out by a church or analogous body, and this was a relevant factor. While it was true that the Liberty Trust was not an actual church, it was established to undertake social welfare and outreach by ministries of the Whakatane Baptist Church and the Whakatane Christian Fellowship church. It was further given authority by its repeated references to Christian principles,[122] and:[123]

114 *Liberty Trust* v. *Charities Commission*, [9]–[25].
115 *Roman Catholic Archbishop of Melbourne* v. *Lawlor* (1934) 51 CLR 1 (HCA).
116 *Liberty Trust* v. *Charities Commission*, [78]–[99].
117 Ibid., [80].
118 *Presbyterian Church (New South Wales) Property Trust* v. *Ryde Municipal Council* [1977] 1 NSWLR 620 (Land and Valuation Court); *Presbyterian Church (New South Wales) Property Trust* v. *Ryde Municipal Council* [1978] 2 NSWLR 387 (NSWCA).
119 *Liberty Trust* v. *Charities Commission*, [85].
120 *Liberty Trust* v. *Charities Commission*, [86], citing *Presbyterian Church (New South Wales) Property Trust* v. *Ryde Municipal Council*, 408.
121 Ibid.
122 Ibid., [88]; Chevalier-Watts and Tappenden, *Equity, Trusts and Succession*, 256.
123 *Liberty Trust* v. *Charities Commission*, [90].

If charitable status is appropriate for churches and their public ceremonies or rituals it seems logical that this status should also apply to their other activities which are carried out as part of the faith to which the church subscribes.

Further, 'the mere fact that others may carry out the very same activities without ascribing to the religion, does not mean that those that are doing the activities for religious purposes are not advancing religion by carrying out that activity'.[124] Consequently, Mallon J concluded that while 'a mortgage scheme in and of itself is not an obvious candidate'[125] to advance religion, its activities were analogous to those in the *Ryde* case, inter alia, therefore the lending scheme advanced religion.[126]

So while, prima facie, this decision appears to be a liberal interpretation of the advancement of religion, in reality, it fits within the rubric of advancement of religion, and is merely a reflection of the application of law in a contemporary context.[127] However, the issue of public benefit within this case is perhaps more challenging, which will be discussed later in the chapter.

A recent Registration Decision of the Charities Services also illustrates this progressive approach towards religion.

K The Jedi Society Incorporated

It is acknowledged that a Registration Decision given by the Board of the Charities Services (the Board) is not binding law,[128] but what this decision does is illustrate the evolutionary nature of New Zealand charity law, especially in relation to advancement of religion. In case there was any doubt, this decision did concern the religious nature of Jediism.[129]

There could be few who are not cognisant of who, or what, is a Jedi. Jediism is a fictional belief system created by George Lucas for the series of Star Wars films, the first of which was released in 1977. Therefore, Jediism, as it is understood today, is an invented religion, with its basis in fiction. It is asserted that George Lucas did not intend to create a religion,[130] although it was acknowledged that

---

124 Ibid.

125 Ibid., [93].

126 *Liberty Trust* v. *Charities Commission*, [91]–[98], referring to *Re Hood* [1931] 1 Ch 240 (CA); *Re Banfield* [1968] 2 All ER 276 (Ch); *Re Charlesworth* (1910) 26 TLR 214 (Ch); *Re Strickland's Will Trusts* [1936] 3 All ER 1027 (Ch); and *Belfast City YMCA* v. *Commissioner of Valuation for Northern Ireland* [1968] NI 3 (CA).

127 However, see Juliet Chevalier-Watts, 'Charitable Trusts and Advancement of Religion: On a Whim and a Prayer?', *Victoria University of Wellington Law Journal* 43(3) (2012), 403–42, for alternative discussion on the advancement of religion.

128 DIAC, 'Jedi Society Incorporated (JED49458)', Decision No: 2015-2, 14 September 2015, DIAC, Charities Services, NZ.

129 See also Juliet Chevalier-Watts, 'Balancing Law and Belief: The Dichotomy of the Moral and the Immortal', *International Journal of Religion and Spirituality in Society*, 7(1) (2017), 1–15.

130 Tom de Castella, 'Have Jedi Created a New "Religion"?', *BBC News* (25 October 2014), www.bbc.com/news/magazine-29753530 [accessed 30 Sept. 2016].

'elements of the doctrine of Jediism can be seen in a variety of other world religions'.[131] While elements of Jediism may be found in other religions, it was still a novel situation being faced in New Zealand, thus the Board stated that the following characteristics would demonstrate a religion when determining a novel set of beliefs:[132]

A body of doctrines that:

- concerns the place of humankind in the universe and its relationship with the infinite;
- goes beyond that which can be perceived by the senses or ascertained through the scientific method; and
- contains canons of conduct around which adherents are to structure their lives.
- The doctrines and canons of conduct must also be sufficiently structured, cogent and serious so as to be capable of advancing religion.

The Board confirmed that Jediism does have a body of doctrines that meets the majority of this criterion, although the doctrines and canons of conduct were not sufficiently structured, cogent, and serious to advance religion at law. In addressing this particular issue, the Board stated that this was not a question of the founder's motives, nor whether the religion was true or false.[133] Instead, the question was whether the religion was 'sufficiently structured to advance religion in a charitable manner'[134] because there 'must be an organised or integrated system of beliefs'[135] for the Board to recognise it as a religion.

One might argue that there can be limited authenticity for a religion whose beliefs are based on films, as opposed to any form of 'divine revelation or inspiration'.[136] However, taking beliefs from such a source may be 'a sometimes more practical means of conveying philosophies applicable to real life'.[137]

This echoes the case therefore of *Liberty Trust*, where a contemporary vehicle for advancing religion was acknowledged in the form of an interest-free loan, and this illustrates New Zealand's liberal interpretation of religion at charity law in order to contextualise an ancient principle within modern society.

While we see evidence of a libertarian jurisprudential approach, the Board confirmed that the Society did not advance religion. It observed that the Society was 'non dogmatic and non-organised',[138] and that Jedi traits may be accepted or rejected, as believers see fit. Indeed, the Jedi code is a mantra that expresses the Jedi aspiration, rather than an obligatory code of conduct.[139] So while the Society

131 DIAC, 'Jedi Society Incorporated (JED49458)', [22].
132 Ibid., [29].
133 DIAC, 'Jedi Society Incorporated (JED49458)', [29], referring to *Church of the New Faith* v. *Commissioner of Pay-roll Tax (Vic)* (1983) 154 CLR 120, 141 and 150.
134 DIAC, 'Jedi Society Incorporated (JED49458)', [34].
135 Ibid.
136 Ibid., [38].
137 DIAC, 'Jedi Society Incorporated (JED49458)', [38], citing letter of 30 April 2015.
138 Ibid., [39], citing www.templeofthejediorder.org/doctrine-of-the-order
139 Ibid.

seeks to advance faith through its website, there is no formal structure to that learning. This meant that:[140]

> The information presented on the quality of Jediism and how it is to be advanced indicates the belief system is merely a collection of interconnected ideas ... rather than structured, cogent and serious religion.

One might presume, therefore, that the door was firmly closed on Jediism being charitable at law; the opposite, however, is true. The Board stated that the Society may 'develop the level of seriousness and structure necessary to advance religion'.[141] It is possible that the Society may develop such criteria to meet the stringent demands of charity law. If this is so, then advancement of religion is likely to acknowledge explicitly fictional religions as being charitable, thus reflecting the development of charity law within New Zealand society.

Therefore, what this collection of cases illustrates is an unusual combination of liberal and conservative jurisprudential approaches, which is perhaps a reflection of the state of flux of charity law generally. It also may be a reflection of New Zealand acknowledging its colonial history in some regards, while also forging its own context-specific charity path that best reflects its own political and socio-economic realities.

L Public benefit

The Charities Act 2005 states that:[142]

> the purpose of a trust, society, or institution is a charitable purpose under this Act if the purpose would satisfy the public benefit requirement.

For the first three heads of charity, the public benefit is presumed, although rebuttable. If the purposes fall within the fourth head, there is no presumption and a court must decide whether the purposes are beneficial to the community, or a sufficient section of it. There is also an additional requirement under the last head that charities must fall within the spirit and intendment of the Statute of Elizabeth, where analogy with existing cases is useful.[143]

The Act does not provide a definition of public benefit, thus courts turn to case law to assess this requirement. New Zealand affirms that there must be a benefit that accrues to the public, which requires the application of the twofold test. That test being that purposes confer a benefit on the public, or a section of the public; and the class of persons eligible to benefit constitutes the public, or a sufficient section of it.[144] This, unsurprisingly, echoes the English approach, reflecting the colonial ancestry.

140 Ibid., [40].
141 Ibid., [41].
142 Charities Act 2005, s 5(2)(a).
143 *Re the Foundation for Anti-Aging Research and the Foundation for Reversal of Solid State Hypothermia*, [16].
144 *Travis Trust* v. *Charities Commission*, [54].

While public benefit sounds like a straightforward concept, it has been stated that 'drawing the line can be exceedingly difficult and there is clearly a degree of interplay between purpose and class'.[145] While there may be difficulties in assessing the public benefit requirement, there is evidence to suggest that the courts in New Zealand have taken a more progressive approach to its interpretation in recent times, and issues relating to Māori and public benefit illustrate this.

M Māori and public benefit

Early case law paints a conservative approach. In *Arawa Māori Trust Board* v. *Commissioner of Inland Revenue*,[146] the Court held that members of a Māori tribe, and their descendants, did not meet the public benefit requirement, because the Court was bound by the *Oppenheim* decision, as discussed in detail in Chapter 4, in relation to blood tie and public benefit. However, with *Latimer* v. *Commissioner of Inland Revenue*[147] came a sea change in the recognition of public benefit in relation to blood tie, specifically, Māori. Chapter 4 discusses this in some detail, but briefly, the Court of Appeal cast doubt on the English notion that there could be no public benefit in benefiting one's family because assisting Māori in these specific circumstances would assist the community generally.

The later High Court case of *Tuhoe Charitable Trust Board*,[148] which concerned the amalgamation of three trusts into one, where all the trusts had broadly similar objects, and operated for the benefit of Ngai Tuhoe,[149] followed a similar path. The Court confirmed that while, historically, doubt had been cast over whether trusts that benefit iwi could be charitable, national law now recognises such trusts as being capable of being charitable.[150] It has been suggested however that 'until there is a court case on the narrower issue of the dividing line between single family whānau and the iwi'[151] it is not yet clear how far public benefit may be extended for Māori.[152]

N Non-Māori and public benefit

Other areas of charity law in New Zealand also reflect a similar progressive approach. For instance, in the Supreme Court case of *Re Greenpeace of New Zealand Inc*,[153] the majority determined that, in relation to the political purpose doctrine, political

---

145 Ibid., [55].
146 *Arawa Māori Trust Board* v. *Commissioner of Inland Revenue* (1961) MCD 391.
147 *Latimer* v. *Commissioner of Inland Revenue*.
148 *Tuhoe Charitable Trust Board* [2012] NZHC 1952 (14 August 2012).
149 A Māori iwi.
150 *Re Tuhoe Charitable Trust Board*, [72].
151 Fiona Martin, 'Convergence and Divergence with the Common Law: The Public Benefit Test and Charities for Indigenous Peoples', in *Not-for-Profit Law: Theoretical and Comparative Perspectives* (Cambridge: Cambridge University Press, 2014), 176.
152 See DIAC, *Nga Uri O Wharetakahia Waaka Whānau Land Trust* (NGA42808) Decision No: 2012-4 19 November 2012 and Deregistration Decision: *Mokorina Whānau Trust* (CC40304) Decision No: D2011-4 25 May 2011.
153 *Re Greenpeace of New Zealand Inc*, [113]–[116].

purposes, even non-ancillary ones, may meet the public benefit test, which was a radical departure from the historical common law approach,[154] thus bringing New Zealand more in line with Australia's approach to this specific matter on public benefit.[155]

The *Liberty Trust* case also reflects this approach, although perhaps in more controversial circumstances. Mallon J asserted that the money-lending scheme conferred a public benefit, even though individuals will benefit from receiving an interest-free loan. Her Honour suggested that such private benefit 'is part and parcel of Christian living'[156] distinguishing it from, inter alia, *Gilmour* v. *Coats*,[157] where the benefits were said to be of a private nature because their purposes focused too narrowly on the adherents. It could be argued that the purposes in *Liberty Trust* were also too narrowly focused on the adherents, because while there was an expectation that beneficiaries would increase their Christian services as a result of being freed from debt, this was also counted with the word 'hope', and not all beneficiaries had done so.[158] Indeed, *Canterbury Development Corporation* states that while purposes may be laudable, they must be more than hopeful.[159] Nonetheless, Mallon J was clear that while a mortgage scheme may not have such acceptance as a religious service, it was a 'public example of what is intended to be a Christian approach'[160] to financial matters. Thus, this case reflects an evolution as to what may now be construed as having public benefit within the advancement of religion.

The recent High Court case of *Re the Foundation for Anti-Aging Research and the Foundation for Reversal of Solid State Hypothermia*[161] also reflects this jurisprudential approach, albeit under the head of advancement of education.[162] In brief, the purposes of the Foundations include providing funding for research into medical therapies to alleviate and eliminate degenerative disease in humans, and the development of technology to repair or regenerate body tissues damaged through illness, ageing, and cryopreservation processes. Public benefit is presumed under this head,[163] although the Board of DIACS considered that controversial purposes, such as those in question, would raise issues pertaining to morality and ethics, and lack public benefit.

154 For example, *Bowman* v. *Secular Society* [1917] AC 406 (HL); *Re Draco Foundation (NZ) Charitable Trust* (201) 25 NZTC 20-032 (HC); and *McGovern* v. *Attorney-General* [1982] Ch 321

155 *Aid/Watch Incorporated* v. *Commissioner of Taxation* [2010] HCA 42.

156 *Liberty Trust* v. *Charities Commission*, 121.

157 *Liberty Trust* v. *Charities Commission*, 118, referring to *Gilmour* v. *Coates* [1949] AC 426 (HL); see also *Cocks* v. *Manners* (1871) LR 12 Esq 574 (HL).

158 Footnote 62 *Liberty Trust v Charities Commision*.

159 *Canterbury Development Corporation* v. *Charities Commission*, [44]; see also Chevalier-Watts, 'Charitable Trusts and Advancement of Religion'.

160 *Liberty Trust* v. *Charities Commission*, [122].

161 *Re the Foundation for Anti-Aging Research and the Foundation for Reversal of Solid State Hypothermia*.

162 Relief of poverty and other purposes beneficial to the community were considered but failed [76]–79].

163 *Re the Foundation for Anti-Aging Research and the Foundation for Reversal of Solid State Hypothermia*, [63], referring to *New Zealand Computer Society Inc* (2011) 25 NZTC 20-033 (HC), [13].

However, Ellis J stated that the Board erred in this matter, stating 'there is no authority that research must be uncontroversial before it can be considered charitable'.[164] This is evidenced with the concept of stem cell research, which has 'been accepted as such'.[165] Traditionally, in advocacy cases, courts have historically been reluctant to judge the public benefit if the subject of the advocacy has been controversial. However, the Supreme Court in *Greenpeace* has now confirmed that 'presence or absence of controversy cannot be determinative'.[166]

In relation to the issues raised by the Board in connection with courts being sceptical about 'alleged downstream benefits'[167] of research, and the potential costs of the research, Ellis J stated the following, respectively. First research 'is an iterative process',[168] meaning that the benefit would not necessarily lie in the end result. Second, the Foundations' purposes do not include a provision of cryogenic services, thus the correct approach is to focus on the research, and the benefit that that yields.[169] Consequently, Ellis J concluded that the public benefit was not rebutted, and indeed, the public benefit was 'readily apparent'.[170]

Thus, this foray into contemporary public benefit reveals that New Zealand appears, generally, to be progressive in its approach, even when faced with novel circumstances that might otherwise call for a more conservative approach. This may then be a reflection of its socially progressive outlook as a nation generally. For instance, in matters such as personal rights and freedoms; schooling and tertiary education; and tolerance and inclusion of minority groups,[171] and charity law underpins this outlook, due to the close correlation between societal progression, requirements, and charity.

---

164 *Re the Foundation for Anti-Aging Research and the Foundation for Reversal of Solid State Hypothermia*, [66].

165 Ibid.

166 *Re the Foundation for Anti-Aging Research and the Foundation for Reversal of Solid State Hypothermia*, [66], referring to *Re Greenpeace of New Zealand Inc*, [75]; see Chapter 11 for discussion on the political purposes doctrine.

167 *Re the Foundation for Anti-Aging Research and the Foundation for Reversal of Solid State Hypothermia*, [66].

168 Ibid.

169 Ibid.

170 Ibid., [67].

171 Simon Collins, 'NZ Ranked #1 for Social Progress', *New Zealand Herald*, 3 April 2014; Michael E. Porter, Scott Stern, and Michael Green, *Social Progress Index 2014*, Non-Profit Organization Report; 'New Zealand Tops New Ranking of the World's Most Socially Progressive Countries', *Business Insider (Australia)* (4 April 2014), www.nzherald.co.nz/nz/news/article.cfm?c_id=1&objectid=11231593 [accessed 6 Oct. 2016], referring to Social Progress Index 2014, www2.deloitte.com/content/dam/Deloitte/cr/Documents/public-sector/2014-Social-Progress-IndexRepIMP.pdf [accessed 6 Oct. 2016]; Astrid Zweynert, 'New Zealand Tops New Ranking of the World's Most Socially Progressive Countries', Business Insider Australia (4 April 2014), www.businessinsider.com.au/r-new-zealand-tops-social-progress-index-worlds-biggest-economies-trail-2014-02?r=US&IR=T [accessed 6 Oct. 2016].

9 Hong Kong

A Introduction

Hong Kong, or the Hong Kong Special Administrative Region of the People's Republic of China (HKSAR), comprises the islands of Hong Kong, the Kowloon Peninsula, the New Territories, and 235 outlying islands; it amounts to a total of 1,075 square miles.[1] The population of Hong Kong in 2016 was approximately 7.3 million people,[2] the majority being ethnic Chinese, and the remaining population made up of a diverse range of Asian and European races.[3]

Hong Kong is said to have a vibrant third sector, with a variety of charitable activities being a mainstay in Hong Kong since its early days as a colony,[4] and its history of charitable activities can be traced to its colonial period, which began in the mid-nineteenth century.[5] Prior to coming under British rule in January 1841, Hong Kong belonged to San On County (of China), and at the time the island of Hong Kong was only inhabited by a few thousand people. Formal cessation to the United Kingdom took place in June 1843, and in July 1997, the People's Republic of China assumed sovereignty over Hong Kong, from which date it was known as HKSAR;[6] for the purposes of this book, 'Hong Kong' will be utilised. While China has indeed assumed sovereignty, Hong Kong has a separate legal and administrative system from China, which is set out in its Basic Law Constitution. The effect of this 'one country, two system' principle has been to retain the conditions that made Hong Kong a commercial success. In addition to preserving the practical conditions within Hong Kong, it also preserves Hong Kong's legal system, which is based on the British common law system,

---

1 William Ahern, 'Trust Law in Hong Kong', *Trust and Trustees* 20(1–2) (February–March 2014), 107.
2 http://countrymeters.info/en/Hong_Kong [accessed 13 Oct. 2016].
3 Ahern, 'Trust Law in Hong Kong', 107.
4 Eric Fichtl, 'An Introduction to the Third Sector in Hong Kong: Historical Developments and Current Outlook' (International Field Program, 2006), www.ericfichtl.org/index.php/texts/article/third_sector_hong_kong [accessed 13 Oct. 2016].
5 Rebecca Lee and Lusina Ho, 'Advocating Public Advocacy: An Opportunity for Charities in Hong Kong?', *Trusts and Trustees* 18(1) (January 2012), 43; see also W. F. Lam and J. L. Perry, 'The Role of the Non-Profit Sector in Hong Kong's Development', *Voluntas* 11(4) (2000).
6 Ahern, 'Trust Law in Hong Kong', 107–8.

and it also has a final court of appeal in Hong Kong. This means, unsurprisingly, that Hong Kong's charity law finds much of its history in the English charity law principles, as opposed to mainland Chinese charity law.[7]

While it is said that the charitable sector has been largely shaped by its colonial history, similar to that of New Zealand, what is also important in this sector in relation to charity, is the makeup of the early local Chinese population, which comprised mainly refugees from mainland China. As a result of lack of resources, colonial rule did little to provide community services to these people, thus self-help and mutual assistance developed in order to fill the gaps left by the ruling parties. Religious and cultural groups, with Chinese cultural traditions, played a large role in supporting communities, and when we consider charitable purposes, later in the chapter, it is evident how many of these purposes are so often context specific to Hong Kong itself, and particularly in relation to Chinese cultural traditions. Indeed, 'charitable giving remains fundamentally inspired by the distinctive Chinese attitude',[8] and the Asian concept of charity has strong foundations in Buddhism, Taoism, Confucianism, and folk culture.[9]

Thus community-based initiatives were key in providing social welfare, and this remained the case up until the 1970s, when rapid economic growth led to a strong business and market sector. With this, the colonial Government was under pressure to improve state welfare provisions, which it began to do. In modern times, the majority of social welfare services are funded by government subvention, and increasingly, the not-for-profit sector, including charity, has become an extension of bureaucracy.[10]

Therefore, the Hong Kong charity sector reflects the altruistic notion of giving, which is deeply rooted in Chinese culture, with such altruism being based on religious thoughts and practices embedded in Chinese custom, as well as being influenced by the Western traditions as a result of colonisation, which included the early social policy of separation.[11] This therefore required ethnic groups to rely on resourcefulness and self-help to assist their social needs, because '[i]n brief, charitable activities were not on the minds of government officials'[12] up until around the mid 1900s in colonial Hong Kong.[13]

While the state may have been lax in its social welfare policies, social unrest in the 1960s caused the Government to invest in education, and social housing and services, and with the transfer of sovereignty to China in 1997, the Government increased its spending on social welfare to enhance its legitimacy. There has subsequently been quite some increase in the number of charitable organisations in Hong Kong.[14]

---

7 Patrick Hamlin and Philip Munro, 'Hong Kong', in *International Charitable Giving*, (Oxford: Oxford University Press, 2012), 301–2.
8 Damian Bethke, 'Charity Law Reform in Hong Kong: Taming the Asian Dragon?', *International Journal of Not-for-Profit Law* 18(1) (May 2016), 16.
9 Bethke, 'Charity Law Reform in Hong Kong', 18, referring to Yu Yue Tsu, *The Spirit of Chinese Philanthropy: A Study in Mutual Aid* (New York: Columbia University, 1912).
10 Terence Yui Kai Yuen, 'Hong Kong' (APPC, 2003), 90–1.
11 Bethke, 'Charity Law Reform in Hong Kong', 18 and 20.
12 Ibid., 21.
13 Ibid.
14 Ibid., 23.

B A potted history of charitable regulations

The increase in charitable organisations in Hong Kong occurred without a broad legal framework. For instance, s 3 of the Ordinance No. 3 1870 incorporated the Tung Wah Hospital, which was the first medical institution in Hong Kong to provide free medical treatment to the local Chinese population, and was supported through voluntary contributions.[15] While this may sound charitable, actually there was no terminology for charity or tax exemption at the time. By way of another example, the Po Leung Kuk Incorporation Ordinance Cap 306 1893, which created a more efficient system for the Po Leung Kuk Institute[16] to operate under, made no reference to charity or tax exemptions, although the latter may be because Hong Kong had no income tax until 1940, thus such a point was irrelevant at the time.[17]

Even today, Hong Kong lacks a comprehensive legal framework for regulating charities, and indeed there is no single piece of legislation that governs charities,[18] which inevitably means that the data available regarding numbers of charities,[19] and their activities, is rather more limited than, for instance, the Western jurisdictions discussed in this book. The rules governing charities are to be found within a variety of laws, including trusts, contracts, and company law, which were predominately created for commercial relationships, but now contain ad hoc additions to encompass charitable organisations.[20]

Hong Kong therefore follows the traditional common law approach to charity law, as addressed below, and in line with its colonial heritage. However, unlike England and Wales, it does not have an independent regulator, such as a Charity Commission. Any entities intending to raise funds for charitable purposes must apply to the Inland Revenue Department (IRD) in order to obtain tax exemption.[21] Section 88 of the Inland Revenue Ordinance (IRO) states that:[22]

> Provided that where a trade or business is carried on by any such institution or trust the profits derived from such trade or business shall be exempt and shall be deemed to have been exempt from tax only if such profits are applied solely

15 Bethke, 'Charity Law Reform in Hong Kong', 21 and 24, referring to John M. Carroll, *Edge of Empires: Chinese Elites and British Colonials in Hong Kong*, 1st edn (New York: Harvard University Press, 2005), 60.
16 This institute was set up to prevent kidnappers from bringing women and children into Hong Kong; Po Leung Kuk, www.poleungkuk.org.hk/en/2009071036/our-history/our-history.html [accessed 13 Oct. 2016].
17 Bethke, 'Charity Law Reform in Hong Kong', 24.
18 Rebecca Lee, 'Charity without Politics? Exploring the Limits of "Politics" in Charity Law', *Journal of Civil Society* 11(3) (2015), 272.
19 Hamlin and Munro, 'Hong Kong', 303.
20 Lee, 'Charity without Politics?', 272.
21 John Kong Shan Ho and Rohan Bruce Edward Price, 'Reform of Charity Law in Hong Kong and Australia: What Lessons Can Be Learned from the United Kingdom', *Asian Journal of Comparative Law* 6(1) (Article 11) (2011), 8; Law Reform Commission of Hong Kong, 'Report on Charities', 6 December 2013, 23–8, www.hkreform.gov.hk/en/docs/rcharities_e.pdf [accessed 27 Jan. 2016].
22 Inland Revenue Ordinance 1950 (Cap 112), s. 88.

for charitable purposes and are not expended substantially outside Hong Kong and either – (Amended 7 of 1986 s. 12)

a   the trade or business is exercised in the course of the actual carrying out of the expressed objects of such institution or trust; or

b   the work in connection with the trade or business is mainly carried on by persons for whose benefit such institution or trust is established.

This IRO was the first law applicable to charitable entities, and was enacted as late as 1950, although it did have the effect of kickstarting the contemporary charitable organisation, and in 2014, there were over 8,000 registered charitable organisations in Hong Kong.[23]

There has been one recent law change that is likely to have an impact on some charitable institutions, although the ordinance's focus is on companies. The Hong Kong Companies Ordinance (Cap 622) came into effect in March 2014, with the aim of, inter alia, enhancing corporate governance and modernising the law. Its impact will be felt by those charitable organisations that are incorporated as Hong Kong companies limited by guarantee. The new law raises the bar on corporate governance requirements, especially with regard to the enforcement regime, and the standard of care expected of directors. Thus, the new provisions may be of particular relevance to directors of such entities who play a passive role, or who have limited business experience.[24] However, it is not within the remit of this book to address specific changes within company law.

So while there has been some limited modernisation of charitable regulation, it has been piecemeal, and it could be said, therefore, that Hong Kong's charity law looks increasingly obsolete,[25] in light of contemporary societal needs and evolution, and especially when considering the changes that have occurred in jurisdictions such as England and Wales and Australia. It is perhaps of little surprise therefore that there have been calls for reform in recent years.

C Law reform

Since the early 1990s there have been calls for greater transparency and accountability with regard to the solicitation and disposal of monies for charitable purposes, and for more stringent control and monitoring of charitable activities.[26] It

23 Bethke, 'Charity Law Reform in Hong Kong', 24; John Nylander, 'Is Hong Kong a Paradise for Charity Fraudsters? It Surely Could Be', *Forbes* (17 September 2015), www.forbes.com/sites/jnylander/2015/09/17/is-hong-kong-a-paradise-for-charity-fraudsters-it-surely-could-be/#1193e0a376e0 [accessed 14 Sept. 2016].

24 Cindy Shammall, 'Assessing the Impact of the New Hong Kong Companies Ordinance on Charitable Institutions' (June 2014), www.skadden.com/newsletters/Assessing_the_Impact_of_the_New_Hong_Kong_Companies_Ordinance_on_Charitable_Institutions.pdf [accessed 13 Oct. 2016].

25 Lee, 'Charity without Politics?', 272.

26 Kai Yuen, 'Hong Kong', 101.

took many years for any movement to gain traction, but in June 2007, the Chief Justice and Secretary for Justice in Hong Kong asked the Law Reform Commission (Commission) to review the law and regulatory framework regarding to charity law in Hong Kong, and to make recommendations for reform. The Charities Sub-Committee of the Commission published a consultation paper in June 2011,[27] and a subsequent report followed in December 2013. The report provided a comprehensive review of national charity law, and provided 18 recommendations for improvement within charity law.

One of the key proposals from the report was for a statutory definition of charitable purpose. This was in response to the view that the adoption of the common law position developed under the *Pemsel* case was outdated. The report recommended that a clear statutory definition be drafted to recognise wider scopes of charitable purpose, which would enhance charities generally, and encourage the public to engage in more charitable activities.[28]

Another recommendation was that additional charitable purposes should be recognised. The IRD already confirms it recognises at least 11 types of charitable purposes,[29] as set out below, but the report recommended an additional three, which would take into consideration the values of a modern society.[30]

Overall, the recommendations generally were said to be 'modest', not least because the most contentious recommendation, that being a centralised regulatory and supervisory authority, had been removed.[31] The Sub-Committee had recommended the establishment of a Charity Commission, in light of such bodies being established by other jurisdictions.[32] However, this suggestion was not supported in the final Law Reform Commission's report due to an apparent lack of consensus among the public.[33] It is said that a number of religious organisations, some with underground activities in mainland China, were fearful of a watchdog that would undermine their religious freedom. Ironically, however, the trust in the Hong Kong Government has been said recently to be at an all-time low, and a charity commission may have improved such trust.

Regardless, just a few years after the release of the Law Commission's report, the Government is yet to take action, or give a response, and since there is no consensus on charity law reform, the authorities have put it on hold.[34] This is said to be because of the current political climate, with other priorities being placed on

27 Kong Shan Ho and Edward Price, 'Reform of Charity Law in Hong Kong and Australia', 8.
28 'Report on Charities', [2.37]–[2.48].
29 IRD, 'A Tax Guide for Charitable Institutions and Trusts of a Public Character' (September 2010), www.ird.gov.hk/eng/tax/ach_tgc.htm [accessed 17 Nov. 2016], at Appendix A.
30 'Report on Charities', 42–74.
31 Bethke, 'Charity Law Reform in Hong Kong', 25.
32 'Report on Charities', [9.1].
33 'Report on Charities', [9.65].
34 Nylander, 'Is Hong Kong a Paradise?'.

the Government. With that in mind, it would be fair to say that any possible law reform has now stalled at the time of writing.[35]

D Inland Revenue Department

As mentioned earlier, the IRD is only responsible for tax exemption aspects of charitable entities. It is not responsible for registering charities, and neither is it responsible for monitoring their conduct. The IRD does keep a public directory of approved charitable entities on its website, but it is not compulsory for charities to have their names placed on this list, and thus this information does not provide a conclusive list of all charities in Hong Kong.[36]

In addition, the Companies Registry also keeps a register. This register covers all charitable organisations created under the Company Ordinance, although it does not differentiate between for-profit organisations or charitable organisations. Therefore, if a charitable entity is not registered with the IRD, the public cannot obtain information about it,[37] thus limiting public awareness and engagement in the third sector. Indeed, such a lack of formal and comprehensive directories is of grave concern for the sector because 'it hinders the public from ascertaining the legal status of an organization. A directory would improve the system and would address the problem of monitoring charitable activities'.[38]

In Hong Kong, unlike England and Wales and New Zealand, for instance, there is no statutory requirement for charitable entities to submit annual records or accounts. Instead, the IRD will, on an ad hoc basis, call for accounts, financial records, or other relevant paperwork to carry out a review as to whether an entity is still charitable and that its activities are still compatible with its objects.[39] However, if a charity exists in the form of a society or unincorporated association, it is only required to submit copies of self-certified accounts. On the other hand, if a charity exists in the form of an incorporated company, it must submit audited accounts to the IRD at least once every four years as part of the IRD's review of charities.[40] However, a charity established as a statutory body may be subject to stringent control. For instance, the Tung Wah Ordinance and the Po Leung Kok Ordinance require their boards to keep proper records of all transactions; the books have to be available for inspection by any director, or persons appointed by the Chief Executive Officer of Hong Kong; and they must be audited by a certified public accountant.[41]

---

35 Stefano Mariani, 'Traditional Chinese Religion Trusts in Hong Kong', *Trust and Trustees* 21(5) (June 2015), 539.
36 Nylander, 'Is Hong Kong a Paradise?'.
37 Bethke, 'Charity Law Reform in Hong Kong', 28.
38 Ibid.
39 'Report on Charities', [9.1], referring to IRD, 'Tax Guide for Charitable Institutions', [17].
40 'Report on Charities', [1.54].
41 Bethke, 'Charity Law Reform in Hong Kong', 29, referring to Tung Wah Group of Hospitals Ordinance 1971 [Cap 1051] (Hong Kong HK); Po Leung Kuk Ordinance 1973 [Cap 1040].

More evidence of the ad hoc basis of scrutiny is seen when a charity applies to conduct fundraising activities, called flag days. Permission is sought through the Social Welfare Department (SWD), or, if funds are raised through a lottery, the entity must first have been granted a licence from the Commissioner for Television and Entertainment Licencing (CTEL). While this does appear to offer some form of accountability, an entity can escape this control if it does not undertake the fundraising during a flag day, and does not engage in activities that may include an element of chance, such as a lottery. Thus, fundraising is only monitored by the Government if the activities fall under the remit of the SWD or the CTEL.[42]

So, while there is some level of accountability, operating on such a limited, and apparently ad hoc basis, provides inadequate scrutiny overall, and is unlikely to increase public confidence in the charitable sector in Hong Kong.

E Charitable purposes

The English common law does not define charity, and as has been discussed in earlier chapters, it 'merely provides a methodology for distinguishing charitable from non-charitable purposes'.[43] Likewise, there is no statutory definition for 'charity', or 'charitable purpose', in Hong Kong;[44] instead, Hong Kong relies on the traditional English approach to determining charitable purpose.[45] This means that for an organisation to be charitable, it must be exclusively charitable, and it must be established for public benefit.[46] Charitable purposes therefore will fall within those mentioned in the Preamble of the Statute of Elizabeth,[47] and subsequently in the condensed purposes set out by Lord Macnaghten in *Commissioners for Special Purposes of Income Tax* v. *Pemsel*, or those analogous to them.[48]

Thus, the purposes that Hong Kong recognises as charitable are:[49]

a   relief of poverty;
b   advancement of education;
c   advancement of religion; and

---

42 Bethke, 'Charity Law Reform in Hong Kong', 28, referring to Summary Offences Ordinance 1933 [Cap 228], s. 4(17)(i); Gambling Ordinance 1977 [Cap 148]; Office Ombudsman – Hong Kong, *Office of the Ombudsman: Investigation Report* (2013), 5.5.
43 Lee and Ho, 'Advocating Public Advocacy', 43–4.
44 Ibid.
45 *Ng Chi (or Tze) Fong* v. *Hui Ho Pui Fun* [1987] HKCFI 42, [87]; *Hong Kong and Shanghai Bank Hong Kong (Trustee) Ltd* v. *The Incorporated Trustees of the Islamic Community Fund of Hong Kong*, No. HCMP 000631/1981.
46 Lee, 'Charity without Politics?', 273; IRD, 'Tax Guide for Charitable Institutions'.
47 See Chapter 2 for further details.
48 Lee, 'Charity without Politics?', 273, referring to *Commissioners for Special Purposes of Income Tax* v. *Pemsel* [1891] AC 531.
49 IRD, 'Tax Guide for Charitable Institutions', [4].

d   other purposes of a charitable nature beneficial to the community not falling
under any of the preceding heads.

This evidently is reflective of its colonial ancestry, although Hong Kong does have
a specific approach to purposes, as the Inland Revenue Department confirms:[50]

> While the purposes under the first three heads may be in relation to activities
> carried on in any part of the world, those under head (d) will only be regarded
> as charitable if they are of benefit to the Hong Kong community.

This came about as a result of *Camille and Henry Dreyfus Foundation Inc* v.
Inland Revenue,[51] whereby the House of Lords held that a charity does not
include a body established under the laws of another legal system because:

> It is at once apparent that the phrase in section 37 (1) (b) 'any body of per-
> sons or trusts established for charitable purposes only' is not expressly limited
> to bodies of persons or trusts established in the United Kingdom, but the
> Court of Appeal held that it should be construed as being so limited.

Thus tax exemption will only be:[52]

> given to charities subject to the jurisdiction of the courts in Hong Kong, that is to
> say, charities established in Hong Kong or Hong Kong establishment of overseas
> charities such as those deemed to be established in Hong Kong under section 4 of
> the Societies Ordinance or registered under Part XI of the Companies Ordinance.

This echoes the original English approach, where a purpose, under what was originally the fourth head of charity, that of any other purposes beneficial to the
community, could not be charitable unless the community, or a section of the
community to be benefited, was in the United Kingdom. However, in 1992,
the Charity Commission for England and Wales determined that it should first
assess as to whether the body operating overseas would be considered a charity if
it operated in the United Kingdom. If yes, then the body would be charitable
even if it operated overseas, unless it was contrary to public policy. This was supported in *Re Carapiet's Trust*, although Hong Kong has not yet considered this
decision. Although it should be noted that English decisions are no more than
persuasive in Hong Kong, thus its relevance may be minor, even if it were considered.[53] Nonetheless, it appears that the IRD adopts a conservative approach

---

50 Ibid.
51 *Camille and Henry Dreyfus Foundation Inc* v. *Commissioner of Inland Revenue*
    [1956] 1 AC 39 (HL), 335; IRD, 'Tax Guide for Charitable Institutions'.
52 IRD, 'Tax Guide for Charitable Institutions', Appendix A.
53 Hamlin and Munro, 'Hong Kong', 303–4, referring to *Re Carapiet's Trust* [1] 2002
    EWHC 1304.

when considering applications under the fourth head and a body is unlikely to be granted charitable status unless its activities are confined to within Hong Kong.[54]

The IRD has made available to the public a set of purposes that have been found to be charitable, and these are:[55]

a   Relief of poor people;
b   Relief of victims of a particular disaster;
c   Relief of sickness;
d   Relief of physically and mentally disabled;
e   Establishment or maintenance of non-profit-making schools;
f   Provision of scholarships;
g   Diffusion of knowledge of particular academic subjects;
h   Establishment or maintenance of a church;
i   Establishment of religious institutions of a public character;
j   Prevention of cruelty to animals;
k   Protection and safeguarding of the environment or countryside.

In addition, the IRD also sets out purposes that have been found to be non-charitable:[56]

a   Attainment of a political object;
b   Promotion of the benefits of the founders or subscribers;
c   Provision of a playing field, recreation ground or scholarship fund for employees of a particular company or industry;
d   Encouragement of a particular sport such as angling or cricket

Utilising the same methodology employed in earlier chapters relating to specific jurisdictions, this chapter will consider a selection of key cases relative to charitable purposes in Hong Kong. This is because such '"leading cases" are a vital part of the chaotic-looking case law tradition',[57] and, indeed, could be said to reflect a uniquely Hong Kong perspective in many regards, while also being grounded in their English heritage.

F   Traditional Chinese religion and ancestor worship

We begin by considering this jurisdictional-specific matter in relation to *Ip Cheung Kwok* v. *Ip Siu Bun*,[58] but before we consider that case, it is worthwhile setting out, briefly, the meanings of traditional Chinese religion (TCR) and ancestor worship.

---

54   Hamlin and Munro, 'Hong Kong', 304.
55   IRD, 'Tax Guide for Charitable Institutions', [8].
56   Ibid., at Appendix A.
57   John Mummery, '*The Commissioners for Special Purposes of the Income Tax* v. *Pemsel*', *Charity Law and Practice Review* 16(1) (2013–14), 1.
58   *Ip Cheung Kwok* v. *Ip Siu Bun* [1990] 1 HKCA 356.

TCR is a 'deceptively general shorthand for the eclectic synthesis of Confucianism, Taoism, and Buddhism predominately practised by ethnic Chinese'.[59] Among its fundamental tenets is ancestor worship as an expression of religious piety. One of the most ritualised and visible forms of ancestor worship takes place in clan halls, called T'ong in Cantonese, where devotional plaques are erected to honour deceased relatives, and their spirits are said to be enshrined collectively therein. A T'ong is typically maintained by a clan, where members share the same surname and claim common descent. Clan membership is numerous and there are many villages within the New Territories that share the same surname, thus they are regarded as having a common clan affiliation.[60] Therefore, it can be said that TCR is a 'religious dimension of traditional Chinese social and kinship structures'.[61] Indeed, ancestor worship has a wider spiritual significance, and failure to make proper obeisance to the dead is said to be calamitous for society at large.[62]

The case of *Ip* concerned a complex dispute relating to the nature and identity of trusts upon which particular properties in Hong Kong were being held. The original settler was a member of the Ip clan, and one of the issues, inter alia, was whether one of the trusts that supplemented an ancestor worship fund was charitable. As has been discussed in earlier chapters, notwithstanding issues relating to the existence of the presumption of public benefit, public benefit in relation to the advancement of religion is said to be presumed, and this does not differ in Hong Kong.[63]

The Court acknowledged that ancestor worship is clearly a bulwark in the religious and social lives of the Chinese, but it was unable to find the charitable nature of such religion due to the absence of public benefit. This is because ancestor worship does not tend 'directly or indirectly towards the instruction or the edification of the public'.[64] Further, the clan raised issues of the second limb of the public benefit test, that of whether ancestor worship benefits a section of the public. In relation to this, the cases of *Re Compton* and *Oppenheim* v. *Tobacco Securities Co Ltd* were discussed in some detail in Chapter 4, but suffice to say here, even if a group of persons is numerous, 'if the nexus between them is their personal relationship to a single propositus or to several propositi, they are neither a community nor a section of the community'.[65] Thus the Court in *Ip* determined that it was 'inescapable that a trust for the benefit of the male descendants of Ip

59 Mariani, 'Traditional Chinese Religion Trusts in Hong Kong', 539.
60 Ibid.
61 Ibid.
62 Ibid., 539–40; see also *Choa Choon Neoh* v. *Spottiswoode* [1869] 1 Kyshe 216.
63 *Ip Cheung Kwok* v. *Ip Siu Bun*, [114]–[116], referring to *National Anti-Vivisection Society* v. *Inland Revenue Commissioners* [1948] 1 AC 31 (HL), 42 and 65; *Gilmour* v. *Coates* [1949] AC 426; *Yeap Cheah Neo* v. *Ong Cheung Neo* (1875) LR 6 PC 381; and *Hoare v Hoare* (1886) 56 LT 147.
64 *Ip Cheung Kwok* v. *Ip Siu Bun* [1990] 1 HKCA 356, [123], referring to *Cocks* v. *Manners* (1871) LR 12 Eq 574.
65 *Ip Cheung Kwok* v. *Ip Siu Bun*, [129]–[130], referring to *Re Compton* [1945] 1 Ch 123 (Civil Division); and *Oppenheim* v. *Tobacco Securities Trust Co Ltd* [1951] 1 AC 297 (HL).

Sze Shing ... falls squarely within the "single propositus" test which makes the requirement of common relationship to Sze Shing an attribute for selection of the class which renders the trusts ... non-charitable'.[66]

However, this decision has been criticised because it does not recognise a fundamental function specific to the Chinese cultural context. Just as in the New Zealand case of *Latimer* v. *CIR*,[67] where Māori tribes were recognised as being an exception to the *Oppenheim* blood-tie rule due to their unique cultural context not being in the consideration of the House of Lords in *Oppenheim*, it is said that the clan affiliation in *Ip* should be eligible for that same exception.[68] Consequently, it is argued that a clan, within a specific Chinese cultural context, 'being a fundamental and self-contained unit of social and religious organization, would constitute an important section of society'.[69]

The *Ip* case also speaks to the earlier aforementioned issues with current Hong Kong charity law, in that this case appears not to recognise fundamental aspects of Chinese life that would appear vital to many communities, thus signalling that reform is perhaps long overdue.

On the other hand, there is evidence that a trust to worship certain deities on T'ong land can be charitable. This was evidenced in the case of *Cheung Man Yu* v. *Lau Yuen Ching*.[70] As with the *Ip* case, *Cheung Man Yu* concerned the advancement of religion in the context of T'ong land. The Court's attention was drawn to the modesty of the temple, with a suggestion that because of its small size, this could only be construed as a vegetarian hall, as opposed to a temple. However, the Court asserted that while vegetarian meals were served there, these were ancillary to its overall charitable purpose and indeed a 'modest chapel can be a place for public worship'.[71] Its size was merely a reflection of the means and size of its congregation and did not reduce its public element. As a result, the Court confirmed that a charity should not be 'defined by its scale or resources. A legal ... charity may be small and run by one of few people. It does not have to be a public organisation'.[72]

What this case therefore shows is that where a T'ong structure houses ancestral plaques, this does not negate its charitability. If the ancestor worship were in a restricted place, this would likely render the trust non-charitable, but identifying a physical space, accessible to the public, such as this temple, regardless of its modest size, will satisfy the public benefit requirement, at least in Hong Kong.[73]

---

66 *Ip Cheung Kwok* v. *Ip Siu Bun* [1990] 1 HKCA 356, [134], also applying *Davies* v. *Perpetual Trustee Company (Limited)* [1959] AC 439.
67 See Chapters 1, 4, and 7 for further discussion.
68 Mariani, 'Traditional Chinese Religion Trusts in Hong Kong', 541–3.
69 Ibid., 543.
70 *Cheung Man Yu* v. *Lau Yuen Ching* [2007] 4 HK314.
71 Ibid., [63].
72 Ibid., [90].
73 Mariani, 'Traditional Chinese Religion Trusts in Hong Kong', 544.

This case is important not just for this reason, but because it also laid down some additional principles applicable to charitable institutions for religious purposes specific to Hong Kong:[74]

a The institution must prove that its religious purposes contain the element of public benefit in order to qualify as a charitable trust,
b Money to be raised specifically for the building of a place for public worship, which satisfies the requirement of a charity,
c Activities for the advancement of religion will not fail to qualify as a charity for lack of publicity or advertising. Religion may be advanced by word of mouth,
d If a building has been built for the advancement of religion, and there is the requisite public benefit, a legal charity can be established. It does not matter whether the person establishing the institution or its keeper knew that they had established a charitable trust. Nor does it matter that no formal declaration of establishment of trust has been made. Subsequent events may throw light on whether a charitable trust has been established, but they cannot by themselves alter the nature of the trust or convert a properly constituted charitable trust or its assets into a private trust or private property.

Thus, the public benefit requirement in relation to TCR appears to be applied rigorously, and with that it fails to acknowledge the cultural importance of this context-specific worship, suggesting therefore that 'the position of a TCR ancestor worship trust urgently requires consideration'.[75]

G Social welfare

The case of *Hong Kong & Shanghai Bank Hong Kong (Trustee) Ltd* v. *The Incorporated Trustees of the Islamic Community Fund of Hong Kong (Alla Ditta)*,[76] provides a unique perspective on the charitability of social welfare in the Hong Kong context.

This case concerned a gift to the Alla Ditta Welfare Society to assist, inter alia, in providing social welfare work to a specific area. It was suggested that the words 'assist in social welfare work' were too vague, as illustrated in *IRC* v. *Baddeley*,[77] where 'social well-being' was considered too vague, and thus not charitable. However, the Court was satisfied that regardless of the English interpretation, the notion of 'social welfare work' was well understood in Hong Kong, and satisfied the concept of charitable at law. This is because in Hong Kong, social welfare is 'coloured by the fact that one of the best known organs of Government in Hong

---

74 *Li Kim Sang Victor* v. *Chen Chi Hsia* HCA 481/2008 24 February [2016] 1 HKLRD 1153, [81], referring to *Cheung Man Yu* v. *Lau Yuen Ching*, [24]–[26], [39], [40], and [46] (footnote pinpoints omitted).
75 Mariani, 'Traditional Chinese Religion Trusts in Hong Kong', 544.
76 *Hong Kong and Shanghai Bank Hong Kong (Trustee) Ltd* v. *The Incorporated Trustees of the Islamic Community Fund of Hong Kong*.
77 Ibid., 5, referring to *Inland Revenue Commissioners* v. *Baddeley* (1955) AC 572.

Kong has long borne the title of the "Social Welfare Department"[78] and the work conducted by this department is concerned with public benefit. Thus 'assist in social welfare work' could only be construed as charitable.[79]

In contrast, however, in the case of *Ip Cheung Kwok* v. *Ip Siu Bun*, as discussed earlier, the Court of Appeal held that the common welfare of a village was not charitable because the meaning of 'welfare' was too wide, and assisting in improving the welfare of a village could involve anything that may enhance the life of the village community.[80] This reflected the approach in *Williams Trustees* v. *IRC*,[81] where Lord Simonds held that promoting the interests of Welsh people in London by social intercourse, and other means, was too wide to be charitable. The Court in *Ip* concluded that there was no direct analogy in charity law with a trust to assist common welfare in the village of Gut Tai, thus putting the trust outside of the spirit and intendment of the Statute of Elizabeth.[82]

At first sight, the *Ip* case appears to be a step backwards in the evolution of charity law in Hong Kong, in comparison with the interpretation of 'welfare' in the *Alla Ditta* case. Perhaps however it is more easily explained by noting that in *Ip*, 'common welfare' can be distinguished from 'social welfare' because the latter had a recognised meaning in Hong Kong, whereas 'common welfare' has no such direct analogy, thus the distinction is made.

Nonetheless, these cases highlight two issues. First, there appears confusion as to some meanings of 'charitable purpose', not least with regard to the comprehension of 'welfare'. Such variances will do little to assist with regard to public confidence and the ability to judge whether a body may be charitable at law. Second, that the state of Hong Kong charity law, in its current manifestation, does not always take into consideration the realities of contemporary society, nor specific cultural aspects. Thus, the earlier calls for reform are still as relevant today as they were when they were first made.

H Public benefit

As has become apparent, Hong Kong's charity law owes much of their heritage to its colonial ancestry, and inevitably this means that the public benefit requirement also follows this approach. However, it follows the pre-2006 English approach,[83]

---

78 *Hong Kong and Shanghai Bank Hong Kong (Trustee) Ltd* v. *Incorporated Trustees of the Islamic Community Fund of Hong Kong*, 5–6.

79 Ibid., 7–8. It should be noted that this gift did fail because it was not a properly constituted entity at the time of the testator's death, despite its general charitable intention.

80 *Ip Cheung Kwok* v. *Ip Siu Bun* [1990] 1 HKCA 356 (HKCA), [162]–[163].

81 Ibid., [166], citing *Williams' Trustees* v. *Inland Revenue Commissioners* [1947] AC 447, 455.

82 *Ip Cheung Kwok* v. *Ip Siu Bun*, [174]–[176], distinguishing *Re Wedgewood* [1911] 1 Ch 113 and *National Anti-Vivisection Society* v.*IRC* [1948] AC 31 (HL).

83 England saw the introduction of the Charities Act 2006 in the same year, which removed the presumption of public benefit for all the heads of charity, including the additional heads of charity that were also introduced at the same time; see Chapter 5

whereby public benefit is presumed, albeit rebuttable, for the first three *Pemsel* heads of charity, those of relief of poverty, advancement of education, and advancement of religion. For the fourth head, that is, any other purposes beneficial to the community, the presumption of public benefit does not exist.[84]

However, it is not always apparent that the public benefit is presumed in the first three heads of charity, as evidenced in some examples relating to the advancement of religion. In the case of *To Kan Chi* v. *Pui Man Yau*,[85] the fact that a temple was set up for the advancement of religion, or that it was set up for religious purposes, did not automatically make it charitable. In the case of *SJ* v. *To Can Chi*,[86] a number of temples were identified, and their ownership was in question. One was said to be held by a clan, family, or t'ong, and thus was held to be in private ownership. As discussed earlier, t'ongs are not generally recognised as falling within the construct of public benefit because:[87]

> The t'ong is an institution of Chinese law and custom. At least as they are generally understood, t'ongs are essentially in the nature of unincorporated associations composed of individuals and with continuous succession through patrilineal descent from their founding members.

What is noted is that the courts in such cases rely on expert extrinsic evidence of the tangibility of the public benefit in order to satisfy the public benefit test, which has strong echoes of the approach taken in *Gilmour* v. *Coates*.[88] This case has been approved by the courts in Hong Kong with regard to public benefit and the advancement of religion, for instance in the case of *Ip Cheung*. Here the Court observed that a:[89]

> celebration of a religious rite in private does not contain the necessary element of public benefit since any benefit by prayer or example is incapable of proof in the legal sense, and any element of edification is limited to a private, not public, class of those present in the celebration.

Such reliance on expert extrinsic evidence to determine public benefit may be because Hong Kong is a 'cosmopolitan city with a diversified religious society',[90]

for further details. See same chapter also for discussion on whether presumption of public benefit is thought to have existed.

84 Mark Hsiao, 'The Beginning and the End of an Era of Charitable Public Benefit in Hong Kong', *Conveyancer and Property Lawyer* 76(3) (2012), 44–5.

85 Ibid., 76 and 49, referring to *To Kan Chi* v. *Pui Man Yau* [1999] 1 CACV 32.

86 Hsiao, 'Beginning and End', 49, referring to *Secretary of Justice* v. *To Chan Chi* [2000] HKLRD 756.

87 *Secretary of Justice* v. *To Chan Chi*, [7].

88 Hsiao, 'Beginning and End', 48–9, referring to *Gilmour* v. *Coats*.

89 *Ip Cheung Kwok* v. *Ip Siu Bun* [1990] 1 HKCA 356 (HKCA), [114(3)], also referring to *Yeap Cheah Neo* v. *Ong Cheung Neo; Hoare* v. *Hoare*.

90 Hsiao, 'Beginning and End', 48.

thus 'there is a need of tangible and extrinsic evidence to support that the purpose of these religions benefit the public'.[91]

However, this approach appears to ignore the notion that public benefit is presumed, as to obtain such expert evidence suggests that the presumption does not exist, and that it is, prima facie, being established, as might occur with the fourth head of charity. Indeed, it could be argued that the House of Lords, in *Gilmour* v. *Coats*, took just that approach, as there is no mention, explicitly, of the presumption of public benefit, merely that the benefit was not explicitly established, thus rendering the convent in question not charitable. It could further be argued that jurisdictions such as Australia and New Zealand are also cosmopolitan, with diverse religious societies. However, their courts have been seen to acknowledge fully the presumption of public benefit, even in challenging circumstances, and recognised public benefit of religious purposes in a contemporary setting. Thus, for example, commercial endeavours, and mortgage schemes, have been recognised as advancing religion.[92]

The concept of public benefit therefore further emphasises the notion that Hong Kong charity law appears increasingly obsolete,[93] with a real need to recognise cultural and societal purposes that are relevant within Hong Kong itself in a modern context. So while Hong Kong might acknowledge, for instance, the social desirability of ancestor worship, the public benefit is not recognised because 'English law would not regard ancestor worship as charitable unless its ceremonies tended ... "directly or indirectly towards the instruction or the edification of the public"'.[94] Thus English law predominates, perhaps at the expense of the Hong Kong social context.

With regard to public benefit, in addition to the presumption of public benefit, or otherwise, a 'purpose is not charitable unless it is directed to the public or a sufficient section of it. An institution cannot generally be charitable if it is in principle established for the benefit of specific individuals'.[95] However, it is not possible to lay down any precise definition of what constitutes a sufficient section of the public. 'Each case must be considered on its own merit.'[96] Therefore, courts will inevitably assess the public nature of the charity through case law because 'charities law in Hong Kong ... largely remains governed by common law jurisprudence'.[97]

---

91 Ibid.
92 *Commissioner of Taxation* v. *Word Investments Ltd*, 236 CLR 204 (High Court of Australia); *Liberty Trust* v. *Charities Commission* [2011] 3 NZLR 68 (High Court). See Chapters 6 and 8 for relevant discussion of these two cases.
93 Lee, 'Charity without Politics?', 272.
94 *Ip Cheung Kwok* v. *Ip Siu Bun* [1990] 1 HKCA 356, [123], citing *Cocks* v. *Manners*, 585.
95 IRD, 'Tax Guide for Charitable Institutions', [5]; see also *Li Kim Sang Victor* v. *Chen Chi Hsia*, [71] and *Cheung Man Yu* v. *Lau Yuen Ching*, [24].
96 IRD, 'Tax Guide for Charitable Institutions', [5].
97 Mariani, 'Traditional Chinese Religion Trusts in Hong Kong', 539.

As we saw earlier in this chapter, this approach was followed in *Ip Cheung Kwok*,[98] where the Court approved the principles of *Oppenheim* v. *Tobacco Securities Trust Co Ltd* with regard to that which may constitute a public benefit as either benefiting an appreciably important or substantial section of the public. Thus, the purpose in the *Ip Cheung-Kwok* case 'fell squarely within the single propositus test',[99] causing the trust to fail for charitable purposes, and the later case of *Li Kim Sang Victor* v. *Chen Chi Hsia* also followed this approach. In the *Li Kim Sang Victor* case, the assets, inter alia, did not benefit an appreciably important section of the public, not least because all the beneficiaries were related to the deceased in question, meaning that the public benefit element was lacking.[100]

This foray into the principle of public benefit in Hong Kong reveals a moderate judicial approach, with a conservative English influence very much in evidence, illustrating that while Hong Kong may be said to be a vibrant and modern cosmopolitan country, its charity law is still firmly embedded in its colonial heritage. As such, it is of little surprise that the calls for reform have been made, and undoubtedly will continue until such time as the Government finds the political will to consider reform.

---

98 *Ip Cheung Kwok* v. *Ip Siu Bun* [1990] 1 HKCA 356.
99 Ibid., [134]; Hsiao, 'Beginning and End', 48. See Chapter 4 for discussion on this test.
100 *Li Kim Sang Victor* v. *Chen Chi Hsia* [2016] 1 HKLRD 1153, [96], referring to *Oppenheim* v. *Tobacco Securities Trust Co Ltd*.

10 Singapore

A Introduction

Singapore is the smallest country in South-East Asia, although it is densely populated, with the population standing at over five million in 2016.[1] It was founded as a British colonial outpost in 1816,[2] becoming a formal British colony in 1824, and it remained so until 1955. During that time, it was regarded as part of the Straits Settlement, along with Malacca and Penang in the Malay Peninsula. The Malays were the indigenous peoples in Singapore, with the Chinese and Indians constituting two large migrant groups. In 1953, the British-appointed Rendal Commission proposed a new constitution, which gave Singapore greater governance. The first election was held in 1955, and in 1959, self-government was attained. The People's Action Party (PAP) won the majority of the seats, and was sworn in as the first government of the state of Singapore, with Lee Kuan Yew as the Prime Minister. In 1963, Singapore joined Malaysia, although this merger ended two years later,[3] and Singapore obtained its independence in 1965.[4]

It is often said that charity begins at home, and this is reflected in the Singapore approach to philanthropy and charity, because the Singaporean Government has always eschewed the role of the state in providing a tax-based welfare system, and instead encouraged its population to assume personal responsibility for their own welfare, although the Government does provide subsidies in some areas, including housing, health, and education. This philosophy of encouraging self-independence in favour of market mechanisms has underpinned its rapid economic growth, making it prosperous on the world stage.[5]

1 www.singstat.gov.sg/docs/default-source/default-document-library/publications/p ublications_and_papers/population_and_population_structure/population2016.pdf [accessed 28 Nov. 2016].
2 Meng-Kin Lim, 'Shifting the Burden of Health Care Finance: A Case Study of Public–Private Partnership in Singapore', *Health Policy* 69(1) (2004), 85.
3 Eliza W. Y. Lee and M. Shamsul Haque, 'Development of the Non-Profit Sector in Hong Kong and Singapore: A Comparison of Two Statist-Corporatist Regimes', *Journal of Civil Society* 4(2) (2008), 101–2.
4 Rachel Leow, 'The Evolution of Charity Law in Singapore: From Pre-Independence to the 21st Century', *Trusts Law International* 26(2) (2012), 83.
5 Lim, 'Shifting the Burden of Health Care Finance', 85.

While it may appear that this is a political policy to avoid a welfare state, the emphasis on personal responsibility for welfare actually underpins the Singaporean sociocultural context of family responsibility and filial piety. The early pioneers of Singapore brought with them a long history of mutual benefit, and neighbourly and clan associations, which all reinforce the notion of family and community support. Thus, the modern-day Government policy merely reinforces early settler values.[6] This approach is perhaps not so surprising if one considers Singapore's politico-social context. Singapore is an island with no natural resources, and even from its outset, it faced an uncertain future. It had a short, but failed, political union with Malaysia until 1965, and its success after that was thought to be as a result of the strong government–people partnership, with a willingness to place the public good above self-interest.

In addition, Singapore has no tradition of state largesse. The early population was made up of migrants escaping poverty and oppression from other countries, and brought with them their own poverty and a desire for success. While Singapore was under British rule for 144 years, the British interest in ensuring health and well-being of its population was limited, and during the British rule, there was much poverty, malnutrition, overcrowding, and disease. Despite these issues, there was virtually no public medical care until 1844, with the building of a charity hospital, the Tan Tock Seng Hospital, although the funds raised for this came from Chinese community leaders, not the British.[7] Thus 'the spirit of self-help is deeply engrained in the Singaporean psyche'.[8]

Nonetheless, Singapore's charitable sector has grown in modern times, and in 2015, there were over 2,200 registered charities, which was an increase from the 1,807 charities in 2005.[9] It is suggested that setting up a charity in Singapore is a two-stage process. First, an organisation must be set up using an existing legal form. The most commonly used legal forms in Singapore for charities are the society, which is governed by the Societies Act 1985; the company limited by guarantee which is governed by the Companies Act 2006; and the trust. This may be subject to the Trustees Act 2005, and possibly the Trust Companies Act 2006.[10]

The second stage is that the organisation must then ensure compatibility with the Charities Act 1994 by ensuring that its purposes are 'exclusively charitable',[11] which inevitably means the application of the common law to determine such

---

6 Ngoh Tiong Tan, 'Regulating Philanthropy: The Legal and Accountability Framework for Singapore Charities', *Asia Pacific Journal of Social Work and Development* 17(1) (June 2007), 75.
7 Lim, 'Shifting the Burden of Health Care Finance', 89.
8 Ibid.
9 Janice Tai, 'Charity Boom: Number of Registered Charities Increase by 23% in 10 Years', *Straits Times*, 27 December 2015, www.straitstimes.com/singapore/charity-boom-number-of-registered-charities-increase-by-23-in-10-years [accessed 28 Nov. 2016].
10 Rachael Leow, 'Four Misconceptions about Charity Law in Singapore', *Singapore Journal of Legal Studies* (1) (2012), 38.
11 Charities Act 1994, s 2(1).

matters. Thus, to be eligible to register as a charity, the entity's governing documents must provide that the entity's purposes are exclusively charitable. There are two further requirements: the entity must have a minimum of three persons to perform the function of governing members, at least two of whom will be Singaporean citizens or permanent residents; and the entity's purposes must benefit wholly or substantially a community in Singapore.[12]

B A potted history of charitable regulations

While its sociopolitical policies are rooted in its own historical context, its charity laws are rooted in its colonial history, with its common law being derived primarily from English law, as well as local case law. By virtue of the Second Charter of Justice 1826, English common law, equity, and statute law came into force and became the applicable law before 27 November 1826, so far as local circumstances permitted, but despite the cut-off date, it was evident that English law continued to be applied long after that date,[13] and is still utilised in contemporary times.[14]

In 1982, the Singaporean legislature enacted the Charities Act 1982, to register and better administer charities in Singapore, and to permit the Commissioner of Charities to determine the charitable status of organisations,[15] and this was modelled on the English 1960 statute.[16]

Under s 2 of the Act, 'charitable purposes' were defined as 'purposes that are exclusively charitable according to the law of Singapore'.[17] There was no further reference to a definition of 'charitable purpose', thus the Commissioner, and the courts, had little option but to turn to former sources to determine charitable status. For instance, in *Choa Choon Neoh* v. *Spottiswoode*, Maxwell CJ said that 'In this Colony, so much of the law of England as was in existence when it was imported here, and is of general ... policy ... is the law of the land'.[18]

---

12 Leow, 'Four Misconceptions about Charity Law in Singapore', 39, referring to Charities (Registration of Charities) Regulations 2008 (Cap 37, Reg 10, 2008 Rev Ed Sing), regs 3(1)(a)–(c); 'Legislative Conditions for Registration as a Charity or IPC', www.charities.gov.sg/setting-up-a-charity/Registering-for-a-new-charity/Pages/Legislative%20Conditions%20for%20Registration%20as%20a%20Charity_IPC.aspx [accessed 7 Dec. 2016].

13 Ter Kah Leng, *The Law of Charities – Cases and Materials: Singapore and Malaysia* (Singapore: Butterworths, 1985), 3.

14 *Koh Lau Keow* v. *Attorney-General* [2014] SGCA 18, [18], referring to *Commissioners for Special Purposes of the Income Tax* v. *Pemsel* [1891] AC 531, 583, making reference to the four heads of charity; see generally *Khoo Jeffrey* v. *Life Bible-Presbyterian Church* [2011] SGCA 18 (26 April 2011).

15 Lim Kien Thye, 'Clearing the Charity Muddle: A Statutory Proposal – The Charities Act 1992', *Malaya Law Review* 26(1) (1984), 133.

16 Kerry O'Halloran, Myles McGregor-Lowndes, and Karla W. Simon, *Charity Law & Social Policy: National and International Perspectives on the Functions of Law Relating to Charities*, vol. 10 (Netherlands: Springer, 2008), 346.

17 Thye, 'Clearing the Charity Muddle', 133.

18 *Choa Choon Neoh* v. *Spottiswoode* (1869) 1 Ky 216, 221.

Thus, the Preamble of the Statute of Charitable Uses 1601 was relied upon, as were, and still are, the classifications laid down by Lord Macnaghten in *The Commissioners for Special Purposes of the Income Tax* v. *Pemsel*,[19] those purposes being the relief of poverty, the advancement of education, the advancement of religion, and any other purposes beneficial to the community.

The Charities Act 1994 was the next key legislative landmark, and was introduced to alleviate concerns expressed by the Commissioner of Charities that tighter regulatory controls and investigative powers were required to address administrative misuses and malpractice. Some indications of abuse related to high administrative expenses; dubious fundraising methods; and abnormally high fundraising costs. The Act did reflect some of the deficiencies highlighted by the Commissioner, and it came into effect, with the exception of Part VII, in January 1995. The Act re-enacts, with amendments, certain provisions of the Charities Act 1982, as well as introducing innovative provisions.[20]

These provisions included increasing the Commissioner's powers of investigation, as well as, inter alia, improving administration of charities.[21] This Act has also evolved over the years, with 'changes reflecting the changing times in Singapore'.[22] Thus revisions in 1995, and amendments in 2001, 2004, and 2005, now provide more effective registration and administration of charities, as well as enhancing the power of the Commissioner to investigate abuses of the system. This included introducing the offence of supplying false or misleading information, or the altering of, or destroying any document.[23]

This Act still remains the key legislation governing charity law in Singapore, although there are other Acts and Regulations that exist to govern charities in Singapore. These are the Charities (Accounts and Annual Report) Regulations; the Charities (Fees) Regulations; the Charities (Fund-Raising Appeals for Local and Foreign Charitable Purposes) Regulations 2012; the Charities (Large Charities) Regulations; the Charities (Registration of Charities) Regulations; and the Charities (Institutions of A Public Character) Regulations.[24]

The 1994 Act was said to be ambitious, and has been, for the most part, welcomed, because it now provides a better framework of supervision, which had

19 Ravindran Ramasamy, 'Charity Law: A Time to Define', *Singapore Law Review* 5 (1984), 230–1, referring to *Commissioners for Special Purposes of Income Tax* v. *Pemsel; In Re Abdul Guny Abdullasa Deceased; Fatima Beebee Amal* v. *Mohamed Abubakar* [1936] 1 MLJ 140, [14]–[15]; *Veerasamy Krishnasamy* v. *Jannaki Ammal* [1947] MLJ 157, [2].
20 Ter Kah Leng, 'Changes to Charity Law', *Singapore Academy of Law Journal* 7(2) (1995), 291–2.
21 O'Halloran, McGregor-Lowndes, and Simon, *Charity Law & Social Policy*, 347; Leng, 'Changes to Charity Law', 291–302 generally and see for instance Charities Act 1994, ss 5, 7, 22, 24, 25, 27, 28 and Parts VII and VIII.
22 Tiong Tan, 'Regulating Philanthropy', 76.
23 Ibid., 77.
24 Legislation governing charities and IPC charity portal, www.charities.gov.sg/set ting-up-a-charity/Registering-for-a-new-charity/Pages/Legislation-governing-Cha rities.aspx [accessed 28 Nov. 2016].

been greatly lacking.[25] Indeed, the Act is 'an evolution over the years, with changes reflecting the changing times in Singapore', as evidenced by the revisions and amendments, mentioned above, that have occurred. Thus, it can be said that the Act now provides a 'solid framework ... to legitimately raise support and enhance accountability'.[26]

C Institutions of Public Character and Charities

Unique to the not-for-profit sector within Singapore are Institutions of Public Character (IPCs). They are described as:[27]

> Institutions of a Public Character (IPCs) are exempt or registered charities which are able to issue tax deductible receipts for qualifying donations to donors. In other words, donors are able to claim tax relief from their assessable income based on the amount donated, at prevailing deduction rate.

As a result, this makes IPCs generally more appealing to donors when attracting donations, because of the higher standards of regulatory compliance and governance.[28]

An IPC must be beneficial to the community in Singapore as a whole, as opposed to sectional interests.[29] IPC status can be granted to organisations that provide social, educational, sports, and even cultural services, although not all organisations that provide direct welfare services will be eligible for IPC status.[30]

There is some thought, incorrectly, that there is a conceptual necessity for IPCs to be charities, and vice versa, for charities to be IPCs. This misconception is perpetuated because the provisions of IPCs are found within the Charities Act 1994, and in subsidiary legislation. However, while an IPC may be a charity, it likewise, may also not be, and there is no legal requirement for an IPC to be a charity, or for a charity to be an IPC. The difference between the two lies in the eligibility criteria for registration as a charity, or approval of an IPC, respectively.[31]

As noted earlier, to be eligible to register as a charity, the entity's governing documents must provide that the entity's purposes are exclusively charitable; the entity must have a minimum of three persons to perform the function of governing members, at

25 Leng, 'Changes to Charity Law', 302.
26 Tiong Tan, 'Regulating Philanthropy', 77.
27 'About Charities and IPCs', www.charities.gov.sg/setting-up-a-charity/Pages/About-Charities-And-IPCs.aspx [accessed 7 Dec. 2016].
28 Ibid.
29 Kerry O'Halloran *et al.*, 'Charity Law Reforms: An Overview of Progress since 2001', in Myles McGregor-Lowndes and Kerry O'Halloran (eds), *Modernising Charity Law, Recent Developments and Future Directions* (Cheltenham: Edward Elgar, 2010), 21.
30 Chung Ming Wong, Vincent C. H. Chua, and S. Vasoo, 'Contributions to Charitable Organizations in a Developing Country: The Case of Singapore', *International Journal of Social Economics* 25(1) (1998), 27.
31 Leow, 'Four Misconceptions about Charity Law in Singapore', 39.

least two of whom will be Singaporean citizens or permanent residents; and the entity's purposes must benefit wholly or substantially a community in Singapore.[32]

On the other hand, to qualify for IPC status, the criteria are different. An entity may be approved if it is a registered charity, or a charity that is exempt, or not required to be registered under the Charities Act 1994, or otherwise falls within s 40A of the Act. This includes hospitals not operated for profit; a public or benevolent or institution not operated, nor conducted, for profit; a public fund established and maintained for the relief of distress of members of the public; and an institution that is established for charitable, benevolent, or philanthropic purposes only. In other words, the key point is that institutions falling within s 40A must ensure that their activities are not conducted for profit. Some entities that fall within that section may also fail as a charity because their purposes are not exclusively charitable.[33]

The distinction between IPCs and charities is important because there are differing fiscal privileges attached to the two statuses. Registered or exempt charities have a clear exemption from their income being subject to income tax under s 13 (1)(zm) of the Income Tax Act 2004. There is no immediate equivalent for IPCs, but they may fall within exemption granted for the income of approved not-for-profit entities under s 13U of the Income Tax Act. Further, provisions for the exemption from income tax for IPCs are more nuanced than those for charities. For instance, income tax exemptions given to a not-for-profit entity cannot be for a period that exceeds ten years, and there are provisions for the Comptroller of Income Tax to make additional assessments on an entity when it appears that income has been exempted when it should not have been.[34]

Another difference between IPCs and charities, as mentioned earlier, is that donors to a charity that is not an IPC are not eligible for tax deductions, while donors to an IPC (regardless of its charitable status) are eligible for tax deductions.[35] The rationale lies in the public benefit. In other words, 'greater public benefit is present where the organisation's purposes are not limited solely to sectoral benefit, which justifies the additional tax privilege of tax deductions to donors'.[36]

D Office of the Commission of Charities

Charities in Singapore are subject to the supervisory regulation of the Commissioner of Charities (COC). The objectives of the COC are:[37]

---

32 Leow, 'Four Misconceptions about Charity Law in Singapore', 39, referring to Charities (Registration of Charities) Regulations 2008, regs 3(1)(a)–(c); 'Legislative Conditions for Registration as a Charity or IPC'.

33 Leow, 'Four Misconceptions about Charity Law in Singapore', 40.

34 Leow, 'Four Misconceptions about Charity Law in Singapore', 40–1, referring to ss 13U(2)–(4) and 13U(6) of the Income Tax Act 2008, respectively.

35 Ibid., 41.

36 Ibid.

37 Singapore Charity Commission, 'About the Commissioner of Charities', www.charities.gov.sg/about/Pages/About-the-Commissioner-of-Charities.aspx [accessed 9 Dec. 2016].

- To maintain public trust and confidence in charities
- To promote compliance by governing board members and key officers with their legal obligations in exercising control and management of the administration of their charities
- To promote the effective use of charitable resources
- To enhance the accountability of charities to donors, beneficiaries and the general public

The COC is assisted in its administration by the Charities Unit under the Ministry of Community Development. The Charities Unit has a broad scope of work, and includes: enforcing regulatory compliance; carrying out field visits and audits on charities and IPCs; developing and reviewing policies within the charitable sector; and promoting good governance and best practice within the sector.[38]

The office of the COC oversees charities and IPCs with charitable objects that relate to:[39]

- Animal welfare
- Environmental protection or improvement
- Religion
- Those which do not fall neatly under the 5 sectors listed below.

There are five sector administrators that assist the COC in the oversight of charities and IPCs within their respective sectors, and they are:[40]

- The Ministry of Education – for charitable objects related to the advancement of education;
- The Ministry of Health – for charitable objects related to the promotion of health;
- The Ministry of Social and Family Development – for charitable objects related to the relief of poverty or those in need by reason of youth, age, ill-health, disability, financial hardship or other disadvantages;
- The People's Association – for charitable objects related to the advancement of citizenship or community development; and
- Sports Singapore (formerly the Singapore Sports Council) – for charitable objects related to the advancement of sport.

The COC also maintains oversight of charities and IPCs that do not fall within any of the above sector administrators,[41] and it also regulates fundraising in Singapore. For instance, for foreign charitable causes, a permit is required and

38 Elaine Seow, 'Singapore', in Anne-Marie Piper (ed.), *Charity Law: Jurisdictional Comparisons* (London: Sweet & Maxwell, 2012), 206.
39 Singapore Charity Commission, 'About the Commissioner of Charities'.
40 Ibid.
41 O'Halloran *et al.*, 'Charity Law Reforms', 22.

conditions will be imposed to ensure proper solicitation and usage of the donations; and for national charitable causes, there are guidelines outlining the requirements for those carrying out public fundraising appeals. In addition, police permits are required for house-to-house and street collections, and other permits may also be required.[42]

It is thought that the introduction of the COC, and various other regulatory regime changes, have been well received, and that they are achieving positive outcomes, which will certainly do much to improve public confidence within this sector. Indeed, data from 2008 shows that public confidence in the sector increased from 83 per cent in 2006 to 90 per cent in 2008, therefore just two years to show a large increase in public confidence.[43]

E The Charity Council

This Council was legally appointed 1 March 2007, after the new Charities Act was brought into operation; each term of the Council lasts for two years.[44] The Council 'acts as an important bridge between regulator and charities',[45] being led by sector representatives, with a focus on good governance and best practice. In addition to the sector administrator representatives, there are eight other members from the people sector. These representatives are selected for their expertise in accountancy, corporate governance, entrepreneurship, and law. In addition, they are involved in volunteer and charity work in a number of fields, for instance, arts and heritage; community; education; health; and social services.[46]

The Council aims to fulfil the following:[47]

- The promotion and encouragement of the adoption of good governance and best practices, to help enhance public confidence and promote self-regulation in the charity sector;
- The building of capabilities of charities and IPCs so that they are able to comply with regulatory requirements and enhance public accountability; and
- To advise the (COC) on key regulatory issues such as proposals on new regulations where there may be broad-ranging impact on charities and IPCs.

---

42 'Fund-Raising Matters', www.charities.gov.sg/manage-your-charity/Fund-raising%20and%20Related%20matters/Pages/Fund-Raising%20Matters.aspx [accessed 9 Dec. 2016]; Charities (Fund-raising Appeals for Local and Foreign Charitable Purposes) Regulations 2012; O'Halloran *et al.*, 'Charity Law Reforms', 23.
43 O'Halloran *et al.*, 'Charity Law Reforms', 24.
44 Singapore Charity Commission, 'About Charity Council', www.charities.gov.sg/about/Pages/About-Charities-Council.aspx [accessed 9 Dec. 2017].
45 O'Halloran *et al.*, 'Charity Law Reforms', 24.
46 Singapore Charity Commission, 'About Charity Council'.
47 Ibid.

F Charitable purposes

The obvious starting point when determining charitable purposes in Singapore is that of the Charities Act 1994.[48] However, this is limited in its assistance because it merely states:[49]

> 'charitable purposes' means purposes which are exclusively charitable according to the law of Singapore.

Therefore, as noted earlier, the courts and associated government bodies rely on the common law, which find its history in English roots.[50] In other words, charitable purposes are derived essentially from the four heads of charity, as defined by Lord Macnaghten in *Commissioners for Special Purposes of the Income Tax* v. *Pemsel*,[51] those of the relief of poverty, the advancement of education, the advancement of religion, and other purposes beneficial to the community, and thus subsequently developed through the application of the spirit and intendment of the Statute of Elizabeth. In other words, and as addressed in earlier chapters, where a novel purpose does not fall within one of the defined charitable purposes, then a court will determine if it can be interpreted as falling within the spirit and intendment of the Preamble of the Charitable Uses Act 1601, or otherwise known as the Statute of Elizabeth.[52]

The COC confirms that an entity's 'objects must be exclusively charitable and must also be clearly and concisely stated. Any power to carry out activities in support of the main objectives should be provided under an incidental clause'.[53] By way of further assistance, the COC confirms that in addition to the recognised four heads of charity, it also recognises the following purposes falling under the fourth head as being charitable:[54]

- Promotion of health;
- Advancement of citizenship or community development;
- Advancement of arts, heritage or science;
- Advancement of environmental protection or improvement;
- Relief of those in need by reason of youth, age, ill-health, disability, financial hardship or other disadvantages;

48 Charities Act 1994, Singapore, revised in 1995, and amended in 1999, 2001, 2004, and 2005.
49 Ibid., s 2(1).
50 Helmut K. Angheier and Stefan Toepler, *International Encyclopaedia of Civil Society* (New York: Springer, 2010), 125.
51 *Commissioners for Special Purposes of Income Tax* v. *Pemsel*; *Koh Lau Keow* v. *Attorney-General*, [18].
52 O'Halloran, McGregor-Lowndes, and Simon, *Charity Law & Social Policy*, 10, 341.
53 'Drafting Your Governing Instrument', www.charities.gov.sg/setting-up-a-charity/Registering-for-a-new-charity/Pages/Drafting%20your%20Governing%20Instrument.aspx [accessed 9 Dec. 2016].
54 Singapore Charity Commission, 'About Charities and IPCs'.

- Advancement of animal welfare; and
- Advancement of sport, where the sport promotes health through physical skill and exertion.

The recognition of these purposes as being charitable echoes much of the extended list of charitable purposes in the United Kingdom's Charities Act 2006, as discussed in Chapter 5, however, Singaporean statute has yet to codify these purposes.

Echoing the approach taken in the earlier jurisdictional-specific chapters, this chapter will consider a selection of cases in relation to charitable purposes, because such '"leading cases" are a vital part of the chaotic-looking case law tradition',[55] and, in doing so, they provide a useful insight into the jurisprudential trends of charitable purposes of Singapore.

G Advancement of religion

One of the most noticeable things concerning charity law within Singapore is the plethora of advancement of religion cases, in comparison with the other heads of charity. This is most likely as a result of the importance and value given to religions by settlers to Singapore. The prominence of religion within Singaporean society has been recognised since the early colonial days, where, in the absence of state welfare, religion-based benevolence institutions, inter alia, were the mainstay of Singapore's social fabric.[56]

Even today, religion is still recognised as having a prominent position in society, with Article 12 of the Singapore Constitution precluding discrimination on the grounds of, inter alia, religion, and Article 15 provides that, in relation to religion, '[e]very person has the right to profess and practise his religion and to propagate it'.[57] However, shoehorning non-Christian purposes within what was traditionally a Christian-focused society in its pre-independence days, has at times been problematic for Singaporean courts. This meant that some courts 'ignored that English law in this area was inappropriate and … applied Christian notions of religion indiscriminately to the local cases'.[58]

For instance, Muslim settlers often settled their property on 'wakaf', which was defined as being 'the dedication or consecration of property, either in express terms or by implication, for any charitable or religious object, or to secure any benefit to human beings'.[59] Unfortunately, such wafaqs did not fit within the

55 John Mummery, '*The Commissioners for Special Purposes of the Income Tax* v. *Pemsel*', *Charity Law and Practice Review* 16(1) (2013–14), 1.
56 Sharifah Maisharah, 'Tracing Singapore's Social Sector' (Social Space, 2008), 17.
57 Li-ann Thio, 'Courting Religion: The Judge Between Caesar and God in Asian Courts', *Singapore Journal of Legal Studies* 1(1) (July 2009), 58–9; Constitution of the Republic of Singapore 1965, arts 12 and 15, respectively.
58 Ramasamy, 'Charity Law', 232.
59 Leow, 'The Evolution of Charity Law in Singapore', 86, citing *Re Syed Sheik Alkaff* (1923) 2 MC 38.

traditional *Pemsel* categories, as they were not limited to charitable objects.[60] Similar difficulties were faced with the concept of 'amur-al khaira', which is translated as 'good works', but essentially includes purposes that are good or pious under Mussalman religion and law, and which would have been approved by the Almighty. However, such purposes were not seen as advancing the Muslim religion, rather they were seen as securing the approval of the Almighty for the settler. Therefore, creating wafaqs, or purposes for amur-al khaira, were invariably not charitable unless they somehow fell within the traditional constructs of the *Pemsel* heads of charity,[61] as was illustrated in *Majlis Ugama Islam Singapura* v. *Saeed Salman*.[62] In this case, the High Court acknowledged that the wakaf in question would be recognised as pious, religious, or charitable under Islamic law. Further, it would be possible to align the notion of a charitable trust with a wakaf because it was for the benefit of another, with a charitable object, and the property was under control or management of a person for another's benefit.

Another example of the difficulties of applying Christian-based English law to a multi-faith society is found in *Re Hadjee Ismail bin Kassim*, where a trust for pilgrimages to Mecca was not charitable as there was no evidence that the benefit extended beyond the pilgrim and their family.[63] It is thought, however, that the Court would have come to a different conclusion had this case been heard after the English case of *MacCarthy's Will Trusts*, where the Court held that a religious pilgrimage to Lourdes was a religious act in the public eye, hence it was charitable as it advanced religion. It is unlikely that the importance of pilgrimages within Singaporean society would have been appreciated by colonial judges at the time of the *Hadjee* case,[64] although it is a useful example of the issues relating to aligning English charity law in a non-English context.

One way of finding such purposes charitable, was to find a generous interpretation under the relief of poverty. For instance, while the wakaf and amur-al-khaira failed in *Re Syed Shaik Alkaff*,[65] because trusts for 'good works' are not charitable as recognised at law, the trusts to provide food to the poor were recognised as charitable. In addition, the cases of *In the Estate of Hadji Daeing Tahira binte Daeing Tedelleh* and *Re Alsagoff Trusts* provide that the burial of poor Muslims can fall within the relief of poverty.[66] This is because while burial is

---

60 See generally Paul Stibbard, David Russell, and Blake Bromley, 'Understanding the Waqf in the World of the Trust', *Trusts and Trustees* 18(8) (September 2012), 785–810.
61 Leow, 'The Evolution of Charity Law in Singapore', 86.
62 *Majlis Ugama Islam Singapura* v. *Saeed Salman* [2016] SGHC 04, [64].
63 Leow, 'The Evolution of Charity Law in Singapore', 87, referring to *Re Hadjee Ismail bin Kassim* (1911) 12 SSLR 74.
64 Leow, 'The Evolution of Charity Law in Singapore', 87, referring to *MacCarthy's Will Trusts* [1958] Ir R 31.
65 *Re Syed Sheik Alkaff*, (1923) 2 MC 38; Leng, *Law of Charities*, 13–17.
66 Leow, 'The Evolution of Charity Law in Singapore', 86, referring to *Hadji Daeing Tahira binte Daeing Tedelleh* (1948) 14 MLJ 62 and *Re Alsagoff Trusts* [1956] 1 MLJ 244.

not a recognised purpose in the Preamble, cemeteries may be charitable, and thus by analogy, a burial may be charitable.[67]

The recent Court of Appeal case of *Koh Lau Keow* v. *Attorney-General*[68] still reflects a relatively strict judicial approach with regard to the advancement of religion, and certainly illustrates the strong reliance on English authority, even in contemporary times, to determine charitable purpose. This case concerned a declaration of a trust, which provided for a property to be used, inter alia, as a temple for vegetarian Chinese women of the Buddhist faith. The question, inter alia, was whether the purpose of the trust advanced religion through passive advancement and personal spiritual contemplation.[69] The Court did not, however, refer to the presumption of public benefit, but stated that purposes to advance religion should have sufficient public benefit, which does not appear to mean the same thing as presuming public benefit,[70] thus suggesting that the presumption of public benefit is weakened. In applying this stringent and restrictive public benefit test, the Court stated that the purpose only benefited a handful of Buddhist vegetarian Chinese women, who need not be poor; were chosen at the discretion of the trustees to live at the property; and were, in fact, simply close friends and relations of the first appellant.[71]

It is said that this case is set to become the *locus classicus* on charity law,[72] no doubt because of its affirmation of the applicability of English authority in contemporary Singapore charity law, and its confirming that conducting private religious worship does not satisfy the public benefit test, even in a context-specific situation within Singapore.

H Ancestor worship

In light of the apparent difficulties of interpreting and applying English charity law principles to religious purposes specific to Singapore, it is not surprising that gifts for religious purposes that fall within the construct of 'ancestor worship', such as Sin Chew (Shenzhu), have also failed to qualify as charitable.[73]

A definition of Sin Chew is found in *Choa Cheow Neoh* v. *Spottiswoode*,[74] as follows:

---

67 *Re Alsagoff Trusts*, [9].
68 *Koh Lau Keow* v. *Attorney-General*.
69 Ibid., [30].
70 *Koh Lau Keow* v. *Attorney-General*, [32]–[37], referring to, inter alia, *Re White* [1893] 2 Ch 41; *Cocks* v. *Manners* (1871) LR Eq 574; *Gilmour* v. *Coats* [1949] 1 AC 426; *Re Warre's Will Trusts* [1953 1 WLR 725; *Re Chionh Ke Hu, Deceased* [1964] MLJ 270.
71 *Koh Lau Keow* v. *Attorney-General*, [39].
72 Hang Wu Tang, 'Equity and Trusts', *Singapore Academy of Law Annual Review of Singapore Cases* 15(1) (2004), 350.
73 *Yeap Cheah Neo* v. *Ong Cheng Neo* (1875) LR 381; *Sir Han Hoe Lim* v. *Lim Kim Seng* [1956] 1 MLJ 142.
74 *Choa Choon Neoh* v. *Spottiswoode*, 3; Lim Pui Huen Wong, 'Ah Fook and Ancestral Trusts', *CHC Bulletin*, 23, http://chc.ntu.edu.sg/Bulletin/Documents/sept03-Pt2.pdf [accessed

The word Sin Chew is composed of Sin, which means a spirit, soul or ghost, and Chew, which means ruler; and the composite word means the spirit ruler, or spiritual head of the house. When a man dies, his name, with the dates of his birth and death, is engraved on a tabled; this is enclosed in an outer casing, on which a new name, which is now for the first time given to him, and the names of his children, are engraved. This tablet is kept either in the house of the worshipper, or in that which has been set apart for the Sin Chew.

This tablet is sacred, and it may only be touched by the male descendants, or the nearest male descendants of the deceased. In other words, it is the representation of the deceased. At certain times, such as the anniversary of his death, gifts are laid at the tablet, such as food and tea, and joss sticks and fire crackers may be lighted. The male relatives worship the Sin Chew, and the primary purpose of the ceremony is to show respect and reverence to the deceased and to preserve his memory in the world; it is said to be agreeable to God. Neglect of such duty is said to bring disgrace on the male whose duty it is to perform it, and will have an adverse impact on the descendants, and humankind generally.[75] Therefore, 'Sin Chew' refers to spirit tablets of ancestors, as well as to the ceremonies held for the worship.[76]

These gifts have generally failed because the courts have 'persistently adhered to the view that the element of "public benefit" was lacking, and that the predominant motive for the gifts was to secure a selfish benefit to the donors (and sometimes their families)'.[77] Thus, in the *Choa Cheow Neoh* case, Maxwell CJ held that the purpose was not charitable because:[78]

> Its object is solely the benefit of the testator himself; and although the descendants are supposed incidentally to derive from the performance of Sin Chew ceremony the advantage of pleasing God and escaping the danger of being haunted, those advantages are obviously not the object of the testator, nor if they were, would they be of such character as to being the devise within the designation of charitable.

Later cases affirmed this approach,[79] and it has been argued, not unreasonably, that the advancement of religion in Singapore should be given a wider consideration, so as to take into consideration the diverse Asian beliefs, practices, and rites that do not fall within the constructs of English law.[80]

---

15 Dec. 2016], referring to J. D. Vaughn, *The Manners and Customs of the Chinese of the Straits Settlements* (Kuala Lumpur: Oxford University Press, 1971), 26.

75 *Choa Choon Neoh* v. *Spottiswoode*, 3–4.
76 Huen Wong, 'Ah Fook and Ancestral Trusts', 23.
77 Ramasamy, 'Charity Law', 233.
78 *Choa Choon Neoh* v. *Spottiswoode*, 6.
79 Ramasamy, 'Charity Law', 233, referring to *Re Khoo Cheng Teow* (1933) 2 MLJ 119 and *Tan Chin Ngoh* v. *Tan Chin Teat* (1946) 12 MLJ 159.
80 Ramasamy, 'Charity Law', 233.

However, it was evident that some judges felt some discomfort with regard to finding local deep-seated cultural and religious beliefs to be non-charitable. For instance, Maxwell CJ in the *Choa Cheow Neoh* case stated:[81]

> I do not doubt that the validity of a bequest for the maintenance or propagation of any Oriental creed, or for building a temple or a mosque, or for setting up or adorning an idol … would be determined in this Court … with the widest regard to the religious opinions and feeling of the various Easter races established here.

He made these remarks at that point 'not because they are necessary to the decision of this case, but to guard against my present judgment being misunderstood as questioning the validity of any Eastern charity'.[82] Nonetheless, and unfortunately for some religious purposes within Singapore, 'the importation of the *Pemsel* categories clearly limited'[83] many of the courts' endeavours to accommodate local practices within charity law.

I Other purposes beneficial to the community

One particular quirk of pre-independence Singapore charity law is 'the extreme paucity of cases falling within the fourth head of *Pemsel* of trusts for other purposes beneficial to the community'.[84] 'While there is abundant authority in English law that this category of trusts is charitable',[85] and, indeed, there were many such cases being heard in English courts during this period,[86] 'there has hardly been a local case in which such trusts have arisen for judicial decision'.[87]

It is thought that this was not an unexpected situation for pre-independence Singapore. This is because while English charity law required purposes to benefit the community at large, instead settlers preferred to direct their wealth with those with whom they shared some kind of relationship, for instance through religious or familial bonds,[88] resulting in a lack of cases falling under this head at this time.

Post-independence Singapore does reflect a change in this position, albeit on a limited basis still, as contemporary Singapore begins to embrace broader philanthropic and charitable visions. In the case of *Lam Joon Shu* v. *Attorney-General*,[89] the Court of Appeal had to consider, inter alia, whether property in Singapore was held on trust for

---

81 *Choa Choon Neoh* v. *Spottiswoode*, 5–6.
82 Ibid., 6.
83 Leow, 'The Evolution of Charity Law in Singapore', 88.
84 Ibid., 90.
85 Leng, *Law of Charities*, 59.
86 Leow, 'The Evolution of Charity Law in Singapore', 90, referring, by way of example, to *Abbott* v. *Fraser* (1874) LR 6 PC 96; *Townley* v. *Bedwell* (1801) 6 Ves 194; and *Re Corbyn* [1941] Ch 400.
87 Leng, *Law of Charities*, 59.
88 Leow, 'The Evolution of Charity Law in Singapore', 90.
89 *Lam Joon Shu* v. *Attorney-General* [1993] 3 SLR 649.

other purposes beneficial to the community to the Chinese Taipoo community, or other communities in Singapore. It was argued that clause 3 of the indenture was too wide, thus rendering it outside the definition of charity, as it read:[90]

> As a classroom, meeting room, or lecture room for any educational, charitable or other purposes beneficial to the Chinese Taipoo community or such community as the trustees shall think fit in Singapore.

However, in relying on *Re Bennett*, the Court confirmed that 'other purposes beneficial to the community' is, of course, a head of charity, thus the clause was not expressed too widely.[91]

A year later, the case of *Hwa Soo Chin* v. *Personal Representatives of the Estate Lim Soon Ban, deceased* was heard.[92] This case concerned the legal status of a crèche to take care of children of poverty-stricken parents while their parents were at work. While it failed under the head of relief of poverty, because there was nothing to indicate that children of affluent parents would be excluded, if for any reason they were denied the care of their parents,[93] it did however fall under the fourth *Pemsel* head, any other purposes beneficial to the community. This was because, relying on *Re Cole* and *In re Sahal's Will Trusts*, the Court found that the crèche fell within the preamble of the Statute of Elizabeth, as a result of the children being helpless and unable to assist themselves.[94]

J Public benefit

Organisations will be charitable in Singapore if they, inter alia:[95]

Are set up exclusively for charitable purposes; and
Carry out activities to achieve these purposes which benefit the public.

Singapore retains the traditional English law, that is, the approach prior to the United Kingdom removing the presumption of public benefit from all its heads of charity in 2006. In other words, public benefit in Singapore is presumed for the first three heads of charity.[96] Similarly to England also, and in contrast to some matters pertaining to blood-tie relations in New Zealand and Australia,[97]

90 Ibid., 653.
91 *Lam Joon Shu* v. *Attorney-General* [1993], 654–5, referring to *Re Bennett* [1960] Ch 18.
92 *Hwa Soo Chin* v. *Personal Representatives of the Estate Lim Soon Ban, deceased* [1994] 2 SLR(R) 1.
93 Ibid., [20].
94 *Hwa Soo Chin* v. *Personal Representatives of the Estate Lim Soon Ban, deceased*, [21]– [24], referring to *Re Cole* [1958] Ch 877 and *In re Sahal's Will Trusts* [1958] 1 WLR 1243.
95 Singapore Charity Commission, 'About Charities and IPCs'.
96 Leng, *Law of Charities*, 10, 30, 38, and 59.
97 See Chapter 4 for discussion on blood-tie and public benefit in Australia and New Zealand.

Singapore retains the concept that because a trust must be beneficial to a community, there should be no dependence on any relationship by blood, or contract, to a particular individual.[98] Such an approach was illustrated earlier in the chapter in relation to some of the advancement of religion, and ancestor worship cases, where the public benefit generally failed because the courts have 'persistently adhered to the view that the element of "public benefit" was lacking'.[99]

One point of interest about public benefit and Singapore in contemporary times appeared in the Charities (Registration of Charities) Regulations 2007. Regulation 31 makes it a condition for eligibility to register as a charity, the entity's purposes must benefit wholly, or substantially, the community in Singapore. This limits the geographical scope of the requirement of public benefit to the community of Singapore.[100] While this does not seem unreasonable, what it does is 'move away from the widespread recognition of overseas public benefit as sufficient to fulfil the requirement of public benefit for charitable status'.[101] Thus the charitable sector in post-independence Singapore, in some respects, is beginning to take on a new character that is specific to its own social and cultural requirements.

K Public benefit and Institutions of Public Character

As noted earlier, IPCs are:[102]

> exempt or registered charities which are able to issue tax deductible receipts for qualifying donations to donors. In other words, donors are able to claim tax relief from their assessable income based on the amount donated, at prevailing deduction rate.

Their creation under the Charities Act created a two-tier structure of activities for public benefit. In situations where the public benefit conferred by an entity is limited to a particular section of the community, and its purposes are deemed charitable within Singapore charity law, then the entity will only be granted charity status. However, where the public benefit is to the Singaporean community as a whole, and clearly other aspects of charity law are fulfilled, then the entity will be granted both charitable status, as well as IPC status.

It is said that the introduction of this system was perhaps necessary 'in light of the development of previous Singaporean charity law along lines based on family, clan and religion'.[103] Thus the development of this two-tier system is entirely unique to the Singapore charity sector, and is a modern reflection of the changing approach to charity law within this contemporary Asian country.

---

98 Leng, *Law of Charities*, 60, referring to *Re Compton* [1945] Ch 123.
99 Ramasamy, 'Charity Law', 233.
100 Leow, 'The Evolution of Charity Law in Singapore', 94.
101 Ibid.
102 Singapore Charity Commission, 'About Charities and IPCs'.
103 Leow, 'The Evolution of Charity Law in Singapore', 94.

11 Political purposes

A Introduction

The doctrine of political purposes within charity law has been said to exist since at least the early 1900s,[1] and is best understood as being supplementary to the general common law definition of charity, as addressed in earlier chapters. Thus, generally speaking, for a purpose to be charitable, it must fall within one of the recognised heads of charity as set out in *Pemsel*, and extended in some jurisdictions,[2] and be for the public benefit.[3] If, however, the purposes are political, and more than secondary to its charitable objects, the purposes will fail as 'a necessary consequence of the requirement of public benefit'[4] because:[5]

> A trust for the attainment of political objects has always been held invalid, not because it is illegal, for everyone is at liberty to advocate or promote by any lawful means a change in the law, but because the court has no means of judging whether a proposed change in the law will or will not be for the public benefit, and therefore cannot say that a gift to secure the change is a charitable gift.

Therefore, it can be said the requirement of public benefit is at the heart of this logic,[6] although it is important to remember that this doctrine will not apply if the entity's political purposes are subsidiary to its dominant non-political purposes.[7]

1 *Bowman* v. *Secular Society Limited* [1917] 1 AC 406 (HL); *McGovern* v. *Attorney-General* [1982] 1 Ch 321; *National Anti-Vivisection Society* v. *Inland Revenue Commissioners* [1948] 1 AC 31 (HL); Juliet Chevalier-Watts, *Law of Charity* (Wellington: Thomson Reuters, 2014), 277–8.
2 For instance, England and Wales, and Australia.
3 Kathryn Chan, 'Backgrounder for Talk on Political Purposes Doctrine', Charities and Not-for-Profit Law Conference, 2014, 2.1.1.
4 Jonathan Garton, 'The Legal Definition of Charity and the Regulation of Civil Society', *King's College Law Journal* 16(1) (2005), 45.
5 *Bowman* v. *Secular Society Limited*, 442; see also *National Anti-Vivisection Society* v. *Inland Revenue Commissioners*.
6 Adam Parachin, 'Charity, Politics and Neutrality', *Charity Law and Practice Review* 18(1) (2015–16), 8.
7 Matthew Harding, *Charity Law and the Liberal State* (Oxford: Oxford University Press, 2014), 177.

It is said that the general starting point for this doctrine is the judgment of Lord Parker of Waddington in the now famous *Bowman* v. *Secular Society*,[8] although his Lordship did state that 'a trust for the attainment of political objects has always been held invalid'. However, it is worth noting that Lord Parker's statement was made in obiter, and at the time of the decision, it was far from clear that in fact political purposes had invariably or mostly been found to be invalid.[9] Indeed, it is rather surprising that politics and charities were said to have been disassociated in such terms because 'charities and politics have long had a symbiotic relationship, starting with the Statute of Elizabeth, which was borne out of a politically charged environment'.[10] Thus, 'where a state may have been unable to provide a function or service, charity could fill that void, and the voids would depend on the government and policies at the time',[11] and it has been argued that the four original heads of charity are themselves rooted in policy.[12] Indeed, if one looks to the history of Victorian Britain, it reveals a strong tradition of charities pursuing a variety of political purposes without suggestion that such purposes were contrary to charity law.[13]

Therefore, while it has been observed that Lord Parker's assertions were an idiosyncratic approach to law at the time,[14] the doctrine was endorsed, and affirmed many times throughout the common law jurisdictions to which this book refers.[15] However, its subsequent varying treatment and interpretation is perhaps a reflection of its challenging and contentious nature. This is likely, at least in part, because while it has been acknowledged for many years that, generally speaking, non-ancillary political purposes are not acceptable, the guidelines and debates surrounding the doctrine have left neither the legal, nor the practical position, of

---

8 *Bowman* v. *Secular Society Limited*, 442.

9 Harding, *Charity Law*, 176, referring to *Farewell* v. *Farewell* (1892) 22 OR 573; *In re Scowcroft* [1898] 2 Ch 638; Adam Parachin, 'Distinguishing Charity from Politics: The Judicial Thinking behind the Political Purposes', *Alberta Law Review* 45(4) (August 2008); *Re Foveaux* [1895] 2 Ch 501.

10 Chevalier-Watts, *Law of Charity*, 278, referring to Juliet Chevalier-Watts and Sue Tappenden, *Equity, Trusts and Succession* (Wellington: Thomson Reuters, 2013), 282; Alison Dunn, 'Demanding Service or Servicing Demand? Charities, Regulation and the Policy Process', *Modern Law Review* 71(2) (2008), 251.

11 Chevalier-Watts, *Law of Charity*, 278, citing Chevalier-Watts and Tappenden, *Equity, Trusts and Succession*, 282.

12 Chevalier-Watts, *Law of Charity*, 278, referring to Juliet Chevalier-Watts, 'Charitable Trusts and Political Activity: Time for a Change?', *Waikato Law Review* 19(2) (2011), 146.

13 Harding, *Charity Law*, 176, referring to Michael Chesterman, *Charities, Trusts and Social Welfare* (London: Weidenfeld & Nicolson, 1979), ch. 4.

14 Harding, *Charity Law*, 176; see also Amherst D. Tyssen, *The Law of Charitable Bequests*, 2nd edn (London: Sweet & Maxwell, 1921), 177; Parachin, 'Distinguishing Charity from Politics', 877–80.

15 For example, *McGovern* v. *Attorney-General; National Anti-Vivisection Society* v. *Inland Revenue Commissioners; Royal North Shore Hospital of Sydney* v. *Attorney-General for New South Wales* (1938) 60 CLR 396; *Molloy* v. *Commissioner of Inland Revenue* [1981] 1 NZLR 688 (CA); *Vancouver Society* v. *MNR* [1999] 1 SCR 10.

the doctrine either settled or clear.[16] For instance, in England and Wales, from where it originates, the effect of the doctrine has been partially mitigated by the inclusion of inherently political purposes, such as the promotion of human rights, within s 3(1)(h) of the Charities Act 2011, and by less restrictive guidance provided by the Charity Commission for England and Wales.[17]

In Canada, much of its law on political purposes is derived from *Bowman*.[18] It is said that the doctrine has been applied strictly, and has been entrenched in its taxation legislation.[19] One of the earliest cases was *Re Knight*,[20] where the Court affirmed the authority of *Bowman*, and later cases confirmed its continued relevance. For instance, in *Positive Action Against Pornography* v. *MNR*,[21] the Court determined that the organisation's objects included achieving social change, and thus were political in nature. In *Human Life International in Canada Inc* v. *MNR*,[22] the Court confirmed that 'that activities primarily designed to sway public opinion on social issues are not charitable activities', and while the appellant argued that its purposes fell outside of the *McGovern* v. *Attorney-General*[23] categories of political purposes (see later in chapter), the Court confirmed that the categories were non-exhaustive. Thus, by inference, the 'kind of advocacy of opinions on various important social issues can never be determined by a court to be for a purpose beneficial to the community'.[24]

---

16 Alison Dunn, 'Charity Law as a Political Option for the Poor', *Northern Ireland Legal Quarterly* 50(3) (1999), 299.

17 Harding, *Charity Law*, 176; Charity Commission *Speaking Out: Guidance on Campaigning and Political Activity by Charities* (2008), www.gov.uk/government/uploads/system/uploads/attachment_data/file/434427/CC9_LowInk.pdf [accessed 13 January 2017].

18 Maurice C. Cullity, 'Charity and Politics in Canada', *The Philanthropist* 25(4) (26 February 2014), 14, http://thephilanthropist.ca/original-pdfs/Philanthropist-25-4-542.pdf [accessed 13 January 2017].

19 Joyce Chia, Matthew Harding, and Ann O'Connell, 'Navigating the Politics of Charity: Reflections on *Aid/Watch Inc* v. *Federal Commissioner of Taxation*', *Melbourne University Law Review* 35(2) (August 2011), 359, referring to Paul Mitchell, 'The Political Purposes Doctrine in Canadian Charities Law', *The Philanthropist* 12(4) (1995), 13, http://thephilanthropist.ca/original-pdfs/Philanthropist-12-4-138.pdf, and the Income Tax Act 1985, 5th Supp., s 149(6.1)–(6.2); Chan, 'Backgrounder for Talk', 2.1.3.

20 *Re Knight* [1937], 1 OR 462; see also *Scarborough Community Legal Services* v. *The Queen*, 85 DTC 5102 [1985] 1 CTC 98 (FCA); Terrance S. Carter and Theresa L. M. Man, 'The Evolution of Advocacy and Political Activities by Charities in Canada: An Overview', *The Philanthropist* 23(4) (2011), 536–7.

21 *Positive Action Against Pornography* v. *MNR*, 88 DTC 6186 [1988] 1 CTC 232 (FCA), [14]–[15], referring to *McGovern* v. *Attorney-General*, 239–40.

22 *Human Life International in Canada Incorporated* v. *MNR* [1998] 3 FCR 202, 1998 CanLII 9053 (FCA), referring to *Positive Action Against Pornography* v. *MNR*; see also *Alliance for Life* v. *MNR* 1998 CarswellNat 625 and *News to You* v. *MNR* 2011 CAF 192, 2011 FCA 192.

23 *Human Life International in Canada Incorporated* v. *MNR*, referring to *McGovern* v. *Attorney-General*; also referring to *Bowman* v. *Secular Society Limited*.

24 *Human Life International in Canada Incorporated* v. *MNR*.

The first Canadian Supreme Court case to consider the doctrine was *Vancouver Society of Immigrant and Visible Minority Women* v. *MNR*,[25] where the Court confirmed that political purposes are generally not charitable. Therefore, Canada reflects, generally speaking, the conservative English approach.

However, the Canadian Charities Directorate has issued guidance which appears to offer a less restrictive approach. For instance, it 'presume[s] an activity to be political'[26] if that activity is confined to explicit types of communication, such as a call to political action, or if its materials 'explicitly indicate ... the intention ... to incite, or organize to put pressure on, an elected representative or public official to retain, oppose, or change the law, policy, or decision'. Further, if an entity fosters 'public awareness about its work or an issue related to that work, it is presumed to be taking part in a charitable activity' so long as it is ancillary to its overall purpose.[27] Although it should be noted that there is one unique restriction to political activities in Canada, and that is that a charity may spend no more than 10 per cent of its income on political activity, with some minor exceptions.[28]

However, Canada does permit the promotion of race relations, which may appear to fall innately within political purposes. Nonetheless, this is still a limited purpose because any such purpose must not include: 'efforts to retain, oppose, or change the law or policy or decisions of any level of government', because this would be deemed political, thus not charitable.[29]

In Hong Kong, which follows the English interpretation of political purpose, the attainment of a political object will not be charitable,[30] although there is a dearth of case law as authority on this matter. Singapore also retains a more restrictive interpretation of political purpose,[31] with reliance on *Bowman* v. *Secular Society*, and, in contrast, Australasia has created sea changes in the doctrine, and

---

25 *Vancouver Society of Immigrant and Visible Minority Women* v. *MNR*, [190], referring to *Positive Action Against Pornography* v. *MNR*.
26 CRA, Political Activities Policy Statement CPS-022, 2 September 2003, [6.2], www.cra-arc.gc.ca/chrts-gvng/chrts/plcy/cps/cps-022-eng.html#politicalactivities6-2 [accessed 13 January 2016].
27 Ibid., [7.1].
28 Chia, Harding, and O'Connell, 'Navigating the Politics of Charity', 360; Canada Revenue Agency Political Activities Policy Statement CPS-022, [9].
29 CRA, 'Registering Charities That Promote Racial Equality', [10], www.cra-arc.gc.ca/chrts-gvng/chrts/plcy/cps/cps-021-eng.html [accessed 19 January 2017].
30 Inland Revenue Hong Kong, A Tax Guide for Charitable Institutions and Trusts of a Public Character Appendix A, www.ird.gov.hk/eng/tax/ach_tgc.htm [accessed 13 January 2016]; Law Reform Commission of Hong Kong, *Report: Charities*, December 2013, www.hkreform.gov.hk/en/docs/rcharities_e.pdf, [2.30] [accessed 18 January 2017]; Patrick Hamlin and Philip Munro, 'Hong Kong', in *International Charitable Giving* (Oxford: Oxford University Press, 2012), 304.
31 Kerry O'Halloran, Myles McGregor-Lowndes, and Karla W. Simon, *Charity Law & Social Policy: National and International Perspectives on the Functions of Law Relating to Charities*, vol. 10 (Netherlands: Springer, 2008), 361; Fiona Martin, '"Advocacy in Charity: A Breakaway from the Common Law" (Impactful Advocacy)', *Lien Centre for Social Innovation (Singapore Management University)* 1(1) (2012), 80; Ter Kah

broadened its scope. For instance, in Australia, s 12 (1) of the Charities Act 2013[32] provides that promoting or opposing matters established by law, policy, or practice nationally and internationally may fall within the definition of charitable purpose. New Zealand now no longer has a blanket exclusion on political purposes within charity law, since the Supreme Court decision of *Re Greenpeace of New Zealand Inc.*[33]

Therefore the treatment of the doctrine varies within jurisdictions, and as a result, it is not surprising that there is a significant body of criticism regarding the exclusion of political purposes within charity law.[34] While some jurisdictions have mitigated some of the limitations of this doctrine, it is still hard to deny that its 'restrictions are arguably based upon unreasoned and misconstrued case law which may owe much to public policy, but little to rigorous jurisprudential analysis'.[35] Indeed, one may wonder why the doctrine still exists today.

Therefore, in order to consider its existence, and its continued relevance today, this chapter will, inter alia, contextualise the historical position of the doctrine from England and Wales, as well as considering some of definitions of politics, and then address some of the fallacies of the doctrine. Leading on from these discussions, the chapter will turn to the jurisprudential changes to the doctrine that were heralded in Australasia.

B History of political purposes and charity law

It appears correct that the now iconic case of *Bowman* v. *Secular Society* ensured that the 'political purpose doctrine sprang fully grown, like Athena from Zeus' forehead',[36] although there is an earlier case that is said to support the same doctrine: *De Themmines* v. *De Bonneval.*[37] *De Themmines* concerned a trust to promote the supremacy of the Pope. The trust was held invalid on the grounds that it

Lang, *The Law of Charities: Cases and Materials: Singapore and Malaysia* (Singapore: Butterworths, 1985), 104, referring to *Bowman* v. *Secular Society Limited*, 442.

32 This recognises the High Court's decision in *Aid/Watch Incorporated* v. *Commissioner of Taxation* [2010] HCA 42; Fiona Martin, 'Has the Charities Act 2013 Changed the Common Law Concept of Charitable "Public Benefit" and, If So, How?', *Australian Tax Forum* 30(1) (2015), 76–7.

33 *Re Greenpeace of New Zealand Inc* [2014] NZSC 105; DIAC, 'Advocacy for Causes', https://charities.govt.nz/apply-for-registration/charitable-purpose/advocacy-for-ca uses [accessed 19 January 2017].

34 Darryn Jensen, 'Charitable Purposes and Political Purposes (or Voluntarism and Coercion)', *Charity Law and Practice Review* 18(1) (2015–16), 39, referring to C. E. F. Rickett, 'Charity and Politics', *New Zealand Universities Law Review* 10(1) (1982); S. Bright, 'Charity and Trusts for the Public Benefit', *Conveyancer and Property Lawyer* 28(1) (1989); Michael Chesterman, 'Foundations of Charity Law in the New Welfare State', *Modern Law Review* 62(3) (1999); Nicola Silke, 'Please Sir, May I Have Some More? Allowing New Zealand Charities a Political Voice', *Canterbury Law Review* 8(2) (2002), 345.

35 Dunn, 'Charity Law as a Political Option for the Poor', 299.

36 Mitchell, 'Political Purposes Doctrine', 6.

37 *De Themmines* v. *De Bonneval* (1828) 5 Russ 288, 38 ER 1035.

would be contrary to the policy of England at the time. However, while policy grounds were cited, and this may have been a political purpose, this is very different from holding that all political purposes generally are void as being contrary to public policy.[38] Indeed, the Master of the Rolls, in this case, did not indicate that the issue before him was one of political purposes, and significantly the trust was not declared absolutely void, rather it was void for superstitious use.[39] As a result, it is difficult to view this case as being authority for political purposes being void generally within charity law. It was suggested that perhaps Lord Parker made 'a mistake to which many law students are still prone',[40] and that was to have read a text and not the case itself, but this is merely conjecture of course,[41] or perhaps Lord Parker was merely just 'a poor historian'.[42] Nonetheless, rely upon this case his Lordship did, and it was cited as sole authority for the prohibition on political purposes within charity law.[43]

This was perhaps a surprising approach for Lord Parker to have taken, because the weight of evidence to support political purposes historically being charitable, is great. For instance, the promotion of the abolition of slavery was held to be a charitable cause;[44] as was a gift to further, inter alia, Conservative principles;[45] and a society to prevent vivisection in animals was also held to be charitable, even though it required the repeal of a specific Act.[46]

Nonetheless, Lord Parker's determination on the doctrine was readily embraced some few years later, not only in England and Wales, but also, unsurprisingly, in Canada, Hong Kong, Singapore, Australia, and New Zealand. However, as will be addressed later in the chapter, the latter two jurisdictions have subsequently adopted more liberal attitudes to this doctrine.

One of the key cases following the *Bowman* decision is *National Anti-Vivisection Society* v. *Inland Revenue Commissioners*,[47] because it cemented the prohibition on political purposes within English jurisprudence.

In this case, the House of Lords found that the Society was not charitable because it sought the full suppression of vivisection practices through the promotion of legislation. Interestingly, Lord Simonds did note that there was 'undoubtedly a

---

38 Jonathan Garton, *Public Benefit in Charity Law* (Oxford: Oxford University Press, 2013), 196, referring also to Lord Parker, dissenting, *National Anti-Vivisection Society* v. *Inland Revenue Commissioners*, 54; Chevalier-Watts, *Law of Charity*, 281.

39 Garton, *Public Benefit in Charity Law*, 196, referring to *De Themmines* v. *De Bonneval*, 1037.

40 Mitchell, 'Political Purposes Doctrine', 6.

41 Chevalier-Watts, *Law of Charity*, 281.

42 Parachin, 'Distinguishing Charity from Politics', 877.

43 *Bowman* v. *Secular Society Limited*; Garton, *Public Benefit in Charity Law*, 197.

44 *Re Greenpeace of New Zealand Inc* [2014], [71], referring to *Jackson* v. *Philips* (1867) 96 Mass 539 14 Allen 539 (Mass SC).

45 Garton, *Public Benefit in Charity Law*, 197, referring to *Re Scowcroft* [1898] 2 Ch 638 (Ch).

46 *Re Foveaux*, although this decision has subsequently been criticised in *National Anti-Vivisection Society* v. *Inland Revenue Commissioners*.

47 *National Anti-Vivisection Society* v. *Inland Revenue Commissioners*.

paucity of judicial authority'[48] although he added that 'in truth the reason of the thing appears to me so clear that I neither expect nor require much authority'.[49] Lord Normand also highlighted difficulties with this doctrine, noting that the 'distinction between political association and a charitable trust has not been defined and I doubt whether it admits of precise definition'.[50] In finding that the Society was 'not a society for the prevention of cruelty to animals generally, but a society for the prevention of cruelty to animals by political means',[51] his Lordship found that the question of degree of political intent was great, requiring legislative change to further its purposes, rendering the Society unequivocally within the realms of the political purpose doctrine.

This was a majority decision, and it is worthwhile considering the dissenting view of Lord Porter,[52] because it illustrates some of the issues associated with this doctrine, even in its early stages of being recognised within English jurisprudence. His Lordship was of the view that 'political objects' had a more limited application and were applicable to objects 'whose only means of attainment is a change in the law'. Therefore, he could not:[53]

> accept the view that the anti-slavery campaign or the enactment of the Factory Acts or the abolition of the use of boy labour by chimney-sweeps, would be charitable so long as the supporters of these objects had not in mind or at any rate did not advocate a change in the laws, but became political and therefore non-charitable if they did so. To take such a view would to me be to neglect substance for form. The object was to stop slavery or the use of boy chimney-sweeps, and to ensure that certain minimum requirements were carried out in factories. All this could be done by common consent, though no doubt the only effective method would be to alter the law. But persuasion not force was a possible means of effecting the desired purpose.

Therefore, his Lordship concluded that the Society's primary object was to prevent animal suffering caused by vivisection, and the main method of bringing that about would be to repeal the relevant legislation that permitted the vivisection.[54] However, Lord Simonds was not of the view that Lord Parker in *Bowman* meant to confine, inter alia, 'political objects' so narrowly.[55]

What this case therefore highlights, when comparing majority and dissenting views, is some of the difficulties that a court faces when determining the nature of the purposes of some organisations;[56] even nearly one hundred years on, such issues still face courts.

---

48 Ibid., 63.
49 Ibid.
50 Ibid., 75.
51 Ibid., 78.
52 Chevalier-Watts, *Law of Charity*, 286–7.
53 *National Anti-Vivisection Society* v. *Inland Revenue Commissioners*, 55.
54 Ibid.
55 Ibid., 62.
56 Chevalier-Watts, *Law of Charity*, 287.

After the *Anti-Vivisection* case came *McGovern* v. *Attorney-General.*[57] While this case did not establish the rule precluding political purposes from being charitable, it was still an important case because it enlarged the application of the political purpose doctrine. In particular, Slade J 'provided the systematic evaluation of what would amount to a political purpose, expanding the notion of "political" through a non-exhaustive test'.[58] The purpose of this case was to determine the charitable nature of Amnesty International. This internationally renowned organisation provides assistance, inter alia, to prisoners of conscience and to relieve their suffering; and endeavours to procure the abolition of torture or inhuman treatment or punishment.[59]

One of the key features of this case was how Slade J addressed the scope and ambit of 'political', which had not been undertaken previously. He set out a fivefold, non-exhaustive classification of purposes that would be political,[60] and thus not charitable:[61]

1   Trusts that further the interests of a political party;
2   Trusts to procure changes in the laws of England and Wales;
3   Trusts to procure changes in the laws of foreign countries;
4   Trusts to procure a reversal of government policy or of particular decisions of government authorities in England and Wales; and
5   Trusts to procure a reversal of government policy or of a particular decision of government authorities in foreign countries.

In particular, the third classification broke new ground, as there was no previous authority for this determination. Slade J justified it on the grounds that it would not be possible for a court in England and Wales to quantify the public benefit of changing the law in a foreign country. While his Honour sought justification on the grounds of public benefit on this point, it has been argued that it would not be difficult, for instance, in circumstances of torture, to see that legislative change to prevent such inhumane actions would be in the public's interest.[62] The other classifications find their authority within previous judgments,[63] and often, in an expansive reading of such case law.[64]

---

57 *McGovern* v. *Attorney-General.*
58 Alison Dunn, '*McGovern* v. *Attorney-General*', *Charity Law and Practice Review* 16 (1) (2013–14), 106.
59 *McGovern* v. *Attorney-General*, 321.
60 Dunn, '*McGovern* v. *Attorney-General*', 109–10.
61 *McGovern* v. *Attorney-General*, 340.
62 Dunn, '*McGovern* v. *Attorney-General*', 114, referring to Richard Nobles, 'Politics, Public Benefit and Charity', *Modern Law Review* 45(6) (1982).
63 Dunn, '*McGovern* v. *Attorney-General*', 111, referring to, the first classification: *Bowman* v. *Secular Society; Re Tetley* [1924] AC 262 (HL) and *Re Strakosch Decd* [1949] 1 Ch 529 (Ch), 111. Referring to the second classification: referring to *Bowman* v. *Secular Society; National Anti-Vivisection Society*; and *Duport Steels Ltd* v. *Sirs* [1980] 1 WLR 142 (HL), 110–11. Referring to the fourth and fifth classifications: *Bowman* v. *Secular Society* and *National Anti-Vivisection Society*, 114–15.
64 Dunn, '*McGovern* v. *Attorney-General*', 116.

One of the key points with regard to this case is that Slade J confirmed that this was a non-exhaustive list, because the legacy of this is that political purposes can be further expanded upon by the courts. Evidence of such expansion is already noticeable. For instance, in *Re Koeppler's Will Trusts*, the Court determined that trusts to oppose a particular change in law, or a change in a particular law; and trusts aimed at better international relations, would not be charitable.[65]

Other evidence of such an expansion is found in *R v. Radio Authority; ex parte Bull*.[66] This was not a case connected with charity, nor the application the *McGovern* classification, but what it did do was transplant Slade J's concept of 'political' within charity law from *McGovern* to another point of law, without 'any meaningful examination of context or the propriety of doing so'.[67] The consequences of such applications, or 'concept creep',[68] may lead to overexpansion of the doctrine, and thus, for instance, may deny organisations charitable status, where once such registration would be of less concern. Such development of charity law can lead to uncertainty and lower public confidence in the sector, which strikes at the very heart of the concept of charity itself.

Therefore, while this case provided a useful classification of political purposes, expanding the doctrine, it also facilitated the extension of the doctrine further, due to the classification's non-exhaustive nature, bringing with it broader consequences for the doctrine for charity law generally, as well as jurisprudentially.

Before we explore some of the fallacies pertaining to the doctrine, it is worthwhile considering some of the definitions of politics and political activities, because such definitions provide further evidence of the difficulties of applying and interpreting this doctrine with any clear certainty.

C Defining politics in charity law

In layperson's terms, 'politics' and 'political activity' have been variously defined. 'Politics' includes 'The activities associated with the governance of a country or area, especially the debate between parties having power'; and 'The activities of governments concerning the political relations between states'; and 'A particular set of political beliefs or principles'.[69] 'Political activity' has been defined as: 'doing something in active support of or opposition to a political party, a candidate for partisan political office ... or a partisan political group',[70] and as:[71]

65 Ibid., 117, referring to *Re Koeppler's Will Trusts* [1984] 1 Ch 243 (HC), 350 and 260–1. It should be noted that the Court of Appeal reversed the High Court decision, but did not remark on these additional purposes.
66 *R v. Radio Authority; ex parte Bull* [1995] 4 All ER 481.
67 Dunn, '*McGovern v. Attorney-General*', 117–18.
68 Ibid., 118.
69 *Oxford Dictionary*, https://en.oxforddictionaries.com/definition/politics [accessed 19 January 2017].
70 US Department of Defense, 'Political Activity' www.dodea.edu/Offices/Counsel/pa.cfm [accessed 19 January 2017].
71 Public Service Commission of Canada, 'Definition of a political activity', www.psc-cfp.gc.ca/plac-acpl/psc-cfp-eng.htm#pol [accessed 19 January 2017].

- Carrying on any activity in support of, within or in opposition to a political party;
- Carrying on any activity in support of, or in opposition to, a candidate before or during an election period; or
- Seeking nomination as, or being, a candidate in an election before or during the election period.

In charity law too, definitions abound, and such definitions are not dissimilar to the layperson's versions,[72] but as with the layperson's, the definitions in charity law are not consistent, and vary within jurisdictions and within different contexts.

As observed by Elias CJ in the New Zealand Supreme Court case of *Re Greenpeace of New Zealand Inc*, the view of the Court in *National Anti-Vivisection Society* was that Lord Parker's reference to 'political objects' in *Bowman* was limited to promoting changes in legislation.[73] However, this view is doubtful because assuming that a political exclusion depends on 'whether a purpose entails legislative change does not explain the general agreement that entities which promote political parties are not charitable, even when they do not promote changes in the law'.[74]

Other definitions were provided by Slade J in *McGovern*, where his Honour provided a non-exhaustive list of classification of purposes that would be political, including procuring changes in national and international laws; and furthering the interests of a political party.[75]

An extension of this has now been provided by the Charity Commission for England and Wales, where political activity may include:[76]

- raising public support for such a change
- seeking to influence political parties or independent candidates, decision-makers, politicians or public servants on the charity's position in various ways in support of the desired change; and
- responding to consultations carried out by political parties

Thus, while definitions may abound, they do not necessarily provide consistency or certainty. The reality is that it is not always easy to distinguish between permissible political activities, advocacy, and indeed subsidiary activities. In fact, even providing definitions may be fraught with difficulties. For instance, the categories

---

72 Alison Dunn, 'Charity Law as a Political Option for the Poor', in *Foundations of Charity* (Oregon: Hart, 2000), 60.
73 *Re Greenpeace of New Zealand Inc* [2014], [61], referring to *National Anti-Vivisection Society* v. *Inland Revenue Commissioners*, 49–50, 55, and 62. However, this view was not adopted in the later New Zealand case of *Molloy* v. *CIR* [1981] 1 NZLR 688 (CA).
74 *Re Greenpeace of New Zealand Inc* [2014], [61].
75 *McGovern* v. *Attorney-General*, 340.
76 Charity Commission for England and Wales, 'Speaking Out: Guidance on Campaigning and Political Activity by Charities', [2.4(2)] www.gov.uk/government/uploads/system/uploads/attachment_data/file/434427/CC9_LowInk.pdf [accessed 19 January 2017].

set out by Slade J in *McGovern*, as set out earlier, have been said to be 'deceptively broad'.[77] This is because it is not confined to institutions established purely to change the law. It can also include institutions that implicitly contemplate law change, and it does not specifically characterise public information campaigns as political. Nonetheless, such campaigns have been found to be political and thus not charitable.[78]

England and Wales has gone some way to alleviate such uncertainty, by including the promotion of human rights in legislation, which legitimises the political engagement in human rights causes.[79] Further, the Charity Commission has provided revised guidelines on the circumstances in which political activities may be permitted.[80] However, these Guidelines may still not meet the needs of charity. For instance, there is an imprecise boundary between permissible and impermissible political activities, which may lead to a chilling effect on charities from carrying out such activities, which may undermine their overall charitable purpose and activities.[81]

Therefore, due to such uncertainties, and added to that, the prohibitive costs of litigation, as well as the publicity that will inevitably arise with such actions, charities may self-censor their public advocacy activities in case they lose their charitable status.[82]

D The fallacies of the doctrine

As is evident, the political purpose doctrine has a long history, however, its critics also have a long history. For instance, nearly 80 years previously, Sir Owen Wilson observed that the 'case law dealing with the distinction between charitable purposes and political objects is in an unsatisfactory condition'.[83] Indeed, the very existence of the doctrine, is, in some respects, difficult to reconcile, because there is a strong historical tradition of charities campaigning to remove political purposes that were deemed objectionable to public welfare. For instance, the originally named

77 Adam Parachin, 'Reforming the Regulation of Political Advocacy by Charities: From Charity under Siege to Charity under Rescue?', *Chicago-Kent Law Review* 91(3) (2016), 1058.

78 Parachin, 'Reforming the Regulation of Political Advocacy by Charities', referring to *Human Life International in Canada Incorporated* v. *MNR; Positive Action Against Pornography* v. *MNR; Alliance for Life* v. *MNR; News to You Canada* v. *MNR*, 2011 CAF 192, 2011 FCA 192.

79 Rebecca Lee, 'Charity without Politics? Exploring the Limits of "Politics" in Charity Law', *Journal of Civil Society* 11(3) (2015), 275.

80 Ibid.; and Charity Commission for England and Wales, 'Speaking Out'.

81 Lee, 'Charity without Politics?', 275.

82 Rebecca Lee and Lusina Ho, 'Advocating Public Advocacy: An Opportunity for Charities in Hong Kong?', *Trusts and Trustees* 18(1) (January 2012), 44–5; Debra Morris, 'Charities and Political Activity in England and Wales: Mixed Messages', *Charity Law and Practice Review* 18(1) (2015–16), 110–11.

83 G. F. K. Santow, 'Charity in Its Political Voice: A Tinkling Cymbal or a Sounding Brass?', *Current Legal Problems* 52(1) (1999), 255–85, citing *Royal North Shore Hospital of Sydney* v. *Attorney-General* (NSW) (1938) 60 CLR 396, 426.

Charity Organisation Society, was founded in 1869 to influence social policies in relation to the poor,[84] and, more recently, internationally recognised groups such as the John Howard League for Penal Reform, Amnesty International, and Oxfam,[85] are advocates for human rights and are critics of various government policies.

Indeed, its application has produced some ironic conclusions over time. For instance, it is charitable to prevent cruelty to animals, but political to seek the abolition of torture of humans.[86] Although with regard to the latter, early case law shows that advocacy to end torture to humans could be charitable.[87] Further ironic results are found where it was charitable to operate an abortion clinic, but political to promote a view on abortion;[88] and where it is charitable to educate the public with regard to finding peace acceptable to war, but political to assist two societies to live harmoniously together.[89]

While the doctrine evidently has wrought some dubious results, its existence has been rationalised. One of the key rationales is that a court cannot determine the public benefit of such purposes, to which Lord Parker in *Bowman* made reference. Leading on from this view is that judges should refrain from deciding political questions, and leave that instead to the legislature.[90]

Another rationale is that '[a] coherent system of law can scarcely admit that objects which are inconsistent with its own provisions are for the public welfare'.[91] In other words, the law must be understood as being correct as it stands, otherwise it risks either being stultified,[92] or made incoherent.[93]

---

84 Now named Family Action, www.family-action.org.uk/who-we-are/our-history [accessed 23 January 2017].

85 Santow, 'Charity in Its Political Voice'.

86 Parachin, 'Distinguishing Charity from Politics', 871–2, referring to *Re Green's Will Trusts* [1985] 3 All ER 455 (Ch D) and *McGovern* v. *Attorney-General*; *Action by Christians for the Abolition of Torture* v. *Canada*, 2002 FCA 499, 225 DLR (4th) 99, respectively.

87 Parachin, 'Distinguishing Charity from Politics', 872, fn. 2, referring to *Jackson* v. *Philips*.

88 Parachin, 'Distinguishing Charity from Politics', 872, referring to *Everywoman's Health Centre Society* (1988) v. *MNR* [1992] 2 FC 52 (CA) and *Human Life International in Canada Inc* v. *MNR* [1998] 3 FC 202 (CA), respectively.

89 Parachin, 'Distinguishing Charity from Politics', 872, referring to *Southwood* v. *A-G* [2000] EWCA Civ 204 and *Anglo-Swedish Society; Buxton* v. *Public Trustee* (1962) 41 TC 235 (Ch D), respectively.

90 Chia, Harding, and O'Connell, 'Navigating the Politics of Charity', 362, referring to *National Anti-Vivisection Society* v. *Inland Revenue Commissioners*, 50 and 62 and *McGovern* v. *Attorney-General*, 337.

91 *Re Collier (Deceased)* [1998] 1 NZLR 81, 89, citing *Royal North Shore Hospital of Sydney* v. *Attorney-General for New South Wales* (1938) 60 CLR 396, 426 and also referring to *Molloy* v. *Commissioner of Inland Revenue*; *National Anti-Vivisection Society* v. *Inland Revenue Commissioners*.

92 Chia, Harding, and O'Connell, 'Navigating the Politics of Charity', 362, referring to *National Anti-Vivisection Society* v. *Inland Revenue Commissioners*, 50 and Tyssen, *Law of Charitable Bequests*, 177.

93 Chia, Harding, and O'Connell, 'Navigating the Politics of Charity', 362, referring to *Royal North Shore Hospital of Sydney* v. *Attorney-General*.

An alternative view, as demonstrated in the US cases, is that courts 'have distinguished between attempts to improve the law and subversion or violation of it, and have held that trusts to secure peaceful and orderly change are in the public interest'.[94] For instance, in the Illinois appellate case, *Garrison* v. *Little*, the Court held that a trust to secure the passage of laws giving women the right to vote was charitable.[95]

With regard to the first rationale, that of public benefit, this can be interpreted as meaning that 'judges are incapable of determining public benefit, or alternatively as reflecting the constitutional claim that judges should not decide political questions'.[96] However, judges are required to determine public benefit all the time in charity law.[97] For instance, in *National Anti-Vivisection Society*,[98] the House of Lords held that abolishing vivisection was not charitable because there would be no public benefit in doing so, evidently judging the public benefit of the matter.

In reality, as observed by Hammond J (as he was), in *Re Collier (Deceased)* this particular view was 'beginning to wear thin',[99] asserting:[100]

> Is it really inappropriate for a Judge to recognise an issue as thoroughly worthy of public debate, even though the outcome of that debate might be to lead to a change in the law? After all, it is commonplace for Judges to make suggestions themselves for changes in the law today, whether in judgments, or extra-curially.

For instance, in *Re Goldwater (Deceased)*,[101] leading on from certain comments in that judgment, the 1979 report of the Property Law and Equity Reform Committee on the Charitable Trusts Act 1957 was commissioned.

The view in relation to the stultification of the law can be said to be 'hopelessly old-fashioned',[102] resting on the 'mythical view of the "eternal correctness" of the law'.[103] Rather, there is evidence that such a strict exclusion of political purposes would actually do the opposite, and stultify the law because:[104]

94 *Re Collier (Deceased)*, 89, citing George Bogert, *The Law of Trusts*, 5th edn (California: Foundation Press, 1973), 236.
95 *Re Collier (Deceased)*, 89, referring to *Garrison* v. *Little* 75 Ill App 402.
96 Chia, Harding, and O'Connell, 'Navigating the Politics of Charity', 362–363, referring to Abraham Drassinower, 'The Doctrine of Political Purposes in the Law of Charities: A Conceptual Analysis', in Jim Phillips, Bruce Chapman and David Stevens (eds), *Between State and Market: Essays on Charities Law and Policy in Canada* (Ottawa: McGill-Queen's University Press, 2011), 288 and 293–4.
97 Chia, Harding, and O'Connell, 'Navigating the Politics of Charity', 363, referring to L. A. Sheridan, 'Charity Versus Politics', *Anglo-American Law Review* 2(1) (1973); Kate Tokeley, 'A New Definition of Charity?', *Victoria University of Wellington Law Journal* 21(1) (February 1991), 51; Helena Kennedy, *Advisory Group on Campaigning and the Voluntary Sector*, government report (May 2007), 11–14.
98 *National Anti-Vivisection Society* v. *Inland Revenue Commissioners*.
99 *Re Collier (Deceased)*, 89.
100 Ibid.
101 Ibid., referring to *Re Goldwater (Deceased)* [1967] 1 NZLR 754 (SC).
102 Chia, Harding, and O'Connell, 'Navigating the Politics of Charity', 363.
103 Ibid., 362.
104 *Re Greenpeace of New Zealand Inc* [2014], [70].

It is likely to hinder the responsiveness of this area of law to the changing circumstances of society. Just as the law of charities recognised the public benefit of philanthropy in easing the burden on parishes of alleviating poverty, keeping utilities in repair and educating the poor in post-Reformation Elizabethan England, the circumstances of the modern outsourced and perhaps contracting state may throw up new need for philanthropy which is properly found to be charitable.

Indeed, examples of charities supporting the 'machinery or harmony of civil society'[105] can be found in England, Australia,[106] and New Zealand[107] where law reporting was held to be charitable. A further example can be found in New Zealand, where the Court of Appeal in *Latimer* v. *Commissioner of Inland Revenue* held that the assistance of Māori in the research, preparation, presentation, and negotiation of claims before the Waitangi Tribunal was charitable.[108] Therefore, it is far from clear why the doctrine should stultify the law. Rather it is more plausible that 'recognising public benefit associated with law reform might draw attention to ways in which the law's aims are frustrated by its inability to keep up with social and economic change and thus help to alleviate any stultification of the law'.[109]

Further, it has been asserted that 'it is clear ... the politically active [civil society organisations] are structurally synonymous with charitable [civil society organisations]',[110] and, as a result, 'there are no theoretical grounds on which to differentiate between the charitable sector and organised civil society when justifying and designing a regulatory strategy'.[111] This suggests therefore that charity and politics should have a close relationship in order to develop a harmonious civil society.

In relation to the argument that the judiciary should remain impartial, and observe the separation of powers between judiciary and legislature, this does not mean that judges cannot engage in the development of the law, and judges are not constitutionally prevented from evaluating the public benefit of political

---

105 Ibid.
106 *Re Greenpeace of New Zealand Inc* [2014], [70], referring to *Incorporated Council of Law Reporting for England and Wales* v. *Attorney-General* [1972] Ch 73 (CA), *Incorporated Council of Reporting (Qld)* v. *Commissioner of Taxation* (Cth) (1971).
107 *Commissioner of Inland Revenue* v. *New Zealand Council of Law Reporting* [1981] 1 NZLR 682.
108 *Re Greenpeace of New Zealand Inc* [2014], [70], referring to *Latimer* v. *Commissioner of Inland Revenue* [2002] 3 NZLR 195 (CA).
109 Harding, *Charity Law*, 184.
110 Matthew Turnour, 'Case Comment – Some Thoughts on the Broader Theoretical Basis for Including Political Purpose within the Scope of Charitable Purpose: The *Aid/Watch* Case', *International Journal of Civil Society Law* 9(2) (April 2011), 88, citing Jonathan Garton, 'The regulation of charities and civil society', London (doctorate thesis, University of London, 2005), 201.
111 Turnour, 'Case Comment – *Aid/Watch*', 88, citing Garton, 'Regulation of charities', 201.

activities.[112] This is evidenced by courts historically observing that public benefit can, or cannot, be denoted from particular political purposes.[113] Indeed, it is a fallacy to suggest that judges do not engage in changing the law, because the reality is that the law in not settled, and judges do propose changes to the law, or depart from precedents, or overrule decided cases as the law evolves.[114]

Therefore, the historical arguments that support the doctrine are difficult to justify on a number of grounds, and while some jurisdictions, such as Canada, are still calling for reform due to the chilling effect of the doctrine, and its negative impact on the sector,[115] it is unsurprising that contemporary charity law has seen a number of sea changes. This is evidenced by decisions from Australasia,[116] as discussed later, and England and Wales also provide some development in this area of law, as illustrated in *Human Dignity Trust* v. *Charity Commission for England & Wales.*[117]

This case is particularly 'relevant to charities that wish to further their objects through strategic litigation'.[118] The Human Dignity Trust (HDT) was established to support those whose human rights have been violated by the criminalisation of private homosexual acts between consenting adults. Its purposes include promoting and protecting human rights, as determined in the Universal Declaration of Human Rights and subsequent UN conventions and declarations, and promoting, inter alia, the sound administration of law.[119]

One of its key activities is bringing litigation to challenge legislation in countries with constitutional human rights protections that appear to contrary to those protections. The Charity Commission rejected HDT's application to register because it deemed HDT's purposes political on the basis that upholding human rights in other jurisdictions would involve changing laws, which the *McGovern* principles exclude as being charitable.

What the Tribunal accepted was that, inter alia, international human rights obligations are a superior law, and HDT's activities were actually enforcing those laws, not changing them. This, it concluded, could be differentiated from the principles expounded by Slade J in *McGovern* because:[120]

> We understand Slade J's analysis ... to be limited to the consideration of a specific constitutional context in which there is a separation of powers with

---

112 Lee, 'Charity without Politics?', 275.
113 *Re Foveaux; National Anti-Vivisection Society* v. *Inland Revenue Commissioners; Aid/ Watch Incorporated* v. *Commissioner of Taxation; McGovern* v. *Attorney-General.*
114 Lee, 'Charity without Politics?', 275; see *Aid/Watch Incorporated* v. *Commissioner of Taxation* and *Re Greenpeace of New Zealand Inc* [2014].
115 Emma Gilchrist, 'Canada's Charity Law Needs Reform: Report', *The Tyee*, 25 March 2015, https://thetyee.ca/News/2015/03/25/Charity-Law-Report-2015 [accessed 23 January 2017].
116 *Aid/Watch Incorporated* v. *Commissioner of Taxation; Re Greenpeace of New Zealand Inc* [2014].
117 *Human Dignity Trust* v. *Charity Commission for England & Wales* CA/2013/0013.
118 Chan, 'Backgrounder for Talk', [2.1.7].
119 *Human Dignity Trust* v. *Charity Commission of England and Wales*, [6].
120 Ibid., [96].

Parliamentary supremacy. His concern about the court usurping the role of the legislature was entirely understandable in that context. However, we find ... HDT's activities take place in a markedly different context, where there is constitutional supremacy and a legitimate role for the court in interpreting and enforcing superior constitutional rights where the domestic law is thought to be in conflict with those rights.

This means that the type of 'constitutional litigation supported and conducted by HDT is fundamentally different in nature from the activities found to be objectionable as political in *McGovern*'.[121] Therefore the Tribunal concluded that such litigation is not political, and additionally there is 'a public benefit in seeking to interpret, clarify and protect superior constitutional rights'.[122]

While on one level this case should be welcomed as a contemporary consideration of the political purpose doctrine, on another it still leaves the doctrine surrounded by uncertainty. The Tribunal was careful not to extinguish the doctrine, and confined its decision to the specific facts of the case,[123] suggesting the decision's overall impact may be limited.

However, in reality, the decision may have far-reaching consequences. For instance, it illustrates that public benefit can be found in activities that would generally be thought of as political.[124] The decision also raises the issue of how a 'political activity' might be reframed as a human right, thus enabling that purpose to fall outside the political purpose doctrine and be charitable, and the implications of this could be very wide. Although it should be noted that once human rights were recognised as being charitable in the Charities Act 2006[125] in England and Wales, it was inevitable that such an issue may arise at some juncture.[126] This case therefore 'leaves a future court with the unenviable task of determining when human rights advocacy is political rather than charitable'.[127] In all likelihood, this is a 'direct product of courts not having articulated a substantive distinction between charity and politics in the first place'.[128]

So, while there is evidence that courts are willing to engage in interpreting the doctrine in contemporary contexts, clarity is still required. Not only that, there is evidence of subversive suppression of political purposes within charities, resulting in an 'atmosphere for charities in relation to their campaigning activities'[129] turning hostile. In 2014, Conservative MP Conor Burns complained to the Charity Commission for England and Wales about Oxfam and its campaign against poverty in Great Britain. The concern was focused on an image entitled 'The Perfect Storm', published by Oxfam on its Twitter account. The image made reference to

121 Ibid., [65].
122 Ibid., [109].
123 Ibid., [113].
124 Lee, 'Charity without Politics?', 278.
125 Charities Act 2006, s 2(2)(h).
126 Morris, 'Charities and Political Activity', 127.
127 Parachin, 'Charity, Politics and Neutrality', 19.
128 Ibid.
129 Morris, 'Charities and Political Activity', 94.

policies relating to poverty, insinuating that the policies forced more people into poverty. The tweet was part of a social media campaign leading up to the release of the report on food poverty.[130]

The Commission investigated, concluding that 'Oxfam should have done more to avoid being seen as politically biased against the Government'.[131] The Commission stated that trustees should have more oversight into the campaigning activities and authorise and sign off procedures for publishing in social media.[132] However, in the same investigation, the Commission concluded that Oxfam's publication in the press relating to ending the blockade in Gaza, and ending the violence so prevalent in that area, was an ancillary political activity, and merely part of its furtherance of its charitable activities.[133]

This investigation goes 'to the heart of the political purpose/activity conundrum'.[134] The Commission has imposed more rigorous requirements of trustees and campaign activities, which will suppress the immediacy of their social media presence, thus striking out many of the benefits of utilising social media. Further, its message is unclear as to how to differentiate between acceptable political campaigns, and those that contravene the political purpose doctrine. Overall therefore what this illustrates is the complexities still surrounding the discourse on the doctrine, which will do little to garner public confidence in the sector.

While there is evidently more clarity required in some jurisdictions, recent Australasian jurisprudence, on the other hand, has added much to the contemporary discourse on the doctrine, to which this chapter now turns.

E Australasia and the winds of change

(1) Australia

(i) Introduction

While it is evident that the political purposes were, once upon a time, contrary to charity law in Australia,[135] 'the position was never as clear-cut as elsewhere'.[136] In *Victorian*

---

130 Morris, 'Charities and Political Activity', 95, referring to N. Cooper, S. Purcell, and R. Jackson, 'Below the Breadline: The Relentless Rise of Food Poverty in Britain' (Church Action on Poverty, Oxfam GB and Trussell Trust, 2014).
131 Morris, 'Charities and Political Activity', 95, referring to Charity Commission, 'Operational Compliance Record: Oxfam' (Registration Number 202918) (2014).
132 Morris, 'Charities and Political Activity', 95.
133 Ibid., 95–6.
134 Ibid., 96.
135 Fiona Martin, 'The Legal Concept of Charity and Its Expansion after the *Aid/Watch* Decision', *Cosmopolitan Civil Societies Journal* 3(2) (2011), 26; Gino Dal Pont, *Charity Law in Australia and New Zealand* (Melbourne: Oxford University Press, 2000), 203; Kerry O'Halloran, *Human Rights and Charity Law: International Perspectives* (Abingdon: Routledge, 2016), 219, referring to *Re Cripps* [1941] Tas SR 19.
136 Garton, *Public Benefit in Charity Law*, 200.

Women Lawyers' Association v. *Commissioner of Taxation*, French J observed that the:[137]

> Political purpose limitation is not well defined and is more difficult of application today having regard to the change in social conditions since 1917 and the involvement of legislatures in areas unthought of at that time.

Earlier Australian jurisprudence reflects equal judicial uncertainty and even explicit criticism of the doctrine.[138] In *Royal North Shore Hospital of Sydney* v. *Attorney-General for New South Wales*,[139] Latham CJ was cautionary about the influence of *Bowman*, stating it should not be 'regarded as making it impossible to establish a trust as charitable merely because the subject matter of the trust might be associated with political activity'. Dixon J, in the same case, stated that the 'case law dealing with the distinction between charitable purposes and political objects is in an unsatisfactory condition',[140] and Rich J thought the doctrine 'vague and indefinite'.[141] Therefore, while the Court in this case did acknowledge the authority of *Bowman* at that time, its unease as to its relevance was evident.[142] In *Public Trustee* v. *Attorney-General of New South Wales*,[143] Santow J also 'lent his voice to the rising tide of criticism being levelled at this doctrine'[144] in Australia, observing that the doctrine does not permit a 'distinction between supplementing the law when it may already be moving in a particular direction, and directly opposing its well established policy'.[145]

With such criticisms being levelled at the doctrine over the course of many years, it was perhaps inevitable that a sea change may occur, and this happened in the High Court case of *Aid/Watch Incorporated* v. *Commissioner of Taxation*.[146] It is true that much has been written about this case, but it would be remiss not to include some discussion on this case because of its fundamental impact on the doctrine.

---

137 *Victorian Women Lawyer's Association* v. *Commissioner of Taxation* [2008] FCA 983, (2008) 170 FCA 318, [128]; see also *Attorney-General (NSW)* v. *NSW Henry George Foundation Ltd* [2002] NSWSC 1128 (27 November 2002).

138 Chevalier-Watts, *Law of Charity*, 291–6.

139 *Royal North Shore Hospital of Sydney* v. *Attorney-General*, 412.

140 Ibid., 427.

141 Ibid., 420.

142 Chevalier-Watts, *Law of Charity*, 294; Chia, Harding, and O'Connell, 'Navigating the Politics of Charity', 357.

143 *Public Trustee* v. *Attorney-General of New South Wales* [1997] 42 NSWLR 600 (NSWSC).

144 Juliet Chevalier-Watts, 'Charitable Trusts and Political Purposes: Sowing the Seeds of Change? Lessons from Australia', *Canterbury Law Review* 19(1) (2013), 59.

145 *Public Trustee* v. *Attorney-General of New South Wales*, 604.

146 *Aid/Watch Incorporated* v. *Commissioner of Taxation*.

(ii) Aid/Watch

Aid/Watch the organisation, is, inter alia, an independent monitor of international and trade policy. It focuses on systems that cause poverty, and it campaigns and challenges national and international government agencies, corporations, and NGOs to utilise aid effectively to benefit those in need.[147]

The Australian Constitution 'played a significant role in underpinning the result'[148] in this case, and it was 'invoked by the majority to support their conclusion that a body can be a "charitable institution" despite engaging in political activities'.[149]

The starting point for the majority was to assert that the remarks of Lord Parker in *Bowman* 'were not directed to the Australian system of government established and maintained by the Constitution itself'.[150] As a result, that was significant in deciding the content of the common law in Australia pertaining to political objects.[151] The majority concluded that the system of law that operates in Australia actually requires the very 'agitation' for legislative and political changes, about which Dixon J spoke in *Royal North Shore Hospital*.[152] The majority rejected the idea that such purposes would stultify the law, which has been a justification for the doctrine, as discussed earlier. This is because it is the 'operation of these constitutional processes which contributes to public welfare'.[153] Therefore, the majority held that generation, by lawful means, of public debate, concerning the efficient use of foreign aid, which is directed to the relief of poverty, was beneficial under the fourth head of charity.[154] It is likely that this decision was 'reinforced by the discussion of the shaky legal foundations of the doctrine, the liberalising effect of the guidance on political purposes issued by the Charity Commission of [sic] England and Wales, and the different position taken in the US'.[155]

(iii) The contemporary Australian political purpose doctrine

The result of this decision is likely to be far-reaching, and overall was celebrated.[156] Organisations in Australia now have an increased ability to carry out campaigning and advocacy, but these activities must be directed to public benefit, and cannot be for illegal purposes, or contrary to public policy.[157] In consequence, the decision

---

147 www.aidwatch.org.au/about/what-we-do [accessed 26 January 2017].
148 George Williams, 'The Australian Constitution and the *Aid/Watch* Case', *Cosmopolitan Civil Societies Journal* 3(3) (special issue) (2011), 1.
149 Ibid.
150 *Aid/Watch Incorporated* v. *Commissioner of Taxation*, [40].
151 Ibid.
152 Ibid., [45], referring to *Royal North Shore Hospital of Sydney* v. *Attorney-General*.
153 Ibid.
154 Ibid., [47].
155 Chia, Harding, and O'Connell, 'Navigating the Politics of Charity', 375, referring to *Aid/Watch Incorporated* v. *Commissioner of Taxation*, [27]–[38].
156 Ibid., 377.
157 Martin, 'Legal Concept of Charity', 31.

broadens the scope of the public benefit requirement so that political purposes 'are indispensable incidents'[158] of the constitutional system. This means that the public benefit test of the fourth head could broaden to include agitation and activism for, and against, political purposes 'that advance Australia's constitutional system of representative democracy'.[159] In turn, this reduces the 'chilling' effect caused by the doctrine that may have deterred charities from engaging in advocacy, and of course, symbolically, advocacy has now been confirmed as a lawful charitable activity.[160]

The Australian legislature has subsequently endorsed the *Aid/Watch* decision by including in the definition of 'charitable purpose' in the Charities Act 2013 'the purpose of promoting of or opposing a change to any matter established by law, policy or practice in the Commonwealth, a State, a Territory or another country, so long as it furthers one or more of its charitable purposes'.[161] This means, therefore, that there continues to be a rule against political purposes in Australian charity law, but its scope is far narrower than the very broad rule developed by jurisdictions such as England and Wales, and Canada.[162]

It may be thought, as a result of this decision, that 'the debate over the application [of] the political purpose doctrine has now been laid to rest in Australia'.[163] However, there are still aspects of the doctrine in Australia that remain unclear, even in light of *Aid/Watch*.

The majority of the Court referred to the 'generation by lawful means of public debate … is a purpose beneficial to the community within the fourth head in *Pemsel*'. The Court does not explain how far the generation of debate may apply in the context of the first three heads of *Pemsel*, nor specifically, when it may apply to charities that fall within the fourth head.[164] In addition, it is not yet clear how far the 'breadth of the implied political communication under the Constitution' may expand.[165] Certainly, 'promoting or opposing a political party or a candidate for political office'[166] will likely disqualify a purpose from being charitable, although the *Aid/Watch* case has not clarified whether or not individual, or isolated activities, might amount to such a disqualification. It is evident, however, that a pattern of such activities may amount to a disqualification, as occurred when the ACNC deregistered Catch the Fire Ministry, an evangelical church, in January 2017 because of its political associations with, and support for, the Rise up Australia party.[167]

---

158 Jenny Beard, 'Charity Law from a Public Law Perspective: The *Aid/Watch* Case Revisited', *Charity Law and Practice Review* 18(1) (2015–16), 75.
159 Ibid.
160 Chia, Harding, and O'Connell, 'Navigating the Politics of Charity', 377–8.
161 Charities Act 2013 (Cth), s 12(1) (Australia AU); Beard, 'Charity Law from a Public Law Perspective', 88.
162 Harding, *Charity Law*, 179.
163 Beard, 'Charity Law from a Public Law Perspective', 88.
164 Martin, 'Legal Concept of Charity', 33.
165 Beard, 'Charity Law from a Public Law Perspective', 89.
166 Charities Act 2013, s 11(b).
167 Christian Siebert and Ann O'Connell, 'Explainer: What Are the Limits to Charities Advancing Political Causes?', 20 January 2017, http://theconversation.com/expla

A further issue is that the majority in *Aid/Watch* did not make it clear whether the public benefit lies 'primarily in the generation of public debate itself, in the charitable purpose which is being publicly debated, or in some combination of the two'.[168] It may be that while there is general value in political speech, the High Court meant that it was the context of the speech that was important in determining the public benefit of the public debate, and this may become evident as other cases bring such an issue to light.[169]

Nonetheless, the *Aid/Watch* case has demonstrated that charity law can adapt in a contemporary context, and while the political purpose doctrine has not been silenced in Australia, its effects are now more limited within the charity sector. Thus, modern charity law in Australia, in which 'advocacy and criticism of government laws and policies is something that is protected',[170] helps to ensure a healthy 'modern, functioning, representative democracy'.[171]

(2) New Zealand

Until recent times,[172] the law pertaining to political purposes in New Zealand was consistent with the traditional approach adopted in England and Wales, that political purposes are contrary to the public benefit requirement of charity law.[173] For instance, in *Molloy* v. *Commissioner of Inland Revenue*,[174] the Court of Appeal held that a society, whose purposes included the objection to legislative change regarding abortion, was not charitable because it was unable to accept 'that the public good in restricting abortion is so self-evident as a matter of law that such charitable prerequisite is achieved'.

In *Re Collier (Deceased)*,[175] Hammond J (as he was then), affirmed that 'there is no warrant to change these well-established principles – which rest on decisions of the highest authority'. However, his Honour did observe, in a critical stance regarding the doctrine, that 'admirable objectives too often fall foul'[176] of the doctrine.

However, with the Supreme Court decision of *Re Greenpeace of New Zealand Inc*,[177] a new legal landscape emerged in New Zealand regarding the doctrine.

iner-what-are-the-limits-to-charities-advancing-political-causes-71466 [accessed 27 January 2017].

168 Chia, Harding, and O'Connell, 'Navigating the Politics of Charity', 384.
169 Ibid., 385.
170 Williams, 'Australian Constitution and *Aid/Watch*', 8.
171 Beard, 'Charity Law from a Public Law Perspective', 89.
172 *Re Greenpeace of New Zealand Inc* [2014] *Family First New Zealand* [2015] NZHC 1493.
173 O'Halloran, *Human Rights and Charity Law*, 254.
174 *Molloy* v. *Commissioner of Inland Revenue*, 697.
175 *Re Collier (Deceased)* [1998] 1 NZLR 81 (HC), 90; see also *Re Draco Foundation (NZ) Charitable Trust* (2011) 25 NZTC 20-032 (HC) and Chevalier-Watts, *Law of Charity*, 307–9.
176 *Re Collier (Deceased)*, 90; Chevalier-Watts, *Law of Charity*, 303–6.
177 *Re Greenpeace of New Zealand Inc* [2014].

This was a much-anticipated decision, especially in light of the *Aid/Watch* decision that had only a short time earlier been released in Australia; would New Zealand follow suit?

Certainly, the majority in the Supreme Court determined that the development of a stand-alone doctrine of exclusion political purposes, which they acknowledged was relatively recent developed and based on little authority,[178] was neither necessary nor beneficial.[179] However, the Court did not follow the same approach of the High Court of Australia in *Aid/Watch* to come to that conclusion.

The majority decision, delivered by Elias CJ, found it difficult to exclude all advocacy for legislative change from being charitable, because:[180]

> Promotion of law reform of the type often undertaken by law commissions which aims to keep laws fit for modern purposes may well be properly seen as charitable if undertaken by private organisations even though such reform inevitably entails promotion of legislation.

'In reality, this type of advocacy might constitute a public good that is analogous to other good works that have been held to be charitable at law.'[181]

The majority concluded that the:[182]

> better approach is not a doctrine of exclusion of 'political' purpose but acceptance that an object which entails advocacy for change in the law is 'simply one facet of whether a purpose advances the public benefit in a way that is within the spirit and intendment of the statute of Elizabeth I'.

However, the Court also affirmed that not all advancement of causes will be charitable, because matters of opinion will not necessarily have sufficient public benefit, and thus fall outside the public benefit rubric.[183] This is in line even with the earlier decision of *Molloy* because 'the viewpoint propounded in that case could not be shown to demonstrate public benefit in the sense that is recognised as law'.[184]

The majority also quashed a point raised in the Court of Appeal *Greenpeace* decision,[185] where that Court suggested that views that are generally acceptable may be charitable, while controversial views may not; the Supreme Court did not

178 Ibid., [59] referring to paragraphs [32]–[47].
179 Ibid.
180 Ibid., [62].
181 Chevalier-Watts, *Law of Charity*, 313; *Re Greenpeace of New Zealand Inc* [2014], [62].
182 *Re Greenpeace of New Zealand Inc* [2014], [72], citing L. A. Sheridan, 'Charitable Causes, Political Causes and Involvement', *The Philanthropist* 2(4) (1980), 16.
183 *Greenpeace of New Zealand Incorporated*, [73] citing *Aid/Watch*, [69] dissenting view); Chevalier-Watts, *Law of Charity*, 313.
184 Chevalier-Watts, *Law of Charity*, 313, referring to *Re Greenpeace of New Zealand Inc* [2014], [73]; see also Sheridan, 'Charitable Causes', 12.
185 *Re Greenpeace of New Zealand Inc* [2012] NZCA 533 [2013] 1 NZLR 339.

agree with this. This would, in effect, 'exclude much promotion of change while favouring charitable status on the basis of majoritarian assessment and status quo'.[186]

Instead, the correct approach should be to establish whether the advocacy, or promotion of a cause, or change in legislation, is actually a charitable purpose, and this will depend on:[187]

> consideration of the end that is advocated, the means promoted to achieve that end and the manner in which the cause is promoted to achieve that end and the manner in which the cause is promoted in order to assess whether the purpose can be said to be public benefit within the spirit and intendment of the 1601 Statute.

As a result, the case has been returned to the Board of the Department of Internal Affairs – Charities Services for further consideration;[188] at the time of writing, the Board has yet to deliver its decision. This means that the law in New Zealand regarding political purposes has been reframed. A blanket ban is unnecessary because political purposes and charitable purposes are not mutually exclusive in all cases, and such an exclusion 'distracts from the underlying inquiry whether a purpose is of public benefit within the sense of the law recognises as charitable'.[189] The true rule is that advocacy 'is charitable in some circumstances and not in others'.[190] Therefore, in relation to Greenpeace's objects of the promotion of nuclear disarmament and elimination of weapons of mass destruction, and taking into account all the local and international consequences, 'the public benefit is not self-evident and ... seems unlikely to be capable of demonstration of evidence'.[191]

The effects of the *Greenpeace* decision were felt swiftly in New Zealand, with the High Court judgment of *Re Family First New Zealand*.[192]

This also was a much-anticipated case because it is the first case to have considered, and applied, the principles set out by the majority in *Greenpeace*, and provides the first consideration of this contemporary approach.

Family First's objects include, inter alia, promoting and advancing research and policy to support marriage and family as foundation for a strong and enduring society. In 2008, the Charities Commission, as it was then, made inquiries as to the extent of Family First's activities, including advocacy, and subsequently deregistered them, because at that time, the traditional English approach to

---

186 *Re Greenpeace of New Zealand Inc* [2014], [75].
187 Ibid., [76].
188 Ibid., [104].
189 Ibid., [3].
190 Chan, 'Backgrounder for Talk', 2.1.7, referring to *Re Greenpeace of New Zealand Inc* [2014], [74], citing Sheridan, 'Charitable Causes', 12; see also *National Anti-Vivisection Society v. Inland Revenue Commissioners*, 75–7.
191 *Re Greenpeace of New Zealand Inc* [2014], [101].
192 *Re Family First New Zealand*.

political purposes was authority. Family First's appeal was deferred until after the Supreme Court gave its judgment in *Greenpeace*.

Collins J observed that the Charities Services Board's decision that Family First's political objects could not be charitable was based on a legal proposition that has now been found to be incorrect. In other words, since *Greenpeace*, political purposes are not irreconcilable with charitable purposes. Thus, the correct approach to take was for the Board to reconsider the charitable position of Family First,[193] which, at the time of writing, is being undertaken.

Interestingly, in relation to the issue of public benefit, his Honour urged the Board to be cautious in referring to analogous cases to determine public benefit:[194]

> it is essential the Charities Board not undertake its analogical assessment by seeking to carefully match Family First's purposes with organisations that have achieved recognition as charitable entities. Doing so would risk undermining the Supreme Court's recognition, for the first time, that political purposes are not excluded from being classified as charitable.

On the other hand, Collins J was careful to note that the Board should not automatically find Family First's purposes are for the purpose of public benefit,[195] rather 'the analogical analysis which the Charities Board must undertake should be informed by examining whether Family First's activities are objectively directed at promoting the moral improvement of society'.[196] A further caution was also given by his Honour, whereby the Board should guard against imposing their own subjective views on the merits of Family First's purposes. Rather, there may be a 'legitimate analogy between [Family First's] role and those organisations that have been recognised as charities. Such an approach would be consistent with the obligation on members of the Charities Board to act with honesty, integrity and in good faith'.[197]

This judgment is useful because it illustrates how the principles enunciated in *Greenpeace* may be applied practically, even to potentially contentious purposes such as Family First's. 'Charity law is therefore not constrained by historical approaches that may not be applicable, or relevant in a contemporary society, but at the same time, the High Court recognises the importance of ensuring that critical legal requirements of charity law are fulfilled.'[198] This, therefore, demonstrates the evolution of charity law in a contemporary context because it reflects that determining a contentious view, that of the promotion of the traditional family, is a matter for the public. If it were otherwise, one would effectively silence

193 Ibid., [84].
194 Ibid., [86].
195 Ibid., [88].
196 Ibid., [89].
197 Ibid.
198 Juliet Chevalier-Watts, 'Case Comment: *Re Family First New Zealand*', *Waikato Law Review* 23(1) (2015), 188.

the public voice by deregistering a charity, which would be a 'loss for democratic discourse'.[199]

F Concluding remarks

Charity and politics have long had a symbiotic relationship, and charities have filled voids left vacant by state policies, or indeed, finances. Thus, charities play a valuable role in society, and have been in a position to help to change law and policies on issues that impact on society generally. Indeed, charities are often uniquely placed to be able to provide a voice for the underrepresented and the vulnerable.[200] However, the doctrine of political purposes is undoubtedly controversial, even today, not least because of its uncertain legal footing, but also because its boundaries are uncertain, and may vary within jurisdictions. Thus, the rules may be seen as vague and imprecise As a result, this can cause uncertainty, and reduced engagement with the public within the sector,[201] so striking at the very effectiveness of charity as a whole.

Nonetheless, the decisions of *Aid/Watch* and *Greenpeace* from the Australasian courts are welcomed because they have reframed the paradigms of the doctrine to some degree, and reflect the doctrine's applicability in a contemporary context. Thus, the legal landscape in relation to charity law may be seen as acting more effectively to support a modern society, which will benefit all within society, which simply reinforces the ethos of charity itself.

199 Rex Tauati Ahdar, 'Charity Begins at the Politically Correct Home? The *Family First Case*', *Otago Law Review* 14(1) (2015), 189; see also *Registration Decision: Society for the Protection of Auckland Harbours* (SO51367) (Decision No. 2016-1), 1 September 2016 and *Registration Decision: Kiwis Against Seabed Mining Incorporated* (KIW49965) (Decision No. 2016-3), 15 December 2016.
200 Morris, 'Charities and Political Activity', 128.
201 Alison Dunn, 'Charities and Restrictions on Political Activities: Developments by the Charity Commission for England and Wales in Determining Regulatory Barriers', *International Journal of Not-for-Profit Law* 11(1) (November 2008), 55.

Bibliography

Legislation

New Zealand

Charities Act 2005
Charities Amendment Act (No. 2) 2012
Explanatory Memorandum Charities Bill 2013
New Zealand Bill of Rights Act 1990

Australia

Australian Charities and Not-for-profits Commission Act 2012
Australian Charities and Not-for-Profits Commission Regulation 2013
Australian Charities and Not-for-Profits Commission (Repeal) (No. 1) Bill 2014
Charities Act 2013 (Cth)
Charities (Consequential Amendments and Transitional Provisions) Bill 2013 (Cth)
Commonwealth of Australia Constitution Act 1901
Extension of Charitable Purpose Act 2004

England and Wales

Charities Act 2006
Charities Act 2011
Co-operative and Community Benefit Societies Act 2014
Human Rights Act 1998
Tribunals, Courts and Enforcement Act 2007

Canada

Constitution Act 1867
Constitution Act 1982
Income Tax Act 1985

Hong Kong

Business Registration Ordinance 1959 (Cap 310)
Gambling Ordinance 1977 [Cap 148]

Inland Revenue Ordinance 1950 (Cap 112)
Po Leung Kuk Ordinance 1973 [Cap 1040]
Registered Trustee Ordinance 1958 (Cap 306)
Societies Ordinance (Cap 151) 1949
Stamp Duty Ordinance 1981 (Cap 117)
Summary Offences Ordinance 1933 [Cap 228]
Tung Wah Group of Hospitals Ordinance 1971 [Cap 1051]

Singapore

Charities Act 1994
Charities (Registration of Charities) Regulations 2008 [Cap 37, Reg 10]
Constitution of the Republic of Singapore 1965
Income Tax Act 2008

Cases

New Zealand

Alocoque *v.* Roache [1998] 2 NZLR 250 (Court of Appeal of New Zealand (NZCA))
Arawa Māori Trust Board *v.* Commissioner of Inland Revenue (1961) 1 MCD 391
Attorney-General for New Zealand *v.* Brown [1917] 393 (PC)
Canterbury Development Corporation *v.* Charities Commission [2010] 2 NZLR 707 (HC)
Commissioner of Inland Revenue *v.* Medical Council of New Zealand [1997] 2 NZLR 297 (CA)
Commissioner of Inland Revenue *v.* New Zealand Council of Law Reporting [1981] 1 NZLR 682 (Court of Appeal of New Zealand (NZCA))
D V Bryant Trust Board *v.* Hamilton City Council [1997] 3 NZLR 342 (HC)
Greenpeace of New Zealand Incorporated (CA) [2013] 1 NZLR 339 (CA)
Hester *v.* Commissioner of Inland Revenue [2005] 2 NZLR 172 (CA)
Institution of Professional Engineers New Zealand Inc *v.* Commissioner of Inland Revenue [1992] 1 NZLR 570 (HC)
Kaikoura County *v.* Boyd [1949] 1 NZLR 233
Laing *v.* Commissioner of Stamp Duties [1948] 1 NZLR 154
Latimer *v.* Commissioner of Inland Revenue [2004] 3 NZLR 157 (PC)
Liberty Trust *v.* Charities Commission [2011] 3 NZLR 68 (HC)
New Zealand Computer Society Inc (2011) 25 NZTC 20-033 (HC)
Molloy *v.* Commissioner of Inland Revenue (1977) 1 TRNZ 211 (SC)
Re Beckbessinger [1993] 2 NZLR 362 (HC)
Re Centrepoint Community Growth Trust [2002] 2 NZLR 325 (HC)
Re Collier (Deceased) [1998] 1 NZLR 81 (HC)
Re Draco Foundation (NZ) Charitable Trust (2011) 25 NZTC 20-032 3 (HC)
Re Education New Zealand Trust CIV-2009485-2301, 29 June 2010) (HC)
Re Family First New Zealand [2015] NZHC 1493 (HC)
Re Foundation for Anti-Aging Research and the Foundation for Reversal of Solid State Hypothermia [2016] 27 NZTC 22 (HC)
Re Goldwater (Deceased) [1967] 1 NZLR 754 (SC)
Re Grand Lodge of Antient Free and Accepted Masons [2011] 1 NZLR 277 (HC)

Re Greenpeace of New Zealand Incorporated [2015] 1 NZLR 169 (SC)
Re Mitchell [1963] 1 NZLR 934 (SC)
Re Queenstown Community Housing Trust [2011] 3 NZLR 502 (HC)
Re Tennant [1996] 2 NZLR 633 (HC)
Re Tuhoe Charitable Trust Board [2012] NZHC 1952 (HC)
Travis Trust *v.* Charities Commission [2009] 24 NZTC 23, 273 (HC)

Australia

Aboriginal Hostels Ltd *v.* Darwin City Council (1985) 75 FLR 197
Aid/Watch Incorporated *v.* Commissioner of Taxation [2010] HCA 42
Attorney General (NSW) *v.* The NSW Henry George Foundation Ltd [2002] NSWSC
    1128 (27 November 2002)
Attorney-General (NSW) *v.* Perpetual Trustee Co Ltd [1940] HCA 12; (1940) 63 CLR
    209 (28 June 1940)
Australian Broadcasting Corporation *v.* Lenah Game Meats Pty Ltd [2001] HCA 63
Bathurst City Council *v.* PWC Properties Pty Ltd [1998] HCA 59
Brisbane City Council *v.* Attorney-General for Queensland [1979] AC 411
Central Bayside General Practice Association Limited *v.* Commissioner of State Revenue
    [2006] HCA 43
Chamber of Commerce and Industry of Western Australia Inc *v.* Commissioner of State
    Revenue [2012] WASAT 146 (WA State Administrative Tribunal (Commercial and
    Civil), Chaney J (President), 18 July 2012)
Church of the New Faith *v.* Commissioner of Pay-Roll Tax (Vic) [1983] HCA 40
Coleman *v.* Power, 220 CLR 1 (High Court of Australia (HCA))
Commissioner of Taxation *v.* The Triton Foundation [2005] FCA 1319
Commissioner of Taxation (Cth) *v.* Word Investments Ltd [2008] HCA 55
Congregational Union of New South Wales *v.* Thistlethwayte [1952] HCA 48
Davies *v.* Perpetual Trustee Co Ltd, 59 NSWSR (New South Wales State Reports) 112
    (NSWSC)
Incorporated Council of Law Reporting (Queensland) *v.* Commissioner of Taxation, 125
    CLR 659 (HCA)
Kruger *v.* Commonwealth [1997] HCA 27
Lange *v.* Australian Broadcasting Corporation [1997] HCA 25
Monds *v.* Stackhouse [1948] HCA 47
Mulholland *v.* Australian Electoral Commission [2004] HCA 41
National Trustees Executors and Agency Company of Australasia Ltd *v.* Jeffrey [1950]
    VLR 382
Nunawading Shire *v.* Adult Deaf and Dumb Society of Victoria [1921] HCA 6
Presbyterian Church (New South Wales) Property Trust *v.* Ryde Municipal Council, 2
    NSWLR 387 (NSWCA)
Presbyterian Church (New South Wales) Property Trust Ryde Municipal Council [1977] 1
    NSWLR 620
Public Trustee *v.* Attorney-General of New South Wales [1997] 42 NSWLR 600
    (NSWSC)
Re Cripps (deceased) [1941] Tas SR 19
Re Hoey [1994] 2 Qd R 510
Re Mathew [1951] 1 VLR 226
Re Municipal Orchestra Endowment Fund (1999) QSC 200, 10 August 1999

Roach *v.* Electoral Commissioner [2007] HCA 43 (HCA)

Roman Catholic Archbishop of Melbourne *v.* Lawlor [1934] HCA 14

Royal North Shore Hospital of Sydney *v.* Attorney-General (NSW) [1938] HCA 39

Salvation Army (Victoria) Property Trust *v.* Fern Tree Gully Corporation [1952] HCA 4

Strathalbyn Show Jumping Club Inc *v.* Mayes [2001] SASC 73 (SASC) 16 March 2001

Tasmanian Electronic Commerce Centre Pty Ltd *v.* Commissioner of Taxation [2005] FCA 439 (FCA) 18 April 2005

Taylor *v.* Taylor [1910] HCA 4 (HCA)

Victorian Women Lawyers' Association *v.* Commissioner of Taxation [2008] FCA 983 (FCA)

England and Wales

Abbott *v.* Fraser (1874) 6 LR PC 96

Anglo-Swedish Society *v.* Inland Revenue Commissioners (1931) 16 TC 34 (KB)

Attorney-General *v.* Brereton (1752) 2 Ves 425

Attorney-General *v.* Clarke [1762] 1 Amb 422

Attorney-General *v.* Fowler (1808) 15 Ves 85

Attorney-General *v.* Skinners' Company (1826) 2 Russ 407

Attorney-General *v.* Sutton (1721) 1 P Wms 754

Baptist Union of Ireland (Northern) Corporation Ltd *v.* Commissioners of Inland Revenue, 26 TC 335

Belfast City YMCA Commissioner of Valuation for Northern Ireland [1969], 1 NI 3 (IRCA)

Biscoe *v.* Jackson [1887] 35 Ch D 460

Bowman *v.* Secular Society Limited [1917] 1 AC 406 (HL)

Brown *v.* Gould [1972] Ch 53

Bruce *v.* Presbytery of Deer (1867) 1 LR, Sc & Div 96 (HL)

Camille and Henry Dreyfus Foundation Inc *v.* Commissioner of Inland Revenue [1956] 1 AC 39 (HL)

Campbell *v.* United Kingdom [1982] 4 EHRR 293 (ECtHR)

Chichester Diocesan Fund and Board of Finance Incorp. *v.* Simpson [1944] 2 All ER 60 (HL)

Cocks *v.* Manners (1871) 12 LR Eq 574

Commissioners of Inland Revenue *v.* Yorkshire Agricultural Society [1928] 1 KB 611

Commissioners for Special Purposes of Income Tax *v.* Pemsel [1891] AC 531 (HL)

Cruwys *v.* Colman (1804) 9 Ves 319

De Themmines *v.* De Bonneval (1828) 5 Russ 288

Dingle *v.* Turner [1972] 1 AC 601 (HL)

Doe d Thompson *v.* Pitcher (1815) 6 Taunt 359

Dunport Steels Ltd *v.* Sirs [1980] 1 WLR 142 (HL)

Gass *v.* White (1834) 32 Ky 170

Gibson *v.* South American Stores (Gath and Chaves) Ltd [1950] 1 Ch 177 (CA)

Gilmour *v.* Coats [1949] 1 AC 426 (HL)

Gilmour *v.* Coats [1948] 1 Ch 340 (CA)

Goodman *v.* Mayor of Saltash (1882) 1 App Cas

Guild *v.* Inland Revenue Commissioners [1992] 2 AC 310 (HL)

Hadaway *v.* Hadaway [1955] 1 WLR 16 (PC)

Hoare *v.* Hoare (1886) 56 LT 147

Houston *v.* Burns [1917] AC 337 (HL)

Howse *v.* Chapman, 4 Ves 542

Human Dignity Trust *v.* Charity Commission of England and Wales CA/2013/0013

In re Harpur's Will Trusts [1962] 1 Ch 78

In re Isabel Joanna James [1932] 1 Ch 25

In re Sahal's Will Trusts [1958] 1 WLR 1243

Incorporated Council of Law Reporting for England and Wales *v.* Attorney-General [1972] 1 Ch 73

Independent Schools Council *v.* The Charity Commission for England and Wales [2011] 1 UKUT 421 (Upper Tribunal)

Inland Revenue Commissioners *v.* Baddeley [1955] 1 AC 572 (HL)

Inland Revenue Commissioners *v.* City of Glasgow Police Athletic Association [1953] 1 AC 380 (HL)

Inland Revenue Commissioners *v.* McMullen [1981] 1 AC 1 (HL)

Ironmonger's Company (1840) 2 Beav 313

James *v.* Allen (1817) 3 Mer 17

Jones *v.* Williams (1767) 1 Ambler 651

Joseph Rowntree Memorial Trust Housing Association Ltd *v.* Attorney-General [1983] 1 Ch 159

Keren Kayemeth Le Jisroel Ltd *v.* Inland Revenue Commissioners [1932] 1 AC 650

Knight *v.* Knight (1840) 3 Beav 148

McGovern *v.* Attorney-General [1982] 1 Ch 321

Mellick *v.* President and Guardian of the Asylum (1821) 1 Jac 180

Mills *v.* Farmer (1815) 1 Mer 55

Morice *v.* Bishop of Durham (1805) 10 Ves 522

National Anti-Vivisection Society *v.* Inland Revenue Commissioners [1948] 1 AC 31 (HL)

Neville Estates Ltd *v.* Madden [1962] 1 Ch 832

O'Hanlon *v.* Logue [1806] 1 IR 247

Oppenheim *v.* Tobacco Securities Trust Co Ltd [1951] 1 AC 297 (HL)

Oxford Group *v.* Inland Revenue Commissioners [1949] 2 All ER 537 (Hl)

Palmer *v.* Simmonds (1854) 2 Drew 221

Pennington *v.* Waine [2002] 4 All ER 215

R (on the application of Independent Schools Council) *v.* Charity Commission [2012] 1 Ch 214 (Upper Tribunal)

R *v.* Radio Authority; *ex parte* Bull [1995] 4 All ER 481

Re Banfield [1968] 2 All ER 276

Re Bennett [1960] 1 Ch 18

Re Bradbury (Deceased) [1951] 1 TLR 130

Re Carapiet's Trust [2002] EWHC 1304

Re Caus [1934] 1 Ch 162

Re Charlesworth (1910) 26 TLR 214

Re Cole [1958] 1 Ch 877

Re Compton [1945] 1 Ch 123

Re Corbyn [1941] 1 Ch 400

Re Corelli [1943] 1 Ch 332

Re Cottam's Will Trusts [1955] 3 All ER 704

Re Coulhurst [1951] 1 Ch 661
Re Delius [1957] 1 Ch 299
Re Driffill [1950] 1 Ch 93
Re Foveaux [1895] 2 Ch 501
Re Good [1905] 2 Ch 60
Re Green's Will Trusts [1985] 3 All ER 455
Re Gulbenkian's Settlement Trusts [1970] 1 AC 508 (HL)
Re Hobourn Aero Components Air Raid Distress Fund [1946] 1 Ch 194
Re Hood [1931] 1 Ch 240
Re Hopkins' Will Trusts [1964] 3 All ER 46
Re Jarman's Estate (1878) 8 Ch D 584
Re Jenkin's Will Trusts [1966] 1 Ch 249
Re King [1923] 1 Ch 243
Re Koeppler's Will Trusts (HC) [1984] 1 Ch 243
Re Koeppler's Will Trusts (CA) [1986] 1 Ch 423
Re Lloyd-Greame (1893) 10 TLR 66
Re Macduff [1896] 2 Ch 451
Re Nottage [1895] 2 Ch 649
Re Pinion [1963] 3 WLR 778
Re Richardson's Will (1887) 58 LT 45
Re Rilands Estate [1881] WN 173
Re Scowcroft [1898] 2 Ch 638 (Court of Chancery)
Re Slevin [1891] 2 Ch 326
Re Stephens (1892) 8 TLR 792
Re Strakosch (Deceased) [1949] 1 Ch 529
Re Strickland's Will Trusts [1936] 3 All ER 1027
Re Tetley [1924] 1 AC 262 (HL)
Re Warre's Will Trusts [1953] 1 WLR 725
Re Watson [1973] 1 WLR 1472
Re Wedgewood [1911] 1 Ch 113
Re Weir Hospital [1910] 2 Ch 124
Re White [1803] 2 Ch 41
Re Wilson [1913] 1 Ch 314
Royal College of Surgeons of England *v.* National Provincial Bank Ltd [1952] 1 AC 631 (HL)
Scottish Burial Reform & Cremation Society Ltd *v.* Glasgow Corporation [1968] 1 AC 138 (HL)
Southwood *v.* Attorney-General [2000] EWCA Civ 204
Thornton *v.* Howe (1862) 31 Beav 14
Townley *v.* Bedwell [1801] 6 Ves 194
Trustees for the Roll of Voluntary Workers *v.* Commissioners of Inland Revenue [1942] 1 SC 47 (SC)
Tucker *v.* Granada [1977] 3 All ER 865 (HL)
Verge *v.* Somerville [1924] 1 AC 496 (PC)
Vezey *v.* Jamson (1822) 1 Sim and Stu 69
Weir *v.* Crum-Brown [1908] 1 AC 162 (HL)
White *v.* White [1893] 2 Ch 41
Williams' Trustees *v.* Inland Revenue Commissioners [1949] 1 AC 447 HL)
Wright *v.* Atkyns (1823) 1 Turn & R 143

Canada

Action by Christians for the Abolition of Torture *v.* Canada (MNR) (2002) 225 DLR (4th) 99

Alliance for Life *v.* MNR [1999] 3 FC 504

Amateur Youth Soccer Association *v.* Canada (Revenue Agency) [2007] 3 SCR 217

Blair Longley *v.* MNR, 2 CTC 382

Credit Counselling Services of Atlantic Canada Inc *v.* Canada (National Revenue) 2016 FCA 193

Everywoman's Health Centre Society (1988) MNR [1992] 2 FC 52

Guaranty Trust Co of Canada *v.* MNR (1967) 60 DLR (2d) 481

Gull Bay Development Corporation *v.* R [1984] 2 FC 3 (TD).

Human Life International in Canada Inc. *v.* MNR [1998] 3 FCR 202

Jones *v.* T Eaton Company [1973] 1 SCR 635

Native Communications *v.* MNR [1986] 3 FC 471 (CA).

News to You Canada *v.* MNR 2011 FCA 192

Positive Action Against Pornography *v.* MNR [1988] 1 CTC 232

Protestant Hold Ladies' Home *v.* Provincial Treasurer of Prince Edward Island (1941) 2 DLR 534

R *v.* Assessors of the Town of Sunny Brae [1952] 2 SCR 76

R *v.* Salituro [1991] 3 SCR 654

Re Bethel (1971) 17 DLR (3d) 652

Re Knight, 1 OR 462

Re LaidLaw Foundation (1984) 13 DLR (4th) 491

Re Robinson, 15 (2d) OR 286

Re Societa Unita and Town of Gravenhurst (1977) 16 OR (2d) 785

Re St Anne's Tower Corporation of Toronto and City of Toronto, 41 DLR (3d) 481

Scarborough Community Legal Services *v.* The Queen [1985] 2 FC 555

Seafarers Training Institute *v.* Williamsburg (1982) 39 OR (2d) 370

Toronto Volgograd Committee *v.* MNR [1988] 3 FC 251

Vancouver Regional Freenet Association *v.* MNR (1996) 137 (4th) DLR

Vancouver Society of Immigrant and Visible Minority Women *v.* MNR [1999] 1 SCR 10

Watkins *v.* Olafson [1989] 2 SCR 750

Wood *v.* R [1977] 6 WWR 273

United States of America

Bivens *v.* Six Unknown Named Agents of Federal Bureau of Narcotics, 403 US 388 (1971)

Garrison *v.* Little (1897) 75 Ill App 402

Jackson *v.* Philips (1867) 96 Mass 539

Hong Kong

Cheung Man Yu *v.* Lau Yuen Ching [2007] 4 HK314

Chinachem Charitable Foundation Ltd *v.* Secretary for Justice [2015] HKCFA 35

Church Body of the Hong Kong Sheng Kung Hui *v.* Commissioner of Inland Revenue [2014] HCCA 445

Hong Kong and Shanghai Bank Hong Kong (Trustee) Ltd *v.* The Incorporated Trustees of the Islamic Community Fund of Hong Kong (HCMP 000631/1981 (HKCFI)

HSBC Trustee (Hong Kong) Ltd *v.* Secretary of Justice, 1 HKCFI 534 (HKCFI)

Ip Cheung Kwok *v.* Ip Siu Bun [1990] 1 HKCA 356 (HKCA)
Ip Cheung-Kwok *v.* Ip Siu-Bun, 2 HKLR 247 (HKHC)
Ip Cheung-Kwok *v.* Sin Hua Bank Trustee Ltd [1990] HKCU 0403 (HKCU)
Li Kim Sang Victor *v.* Chen Chi Hsia [2015] HKCFI 259; HCA 481/2008 (HKCFI)
Li Kim Sang Victor *v.* Chen Chi Hsia [2016] 1 HKLRD 1153 (HKCFI
Ngi Chi Fong *v.* Hui Ho Pui Fun [1987] HKCFI 42
Secretary for Justice *v.* Joseph Lo Kin Ching, 1 HKCFI 233
To Kan Chi *v.* Pui Man Yau [1999] 1 CACV 32 (HKCA)
Yeap Cheah Neo *v.* Ong Cheung Neo [LR PC] 6 1875 381 (PC)

Singapore and Malaysia

Hwa Soo Chin *v.* Personal Representatives of the Estate Lim Soon Ban, deceased [1994] 2 SLR(R) 1
In Re Abdul Guny Abdullasa Deceased; Fatima Beebee Amal *v.* Mohamed Abubakar 1936 MLJ 140
Khoo Jeffrey *v.* Life Bible-Presbyterian Church [2011] SGCA 18 (26 April 2011)
Koh Lau Keow *v.* Attorney-General [2014] SGCA 18
Lam Joon Shu *v.* Attorney-General [1993] 3 SLR 649
Life Bible-Presbyterian Church *v.* Khoo Eng Teck Jeffrey [2010] 1 SGHC 187
Majlis Ugama Islam Singapura *v.* Saeed Salman [2016] SGHC 4
Re Alsagoff Trusts [1956] 1 MLJ 244
Re Chinonh Ke Hu (Deceased) [1964] MLJ 270
Re Hadji Daeing Tahira Binte Daeing Tedelleh [1948] MLJ 62
Re Khoo Cheng Teow [1933] MLJ 119
Re Syed Shaik Alkaff (1923) 2 MC 38
Sir Han Hoe Lim *v.* Lim Kim Seng [1956] MLJ 142
Tan Chin Ngoh *v.* Tan Chin Teat [1946] MLJ 159
Veerasamy Krishnasamy *v.* Jannaki Ammal [1947] MLJ 157

Sources

Ahdar, Rex Tauati, 'Charity Begins at the Politically Correct Home? The Family First Case'. *Otago Law Review* 14(1) (2015): 171–190
Ahern, William, 'Trust Law in Hong Kong'. *Trust and Trustees* 20(1–2) (February–March 2014)
Aid/Watch, 'What We Do', 2017. www.aidwatch.org.au/about/what-we-do
Alexander, Cox, et al., *Charity Governance*, 2nd edn. Bristol: Jordans, 2014
Andrews, Kevin, 'Explanatory Memorandum to the ACNC Repeal Bill: Regulation Impact Statement'. Parliament of the Commonwealth of Australia, 2013–14. http://parlinfo.ap h.gov.au/parlInfo/download/legislation/ems/r5202_ems_43c2f9ce-f4c7-4c4 d-89ee-528d39b09619/upload_pdf/392326.pdf;fileType=application%2Fpdf
Angheier, Helmut K. and Stefan Toepler, *International Encyclopaedia of Civil Society*, 1st edn. New York: Springer, 2010
Atkinson, R., 'Reforming Cy Pres Reform'. *Hastings Law Journal* 44 (1992)
Attwater, Rachael (ed.) and William Langland, *The Book Concerning Piers Plowman*, 1st edn. New York: Dent, 1957
Australian Charities and Not-for-Profit Commission [ACNC], 'ACNC's Role', accessed 19 Jan. 2016. www.acnc.gov.au/ACNC/About_ACNC/ACNC_role/ACNC/Edu/ACNC_role. aspx?hkey=88635892-3c89-421b-896d-d01add82f4fe

ACNC, 'Legal Meaning of Charity', 12 Jan. 2015. www.acnc.gov.au/ACNC/Register_m y_charity/Who_can_register/Char_def/ACNC/Edu/Edu_Char_def.aspx

ACNC, *Not-for-Profit and the Australian Government* (2013)

ACNC, 'Register My Charity', 13 Jan. 2016. www.acnc.gov.au/ACNC/Register_my_cha rity/Why_register/Charity_tax/ACNC/FTS/Fact_ConcAvail.aspx?hkey= c9347d53-e040-4ab0-81be-9f3e5193ad40

Australian Federal Senate, *Disclosure Regimes for Charities and Not-for-Profit Organisations* ['Disclosure Regimes for Charities Report'] (2008)

Australian government, *Final Report: Scoping Study for a National Not-for-Profit Regulator.* April 2011

Barker, Susan, 'The Myth of "Charitable Activities"'. *New Zealand Law Journal* 1(8) (September 2014)

Barker, Susan, 'The Presumption of Charitability'. *New Zealand Law Journal* (9 October 2012)

Barker, Susan and Kate Yesberg, 'Charities Act Review'. *NZLawyer*, April 2011. http:// ndhadeliver.natlib.govt.nz/ArcAggregator/arcView/frameView/IE5308872/www.nzla wyermagazine.co.nz

Barker, Susan, 'Are All Charities Equal?' *Chartered Accountants Journal* 90(5) (June 2011)

Barker, Susan, Michael Gousmett, and Ken Lord. *The Law and Practice of Charities in New Zealand*, 1st edn. Wellington: LexisNexis, 2013

Barrett, Jonathan and John Veal, '"Charities" Tax Privileges in New Zealand: A Critical Analysis'. *Journal of Australasian Tax Teachers Association* 7(1) (2012)

Bassett, John, 'Charity Is a General Public Use'. *New Zealand Law Journal* 1(2) (2011)

Baumgarnter, Frank B. and Bryan D. Jones, 'Agenda Dynamics and Policy Subsystems'. *Journal of Politics* 53(4) (1991)

Beard, Jenny, 'Charity Law from a Public Law Perspective: The Aid/Watch Case Revisited'. *Charity Law and Practice Review* 18(1) (2015–16)

Bethke, Damian, 'Charity Law Reform in Hong Kong: Taming the Asian Dragon?' *International Journal of Not-for-Profit Law* 18(1) (May 2016)

Biehler, Hilary, 'Trusts for the Relief of Poverty and Public Benefit: Time for a Reappraisal?' *Trust Law International* 28(3) (2014)

Bogert, George, *The Law of Trusts*, 5th edn. California: Foundation Press, 1973

Bourgeois, Donald J., *The Law of Charitable and Non-Profit Organizations*, 2nd edn. London: Butterworths, 1995

Bridge, Richard, 'The Law Governing Advocacy by Charitable Organizations: The Case for Change'. *The Philanthropist* 17(2) (July 2002)

Bright, S., 'Charity and Trusts for the Public Benefit'. *Conveyancer and Property Lawyer* 28 (1) (1989)

Broder, Peter, The Legal Definition of Charity and Canada Customs and Revenue Agency's Charitable Registration Process. Canadian Centre for Philanthropy Public Affairs. August 2011

Broder, Peter, 'Pemsel Case Foundation Launched to Foster Canadian Charity Law'. *The Philanthropist* 25(4) (2014)

Bromley, Kathryn, 'The Definition of Religion in Charity Law in the Age of Fundamental Human Rights'. *International Journal of Not-for-Profit Law* 3(1) (September 2000)

Brooks, Neil, *Charities: The Legal Framework*, 1st edn. Ottawa: Policy Coordination Directorate (Secretary of State – Canada) 1983

Business Insider (Australia), 'New Zealand Tops New Ranking of The World's Most Socially Progressive Countries', 4 April 2014. www.businessinsider.com.au/r-new-zeala nd-tops-social-progress-index-worlds-biggest-economies-trail-2014-02?r=US&IR=T

Butler, Andrew, 'The Trust Concept, Classification and Interpretation', *Equity and Trusts in New Zealand*, 2nd edn. Wellington: Thomson Reuters, 2009

Butler, Andrew and Tim Clarke, 'Charitable Trusts', *Equity and Trusts in New Zealand*, 2nd edn. Wellington: Thomson Reuters, 2009

Canadian Government, 'Guidelines for Registering a Charity: Meeting the Public Benefit Test'. 30 May 2014. www.cra-arc.gc.ca/chrts-gvng/chrts/plcy/cps/cps-024-eng.html

Canadian Obesity Network, 'Obesity in Canada'. www.obesitynetwork.ca/obesity-in-canada

Canadian Revenue Agency [CRA], 'General Requirements for Charitable Registration', 2 November 2012. www.cra-arc.gc.ca/chrts-gvng/chrts/plcy/cgd/gnrlrqrmnts-eng.html

CRA, 'Guidelines for Registering a Charity: Meeting the Public Benefit Test', 1 May 2016. www.cra-arc.gc.ca/chrts-gvng/chrts/plcy/cps/cps-024-eng.html#N1020F

CRA, 'What Is Charitable?', 30 April 2009. www.cra-arc.gc.ca/chrts-gvng/chrts/pplyng/cpc/wtc-eng.html

CRA, 'Who We Are', 6 January 2011. www.cra-arc.gc.ca/chrts-gvng/chrts/bt/mssn_vsn-eng.html

Carroll, John M., *Edge of Empires: Chinese Elites and British Colonials in Hong Kong*, 1st edn. New York: Harvard University Press, 2005

Carter, Terrance S. and Theresa L. M. Man, 'The Evolution of Advocacy and Political Activities by Charities in Canada: An Overview'. *The Philanthropist* 23(4) (2011)

Chan, Kathryn, 'Backgrounder for Talk on Political Purposes Doctrine', Charities and Not-for-Profit Law Conference, 2014

Chan, Kathryn, 'The Function (or Malfunction) of Equity in the Charity Law of Canada's Federal Courts'. *Canadian Journal of Comparative and Contemporary Law* 2(1) (2016)

Charity Commission for England and Wales, 'Application for the Registration of the Church of Scientology (England and Wales)', 17 November 1999. www.gov.uk/government/uploads/system/uploads/attachment_data/file/324214/cosdecsum.pdf

Charity Commission for England and Wales, 'About Us', accessed 18 Jan. 2016. www.gov.uk/government/organisations/charity-commission/about

Charity Commission for England and Wales, 'The Advancement of Religion for the Public Benefit', December 2011. www.gov.uk/government/uploads/system/uploads/attachment_data/file/358531/advancement-of-religion-for-the-public-benefit.pdf

Charity Commission for England and Wales, 'Application for Registration of the Gnostic Centre', 16 December 2009. www.gov.uk/government/uploads/system/uploads/attachment_data/file/324274/gnosticdec.pdf

Charity Commission for England and Wales, 'Application for the Registration of the Druid Network', 21 September 2010. www.gov.uk/government/uploads/system/uploads/attachment_data/file/324236/druiddec.pdf

Charity Commission for England and Wales, 'Charities in England and Wales – 31 March 2016 (An Overview)'. http://apps.charitycommission.gov.uk/showcharity/register ofcharities/SectorData/SectorOverview.aspx

Charity Commission for England and Wales, 'Public Benefit: The Public Benefit Requirement (PB1)', September 2013. www.gov.uk/government/uploads/system/uploads/attachment_data/file/383871/PB1_The_public_benefit_requirement.pdf

Charities Commission – New Zealand, 'Registration Decision: Kiwis Against Seabed Mining Incorporated (KIW49965)', 15 December 2016. www.charities.govt.nz/assets/Uploads/Kiwis-Against-Seabed-Mining-Incorporated.pdf

Charities Commission – New Zealand, 'Registration Decision for Northern Region Equestrian Trust (NOR44300)', 15 April 2013. www.charities.govt.nz/assets/Uploads/2013-6-Northern-Region-Equestrian-Trustv1.pdf

Chesterman, Michael, 'Foundations of Charity Law in the New Welfare State'. *Modern Law Review* 62(3) (1999)

Chesterman, Michael, *Charities, Trusts and Social Welfare*, 1st edn. London: Weidenfeld & Nicolson, 1979

Chevalier-Watts, 'Balancing Law and Belief: The Dichotomy of the Moral and the Immortal'. *International Journal of Religion and Spirituality in Society*, 7(1) (2017), 1–15.

Chevalier-Watts, 'Case Comment: *Re Family First New Zealand*'. *Waikato Law Review* 23 (1) (2015)

Chevalier-Watts, 'Charitable Trusts and Advancement of Religion: On a Whim and a Prayer?' *VUWLR* 43(3) (2012): 403–442

Chevalier-Watts, 'Charitable Trusts and Political Activity: Time for a Change?' *Waikato Law Review* 19(2) (2015): 145–159

Chevalier-Watts, 'Charitable Trusts and Political Purposes: Sowing the Seeds of Change? Lessons from Australia'. *Canterbury Law Review* 19(1) (2013)

Chevalier-Watts, 'Post Re Greenpeace Supreme Court Reflections: Charity Law in the 21st Century in Aotearoa (New Zealand)'. *Bond Law Review* 28(1) (2016): 63–82

Chevalier-Watts, 'The Public Benefit Requirement in Charity Law: The Mystery of the Balancing Act'. *Trust and Trustees* 21(4) (2015)

Chevalier-Watts, *Law of Charity*, 1st edn. Wellington: Thomson Reuters, 2014

Chevalier-Watts, Juliet and Sue Tappenden, *Equity, Trusts and Succession*, 1st edn. Wellington: Thomson Reuters, 2013

Chia, Joyce, Matthew Harding, and Ann O'Connell, 'Navigating the Politics of Charity: Reflections on *Aid/Watch Inc v. Federal Commissioner of Taxation*'. *Melbourne University Law Review* 35(2) (August 2011)

Church Properties.co.uk, 'About the Charities Act 2011', 2017. http://churchproperties.co.uk/about-the-charities-act-2011

Clayton Utz, 'Does Government Funding with Strings Attached Affect a Body's Charitable Status?', 2017. www.claytonutz.com/publications/news/200612/12/does_government_funding_with_strings_attached_affect_a_bodys_charitable_status.page

Collins, Simon, 'NZ Ranked #1 for Social Progress'. *New Zealand Herald*, 3 April 2014. www.nzherald.co.nz/nz/news/article.cfm?c_id=1&objectid=11231593

Commonwealth Board of Taxation, *Consultation on the Definition of a Charity: A Report to the Treasurer* (2003)

Cordery, Carolyn, Carolyn J. Fowler, and Gareth G. Morgan, 'The Development of Incorporated Structures for Charities: A 100-Year Comparison of England and New Zealand'. *Accounting History* 21(2–3) (2016): 281–303

Cordery, Carolyn, *Light Handed Charity Regulation: Its Effect on Reporting Practice in New Zealand*. Working paper no. 83, Centre for Accounting, Governance, and Taxation Research. December 2011

Countrymeters, 'Hong Kong Population', 2017. http://countrymeters.info/en/Hong_Kong

Cranmer, Frank, 'Government and Parliament 2010–2011'. *Christian Law Review* 80(1) (2011)

Craton, Margaret, 'Independent Schools *v.* Charity Commission – and the Winner Is?' Asblaw, 13 March 2012. www.asb-law.com/what-we-say/articles/articles/2012/independent-schools-v-charity-commission-and-the-winner-is#.WI6GOxh7E_V

Cullity, Maurice, 'Charity and Politics in Canada'. *The Philanthropist* 25(4) (26 February 2014) http://thephilanthropist.ca/original-pdfs/Philanthropist-25-4-542.pdf

Cullity, Maurice, 'Charities and Politics in Canada – A Legal Analysis'. Pemsel Case Foundation. December 2013

Cutbill, Clive, Alison Paines, and Murray Hallam. *International Charitable Giving*, 1st edn. Oxford: Oxford University Press, 2012

Cullity, Maurice, 'The Myth of Charitable Activities'. *Estates Trust Journal* 10(1) (1990–1): 7–29

d'Apice, Bill and Ann Lewis, 'Government to Repeal the ACNC'. Charities & Not-For-Profits Law in Australia, 19 March 2014. www.charitiesnfplaw.com.au/2014/03/19/government-to-repeal-the-ACNC

Dadelszen, Mark Von. *Law of Societies*, 3rd edn. Wellington: LexisNexis, 2009

Dal Pont, Gino, 'Charity Law: "No Magic in Words"?' *Not-for-Profit Law: Theoretical and Comparative Perspectives*, 1st edn. Cambridge: Cambridge University Press, 2014

Dal Pont, Gino, *Charity Law in Australia and New Zealand*, 1st edn. Melbourne: Oxford University Press, 2000

Dal Pont, Gino, *Law of Charity*, 1st edn. Chatswood: LexisNexis, 2000

de Castella, Tom, 'Have Jedi Created a New "Religion"?' *BBC News*, 25 October 2014. www.bbc.com/news/magazine-29753530

Demczur, Jacqueline M. and Terrance S. Carter, 'FCA Holds that the Prevention of Poverty Is Not a Charitable Purpose'. Carters law firm, 25 August 2016. www.carters.ca/pub/bulletin/charity/2016/chylb390.pdf

Department of Internal Affairs [DIAC] 'Charities Commission Functions Moved to Internal Affairs', 2016. www.dia.govt.nz/Charities-Commission-functions-moved-to-Internal-Affairs

DIA, 'Office for the Community and Voluntary Sector Website', 2016. www.dia.govt.nz/Decommissioned-websites—Office-of-the-Community-and-Voluntary-Sector-website

Department of Internal Affairs – Charities Services [DIAC] 'Charitable Purpose', 2017. https://charities.govt.nz/apply-for-registration/charitable-purpose

DIAC, 'Mokorina Whānau Trust (CC40304) Decision No: D2011', 25 May 2011. https://charities.govt.nz/assets/Uploads/mokorina-whanau-trust.pdf

DIAC, 'Nga Uri O Wharetakahia Waaka Whānau Land Trust (NGA42808) Decision', 19 November 2012. www.charities.govt.nz/assets/Uploads/2012-4-Nga-Uri-O-Wharetakahia-Waaka-Whanau-Land-Trust.pdf

DIAC, 'Registration Decision: The Jedi Society Incorporated (JED49458)', 14 September 2015. www.charities.govt.nz/assets/Uploads/Jedi-Society-Incorporated.pdf

DIAC, 'Registration Decision: Society for the Protection of Auckland Harbours (SO51367)', 1 September 2016. www.charities.govt.nz/assets/Uploads/Society-for-the-Protection-of-Auckland-Harbours-decision.pdf

Department of Statistics Singapore, *Population Trend 2016*. Government report, September 2016

Drache, Arthur, 'Canadian Charity Tribunal: A Proposal for Implementation'. Brisbane: Queensland University of Technology, 1996

Drache, Arthur and Frances K. Boyle, *Charities, Public Benefit and the Canadian Income Tax System*, 1st edn. Brisbane: Queensland University of Technology, 1999

Drassinower, Abraham, 'The Doctrine of Political Purposes in the Law of Charities: A Conceptual Analysis', *Between State and Market: Essays on Charities Law and Policy in Canada*, 1st edn. Ottawa: McGill-Queen's University Press, 2011

Dunn, Alison, 'Charity Law as a Political Option for the Poor'. *Northern Ireland Legal Quarterly* 50(3) (1999)

Dunn, Alison, 'Charity Law as a Political Option for the Poor', *Foundations of Charity*, 1st edn. Oregon: Hart, 2000

Dunn, Alison, 'Charities and Restrictions on Political Activities: Developments by the Charity Commission for England and Wales in Determining Regulatory Barriers'. *International Journal of Not-for-Profit Law* 11(1) (November 2008)

Dunn, Alison, 'Demanding Service or Servicing Demand? Charities, Regulation and the Policy Process'. *Modern Law Review* 71(2) (2008): 247–270

Dunn, Alison, 'Lord Hogdson's Charities Act Review'. *Voluntary Sector Review* 4(1) (2013)

Dunn, Alison, '*McGovern* v. *Attorney-General*'. *Charity Law and Practice Review* 16(1) (2013–14)

Dunn, Alison, 'Regulatory Shifts: Developing Sector Participation in Regulation for Charities in England and Wales'. *Legal Studies* 34(4) (2014)

Dunn, Joanne, 'What Is the Future of the ACNC under the New Government?' *The Lawyer*, 1 November 2013. www.thelawyer.com/what-is-the-future-of-the-acnc-under-the-new-government

DWF Law, '*Independent Schools Council* v. *Charity Commission for England & Wales*', 17 November 2011. www.dwf.law/news-events/legal-updates/2011/11/independent-schools-council-v-charity-commission-for-england-wales

Elson, Peter R., 'A Short History of Voluntary Sector–Government Relations in Canada'. *The Philanthropist* 21(1) (2007)

Elson, Peter R., 'The Origin of Species: Why Charity Regulations in Canada and England Continue to Reflect Their Origins'. *International Journal of Not-for-Profit Law* 12(3) (May 2010)

English Oxford Living Dictionaries [2007], definition of *politics*. Oxford University Press. https://en.oxforddictionaries.com/definition/politics

Family Action, 'Who We Are', 2014. www.family-action.org.uk

Farrow, Trevor, 'The Limits of Charity: Redefining the Boundaries of Charitable Trust Law'. *Estates and Trust Journal* 13(1) (1999)

Federal Senate of Australia Tax Laws Amendment (Public Benefit Test) Bill 2010 (Comm. Print 2010)

Federal Treasury of Australia, *Consultation Paper: Scoping Study for a National Not-Profit-Regulator* (2011)

Federal Senate of Australia, Industry Commission on the Not-for-Profit Sector: Industry Commission, *Charitable Organisations in Australia*, Government Report No. 45 (1995)

Fichtl, Eric, 'An Introduction to the Third Sector in Hong Kong: Historical Developments and Current Outlook'. International Field Program, 2006. www.ericfichtl.org/index.php/texts/article/third_sector_hong_kong

Fish, Edith L., 'The Cy Pres Doctrine and Changing Philosophies'. *Michigan Law Review* 51(3) (1953)

Garton, Jonathan, 'The Legal Definition of Charity and the Regulation of Civil Society'. *King's College Law Journal* 16(1) (2005)

Garton, Jonathan, *Public Benefit in Charity Law*, 1st edn. Oxford: Oxford University Press, 2013

Garton, Jonathan, 'The Regulation of Charities and Civil Society'. D Phil thesis, University of London, 2005

Garton, Jonathan, 'Charitable Purposes and Activities'. *Current Legal Problems* 67(1) (2014)

Gilbert, M., 'The Work of Lord Brougham for Education in England'. University of Pennsylvania, 1922

Gilchrist, Emma, 'Canada's Charity Law Needs Reform: Report'. *The Tyee: News, Culture, Solutions*, 25 March 2015. https://thetyee.ca/News/2015/03/25/Charity-Law-Report-2015

Gousmett, Michael, 'Charity and Economic Development'. *New Zealand Law Journal* 1(2) (2011)

Gousmett, Michael, 'Fiscal Issues for Charities'. *New Zealand Law Journal* 1(3) (2014)

Gousmett, Michael, 'The History of Charitable Purpose Tax Concessions in New Zealand Part I'. *New Zealand Journal of Taxation Law and Policy* 19(2) (2013)

Government of Canada [CRA], 'How to Draft Purposes for Charitable Registration', 25 July 2013. www.cra-arc.gc.ca/chrts-gvng/chrts/plcy/cgd/drftprpss-eng.html#N103DF

CRA, 'Political Activities', 2 September 2003. www.cra-arc.gc.ca/chrts-gvng/chrts/plcy/cps/cps-022-eng.html#politicalactivities6-2

CRA, '*Registering Charities That Promote Racial Equality*', 2 September 2003. www.cra-arc.gc.ca/chrts-gvng/chrts/plcy/cps/cps-021-eng.html

Government of Canada, *Royal Commission on Taxation*. Ottawa: Queen's Printer, 1966

Government of Hong Kong, *The Law Reform Commission of Hong Kong Report: Charities*. Hong Kong Law Commission, 6 December 2013

Government of the United Kingdom, 'Charities and Tax', accessed 25 Oct. 2016. www.gov.uk/charities-and-tax/tax-reliefs

Government of the United Kingdom, 'Charity Commission of England and Wales', 2017. www.gov.uk/government/organisations/charity-commission

Government of the United Kingdom, 'Operational Compliance Case: Oxfam'. Charity Commission for England and Wales, 19 December 2014. www.gov.uk/government/news/operational-compliance-case-oxfam

Government of the United Kingdom, 'Speaking Out: Guidance on Campaigning and Political Activity by Charities'. Charity Commission for England and Wales, March 2008.   www.gov.uk/government/uploads/system/uploads/attachment_data/file/591353/CC9.pdf

Government of the United Kingdom, 'Strategy Unit Public Bodies Reform – Proposals for Change'. 14 December 2011

Government of the United States, 'Political Activity and the Federal Employee'. United States Department of Defense, 2017. www.dodea.edu/Offices/Counsel/pa.cfm

Guardian, 'New Zealand Housing Crisis Forces Hundreds to Live in Tents and Garages', 17 May 2016. www.theguardian.com/world/2016/may/17/new-zealand-housing-crisis-forces-hundreds-to-live-in-garages-tents-and-cars

Hackney, Jeffrey, 'Charities and Public Benefit'. *Law Quarterly Review* 124(1) (2008)

Hamlin, Patrick and Philip Munro, 'Hong Kong', *International Charitable Giving*, 1st edn. Oxford: Oxford University Press, 2012

Harding, Matthew, *Charity Law and the Liberal State*, 1st edn.Oxford: Oxford University Press, 2014

Harpur, Paul, 'Charity Law's Public Benefit Test: Is Legislative Reform in the Public Interest?'. *Queensland University of Technology Law Journal* 3(2) (November 2003): 422–437

Henry Review Panel, *Report to the Treasurer* ['Australia's Future Tax System Report'] (2009)

Hodgson, Robin, *Trusted and Independent: Giving back to Charities – Review of the Charities Act 2006*, 1st edn. London: TSO, 2012

Hong Kong Law Reform Commission, 'The Law Reform Commission of Hong Kong Charities Sub-Committee Consultation Paper: Charities', June 2011. www.gov.hk/en/residents/government/publication/consultation/docs/2011/Charities.pdf

Horwitz, Jill, 'Nonprofits and Narrative: Piers Plowman, Anthony Trollope, and Charities Law'. *Michigan State Law Review* 1(4) (2009)

Howden-Chapman, Philippa, *Home Truths Confronting New Zealand*, 1st edn. Wellington: Bridget Williams Books, 2015

Hsiao, Mark, 'The Beginning and the End of an Era of Charitable Public Benefit in Hong Kong'. *Conveyancer and Property Lawyer* 76(3) (2012)

Huen Wong, Lim Pui, 'Ah Fook and Ancestral Trusts'. *CHC Bulletin*, accessed 15 Dec. 2016. http://chc.ntu.edu.sg/Bulletin/Documents/sept03-Pt2.pdf

Inland Revenue Department of Hong Kong, 'A Tax Guide for Charitable Institutions and Trusts of a Public Character', September 2010. www.ird.gov.hk/eng/tax/ach_tgc.htm

Irvine, Helen, Christine Ryan, and Myles McGregor-Lowndes, 'An International Comparison of Not-for-Profit Accounting Regulation'. School of Accountancy (Queensland University of Technology) 2010. http://apira2010.econ.usyd.edu.au/conference_p roceedings/APIRA-2010-092-Irvine-Not-for-profit-accounting-regulation.pdf

Jensen, Darryn, 'Charitable Purposes and Political Purposes (or Voluntarism and Coercion)'. *Charity Law and Practice Review* 18(1) (2015–16)

Johnson, S. E. A., 'A New Look for Public Benefit in the Law of Charities'. *Modern Law Review* 36(5) (1973)

Jones, Gareth, *History of the Law of Charity 1532–1827*, 1st edn. Cambridge: Cambridge University Press, 1969

Kai Yuen, Terence Yui, 'Hong Kong'. APPC, 2003

Kennedy, Helena, *Advisory Group on Campaigning and the Voluntary Sector*. Government report, May 2007

King's School, 'The History of King's'. King's School, Canterbury, 2017. www.kings-school.co.uk/about/history

Kingdon, John W., *Agendas, Alternatives and Public Policies*, 2nd edn. New York: Harper Collins, 1995

Kirkness, Martin, 'Life Cycle Issues for Charities'. *Taxation in Australia* 50(5) (November 2015)

Kitching, Andrew, 'Charitable Purpose, Advocacy, and the Income Tax Act'. Parliamentary Information and Research Service (Canada), 28 February 2006. www.lop.parl.gc.ca/content/lop/researchpublications/prb0590-e.pdf

Kong Shan Ho, John and Rohan Bruce Edward Price, 'Reform of Charity Law in Hong Kong and Australia: What Lessons Can Be Learned from the United Kingdom'. *Asian Journal of Comparative Law* 6(1) (2011)

Lam, W. F. and J. L. Perry, 'The Role of the Non-Profit Sector in Hong Kong's Development'. *Voluntas* 11(4) (2000)

Lang, Ter Kah, 'Changes to Charity Law'. *Singapore Academy of Law Journal* 7(2) (1995)

Lang, Ter Kah, *The Law of Charities: Cases & Materials – Singapore and Malaysia*, 1st edn. Singapore: Butterworths, 1985

Lee, Rebecca, 'Charity without Politics? Exploring the Limits of "Politics" in Charity Law'. *Journal of Civil Society* 11(3) (2015)

Lee, Rebecca and Lusina Ho, 'Advocating Public Advocacy: An Opportunity for Charities in Hong Kong?' *Trusts and Trustees* 18(1) (January 2012): 43–47

Leow, Rachael, 'The Evolution of Charity Law in Singapore: From Pre-Independence to the 21st Century'. *Trusts Law International* 26(2) (2012)

Leow, Rachael, 'Four Misconceptions About Charity Law in Singapore'. *Singapore Journal of Legal Studies* (1) (2012)

Levasseur, Karine, 'In the Name of Charity: Institutional Support for and Resistance to Redefining the Meaning of Charity in Canada'. *Canadian Public Administration* 55(2) (June–July 2012)

Levin, Adam, 'Observations on the Development of Native Title Trusts in Australia'. *Trusts and Trustees* 22(2) (March 2016): 241–264

Lim, Meng-Kin, 'Shifting the Burden of Health Care Finance: A Case Study of Public-Private Partnership in Singapore'. *Health Policy* 69(1) (2004): 83–92

Little, Andrew, 'Housing Crisis Affecting More than 98 per Cent of NZ'. Labour Party of New Zealand, 14 July 2016. www.labour.org.nz/housing_crisis_affecting_more_than_98_per_cent_of_nz

Luxton, Peter, '*Dingle v. Turner* Forty Years on'. *Charity Law and Practice Review* 16(1) (2013–14)

Luxton, Peter, *The Law of Charities*, 1st edn. Oxford: Oxford University Press, 2001

Luxton, Peter, 'Making Law: Parliament *v.* The Charity Commission', *Politeia* 64 (June) (2009)

Luxton, Peter and Nicola Evans, 'Cogent and Cohesive? Two Recent Charity Commission Decisions on the Advancement of Religion'. *Conveyancer and Property Lawyer* 75(2) (2011): 144–151

McKenzie, Peter, 'Charitable Trusts', *Master Trusts Guide*, 3rd edn. Auckland: Wolters Kluwer, 2011

Maisharah, Sharifah, 'Tracing Singapore's Social Sector'. *Social Space*, 2008. http://ink.library.smu.edu.sg/cgi/viewcontent.cgi?article=1014&context=lien_research

Mandarin, 'Charities Regulator Reprieve a Call to Get back to Work', 9 April 2015. www.themandarin.com.au/28930-acnc-charities-regulator-reprieve/?pgnc=1

Māori Dictionary [2016], definition of *hapū*, http://maoridictionary.co.nz/search?idiom=&phrase=&proverb=&loan=&histLoanWords=&keywords=hapu; definition of *iwi*; http://maoridictionary.co.nz/search?idiom=&phrase=&proverb=&loan=&histLoanWords=&keywords=iwi; definition of *marae*, http://maoridictionary.co.nz/search?idiom=&phrase=&proverb=&loan=&histLoanWords=&keywords=marae; definition of *tangata whenua*, http://maoridictionary.co.nz/search?keywords=tangata+whenua

Māori Dictionary [2017], 'Whakapapa Māori: Structure, Terminology and Usage', http://maaori.com/whakapapa/whakpap2.htm

Mariani, Stefano, 'Traditional Chinese Religion Trusts in Hong Kong'. *Trust and Trustees* 21(5) (June 2015)

Martin, Fiona, 'Advocacy in Charity: A Breakaway from the Common Law' (Impactful Advocacy)'. *Lien Centre for Social Innovation (Singapore Management University)* 1(1) (2012)

Martin, Fiona, 'Charities for the Benefit of Employees: Why Trusts for the Benefit of Employees Fail the Public Benefit Test'. *Social Science Research Network* 1(1) (2009)

Martin, Fiona, 'Convergence and Divergence with the Common Law: The Public Benefit Test and Charities for Indigenous Peoples', *Not-for-Profit Law: Theoretical and Comparative Perspectives*, 1st edn. Cambridge: Cambridge University Press, 2014

Martin, Fiona, 'Has the Charities Act 2013 Changed the Common Law Concept of Charitable "Public Benefit" and, If So, How?'. *Australian Tax Forum* 30(1) (2015)

Martin, Fiona, 'The Legal Concept of Charity and Its Expansion after the Aid/Watch Decision'. *Cosmopolitan Civil Societies Journal* 3(2) (2011)

Martin, Fiona, 'Recent Developments in Australian Charity Law: One Step Forward and Two Steps Backward'. *Charity Law and Practice Review* 17(1) (2014–15)

Millman, Bryan, 'Prevention vs. Relief of Poverty: Not a Difference without a Distinction in the Eyes of the Law'. Norton Rose Fulbright, July 2016. www.nortonrosefulbright.com/knowledge/publications/144119/prevention-vs-relief-of-poverty-not-a-difference-without-a-distinction-in-the-eyes-of-the-law

Mitchell, Paul, 'The Political Purposes Doctrine in Canadian Charities Law'. *The Philan-thropist* 12(4) (1995) http://thephilanthropist.ca/original-pdfs/Philanthrop ist-12-4-138.pdf

Morris, Debra, 'Charities and Political Activity in England and Wales: Mixed Messages'. *Charity Law and Practice Review* 18(1) (2015–16)

Morris, Debra, 'The Charity Commission for England and Wales: A Fine Example or Another Fine Mess?'. *Chicago-Kent Law Review* 91(3) (2016)

Mummery, John, '*The Commissioners for Special Purposes of Income Tax v. Pemsel*'. *Charity Law and Practice Review* 16(1) (2013–14)

Morris, Debra, 'Public Benefit: The Long and Winding Road to Reforming the Public Benefit Test for Charity: A Worthwhile Trip or "Is Journey Really Necessary?"', *Modernising Charity Law: Recent Developments and Future Directions*, 1st edn. Cheltenham: Edward Elgar, 2010

Murray, Ian, 'The Australian Charities and Not-for-Profits Commission: Reform or Unreform?' *Charity Law and Practice Review* 17(1) (2014–15)

Murray, Ian, 'Charity Means Business: *Commissioner of Taxation v. Word Investments Ltd*: Case Note'. *Sydney Law Review* 31(2) (June 2009): 309–329

Murray, Ian, 'Not-for-Profit Reform: Back to the Future?' *Third Sector Review* 20(1) (2014)

Nehme, Marina, 'Regulation of the Not-for-Profit Sector Is Another Change Really Needed?' *Alternative Law Journal* 39(1) (2014)

New Zealand Government, 'Advocacy for Causes'. DIAC, 2017. https://charities.govt. nz/apply-for-registration/charitable-purpose/advocacy-for-causes

New Zealand Government, 'Charities Commissions Functions Moved to Internal Affairs', June 2012. www.dia.govt.nz/Charities-Commission-functions-moved-to-Internal-Affairs

New Zealand Government, 'No Review of the Charities Act at this Time', 16 November 2012. www.beehive.govt.nz/release/no-review-charities-act-time

New Zealand Parliament, *Report of the Social Services Select Committee Considering the Charities Bill 108–2*, 17 December 2004

Nobles, Richard, 'Politics, Public Benefit and Charity'. *Modern Law Review* 45(6) (1982)

Nylander, John, 'Is Hong Kong a Paradise for Charity Fraudsters? It Surely Could Be'. *Forbes*, 17 September 2015. www.forbes.com/sites/jnylander/2015/09/17/is-hong-kong-a-paradise-for-charity-fraudsters-it-surely-could-be/#3c8c47cb76e0

O'Connell, Ann, Fiona Martin, and Joyce Chia, 'Law, Policy and Politics in Australia's Recent Not-for-Profit Sector Reforms'. *Australian Tax Reform* 28(2) (2013)

O'Halloran, Kerry, *Charity Law and Social Inclusion: An International Study*, 1st edn. Oxon. and New York: Routledge, 2007

O'Halloran, Kerry, *Human Rights and Charity Law: International Perspectives*, 1st edn. Abingdon: Routledge, 2016

O'Halloran, Kerry, Myles McGregor-Lowndes, and Karla W. Simon, *Charity Law & Social Policy: National and International Perspectives on the Functions of Law Relating to Charities*, 1st edn, vol. 10. Netherlands: Springer, 2008

O'Halloran, Kerry, *The Profits of Charity: International Perspectives on the Law Governing the Involvement of Charities in Commerce*, 1st edn. New York: Oxford University Press, 2012

O'Halloran, Kerry, Bob Wyatt, Laird Hunter, Michael Gousmett, and Myles McGregor-Lowndes, 'Charity Law Reforms: An Overview of Progress Since 2001', *Modernising Charity Law: Recent Developments and Future Directions*, 1st edn. Cheltenham: Edward Elgar, 2010

Office Ombudsman – Hong Kong, *Investigation Report* (2013)

Ontario Law Reform Commission, *Report on the Law of Charities* (1996)

Open Charities, 'The Laugharne Corporation Lands', 1 December 2016. http://opencha rities.org/charities/218121

Owen, Suzanne and Teemu Taira, 'The Category of Religion in Public Classification: Charity Registration of The Druid Network in England and Wales', *Religion as a Category of Governance and Sovereignty*, 1st edn. Chester: Brill, 2015

Oxfam UK, 'Below the Breadline: The Relentless Rise of Food Poverty in Britain'. *Policy and Practice*, 9 June 2014. http://policy-practice.oxfam.org.uk/publications/below-the-breadline-the-relentless-rise-of-food-poverty-in-britain-317730

Panel on Accountability and Governance in the Voluntary Sector, *Building on Strength: Improving Governance and Accountability in Canada's Voluntary Sector* (1999)

Parachin, Adam, 'Charity, Politics and Neutrality'. *Charity Law and Practice Review* 18(1) (2015–16)

Parachin, Adam, 'Distinguishing Charity from Politics: The Judicial Thinking Behind the Political Purposes'. *Alberta Law Review* 45(4) (August 2008)

Parachin, Adam, 'Legal Privilege as a Defining Characteristic of Charity'. *Canadian Business Law Journal* 48(1) (2009)

Parachin, Adam, 'Reforming the Regulation of Political Advocacy by Charities: From Charity under Siege to Charity under Rescue?' *Chicago-Kent Law Review* 91(3) (2016)

Phillips, Andrew, 'Charities Services 'Registration, Deregistration and Applying the Eligibility Test'. 4 October 2016

Phillips, Susan D., '"Canadian Leapfrog" From Regulating Charitable Fundraising to Co-Regulating Good Governance', *Voluntas* 23(3) (2012)

Phillips, Susan D., 'Shining Light on Charities or Looking in the Wrong Place? Regulation-by-Transparency in Canada'. *International Journal of Voluntary and Nonprofit Organisations* 24(3) (2013)

Picarda, Hubert, 'Charities Act 2011: A Dog's Breakfast or Dream Come True? A Case for Further Reform', *Not-for-Profit Law: Theoretical and Comparative Perspectives*, 1st edn. Cambridge: Cambridge University Press, 2014

Picarda, Hubert, *The Law and Practice Relating to Charities*, 4th edn. Haywards Heath: Bloomsbury, 2010

Picarda, Hubert, *Written Evidence on the Joint Committee on the Draft Charities Bill 2004*, Government Report No. 167–2; 662, DCH 297 (2004)

Piper, Anne-Marie, *Charity Law*, 1st edn. London: Sweet & Maxwell, 2012

Poirier, Donald, *Charity Law in New Zealand*, 1st edn. Wellington: Department of Internal Affairs, 2013

Porter, Michael E., Scott Stern, and Michael Green, *Social Progress Index 2014*, 6 October 2016

Productivity Commission of Australia, *Contribution of the Not-for-Profit Sector* ['Contribution of the Not-for-Profit Sector Report'] (2010)

Ramasamy, Ravindran, 'Charity Law: A Time to Define', *Singapore Law Review* 5 (1984)

Rickett, C. E. F., 'Charity and Politics'. *New Zealand Universities Law Review* 10(1) (1982)

Russell, Clive, 'A Word to the Wise'. *Keeping Good Companies* 61(3) (April 2009): 179–181

Sandberg, Russell, 'Defining the Divine'. *Ecclesiastical Law Journal* 16(2) (2014)

Sanders, Anne, 'The Mystery of Public Benefit'. *Charity Law and Practice Review* 10(2) (2007)

Santow, G. F. K., 'Charity in Its Political Voice: A Tinkling Cymbal or a Sounding Brass?' *Current Legal Problems* 52(1) (1999): 255–285

Seow, Elaine, 'Singapore', *Charity Law: Jurisdictional Comparisons*, 1st edn. London: Sweet & Maxwell, 2012

Seymour, Elen and Marina Nehme, 'The ACNA, The Senate, The Commission of Audit and the Not-for-Profit Sector'. *UNSW Law Journal* 38(3) (2015)

Shammall, Cindy, 'Assessing the Impact of the New Hong Kong Companies Ordinance on Charitable Institutions'. Shadden LLP, June 2014. www.skadden.com/newsletters/Assessing_the_Impact_of_the_New_Hong_Kong_Companies_Ordinance_on_Charitable_Institutions.pdf

Sheppard, Ian F., *Commonwealth Inquiry into the Definition of Charities and Related Organisations Report* ['Definition of Charities' Report'] (2001)

Sheridan, L. A., 'Charitable Causes, Political Causes and Involvement'. *The Philanthropist* 2 (4) (1980)

Sheridan, L. A., 'Charity Versus Politics'. *Anglo-American Law Review* 2(1) (1973)

Siebert, Christian and Ann O'Connell, 'Explainer: What Are the Limits to Charities Advancing Political Causes?' *The Conversation*, 20 January 2017. http://theconversation.com/explainer-what-are-the-limits-to-charities-advancing-political-causes-71466

Silke, Nicola, 'Please Sir, May I Have Some More? Allowing New Zealand Charities a Political Voice'. *Canterbury Law Review* 8(2) (2002)

Singapore Charity Commission, 'About Charities and IPCs'. 11 January 2016. www.charities.gov.sg/setting-up-a-charity/Pages/About-Charities-And-IPCs.aspx

Singapore Charity Commission, 'About Charity Council'. 11 January 2016. www.charities.gov.sg/about/Pages/About-Charities-Council.aspx

Singapore Charity Commission, 'About the Commissioner of Charities'. 1 November 2016. www.charities.gov.sg/about/Pages/About-the-Commissioner-of-Charities.aspx

Singapore Charity Commission, 'Drafting Your Governing Instrument'. 11 January 2016. www.charities.gov.sg/setting-up-a-charity/Registering-for-a-new-charity/Pages/Drafting%20your%20Governing%20Instrument.aspx

Singapore Charity Commission, 'Fund-Raising Matters'. 11 January 2016. www.charities.gov.sg/manage-your-charity/Fund-raising%20and%20Related%20matters/Pages/Fund-Raising%20Matters.aspx

Singapore Charity Commission, 'Legislative Conditions for Registration as a Charity or IPC', 11 January 2016. www.charities.gov.sg/setting-up-a-charity/Registering-for-a-new-charity/Pages/Legislative%20Conditions%20for%20Registration%20as%20a%20Charity_IPC.aspx

Singapore Charity Commission, 'Legislation Governing Charities and IPC'. 11 January 2016. www.charities.gov.sg/setting-up-a-charity/Registering-for-a-new-charity/Pages/Legislation-governing-Charities.aspx

Singapore Government, 'About Charity Council', 1 November 2016. www.charities.gov.sg/about/Pages/About-Charities-Council.aspx

Singapore Government, 'About the Commissioner of Charities', accessed 1 Nov. 2016. www.charities.gov.sg/about/Pages/About-the-Commissioner-of-Charities.aspx

Singapore Government, 'Charity Transparency Framework', 28 January 2016. www.charities.gov.sg/about/Pages/About-Charities-Council.aspx

Singapore Government, 'Other Requirements for Registration as a Charity or IPC', 1 November 2016. www.charities.gov.sg/setting-up-a-charity/Registering-for-a-new-charity/Pages/Other%20Requirements%20for%20Registration%20as%20a%20Charity_IPC.aspx

Smerdon, Xavier, 'Turnbull Government Makes Plans for ACNC's Future'. *Probono Australia*, 23 December 2015. https://probonoaustralia.com.au/news/2015/12/turnbull-government-makes-plans-for-acncs-future

Smith, B. H., *Traditional Imagery of Charity in Piers Plowman*, 1st edn. The Hague: Mouton, 1966

Sossin, Lorne, 'Regulating Virtue: A Purposive Approach to the Administration of Charities', *Between State and Economy: Essays on Charities Law and Policy in Canada*, 1st edn. Montreal and Kingston: McGill-Queen's University Press, 2001

Spells, Judith, 'Trust Essentials', *New Zealand Master Trusts Guide*, 3rd edn. Auckland: Wolters Kluwer, 2011

Stevens, David and Margaret Mason, 'Tides Canada Initiatives Society: Charitable Venture Organizations: A New Infrastructure Model for Canadian Registered Charities'. *The Philanthropist* 23(2) (2010)

Stibbard, Paul, David Russell, and Blake Bromley, 'Understanding the Waqf in the World of the Trust'. *Trusts and Trustees* 18(8) (September 2012)

Synge, Mary, '*The 'New' Public Benefit Requirement Making Sense of Charity Law?*1st edn. Oxford: Hart, 2015

Synge, Mary, 'A State of Flux in the Public Benefit Across United Kingdom, Ireland and Europe'. *Charity Law and Practice Review* 16(1) (2013)

Tai, Janice, 'Charity Boom: Number of Registered Charities Increase by 23% in 10 Years'. *Straits Times*, 27 December 2015. www.straitstimes.com/singapore/charity-boom-num ber-of-registered-charities-increase-by-23-in-10-years

Tang, Hang Wu, 'Equity and Trusts'. *Singapore Academy of Law Annual Review of Singapore Cases* 15(1) (2004)

Tax Adviser, 'Not-for-Profit, Not for Tax?', 8 January 2015. www.taxadvisermagazine. com/article/not-profit-not-tax

Tennant, Margaret, Mike O'Brien, and Jackie Sanders, *The History of the Non-Profit Sector in New Zealand*, 1st edn. Wellington: Office for the Community and Voluntary Sector, 2008

Tennant, Margaret, Jackie Sanders, Michael O'Brien, and Charlotte Castle, 'Defining the Non-Profit Sector: New Zealand'. Parliament of New Zealand, September 2006. www. parliament.nz/resource/0000115088

Thio, Li-ann, 'Courting Religion: The Judge between Caesar and God in Asian Courts'. *Singapore Journal of Legal Studies* 1(1) (July 2009)

Thye, Lim Kien, 'Clearing the Charity Muddle: A Statutory Proposal – The Charities Act 1992'. *Malaya Law Review* 26(1) (1984)

Tiong Tan, Ngoh, 'Regulating Philanthropy: The Legal and Accountability Framework for Singapore Charities'. *Asia Pacific Journal of Social Work and Development* 17(1) (June 2007): 69–78

Tokeley, Kate, 'A New Definition of Charity?'. *Victoria University of Wellington Law Journal* 21(1) (February 1991): 41–58

Tsu, Yu Yue, *The Spirit of Chinese Philanthropy: A Study in Mutual Aid*, 1st edn. New York: Columbia University Press, 1912

Turnour, Matthew, 'Case Comment – Some Thoughts on the Broader Theoretical Basis for Including Political Purpose within the Scope of Charitable Purpose: The Aid/Watch Case'. *International Journal of Civil Society Law* 9(2) (April 2011)

Turnour, Matthew and Elizabeth Turnour, 'Archimedes, Aid/Watch, Constitutional Leavers and Where We Now Stand', *Not-for-Profit Law: Theoretical and Comparative Perspectives*, 1st edn. Cambridge: Cambridge University Press, 2014

Tyssen, Amherst D., *The Law of Charitable Bequests*, 2nd edn. London: Sweet & Maxwell, 1921

UK Government, *The Committee on the Law and Practice Relating to Charitable Trusts (The Nathan Committee)* Government Report No. 8710. London: HMSO, 1952

UK Government, 'Tax Relief When You Donate to a Charity', 9 July 2016. www.gov.uk/donating-to-charity/overview

Underhill, A. and D. J. Hayton, *Underhill & Hayton: The Law Relating to Trusts and Trustees*, 15th edn. London: Butterworths, 1995

Vaughn, J. D., *The Manners and Customs of the Chinese of the Straits Settlements*, 1st edn. Kuala Lumpur: Oxford University Press, 1971.

Victoria State Services Authority, *Review of the Not-for-Profit Regulation* (2007)

Volunteer Sector Initiative Secretariat, and Laurie Rektor, 'Advocacy: The Sound of Citizen's Voices'. Government of Canada. September 2002. www.vsi-isbc.org/eng/policy/pdf/position_paper.pdf

Von Dadelszen, Mark, 'Moving the Charitable Goal Posts'. *NZLawyer*, March 2011. http://ndhadeliver.natlib.govt.nz/ArcAggregator/arcView/frameView/IE5308872/www.nzlawyermagazine.co.nz

W. Y. Lee, Eliza and M. Shamsul Haque, 'Development of the Non-Profit Sector in Hong Kong and Singapore: A Comparison of Two Statist–Corporatist Regimes'. *Journal of Civil Society* 4(2) (2008)

Warburton, Jean, *Tudor on Charities*, 9th edn. London: Sweet & Maxwell, 2003

Waters, Donovan, '"Singapore and Hong Kong Also Retain the presumption": 'The Advancement of Religion in a Pluralist Society (Part II): Abolishing the Public Benefit Element'. *Trust & Trustees* 17(8) (September 2011)

Watt, Gary, *Trusts & Equity*, 6th edn. Oxford: Oxford University Press, 2014

Weinert, Kim, 'Is It a Not-for-Profit Organisation or a For-Profit Organisation? The Case for a CIC Structure in Australia'. *Journal of Australasian Law Teachers Association* 7(1) (2014)

Wikipedia, 'Po Leung Kuk', 1 December 2016. https://en.wikipedia.org/wiki/Po_Leung_Kuk

Wikipedia, 'Transfer of Sovereignty over Hong Kong', 17 January 2017. https://en.wikipedia.org/wiki/Transfer_of_sovereignty_over_Hong_Kong

Williams, George, 'The Australian Constitution and the Aid/Watch Case'. *Cosmopolitan Civil Societies Journal* 3(3) (2011)

Withersworldwide, 'Review of the Charities Act 2006 – Giving Charity back to Charities?' 17 July 2012. www.withersworldwide.com/news-publications/review-of-the-charities-act-2006-%E2%80%93-giving-charity-back-to-charities–2

Wong, Chung Ming, Vincent C. H. Chua, and S. Vasoo, 'Contributions to Charitable Organizations in a Developing Country: The Case of Singapore'. *International Journal of Social Economics* 25(1) (1998)

Working Party on Charities and Sporting Bodies, *Report to the Minister of Finance and the Minister of Social Welfare* (1989)

Zwiebel, Ellen, 'A Truly Canadian Definition of Charity and a Lesson in Drafting Charitable Purpose'. *The Philanthropist* 7(1) (1987)

Index

For Product Safety Concerns and Information please contact our EU
representative GPSR@taylorandfrancis.com
Taylor & Francis Verlag GmbH, Kaufingerstraße 24, 80331 München, Germany

www.ingramcontent.com/pod-product-compliance
Ingram Content Group UK Ltd.
Pitfield, Milton Keynes, MK11 3LW, UK
UKHW021007180425
457613UK00019B/835